GROUP PROBLEMS
IN CRIME AND PUNISHMENT

PATTERSON SMITH REPRINT SERIES IN
CRIMINOLOGY, LAW ENFORCEMENT, AND SOCIAL PROBLEMS

A listing of publications in the SERIES *will be found at rear of volume*

PUBLICATION NO. 117: PATTERSON SMITH REPRINT SERIES IN
CRIMINOLOGY, LAW ENFORCEMENT, AND SOCIAL PROBLEMS

GROUP PROBLEMS IN CRIME AND PUNISHMENT

and Other Studies in
Criminology and Criminal Law

by

HERMANN MANNHEIM

Second Edition Enlarged

MONTCLAIR, N. J.
PATTERSON SMITH
1971

Originally published 1955
*Reprinted 1971 with the permission of
Routledge and Kegan Paul, Ltd.*
**Patterson Smith Publishing Corporation
Montclair, New Jersey 07042**
*New material copyright ©1971 by
Patterson Smith Publishing Corporation*

SBN 87585-117-7

Library of Congress Catalog Card Number: 73-108234

This book is printed on three-hundred-year acid-free paper.

TO MY WIFE

PREFACE TO THE SECOND EDITION

IT has given me great pleasure to accept the suggestion of the publisher of this edition to write a new and possibly more detailed Preface to my volume of essays. *Group Problems in Crime and Punishment* is a book somewhat difficult to introduce in a few sentences as the essays here collected not only belong to different periods of time but also deal with a great variety of subjects. While, as stressed in the original Preface, the problems of groups are clearly the *leitmotiv* of the book, there are, as indicated in the subtitle of the book, a few chapters in it dealing with other matters. The reviewers of the first edition did, with only one or two exceptions, willingly accept the organization of the book as quite legitimate. Similarly, whether they were academic lawyers, criminologists or sociologists, or practitioners such as prison medical officers or probation officers in Great Britain or abroad, they also accepted the difficulties which the diversity of topics must have given them in reviewing the material covered. Only a few reviewers (otherwise very friendly) made mention of the inconvenience of having to express their views on a number of subjects for which they felt themselves ill-equipped—a process described by one of them as "changing hats" from one chapter to the next. In the subsequent fifteen years, however, the various scientific disciplines concerned have, I think, drawn more closely together, and their representatives have got more used, if not to "changing hats" completely, at least to showing more tolerance of others' headgear. Moreover, there is an increasing number who wear no hats at all or more than one. What I did find disappointing was not the tone of the reviews, which was with one exception extremely friendly, but the fact that hardly any of them even touched on those sections which I personally regarded as among the most important of the volume. This applies in particular to the chapter on "Collective Responsibility," admittedly a very awkward subject to deal with, and on "The Socio-

PREFACE TO SECOND EDITION

logical Aspects of the Criminal Law," also a rather complex subject to tackle. The explanation may be that these two chapters are legal-philosophical rather than criminological and therefore lie outside the traditional domain of the criminologist.

More important than all this, however, are the questions, first, what changes if any have occurred regarding the subjects under discussion in the fifteen years since this volume was first published and, second, to what extent might it be said that any of my suggestions or criticisms had impact? To the second question a convincing answer is almost impossible to give, since even where the actual changes seem to be in line with my personal trend of thought, they might just as well have taken place independently and it would be presumptuous on my part to claim any credit for them. In the following pages I propose therefore to say a few words on each chapter in order to answer the first of my questions. In some instances it has seemed advisable to group comments on a few chapters. Incidentally, it goes without saying that the chapters "Collective Responsibility and Collective Punishment" and "The Sociological Aspects of the Criminal Law" have been less in danger of becoming dated than, for example, those on "American Prisons," "American Criminology," and "Short-Term Imprisonment." In the case of the final chapter, "The Treatment of Mental Disorders in Continental Criminal Law," the changes in the legal position have become so numerous since the lecture was delivered in 1936 that I thought it advisable to add as an Appendix a lecture delivered in 1960. While this does not claim to present a complete up-to-date picture it gives at least an idea of the general trends of development in legal thinking over a quarter of a century, and I am grateful for the opportunity of publishing the two lectures side by side.

To preface my comments on the various chapters I might perhaps make a few more general points. Most of my criminological writings, and particularly large parts of *Group Problems,* produced within the past thirty-five years may be regarded as preliminary steps towards my textbook, *Comparative Criminology.*[1] To give but two illustrations from my earlier works: First, methodological questions played an important part in my writings as early as *Social Aspects of Crime in England between the Wars* (1940),[2] with its emphasis on the diffi-

[1] Hermann Mannheim, *Comparative Criminology* (London: Routledge & Kegan Paul, 1965; Boston: Houghton Mifflin Company, 1965).
[2] Hermann Mannheim, *Social Aspects of Crime in England between the Wars* (London: George Allen & Unwin, 1940).

PREFACE TO SECOND EDITION

culties of correctly interpreting criminal statistics. Fifteen years later appeared *Prediction Methods in Relation to Borstal Training*,[3] produced for the Home Office jointly with that master of statistical techniques Leslie T. Wilkins, which was directly concerned with methods. Turning to the present work, the whole of Part Two is, as its title indicates, devoted to methodological questions. To give only two examples, the centenary essay on Lombroso was largely a critique of his methods, and my contribution to "Why Delinquency?" was an outcry directed against the all too primitive techniques then often used in criminological research. Primitive methods have now become largely a thing of the past, and the complaint is occasionally heard that overly refined techniques are sometimes employed to crack empty nuts. In *Comparative Criminology* I have tried to present an all-round picture of the subject.

My second general point referred to what I regarded as the provincialism and lack of interest in international developments found among criminologists and criminal lawyers, especially in Anglo-Saxon countries.[4] Here again considerable progress can be reported. In the United States the historical series featuring eminent European criminologists begun in 1954 by the *Journal of Criminal Law, Criminology and Police Science* has been continued and has led to the publication of the widely known symposium *Pioneers in Criminology*. Edited by the present writer for the Law School of Northwestern University, Chicago, a first edition appeared in 1960 and a second enlarged edition is soon to be published.[5] This revival of American interest in European developments has been further encouraged by the International Congresses held every five years; additionally in Britain a reciprocal strengthening of the links with American criminology has taken place thanks to the work of the *British Journal of Criminology*, the British Society of Criminology, and the Cambridge Institute of Criminology. On the European continent it has been mainly in Germany, Italy, and the Scandinavian countries where international contacts have of late become more frequent and intensive, with some of the other countries also showing an active interest. It is in the field of

---

[3] Hermann Mannheim and Leslie T. Wilkins, *Prediction Methods in Relation to Borstal Training* (London: H.M.S.O., 1955; 2d ed., 1965).

[4] *Infra*, pp. 208–10.

[5] Hermann Mannheim, ed., *Pioneers in Criminology*, 1st ed. (London: Stevens & Sons, 1960); 2d ed. (Publication No. 121, Patterson Smith Reprint Series in Criminology, Law Enforcement, and Social Problems [Montclair, N.J., 1971]).

PREFACE TO SECOND EDITION

criminal law where, as I said in my Hague lecture,[6] we are still rather far from a "Common Market," nor is this surprising, as assimilation of ideas in this field usually requires coordinated legislation for which the consent of the various national legislatures is needed.

In my lecture of December 1951 at the "European Seminar" in Brussels,[7] I felt somehow on the defensive as the lone spokesman for the "sociological study of the adult offender." In the meantime, however, the tendency to which I could even then refer[8] has made further progress—the gradual drawing together of the individual/psychological and the sociological/group approaches to the study of the offender. Following the pioneer work of Donald Clemmer[9] there have been several important sociological surveys of the populations of American and British prisons, such as Gresham Sykes' work in the Trenton Penitentiary, New Jersey,[10] and the Pentonville research by Terence and Pauline Morris.[11] Moreover, there have been valuable prison and Borstal studies of a more general nature which have given penetrating pictures of the sociological problems confronting more or less every institution for lawbreakers.[12] Nor should the numerous official or officially sponsored publications in this field be forgotten,[13] or similar sociological studies of probationers.[14] All these researchers have been of a theoretical character, most of them carried out by academics and, possibly, read mainly by academics. How far have they been able to achieve the object so aptly described by John Conrad of narrowing the gap between the "thinker" and the "doer"?[15] In

---

[6] See Appendix to Chapter 13.
[7] *Infra*, pp. 3–18.
[8] *Infra*, pp. 9–10, 15–16.
[9] *Infra*, pp. 35–41.
[10] Gresham Sykes, *The Society of Captives* (Princeton University Press, 1958).
[11] Terence and Pauline Morris, *Pentonville* (London: Routledge & Kegan Paul, 1963).
[12] To cite only a few of them: Donald R. Cressey, ed., *The Prison* (New York: Holt, Rinehart and Winston, 1961); Hugh J. Klare, *Anatomy of Prison* (London: Hutchinson, 1960); and John P. Conrad, *Crime and Its Correction* (University of California Press, 1965).
[13] See, e.g., for England and Wales, the lists of such researches in *People and Prisons* (London: H.M.S.O., Cmnd. 4214, 1969), pp. 57–59; and *Report on the Work of the Prison Department, 1968* (London: H.M.S.O., Cmnd. 4186, 1969), pp. 24–25.
[14] E.g., *Probationers in Their Social Environment: A Home Office Research Unit Report* (London: H.M.S.O., 1969).
[15] Conrad, pp. 3–4.

PREFACE TO SECOND EDITION

my Brussels lecture I stressed the need not only for theoretical studies of a sociological kind but also for sociologists doing practical work at least in a few selected penal and reformative institutions, side by side with psychologists, psychiatrists and social workers. How far has the position in this respect improved? Not very much, I fear.

Closely connected with this, my attempt to draw attention to the pioneer work of an eminent Dutch judge, Dr. N. Muller, has as far as I can see met with no response[16] and the same is true of my suggestion that side by side with "Intelligence and Personality Tests, Prediction Tables and Electro-Encephalograms" we may have to place at the disposal of Courts and penal administrators a "Table of Group Values and Group Attitudes." I originally called this proposal utopian, and it has remained so. The recent efforts in the field of group counseling, to be discussed below, have of course some bearing on this, but at best they can only touch offenders sent to institutions or placed on probation, not those merely fined, who form the majority of those whom Muller had in mind,[17] nor can this counseling have any impact on the attitudes of the Courts themselves.

We come now to the grave and complex topic of "Collective Responsibility and Punishment." Here a great deal of important work has been done, notably in West Germany in connection with the detailed analysis of the closely related subject of Nazi crimes,[18] and the matter has recently gained special topicality in the United States in view of certain much-publicized happenings during the war in Vietnam. Various instances are quoted in the book of the imposition of collective penalties in colonial territories, but these penalties do not seem to have included wholesale executions.[19] As recent discussions in connection with the Vietnam War have shown, the remnants of the idea of collective punishment are particularly difficult to eradicate in the military mind; even in this field, however, something may have been learned in the past thirty years. Whether, on the other hand, Karl Jaspers' brilliant analysis of the philosophical problems has been constructively continued, I do not know.[20]

---

[16] *Infra*, pp. 16, 19–27.
[17] See, e.g., *infra*, p. 20.
[18] Herbert Jäger, *Verbrechen unter totalitärer Herrschaft* (Olten und Freiburg i.B.: Walter-Verlag, 1967); Heinz Höhne, *The Order of the Death's Head* (London: Secker and Warburg, 1969).
[19] *Infra*, pp. 48 ff.
[20] *Infra*, pp. 61–65.

PREFACE TO SECOND EDITION

There is not much to be added to the discussions on Lombroso and the history of crime in the Second World War, except that the former has been the subject of a lengthy contribution to *Pioneers in Criminology*[21] and that the whole biological approach to criminality has been discussed by Professor di Tullio in *Horizons in Clinical Criminology*.[22] Moreover, a large and important literature has come into existence in the past ten years or so on the significance of abnormal chromosomes (XYY) in male offenders.[23] In the chapter on crime in the Second World War readers may well discover many factors which could serve as explanations for the present crime wave.

One might easily be tempted to write another book to continue the story in Part Three, "American Impressions of a Criminologist," but the temptation has to be firmly resisted. That in a period of seventeen years innumerable changes must have taken place in a prison structure so vast and complicated as that of the American federal and state systems is obvious, but here attention can be drawn to very few of them, and as the author's subsequent visit to the United States was not primarily concerned with the institutional side, even the brief observations offered here are only secondhand and tentative. There is first the decline in the frequency and seriousness of prison riots which had been extremely disturbing in the years 1951–53,[24] and their place was, for a while at least, taken by street rioting until the recent recurrence of violence in prisons. Apart from such phenomena easily recognizable to the outside, however, one has to tread most warily, considering that even an expert with the experience of John Conrad describes the "dominant correctional pattern in the United States as an impersonal monster."[25] In Chapter 7 I emphasized the immense variety of state and local systems; Conrad, on his part, while stressing the similarities, also concludes that "conformity" has not been attained. Certain details are of course not too difficult to ascertain. I ventured to criticize the fact that most American prison officials were

---

[21] Marvin E. Wolfgang, "Cesare Lombroso," in Hermann Mannheim, ed., *Pioneers in Criminology*.
[22] Benigno di Tullio, *Horizons in Clinical Criminology*, New York University Criminal Law Education and Research Center. Monograph Series v. 3 (South Hackensack, N.J.: Fred B. Rothman, 1969).
[23] See, among others, B. di Tullio, pp. 129-30, and the Research Reports in *British Journal of Criminology* 8, no. 2 (April 1968), 186 ff.
[24] *Infra*, pp. 183 ff.
[25] Conrad, pp. 59-60.

PREFACE TO SECOND EDITION

still political appointees,[26] and according to a recent survey this seems to apply even today.[27] Nor has there been much improvement in the local jails.[28] There has been one important recent development, however, which should not be passed over in silence. When in 1953 its originator, Dr. Norman Fenton, showed me the exterior of Folsom Prison in California, he was reluctant to have me enter because he thought it too grim. In the following year, however, he embarked on his group-counseling movement in that "grim old bastille for maximum-security recidivists" and an enthusiastic, though cautious, report on its growth and effect can be found in Conrad's book.[29] This does not imply that nothing had been done in this field before 1954,[30] only that this year has special significance.

To pinpoint other developments of American criminology since 1953 is also well-nigh impossible. In my book I mentioned eight types of research as the most outstanding,[31] and most of them are still receiving much attention in contemporary publications. Nevertheless the emphasis has shifted somewhat. Crimes of violence, though always predominant in the United States, did not yet occupy the unique place they now hold in present-day life and in criminological research as witnessed by the Reports of the Presidential Commissions and of the Chicago Riot Commission of 1968 and the immense private literature on the criminal subculture which has been produced since Albert K. Cohen's *Delinquent Boys* of 1955.[32] Prediction studies

[26] *Infra*, p. 171.
[27] Stephen G. Seliger, "Towards a Realistic Reorganization of the Penitentiaries," *Journal of Criminal Law, Criminology and Police Science* 60, no. 1 (March 1969), 49.
[28] Hans W. Mattick and Alexander B. Aikman, *Annals of the American Academy of Political and Social Science* 381 (January 1961), 109 ff.
[29] Conrad, pp. 237–47, 265, and 219 ff. on the Van der Hoeven Kliniek in Utrecht.
[30] See the survey, "Group Treatment Literature in Correctional Institutions: An International Bibliography, 1945–67," by Logan D. Akman, André Normandeau, and Marvin E. Wolfgang, *Journal of Criminal Law, Criminology and Police Science* 59, no. 1 (March 1968), pp. 41–56. Also, Albert Elias, *Federal Probation* (December 1968), pp. 38 ff.; and Elizabeth H. Gorlich, *Federal Probation* (December 1968), pp. 46 ff. For English institutions, see *People and Prisons* (London: H.M.S.O., Cmnd. 4214, 1969), para. 211.
[31] *Infra*, p. 191.
[32] *Report of the National Commission on the Causes and Prevention of Violence* (Washington, D.C.: G.P.O., January 1969); *Rights in Conflict ... A Report Submitted by Daniel Walker ... to the ... Commission* (New York: Dutton, 1968). Especially representative of the private literature is Marvin E. Wolfgang and Franco Ferracuti, *The Subculture of Violence* (London: Tavistock, 1967).

PREFACE TO SECOND EDITION

continue to flourish under the untiring leadership of the Gluecks, but new theories and "schools"—often merely old ideas under new names, such as what is now called the "interactional" school—have recently gained much support.

Throughout the world the movement towards abolition of capital punishment[33] has made considerable, though uneven, progress since the first appearance of *Group Problems*. In Great Britain it was completely abolished in 1969, and in several other countries at various times after 1955. Perhaps the best recent international surveys are those presented in the multilingual Portuguese publication on the centenary celebration of the abolition of capital punishment in that country and in a special number of the American journal *Crime and Delinquency*.[34] However, progress has by no means been uniform; France, Spain, Greece and Turkey are still important exceptions, and such an international expert as Marc Ancel seems to be rather pessimistic.[35] Perhaps more important though less impressive than the increase in the number of abolitionist countries is the decline in the number of capital crimes and actual executions in recent decades.[36] Even so the possibility of a sudden reverse movement cannot be ruled out as a reaction to the growing increase in violent crime.

Similarly, with regard to the frequency of very short prison sentences[37] the overall picture, though not unfavorable, is not everywhere optimistic. Post-war legislation in England and Wales, for instance, has persistently tried to reduce the number of offenders, especially young ones, sent to prison for very short periods, and the corresponding percentage figures have declined from 51.4 in 1948 to 37.8 in 1968 for sentences of up to three months, whereas the figures for longer sentences have risen.[38] Moreover, the Criminal Justice Act 1967, by introducing the suspended sentence, will further reduce the number of offenders actually serving short prison sentences. In another direction, proposals made in *Group Problems* have to some

---

[33] *Infra*, pp. 223–41.
[34] *Pene de Morte*, Faculdade de Direito da Universidade de Coimbra, 1967, 2 vols.; *Crime and Delinquency* 15, no. 1 (January 1969), especially Walter C. Reckless, pp. 43–56.
[35] *Pene de Morte*, 2: 415 ff.
[36] See, e.g., Thorsten Sellin, *Pene de Morte*, 1: 153 ff.; Sheldon and Eleanor Glueck, *Pene de Morte*, 1: 266; Norval Morris, *Pene de Morte*, 2: 411 ff.; and other contributors.
[37] *Infra*, pp. 242–56.
[38] *People and Prisons*, p. 17.

PREFACE TO SECOND EDITION

extent materialized insofar as an attempt has been made to carry out resarch of the kind there envisaged.[39] The results have been presented in R. G. Andry's book *The Short-term Prisoner*.[40] Internationally, the Council of Europe in Strasbourg has recently undertaken to collect information on the situation as it exists today and to offer suggestions for improvement.

As already indicated, there is very little I would wish to change, or to add, to the chapter on "The Sociological Aspects of the Criminal Law," but I should like to underline, as already done in *Comparative Criminology*, the view that criminology is essentially an idiographic, not a nomothetic, discipline. This means that its principal concern is the discovery and interpretation of facts, possibly also of causal connections, far more than the discovery of scientific "laws" of a general nature, and that it has to leave the legislative and administrative conclusions to be derived from those facts to *Kriminal-Politik,* that is, to the politician who may have to take into account many other considerations in addition to the criminological and penological ones.[41] I fully appreciate the arguments for the opposite view, more and more stressed in recent years with regard to many scientific disciplines, in particular to the natural sciences,[42] but my faith in the competence of the expert is not strong enough to concede him more power than he already possesses.

HERMANN MANNHEIM

January, 1971

---

[39] *Infra*, pp. 253 ff.
[40] R. G. Andry, *The Short-term Prisoner* (London: Stevens & Sons, 1963).
[41] *Infra*, pp. 263, 273; and my *Comparative Criminology*, pp. 13, 77–78. See also my article, "Criminology," in the forthcoming edition of *Encyclopaedia Britannica*.
[42] For criminology, see the weighty arguments put forward in Tadeusz Grygier's review of my *Comparative Criminology*, in *Ottawa Law Review* 2, no. 2 (Spring 1968), p. 510. For the natural sciences, see the lecture, "The Conscience of the Scientist," by the biologist John Maynard Smith, *The Listener*, 7 August, 1969, and, more general, Sir Eric Ashby's lecture, *The Academic Profession* (published for the British Academy by Oxford University Press, 1969).

PREFACE TO THE FIRST EDITION

IN the present volume material has been collected written in the course of the past twenty years and, with a few exceptions, already published in various periodicals in the form of articles, reports or reviews. Many of these papers are enlarged versions of special lectures delivered at Universities or to other scientific bodies in this country and abroad. The material has throughout been revised and brought up to date by adding brief introductory or concluding remarks and further references to recent legislation, literature, and other subsequent developments. An attempt has also been made to revise the writer's English style which, naturally, was particularly atrocious in papers written in the early period before the war. In the case of lectures or addresses traces of the version in which they were originally delivered have, here and there, been preserved as a reminder that the occasion for which the material was first prepared should not be entirely ignored. While the title of the volume has been taken from the theme of its first Part, it will be apparent to readers of other Parts, in particular of Chapters 5, 6, 8 and 12, that 'group problems' are in fact the *leitmotiv* of the whole book. To some extent the Chapters dealing with criminal law will appeal to a public somewhat different from that interested in criminological and penological subjects. There can be little doubt, however, that a process of drawing nearer is slowly taking place between the legal and the sociological-penological ways of approach to problems of crime, a process which greatly facilitates mutual understanding and justifies the inclusion in the same volume of papers belonging to these different disciplines. Even so, several lengthy essays of a predominantly legal character had to be omitted for reasons of space. Moreover, material of mainly ephemeral interest has been excluded or drastically pruned.

PREFACE TO FIRST EDITION

The author's acknowledgments and thanks for permission to reprint are due to the following:

The Secretariat of United Nations, Department of Social Affairs, New York, Editors of the *International Review of Criminal Policy* (Chapter 1).

Messrs. Baillière, Tindall & Cox, London, Publishers, and the Editorial Board of *The British Journal of Delinquency* (Chapters 2, Section I; 6 Section IIIa and b; 7 and 10, Section II).

Dr. Marjorie Franklin and the Q Camps Committee, London (Chapter 2, Section II).

Lord Chorley, London, General Editor of *The Modern Law Review* (Chapters 2, Section III, and 6, Section IIIc).

The Managing Editor of *The Sociological Review*, University College of North Staffordshire, Keele (Chapter 4).

Mr. John Armitage, London, Editor of *The Fortnightly* (Chapters 5, Section I, and 10, Section I).

Professor Thorsten Sellin, Philadelphia, Editor of *The Annals of the American Academy of Political and Social Science* (Chapter 5, Section I).

Mr. Victor H. Evjen, Washington, Editor of *Federal Probation* (Chapter 5, Section III).

The National Association for Mental Health, London (Chapter 6, Section II).

Messrs. Routledge & Kegan Paul Ltd., London, and the Editorial Board of *The British Journal of Sociology* (Chapter 8).

Professor Thorsten Sellin, Secretary General of the Twelfth International Penal and Penitentiary Congress, The Hague, 1950 (Chapter 11).

The Editorial Board of *Mens en Maatschappij*, Amsterdam (Chapter 12).

Dr. G. W. T. H. Fleming, Editor-in-Chief of *The Journal of Mental Science*, London (Chapter 13).

HERMANN MANNHEIM

THE LONDON SCHOOL OF ECONOMICS
AND POLITICAL SCIENCE
(University of London)
February, 1955

CONTENTS

PART ONE: GROUP PROBLEMS IN CRIME AND PUNISHMENT

1 The Sociological Study of the Adult Offender — *page* 3
2 The Group Factor in Crime and Punishment — 19
   i. *Comments on an Article by Dr. N. Muller* — 19
   ii. *Reflections on the Place of Q Camps in Penal Reform* — 27
   iii. *Review of Donald Clemmer's* The Prison Community — 35
3 Collective Responsibility and Collective Punishment — 42

PART TWO: CRIMINOLOGY AND ITS METHODS

4 Lombroso and his Place in Modern Criminology — 69
5 Three Contributions to the History of Crime in the Second World War and After — 85
6 Methodological Problems of Criminology — 115
   i. *Methodological Problems of Criminology* — 115
   ii. *'Why Delinquency? The Limits of Present Knowledge'* — 128
   iii. *The Study of the Young Offender* — 139
      (a) *Erwin Frey*, Der Frühkriminelle Rückfallsverbrecher — 139
      (b) *Edwin Powers and Helen Witmer*, An Experiment in the Prevention of Delinquency — 146
      (c) *S. and E. Glueck*, Juvenile Delinquents Grown Up — 155

CONTENTS

PART THREE: AMERICAN IMPRESSIONS OF A CRIMINOLOGIST

7 American Prisons (with a Note on British Columbia) *page* 165
8 American Criminology 190
9 Miscellaneous Topics 211

PART FOUR: TWO PENOLOGICAL PROBLEMS

10 Capital Punishment: What Next? 223
11 Short-Term Imprisonment and its Alternatives 242

PART FIVE: CRIMINAL LAW

12 The Sociological Aspects of the Criminal Law 259
13 The Treatment of Mental Disorders in Continental Criminal Law 282
Appendix to Chapter 13: The Criminal Law and Mentally Abnormal Offenders 300

Index of Subjects 319
Index of Authors 324

PART ONE

GROUP PROBLEMS IN CRIME AND PUNISHMENT

CHAPTER 1

THE SOCIOLOGICAL STUDY OF THE ADULT OFFENDER

[In December, 1951, a 'European Seminar' was held in Brussels at the invitation of the Belgian Government, organized by United Nations in collaboration with the World Health Organization. Its subject was 'The Medico-Psychological and Social Examination of Offenders'. Its Director was Professor Paul Cornil, Secretary-General of the Belgian Ministry of Justice and Professor of Criminal Law at the University of Brussels. Reports were submitted by experts on various legal and procedural questions related to the scientific examination of offenders; on the selection of offenders for examination; and on the specific problems of their biological, physical, psychiatric, social and sociological examination. These Reports, together with other documents related to the Seminar, have been published by the United Nations Department of Social Affairs, New York, in their periodical *International Review of Criminal Policy*, No. 3, January, 1953.

The author was invited to submit the Report on 'The Sociological Study of the Adult Offender' (see pp. 70 et seq. of the *International Review*). The following article is a slightly revised reproduction of the Report which was read at the Seminar on the 8th December, 1951.

When approaching this task the author was fully aware of the peculiar difficulties of his subject. No doubt, his colleagues who had to deal with other specific techniques of examination had their full share of problems, too, and in addition many controversial aspects of a more general character, as outlined in Dr. Cornil's lucid introductory survey, required attention: the criteria for the selection of cases for examination; the stage in the proceedings when the examination should be carried out; how far any examination could be allowed to go without violating certain fundamental personality rights of the offender; whether certain techniques, such as narco-analysis, should be entirely prohibited; the subject of professional secrecy—and many more. All these problems, however, could not only be clearly defined, they also had in common that their bearing on the subject of the Seminar was direct and obvious and almost beyond dispute. It was the person of the individual offender and his biological, physical, psychological and psychiatric examination that stood in the centre of interest, and in spite of some opposition on the part of the 'classic jurists' as reported by Cornil, the need for such examinations was in principle admitted. It was the 'how to do it' and 'how far to go' rather than the 'whether' of such examinations that were debated, and the same applied to 'social observation' on which a separate report was submitted by a distinguished Belgian social worker. With regard to the sociological study, as distinguished from the social observation of the offender, the position was different. Just as, with the exception of some States of U.S.A., there are no sociologists in prisons but only social workers, it is still fairly universally taken for granted that the social case work approach is all that is required in the study of the individual offender. The essential difference in emphasis and techniques between social work and sociological investigation—a distinction which is after all one of the reasons for the existence of separate Departments of Sociology and of Social Science in many Universities—is still frequently ignored. While they are both concerned with the relationship between the individual and social groups the sociologist will place the main emphasis on the problems of the group and the social worker on the problems of the individual; and their techniques will differ correspondingly. This can be admitted without implying any discrimination. When James Bossard, writing as a sociologist, twenty years ago criticized the social worker's approach as 'seriously unbalanced' because of its 'concentration upon the individual',[1] social workers might possibly have reciprocated by calling the sociologist's 'concentration upon society' equally unbalanced. In fact, both ways of approach, with their corresponding techniques, are indispensable and complementary. Whereas, however, the social worker has become accepted as an essential link in the practical administration of criminal justice, the sociologist has in this field still to fight for his recognition.

These are some of the considerations to be borne in mind by the reader of the following paper who may not be familiar with the general atmosphere and design of the Brussels Seminar.]

[1] James H. S. Bossard, *The Fields and Methods of Sociology*, edited by L. L. Bernard (New York, Farrar & Rinehart, Inc., 1934), p. 208. See also Herbert Bisno, *The Philosophy of Social Work* (Washington, Public Affairs Press, 1952), p. 75.

STUDY OF THE ADULT OFFENDER

I

WHICH factors are relevant in the sociological study of the adult offender? The answer depends (1) on our views regarding the *general objects* of the sociological study of an offender; (2) on the *specific purpose* pursued and on the specific *stage* of the enquiry; (3) on the special *characteristics of the sociological method* of study.

(1) The objects of the sociological study of the adult offender are fundamentally the same as the objects pursued by the other methods of study covered by the programme of the Seminar. There is, first, the practical object of collecting the knowledge which is indispensable for a just and effective sentencing policy of the Courts and for an equally just and effective technique of treatment on the part of penal administrators, probation officers, etc. And there is, secondly, the theoretical object of collecting data for research. From this, it follows that, in order to define the scope of our studies, we have to reach at least some approximate agreement on the character and objects of our judicial sentencing policy and of our administrative policy of treatment. Such an agreement has to be based not on our subjective ideas of what we would wish those objects to be, but on their actual character which, largely determined as it is by public opinion, still shows a mixture of retributive, deterrent and reformative elements. In some countries, within some occupational groups or social classes and in the minds of some individuals, the retributive and deterrent elements are still predominant, whereas in others reformative ideas take preference. Similarly, while the former elements play a more important part in our dealings with adult offenders, the idea of reformation is more generally accepted in our attitudes to juveniles. Where the idea of reformation prevails greater efforts will be made to study the individual offender than in a retributive or deterrent system, and this difference may even find its expression in the law. In English law, for example, pre-sentence enquiries into the home surroundings, school records, health and character have to be made in all, except trivial, cases where juveniles are to be charged before a Juvenile Court, whereas no such general provision exists with regard to adults. In recent English legislation, it is true, the tendency is becoming more and more noticeable to extend the principle of pre-sentence enquiries to adolescents and adults (see Criminal Justice Act, 1948, sections 17(2), 20(7), 21(4)), but the

contrast between the position in Juvenile Courts and Courts for adult offenders is still marked.

One of the most important objects of studying the individual offender is to collect information which might make it easier for the Courts and administrators to *predict* his future conduct, to provide them with 'Prediction' Tables (Glueck) or 'Experience' Tables (Ohlin)[1] which would enable them to select for each individual offender the kind of treatment that would make adjustment more likely than other forms of treatment.

(2) (*a*) The relevance of a factor also depends upon the specific purpose and the stage of enquiry. As Sheldon Glueck points out in his General Report on 'Pre-sentence Examination', submitted to the International Congress of Criminology of 1950,[2] the scope and content of the pre-sentence examination 'ought to depend on whether the report is to be used solely for the rough original classification involved in the sentencing process or also as a detailed plan of peno-correctional treatment thereafter'. Naturally, in view of the limited time and inadequate facilities available as well as of the failure of some legislations to place sufficient emphasis on the need for adequate pre-sentence enquiries the tendency may easily develop to leave too much to the post-sentencing stage. This may have the unfortunate result that the Court may not be able to select the most appropriate method of treatment. A probation order may be made, for example, because the information presented to the Court may merely show that the offender has no previous convictions, but fail to reveal that he comes from a criminal milieu in which probation is bound to fail. It seems essential, therefore, that at least in every more serious case all the sociological factors referred to below under (3) should be adequately investigated already before the sentence.

(*b*) Naturally, the scope of the information available will widen with each successive stage of the penal process, i.e. the Prison Authorities or Board of Parole who have to decide at what stage a prisoner may be safely discharged should know more about him than the Court that committed him to prison; similarly, the After-care organizations who may have to look after him perhaps for

[1] Lloyd E. Ohlin, *Selection for Parole* (New York, Russell Sage Foundation, 1951).
[2] *The Journal of Criminal Law and Criminology*, Vol. XLI, No. 6, March–April, 1951.

several years after his discharge should know more than the Prison Authorities. Prediction instruments would have to be constructed on different lines, therefore, according to the stage in the whole process for which they are intended. On the other hand, the Glueck studies seem to have shown that factors which might be regarded as likely causes of crime in an individual case may well lose their causal and in particular their predictive significance for subsequent stages of the individual's career.[1] Nevertheless, it has been stressed by the Gluecks that as many factors as possible should be studied and included in case histories. There are obvious limitations, however, to the thoroughness and scope of investigations which can be made for the practical purposes of individual cases. The special needs of the research worker can be met only by separate sample enquiries. It also follows that no list of relevant factors can be drawn up regardless of time, place, and other circumstances. In a recent American prediction study it has been found that the marital status of the parents was significant as a predictive factor for white boys, not however for negroes.[2] Similar differences are likely to exist in other respects, but they cannot be brought to light unless the factor in question is first included in the list of potentially relevant factors. Comprehensiveness should, of course, not be allowed to go so far as to become a danger to accuracy. As recent investigations have shown, the primary need of the research worker is quality rather than quantity, i.e. more *reliable* information rather than *more* information.[3]

(3) In spite of the essential identity of their objects (see above under (1)), certain obvious differences in approach do exist between the sociological and the psychological methods of study. These differences are mainly due to the fact that the scope of the sociological study of crime is wider, including as it does many more factors besides those relating to the personality of the individual offender to his family and his narrowest circle. While the

[1] Sheldon and Eleanor Glueck, *500 Criminal Careers* (New York, Alfred A. Knopf, 1950), p. 257; *After-Conduct of Discharged Offenders* (London, Macmillan & Co., 1945), p. 75, note 1.
[2] Albert I. Reiss, *American Journal of Sociology*, Vol. 56, 1950–1, p. 559.
[3] See H. Mannheim and Leslie T. Wilkins, *Prediction Methods in Relation to Borstal Training*, Vol. I of 'Studies in the Causes of Delinquency and the Treatment of Offenders', (London, published for the Home Office by H.M.S.O., 1955), p. 215; T. Grygier, *The British Journal of Delinquency*, Vol. V, No. 3, January, 1955.

GROUP PROBLEMS

activities of the psychologist and psychiatrist, as those of the social worker, are directly focused on the individual offender, the sociologist can deal with the latter only in more indirect ways, i.e. via Society or the groups and institutions existing within Society. Whereas psychologists and psychiatrists are mainly interested in the problems and tensions arising in the individual and through his relations with his family which is, at least in European Society, the smallest of all sociological groups, sociologists will stress the fact that the individual is a member not only of his family but also of many wider groups: neighbourhood ('street-corner society')—School—Church—Clubs and similar groups catering for his leisure time activities—occupational groups (factory, office, etc.)—political and military organizations—communities which he enters as the consequence of his anti-social activities (Prisons, Reformatories)—and throughout he is a citizen of the State. The main criticism which the sociologist has to make of the views of certain more extreme psycho-analysts is that they tend to ignore the possibility that some of the difficulties arising in the family may be mere reflections of the tensions existing within those wider groups. Another point of difference is this: whenever the sociologist deals with family problems in the causation of delinquency, he will do so primarily not in terms of individual conflict between parents and children, but in a wider setting, considering the social functions of the family in a given society and examining whether, in that society, the family is actually fulfilling these functions.[1]

What are the consequences of the existence, side by side, of so many different social groups to which the individual belongs? We have to realize that each of these groups may have developed a code of social conduct of a nature very different from, or even contradictory to, those of the other groups. What the child has learnt from its parents may not hold good in his school or at the street corner; what he hears in the Sunday School will almost certainly differ from his factory or army code—at least the 'underground' codes—and so forth. Such divergencies must inevitably create bewilderment and may easily undermine the individual's confidence in the binding force of any existing code of conduct. Bewilderment and cynicism, however, may breed crime.

The position may become even more dangerous when the in-

[1] See, e.g., S. N. Eisenstadt, 'Delinquent Group Formations among Immigrant Youth', *The British Journal of Delinquency*, Vol. II, 1951, pp. 34 et seq.

STUDY OF THE ADULT OFFENDER

dividual moves from one civilization to another. The problems of the foreign immigrant and of the child evacuated in war-time from a big city to a village and later back again are striking examples. Another interesting criminogenic situation arises where a certain civilization produces a uniform ideology unsuitable for some of the social classes in it, without at the same time offering any kind of material or ideological compensation to these classes.[1]

It will be obvious that none of these sociological problems can be adequately studied if we limit our field to the individual offender and his family. What we are concerned with is the effect which group values and attitudes have on the individual, and we have therefore to study these values and attitudes. This applies not only to offences committed by groups such as crowds or gangs, where the importance of the group factor is too obvious to be overlooked, but equally to offences committed by individuals acting singly but being nevertheless entirely under the influence of their group. Lindesmith and Dunham[2] distinguish between the 'individualized' and the 'social' criminal and contrast types of crime committed mainly by either the one or the other. The 'social' criminal acts in accordance with his group culture and is backed by it, the 'individualized' criminal not. Lynching may be an extreme example of the former, but it is useful as an illustration because of the existence of a considerable body of criminological literature on the subject and because it shows, perhaps more clearly than any other example, how futile it would be in such cases to confine our examination to a study of the individual offender. Crimes of violence, among others, are greatly influenced and can be shaped by communal patterns and standardized group attitudes. In certain villages, some days are reserved every year by custom for communal violence.

All this does not, of course, mean that there is an unbridgeable gap between the sociological and the psychological study of crime. Whatever differences do exist are mainly differences in emphasis, and even they have been greatly reduced in recent years. There is probably common agreement now that, for example, the study of individual cases has to be supplemented by statistical and

[1] See Robert K. Merton, *Social Theory and Social Structure*, pp. 134 et seq.; also *American Sociological Review*, Vol. III, 1938, pp. 672 et seq.
[2] A. R. Lindesmith and H. Warren Dunham, *Social Forces*, Vol. 19, March, 1941, pp. 307 et seq.

sociological research and vice versa, or that the study of objective values and that of subjective attitudes cannot be separated from each other, or that the individual and the group are nothing but different aspects of the same problem. Ernest W. Burgess, writing in 1923,[1] tried to express the contrast between the psychological and the sociological approach to the study of the offender in the terms 'individual' and 'person', which latter concept he described as 'the individual who has status, i.e. position in society', and among the points he regarded as essential for the study of the 'person' were the extent and intimacy of his membership of groups, and so forth. When, fifteen years ago, two experienced American research workers, the sociologist Walter C. Reckless and the psychiatrist Lowell S. Selling, tried to elucidate the actual differences between a sociological and a psychiatric interview, conducted independently with the same person (a coloured prostitute), it was found—as had to be expected—that, whereas the sociologist had 'obtained a life history', the psychiatrist had 'made a personality trait inventory'; that the former showed 'much less interest in the mental reactions at the sensitive zones of the subject's life', whereas the latter was much less interested in situational details; that the typical aspects of the case and the socio-legal implications of prostitution were more important to the sociologist than to the psychiatrist to whom, as Reckless thinks, it would have made but little difference whether the subject was a prostitute or anything else. Nevertheless, there was 'one important exception to the objective-subjective contrast. . . . Both the sociologist and the psychiatrist try to capture the subject's attitudes towards her experiences.'[2] We might perhaps add that, if this interesting experiment were repeated to-day, it would probably show that in the meantime the contrast has been even further reduced.

II

(1) The *methods* used in the sociological study of the offender are mainly (*a*) the statistical technique, (*b*) the sociological, ecological and typological study of an area or of a social group, (*c*) the socio-

[1] Ernest W. Burgess. 'The Study of the Delinquent as a Person', *American Journal of Sociology*, Vol. 28, May, 1923, pp. 657 et seq.
[2] Walter C. Reckless and Lowell S. Selling, 'A Sociological and Psychiatric Interview compared', *American Journal of Orthopsychiatry*, Vol. 7, 1937, pp. 532 et seq.

STUDY OF THE ADULT OFFENDER

metric technique of studying the inter-personal structure of communities or groups, (*d*) the individual interview or group discussion, (*e*) the questionnaire technique, (*f*) the use of the life history and of other personal documents, (*g*) the follow-up study, (*h*) the experimental method, (*i*) the operational method.

All these techniques are generally known, and for reasons of space only a few brief remarks may be added about some of them. It should be understood that, in theory and in practice, the use of any one of them does not exclude the use of the others. In a sociological study, for example, the interview, the life history and the questionnaire techniques may be employed. A follow-up study may involve the use of statistical methods, interviews, life histories, questionnaires, etc.

(*a*) The *statistical* technique can, here as in other fields of study, provide certain broad initial hypotheses which may be useful as indicating the direction for further investigation. If statistical studies show, for example, striking accumulations of criminal conduct in certain geographical areas, certain age groups or certain occupations, the sociological examination of an individual case will have to take account of such facts.

(*b*) The *sociological, ecological* and *typological* methods are closely related to each other.

The sociological method will, in the first place, aim at a comprehensive examination and evaluation of the social life of the community or other groups with which the offender is connected; its system of values, ideologies, attitudes, and the way in which it affects this particular offender. This community or group may be small, a village or street corner group, or fair-sized, such as Thomas and Znaniecki's Polish peasant immigrants in U.S.A. or the 'Middletown' of the Lynds or Nagel's Oss, or Sutherland's 'White collar criminals'; or it may be as vast as the whole of the United States. In every case, however, is the sociological study of these areas or groups likely to make a vital contribution to the understanding of the individual offender belonging to them. Robert K. Merton's analysis of the specific sociological conditions which make poverty a stronger criminogenic factor in U.S.A. than elsewhere and Clifford Shaw's study of five *Brothers in Crime* may be quoted as further illustrations. The ecological method, also mainly developed by Clifford Shaw, is too well-known to require any further comment.

GROUP PROBLEMS

The typological method, although more frequently employed by psychologists, psychiatrists and biologists, plays a certain part in sociological studies as well. Almost inevitably, the sociologist thinks in terms of type of family structure, of communities, etc., and tries to distinguish sociological types of criminal or otherwise maladjusted persons. Howard Becker, in his recent book *Through Values to Social Interpretation*,[1] distinguishes the 'unsocialized', the 'semi-socialized', the 'transitionally socialized', and other sociological types of adjustment or maladjustment to society. One of the objects of such typological work is to make it easier to find the most appropriate pigeon-hole for each individual for purposes of diagnosis, classification and treatment.

(c) The *sociometric technique*, developed by Ludwig Moreno,[2] was, significantly enough, first used for the detailed study of a community of delinquent girls. It is, however, not confined to the study of closed communities as its application to classes of schoolchildren shows. Whether it can be equally valuable for the study of adult offenders in prisons or elsewhere remains still to be seen.

(d) The *individual interview* technique is still probably the most popular with psychologists, psychiatrists, probation officers and other social workers. Sociologists, too, have made frequent use of it, for example, Donald Clemmer for his study *The Prison Community*,[3] Lunden[4] and Sorensen[5] in U.S.A., Norval Morris[6] for his recent book *The Habitual Criminal*, and J. Spencer[7] for his study of the effect of service life on criminal behaviour, Sir Leo Page for his book *The Young Lag*,[8] and Karl O. Christiansen[9] for his *Mand-*

[1] Howard Becker, *Through Values to Social Interpretation*, (Durham, North Carolina, Duke University Press, 1950), pp. 79 et seq.
[2] J. L. Moreno, *Who shall survive? A new Approach to the Study of Human Interrelations* (Washington D.C., Nervous and Mental Disease Publishing Co., 1934; new ed., 1953, Beacon House Inc., Beacon, New York).
[3] Donald Clemmer, *The Prison Community* (Boston, Mass., The Christopher Publishing Co., 1940). See below, Chapter 2, Sect. III.
[4] W. A. Lunden, *The Tyranny of Time*, The Presidio, March, 1950.
[5] Robert C. Sorensen, 'Interviewing Prison Inmates', *The Journal of Criminal Law and Criminology*, Vol. XLI, No. 2, July–August 1950.
[6] Norval Morris, *The Habitual Criminal* (The London School of Economics and Political Science and Longmans, Green & Co., London, New York, Toronto, 1951).
[7] John C. Spencer, *Crime and the Services* (London, Routledge & Kegan Paul, Ltd., 1954).
[8] Sir Leo Page, *The Young Lag* (London, Faber and Faber, 1950).
[9] Karl O. Christiansen, *Mandlige Landssvigere i Danmark under Besaettelsen* (I kommission hos G.E.C. Gads Forlag, København, 1950).

STUDY OF THE ADULT OFFENDER

lige Landssvigere i Danmark under Besaettelsen (Male Collaborators with the Germans in Denmark during the Occupation). W. F. Roper's survey of the Wakefield prison population,[1] although done by a Prison Medical Officer, might also be mentioned on account of the various sociological factors included. In most cases, these studies have been undertaken mainly for purposes of research; to some extent, however, also for practical objects such as improvements in judicial sentencing policy or in prison administration. Throughout, the interview has been regarded as a supplement to the information contained in case records and similar documents. Attention to the technical problems and pitfalls in interviewing prisoners has been drawn by Sorensen and Spencer. It is essential, for example, to take the peculiar 'interview situation' carefully into account; otherwise, as for example in the case of Sir Leo Page, the information obtained may only scratch the surface.

(*e*) The *questionnaire* method has recently lost some of its popularity, but there are certain research situations where it may be difficult to replace, at least for the initial stages of an investigation.

(*f*) The *life history*, especially the auto-biographical, technique has become prominent in the field of criminology in the past twenty-five years, mainly through the various publications of Clifford Shaw. The general theory of the subject has been developed by John Dollard[2] and Ernest W. Burgess[3] from the sociological and by Gordon W. Allport[4] from the psychological angle. There can be no doubt as to its value for research purposes, but it has also its more immediate merits for the understanding of individual offenders and their background, the system of values and attitudes which they have received and absorbed as a matter of course from their social groups. One of the disadvantages of the auto-biographical technique is that it requires a certain minimum of intelligence and education on the part of the offender.

(*g*) As already indicated, *follow-up studies* are dependent upon

[1] W. F. Roper, 'A Comparative Survey of the Wakefield Prison Population in 1948 and 1949', *The British Journal of Delinquency*, Vol. I, Nos. 1 and 4, July, 1950, and April, 1951.
[2] John Dollard, *Criteria for the Life History* (New Haven, Yale University Press, 1935).
[3] Ernest W. Burgess in Clifford R. Shaw *et al.*, *Brothers in Crime* (Chicago, The University of Chicago Press, 1938). See also George A. Lundberg, *Social Research* (New York, London, Toronto, 2nd ed. 1942).
[4] Gordon W. Allport, *The Use of Personal Documents* (New York, Social Science Research Council, Bulletin 49, 1942).

a number of other techniques. They should become a regular feature of an efficient treatment and after-care programme. The various Glueck studies and many of the other American prediction studies which have been conveniently summarized in Monachesi's report for the Second International Congress of Criminology, Paris, 1950,[1] have shown that, in addition to their predictive value, such follow-up investigations are likely to throw light on the development of individual criminal careers, to show where the danger spots are and to enable those concerned with individual offenders to employ their resources in the most effective manner. In this respect, life histories such as Shaw's *Brothers in Crime* provide an interesting supplement to the follow-up study by demonstrating how individual offenders whose prognosis would have been very poor according to actuarial prediction might nevertheless be diverted from further crime through special attention. It is here that we approach the fields of experimental and operational research which seems, however, to lie outside the scope of the present report.

One of the most important lessons of the research so far undertaken into the methodology of sociological studies of offenders seems the need for a judicious blending of all these different techniques.

(2) *Some technical difficulties in the sociological study of the adult offender.* (a) No collection of information regarding the adult offender can be adequate that would not go back to his childhood. 'Life', as Dollard says,[2] 'begins at zero and not at seven or fourteen or forty or otherwise, at the option of the theorist.' This dependence on early childhood experiences is indisputable not only in the field of psychological and especially psycho-analytical interpretation, but also in that of sociological analysis. Whether it is mobility or family or class structure or criminal associations or the effect of a certain group ideology that the criminologist wishes to study, his picture will be seriously incomplete and very often even distorted if he has to be content with information covering perhaps only the last few months or years before the commission of the crime which provides the occasion for his study. In *Brothers*

---

[1] Elio D. Monachesi, 'American Studies in the Prediction of Recidivism', *The Journal of Criminal Law and Criminology*, Vol. XLI, No. 3, September–October, 1950.

[2] *Criteria for the Life History*, (above p. 13, note 2), p. 26.

STUDY OF THE ADULT OFFENDER

in Crime it is shown how the continuity of contacts with criminal associations could, in one case, be traced back over a period of approximately eighteen years. In the daily routine of ordinary practical work, however, such information is hardly ever available, except perhaps occasionally in cases of offenders brought up in institutions or dealt with by Child Guidance Clinics where full case records were kept. In particular in cases of adult offenders who had never been in contact with any official agency before the commission of the crime nothing may be known about such essential factors as illegitimate birth, social, economic and criminal background of his family, etc. However, even where the offender had been dealt with by a Juvenile Court many years before his most recent crime, this fact and the information previously collected may remain unknown to the authorities either because of an understandable reluctance to include offences committed in childhood in the criminal record of a person or because of the operation of a system of rehabilitation which requires the destruction of criminal records after a period of good conduct.

(*b*) While there has been, in the course of the past thirty years or so, a considerable improvement in the psychological training of persons who have to deal with offenders, the sociological counterpart of such training is still in its infancy. When, in his article quoted above on 'The Study of the Delinquent as a Person', published in 1923,[1] Ernest W. Burgess paid tribute to William Healy's pioneer work and in particular to his recognition of the importance of the social worker in delinquency studies, he added that there was no place as yet in that field for the technique of the sociologist. It is mainly in connection with Moreno's sociometric studies and the work of sociologists employed in American prisons, notably Donald Clemmer, that sociological techniques have been used to examine the human relationships existing in closed communities such as prisons and reformatories. To the study of crime in the open, sociological techniques have been employed mainly by Clifford Shaw and his followers, by W. I. Thomas and F. Znaniecki, and by Frederick Thrasher in U.S.A. and, to mention only a few recent Continental investigations, by W. H. Nagel in *De Criminaliteit van Oss*[2] and H. van Rooy in *Criminaliteit*

[1] See note 1, p. 10 above.
[2] W. H. Nagel, *De Criminaliteit van Oss* (S-Gravenhage, D. A. Daamen's Uitgeversmaatschappij N.V., 1949).

GROUP PROBLEMS

van Stad en Land.[1] Studies of this kind have led to a growing recognition of the importance of the sociological approach for the better understanding not only of crime in general, as a mass phenomenon, but also of the development of individual criminal personalities. This, in connection with recent improvements in sociological training, may eventually lead to the employment of trained sociologists in penal and reformatory institutions, which still seems to be very rare outside the United States.

III

Finally, there arises the practical issue: how can the necessary knowledge of these group values and attitudes be acquired by the Criminal Court and used in its dealings with the individual offender?

In many cases the values and attitudes in question will be common knowledge and no special study needed. In other cases, however, the learned judge cannot be expected to be sufficiently familiar with the position existing in social classes with which he may have little or no contact. Moreover, local customs unknown outside the district in which the offender lives may be important. Where laymen are members of the Court they may possess the necessary knowledge, but they too may come from different classes or areas. With the growth of sociological and criminological literature the latter may, to some extent, take the place of the expert witness who may otherwise have to be called in future in the same way as the psychiatrist is now called. So far, use has been made of Intelligence and Personality Tests, Prediction Tables and Electro-Encephalograms. The time may come when we shall, as a matter of course, place at the disposal of the Court and the penal administrator a 'Table of Group Values and Group Attitudes'. These tables would have to answer questions such as the following: 'This offender is a worker in this particular factory— what are the standards of conduct prevailing in this factory in this particular situation?', or corresponding questions with regard to a greengrocer in this or that village or a company director in this or that city. This may seem Utopian at present, but in fact it is

---

[1] H. van Rooy, *Criminaliteit van Stad en Land* (Utrecht and Nijmegen, Dekker & van de Vegt N.V., 1949).

hardly more so than those other developments to which I have just referred may have been regarded fifty years ago.

Needless to say, the object of such specialized enquiries is not simply to provide excuses, mitigating circumstances for the accused, but to enable the Court correctly to assess guilt and to select the best possible method of treatment. Where the crime has to be regarded as mainly the outcome of values and attitudes prevailing in the community or smaller group to which the offender belongs, one of the following three courses might be adopted with regard to treatment:

(a) An attempt might be made to change those values and attitudes, for example by tackling the workers of the factory concerned through their representatives[1] or by providing new and more constructive outlets to a juvenile gang.[2]

(b) An attempt might be made to separate the individual offender from his group, for example by moving him to another district or making him join a group with better social standards.

(c) Finally, an attempt might be made to change the values and attitudes of the individual while he remains a member of his unchanged group, for example through probation without group work or work with the family. Obviously, this technique is unlikely to succeed. As social psychology has amply shown, individual attitudes can be changed, but—as among others Kurt Lewin has demonstrated[3]—this is much easier if we first change the attitudes of the group to which the individual belongs. With regard to a group of psychopathic and similar severely maladjusted patients, Maxwell Jones also expresses the view that their antisocial attitudes can be changed 'provided they are treated together in a therapeutic community'.[4] As all our findings, this, too, may of course hold good only in a social and psychological atmosphere similar to our own. For a community so profoundly different from it as the Japanese, Margaret Mead maintains that psychological

[1] See N. Muller and H. Mannheim, 'The Group Factor in Crime and Punishment', *The British Journal of Delinquency*, Vol. I, 1950, pp. 85 et seq. (see below, Chapter 2, Sect. I).
[2] See John Spencer, 'The Unclubbable Adolescent', *The British Journal of Delinquency*, Vol. I, 1950, pp. 113 et seq.
[3] Kurt Lewin, *Group Decisions and Social Change*, in T. M. Newcomb, Hartley and others, *Readings in Social Psychology* (New York, Henry Holt, 1947), pp. 337 and 343.
[4] Maxwell Jones, et al., *Social Psychiatry* (London, Tavistock Publications, 1952), p. 156.

GROUP PROBLEMS

changes could be affected only in individuals isolated from their groups.[1]

Whether the developments to which we have referred are 'good' or 'bad' is a matter of personal opinion with which we are not at present concerned. And, whatever our views may be, in spite of all the emphasis placed in this paper on the strength of group influences, the existence of personal factors should never be ignored. Recent psychological studies, such as Ruth Berenda's,[2] of children exposed to specific forms of group pressure have shown that, however strong the effect of such pressure may be, acceptance of group values and judgements is not invariably blind and complete, and age and many other factors may determine the outcome. It is here that individual lines of approach such as probation are able to make a real contribution.

[1] Margaret Mead, *Collective Guilt, in Proceedings of the International Conference on Medical Psychotherapy* (London, H. K. Lewis; New York, Columbia University Press), Vol. III, 1948, p. 61.

[2] Ruth W. Berenda, *The Influence of the Group on the Judgments of Children. An Experimental Investigation* (New York, King's Crown Press, Columbia University, 1950), pp. 19, 76 et seq.

CHAPTER 2

THE GROUP FACTOR IN CRIME AND PUNISHMENT

I. COMMENTS ON AN ARTICLE BY DR. N. MULLER

[In October, 1950, *The British Journal of Delinquency* (vol. I, No. 2), published an abridged version of articles by the Dutch judge Dr. N. Muller, Amsterdam, selected by the present writer from material which had appeared over a number of years in Dr. Muller's journal, *Maandblad voor Berechting en Reclasseering*. The translation, the work of Mr. A. D. K. Brantenaar, was financed by a grant of the Social Research Division of the London School of Economics and Political Science. The essential point made in these articles was that crime was often due to group influences rather than to any personal characteristics of the offender and that those concerned with his punishment and treatment should draw the inescapable conclusions from this. The most important features of Dr. Muller's argument are referred to in the following 'Commentary', published by the present writer in the same number of *The British Journal of Delinquency*.]

DR. MULLER deserves every praise for the wisdom and courage with which he has tackled, both as a theorist and as a practising judge of very long experience, one of the most urgent criminological problems of our time: petty stealing as a mass phenomenon, committed by so-called 'honest' people, and one of its particularly disturbing aspects: pilfering from employers.[1] He has made not only a distinct contribution to our understanding of the causes of this phenomenon, but also an interesting and

[1] See Claud Mullins, *Fifteen Years Hard Labour* (London, Victor Gollancz Ltd., 1948), p. 107: stealing from railways by men and women employed in transport work, 'presumably respectable people'.

unorthodox attempt to check it. Similar conditions exist in many other countries, including Great Britain, and there is a widespread feeling of dissatisfaction with the working of the traditional penal system and a search for more efficient counter-measures. It is in particular the Probation system that has come under fire recently as being incapable of coping with a problem apparently rooted more in group than in individual factors. Consequently, probation seems to be very rarely used in such cases, and this may be one of the many reasons for the proportionate decline in the number of persons placed on probation in recent years. It may be symptomatic of the overall picture to find that fifty-four cases of pilfering from the London Docks between May and September, 1948, dealt with by various Magistrates Courts in the Metropolitan Area, were disposed of as follows: fines, 41 cases; imprisonment, 4; dismissed with costs, 8; bound over, 1; probation, nil. No information is available regarding the number of first offenders among these pilferers, but the fact that only a few prison sentences were imposed seems to indicate that not many of them were recidivists.

Quite rightly, Muller stresses the difference between widely scattered, unco-ordinated social groups of offenders, such as those who steal electric power or the money contained in gas meters, and a more or less closely knit group such as the employees of one firm, and he points out that the method of attack has to differ accordingly. Whereas in cases of the first category any conceivable use of publicity, any appeal to the community spirit and sense of honour of actual or potential offenders would necessarily have to be of a character too vague and general to be successful, in cases of the second group the whole arsenal of sociological and psychological stimuli operating within a closely-knit group of workers can, at least in theory, be employed for purposes of crime prevention. Whether the use of these various stimuli will in actual practice be effective will, however, depend on a number of factors which have been the object of study by industrial psychologists, sociologists and criminologists for the past twenty or thirty years. Muller's reference to the famous Hawthorne experiment is very much to the point, and the fact that a practising magistrate has been trying to apply its lessons within his own sphere of work is in itself encouraging enough. It now becomes the task of the theorist to build upon these foundations.

GROUP FACTOR IN CRIME AND PUNISHMENT

The starting-point for our analysis has to be the fact that within certain groups the commission of certain types of offences is not only not disapproved and stigmatized but, on the contrary, expected and applauded. In the case of members of the so-called Underworld of our traditional Criminology, Mark Benney's 'wide people' or perhaps even the 'perfectly happy family' described by Mass-Observation,[1] this state of mind has to be taken for granted almost by definition not only in some of their relations with society but throughout; they are professional criminals with a 'criminal superego'. Now, however, we find that there are groups within society, probably much larger and more deeply affecting its well-being than the small stage-army of professionals: people neither downright anti-social nor altogether honest, but honest in certain situations and dishonest in others. There is no such thing as 'honesty' or 'dishonesty' in general. This, the 'specificity' of conduct and of attitudes, was one of the principal conclusions reached already many years ago by Hartshorne and May in their painstaking investigation of cheating, lying and stealing in some 11,000 American schoolchildren aged eight to sixteen.[2] It was also found in that study, among many other discoveries, that friends who were together in the same class of a school resembled one another more closely in deception than friends who did not attend the same class;[3] that the group atmosphere, the 'code of the classroom', seemed to be more important in matters of honesty than home background or abstract teaching,[4] and that in an atmosphere of conflict between the teacher and the class deception was bound to flourish.[5]

These facts, the 'specificity' of social and anti-social conduct, its dependence on the situation and on the general climate within the group, have more recently been confirmed by Professor Sutherland's studies of 'White Collar Crime'. Miles apart in its sociological and psychological setting as it is from both, deceit in schoolchildren and stealing by otherwise honest factory workers,

---

[1] *Report on Juvenile Delinquency* (The Falcon Press, London, 1949), pp. 73 et seq.
[2] *Studies in the Nature of Character*, Vol. I, 'Studies in Deceit', by Hugh Hartshorne and Mark A. May (New York, Columbia University Teachers College, 1930), Book I, pp. 411 et seq.
[3] Ibid., Book I, p. 275.
[4] Ibid., I, Chapters XV, XVII to XX, and p. 413.
[5] Ibid., p. 400.

GROUP PROBLEMS

white collar crime has, nevertheless, this in common with them that it is practised with the approval of the inner group by individuals who are not likely to commit crime outside the one specific setting in which they can be sure of that approval. Prestige in the world of American big business as described by Sutherland is lost not through any violations of the State criminal law but only by violations of the code of behaviour prevailing in the business world.[1] An important consequence of this is that white collar criminals, just as factory workers pilfering from their employers, do not regard themselves as criminals, that they are not ashamed of their unlawful activities, and that they are highly successful in rationalizing their conduct. There are of course many points of difference between the pilfering factory worker and the business man who fleeces the public, especially in that the victim of the former is, on the whole, better able to protect himself than can the public, and that American white collar criminals, according to Sutherland, to some extent even enjoy the protection of the Government machine.[2] Even so, however, it is essential for our whole approach to the matter to realize that the phenomenon described by Muller is only one aspect of a wider problem: that of habitual crime committed by 'otherwise honest' people who apparently experience no feeling of guilt because in their limited sphere of anti-social activities they are sure of the approval of their group which is more important to them than the disapproval of the State or of society at large and of the other groups in it. Some doubt has been expressed as to the possibility of a mentally normal criminal without a feeling of guilt towards society.[3] The profound friction, the cracks and disharmonies characteristic of modern society, however, are bound to throw up representatives of this type.

At a recent 'Conference on the Scientific Study of Juvenile Delinquency' certain points were stressed which seem to have a distinct bearing on our problem:[4] Sociological research was sug-

---

[1] Edwin H. Sutherland, *White Collar Crime* (New York, The Dryden Press, 1949), p. 219 et seq.
[2] Sutherland, p. 247.
[3] Paul Reiwald in *Die Prophylaxe des Verbrechens*, edited by Heinrich Meng, (Basel, Benno Schwabe, 1948), p. 160; also in his *Die Gesellschaft und ihre Verbrecher* (Zurich, Pan-Verlag, 1948), p. 165 (p. 150 of the English edition, *Society and its Criminals* (London, Heinemann, 1949)).
[4] *Why Delinquency?* (Published by the National Association for Mental Health), 1949. See below, Chapter 6, Sect. II.

gested into the 'attitudes of dominant social groups and individuals towards the less successful members of the community'.[1] Agreed; but why only of 'dominant' social groups? A study of attitudes of all important social groups to one another and to the various social institutions, such as property, is required. Or, as another speaker put it,[2] we have no information at present as to 'the extent to which delinquent tendencies are manifest in the behaviour of each of us in the daily round of our lives', and 'the social problem that requires investigation is the relationship between environment, group, and group member'.

For the solution of our special problem, stealing from employers, an analysis is required of the attitudes of different groups of people to property in its various forms and, more specifically, of the relationships existing between management and workers and between the workers, or groups of workers, themselves. On the first of these aspects, very little systematic research seems to have been done so far, although various writers have made some interesting observations on it of a more general character.[3] For the second aspect we have, as Muller indicates,[4] to turn to Industrial Psychology and Business Administration, knowing that our criminological problem is part and parcel of the wider one of industrial relations and morale. We cannot expect to obtain from the literature on these subjects a great deal of material bearing directly upon our own problem—stealing from employers is too delicate a subject to be taken up enthusiastically by research workers mainly interested in the wider aspects of industrial relations. Nevertheless, their findings are, indirectly, of the greatest value by enabling us to see the criminological situation in its general setting. Hartshorne and May, as already mentioned, came to the conclusion for their particular field of investigation that deception is inevitable in schools as long as there is friction between the children and their teachers and school authorities, but that even given such friction some of

[1] John Bowlby, op cit., p. 42.
[2] T. S. Simey, p. 45 et seq.
[3] See, in addition to the references given in the present writer's *Criminal Justice and Social Reconstruction* (1946), pp. 105–6, W. J. H Sprott's article, 'Psychology and the Moral Problems of our Time', *Philosophy*, July, 1948; also Mass-Observation's *Report on Juvenile Delinquency*, pp. 31 and 72.
[4] For descriptions of the Hawthorne Experiment see Elton Mayo, *Social Problems of an Industrial Civilization* (1948); F. J. Roethlisberger, *Management and Morale* (1941); F. J. Roethlisberger and W. J. Dickson, *Management and the Worker* (Harvard University Business Research Studies No. 9, 1934).

GROUP PROBLEMS

the children, because of the general background from which they come or for other individual reasons, do not cheat. Similarly, in industrial relations 'the first human problem of any business organization', as Roethlisberger has pointed out, 'is how to secure the co-operation of people in attaining its collective purpose',[1] or, in other words, how to avoid friction between management and workers. Stated in such a very general way, this is of course a commonplace hardly in need of any scientific backing. To achieve this object, more than good intentions or even intuitive insight is required, however: a systematic study not only of the 'formal', technical, but also of the 'informal' organization and the codes of behaviour existing within an industrial unit which largely determine the ways of thinking and of acting of the individual worker. For him, it may be much more important to conform with those codes than with the laws of the State or the intentions of the management, and less risky to be regarded as a 'poor worker' than as a 'rate buster'.[2] Where pilfering is practised by an influential section of the workers, those who do not take part will be not only unpopular as non-conformists but even suspect as traitors, with all the unpleasant consequences which this entails.

As far as the counter-offensive is concerned, one cannot but agree with Dr. Muller that neither the various penalties of the traditional penal system nor probation have so far proved particularly successful. They are inflicted in only a tiny fraction of offences committed, and where actually imposed they are largely ineffective because of the overwhelming encouragement which the offender receives in his illegal activities from his group. The State cannot cope with such problems without the active support of that group. Once more, an analogy might be drawn between the working population of a factory and other closely-knit communities. The idea of enlisting the participation of the group members in the administration of criminal justice in schools and reformatory or penal institutions has similar roots as the attempt

[1] *Management and Morale*, p. 110. In a series of articles on 'Dockers at Work' (*The Times*, 10th and 11th March, 1950) it was stated that 'pilferage, which assumed alarming proportions during the war and immediately afterwards, seems to have been substantially reduced in most ports, though it still causes concern'. This improvement may be due to the introduction of the post-war dock labour scheme, although the leading article in *The Times* on 11th March, 1950, complains that 'little or nothing has been done to secure from the docker a sense of loyalty to, and partnership in, the enterprise for which he works.'

[2] Roethlisberger, pp. 122 et seq.

GROUP FACTOR IN CRIME AND PUNISHMENT

to establish 'Comrades Courts' in Soviet Russia or Munition Tribunals in Great Britain during the first World War.[1] In the Rowntree Cocoa Works at York, 'with a view to creating a public opinion throughout the works which would condemn pilfering, it was arranged, in 1920, that all cases of pilfering, instead of being dealt with by the management, should be referred to a committee consisting of three elected workers' representatives and three representatives of the management, with an agreed chairman. This committee acts as a Court of Justice, trying all cases brought before it and inflicting all punishments.'[2] The interesting point here is that the third possibility, i.e. charging pilferers before the ordinary criminal courts, is not even mentioned.

There will probably be a considerable amount of agreement with Muller's diagnosis and also with his recommendation to establish Factory Courts, particularly in view of the rather rigid limitations of their competence which he proposes. If it is true that 'the major malaise of industry is the lack of participation on the part of the many'[3], anything likely to improve such participation should be welcomed. Opposition is likely to be directed against Muller's method of making the final fate of workers found guilty by the criminal court dependent not only upon their own after-conduct but also upon that of their fellow workers. Such opposition has already been voiced by another Dutch expert, Professor van Bemmelen-Leiden.[4] He stresses, in particular, that under Muller's scheme the offender in whose factory no workers' committee exists seems to be worse off than the one who can in the first instance be dealt with by his committee—a distinction which, he thinks, has as little bearing upon individual guilt as the conduct of the offender's fellow workers. Van Bemmelen prefers the traditional system of punishment strictly according to individual guilt. Clearly, no collective punishment in the technical sense is involved in Muller's scheme as the workers concerned had, each of them individually, been found guilty of an offence. Only the choice of the sentence was, to some extent, made dependent on the behaviour of other persons, over which the offender may have had

[1] See *Criminal Justice and Social Reconstruction*, pp. 178 and 245.
[2] Patricia Hall and H. W. Locke, *Incentives and Contentment*, 1938, p. 13.
[3] Wilfred B. D. Brown and Winifred Raphael, *Managers, Men and Morale*, 1948, p. 158.
[4] J. M. van Bemmelen, *Tijdschrift voor Strafrecht*, Vol. LVII, 1948, pp. 255 et seq.

GROUP PROBLEMS

no control.[1] One might perhaps argue, however, that certain further distinctions are needed to make the introduction of collective factors more effective and palatable. These collective elements might indeed, to a considerable extent, be reconciled with the idea of individual guilt—and it is highly desirable that such a reconciliation should be achieved—if the group to which the individual offender belongs becomes so well integrated that he can justly be given the credit or otherwise for its conduct. Criteria of such integration might be the average labour turnover in the factory, the size of its working population, the whole character of its 'informal' organization, including the existence of a workers' committee. Only where we have to deal with a well integrated group can judicial appeals to its collective conscience be justified and meaningful; otherwise, they would be out of place since integration which did not exist before can hardly be created by official action. Another *conditio sine qua non* is that the judge who makes the appeal should enjoy the full confidence of the group.

While Muller's plea for better group education deserves every support, one should not rely too much on the effect of degrading penalties, nor even of press publicity. Their history, from Bentham to the Nazis, is not altogether encouraging, and they should be applied, if at all, with the greatest caution and discrimination.[2] Group education should be of a constructive rather than of a punitive and destructive character. Moreover, individual treatment should go hand in hand with it. The individual offender must be made to feel that he matters as much as his group. To refer once more to the principles of industrial management, even here one of the aims is to discover the particular problems of a particular individual in a particular situation.[3] This means that there is a place for probation very often even in cases of this kind, provided it is well adapted to the specific needs of group education. Such adaptation may have to be attempted in two ways: first, probation officers have to be trained to deal more intensively with group problems themselves, and, secondly, they and group workers have to participate in a joint plan of action. A good beginning in this direction seems to have been made recently, also in Holland,

[1] As Dr. Muller makes it clear in some of his writings, his ideas should not be confused with 'collective responsibility'.
[2] Sutherland, *White Collar Crime*, pp. 39–40, emphasizes the importance of the element of public shame in the penalties imposed on white-collar criminals.
[3] Roethlisberger, *Management and Morale*, p. 133.

GROUP FACTOR IN CRIME AND PUNISHMENT

by the Juvenile Court magistrate at Utrecht, Dr. M. B. van de Werk, by further developing the basic ideas of Dr. Muller.[1] In his experience, factory work gives no feeling of satisfaction and no sense of responsibility to the boys and girls employed in it; the management very often shows but little understanding of their peculiar difficulties; and existing methods of control have no effect. He therefore decided to tackle the problem through the combined efforts of the probation officer, the factory welfare officer and a workers' committee. The probation officer, by permission of the management, discussed with the workers problems of honesty in their various aspects, and as a result a committee was elected by the workers which is now closely co-operating with the factory welfare officer and the probation officer, thus relieving the latter of those aspects of group education which may be regarded as being somewhat outside his own sphere. It remains to be seen whether this system will, in the long run, prove to be successful and whether it can also be applied to adult offenders.

II. REFLECTIONS ON THE PLACE OF Q CAMPS IN PENAL REFORM

[In 1936, a small organization was founded in London, called 'Q Camps', whose object it was to provide facilities for the training of young people and children who presented difficulties in social adjustment or behaviour. It had the moral support of a number of larger bodies working in the same or neighbouring fields such as the Central Association for Mental Welfare, the Howard League for Penal Reform, and the Institute for the Scientific Treatment of Delinquency (I.S.T.D.). This Q Camps Committee established a small open camp for young men, the Hawkspur Camp in Essex, which existed for four years when wartime difficulties enforced its closure. The Camp Chief, Mr. David Wills, has described this venture in his book *The Hawkspur Experiment*,[2] and the Q Camps Committee published a booklet *Q Camp. An Epitome of Experiences at Hawkspur Camp*, edited by the Hon. Secretary, Dr. Marjorie E.

---

[1] The following is based on personal information from Dr. van de Werk and on an article by his secretary, Miss Sluiter, in *Maandblad voor Berechting en Reclasseering*, June, 1948.
[2] London, George Allen & Unwin, Ltd., 1941. A brief description is also to be found in Teeters and Reinemann, *The Challenge of Delinquency* (New York, Prentice-Hall, Inc., 1950), pp. 508 et seq.

GROUP PROBLEMS

Franklin, to which several members of the Committee contributed. In the following, the author's contribution, which is a brief commentary on some of the points made by his colleagues, is reproduced with some cuts.

On further reflection, after a lapse of fifteen years since the closing down of Hawkspur Camp, it can be said without exaggeration that many of the ideas upon which the Camp was founded have gained widespread acceptance. 'Instruments of Treatment', as Dr. Franklin calls them in her section, such as 'pioneering', absence of regular use of punishment, informal relations between members and staff, shared responsibility (not 'self-government'), to the development of which David Wills has made lasting contributions, and many others have become integral parts of the programme of every progressive training school. No doubt, some of these principles had been known and applied before Q Camp by the pioneers to whom acknowledgment is made throughout the booklet. The work of Hawkspur Camp, however, carried on up to the present day with due adaptations in different places by David Wills [1] and his pupils and by Marjorie Franklin, has helped to keep those ideas alive and to demonstrate their practical worth. In particular, the Schools for Maladjusted Children, established in connection with sect. 33 of the Education Act, 1944, have taken over some of the principles and of the staffs trained by former members of the Q Camp Committee.]

My qualification for writing this concluding section is mainly the negative one that I have been connected with Q Camps much less intimately than my colleagues and may, for this very reason, perhaps be able to give a more detached and impersonal estimate of its activities than those who are its parents or godparents. My interest in Q Camps, it is true, goes back, if not to its pre-historic days, at least to the year 1937, when I began to attend some of its meetings. In the following year, I visited the Camp and the 'White House' and invited the Camp Chief to talk about his work to members of my Seminar at the London School of Economics. This first, and very successful, contact between the University study of delinquency and Q was soon renewed and may have given many of the students some foretaste of certain practical difficulties which beset the path of the penal reformer who has to rely mainly upon his own resources. Such experiences, together

[1] See W. David Wills, *The Barns Experiment* (London, George Allen & Unwin, Ltd., 1945).

with frequent discussions with leading members of the organization, convinced me of the great potentialities of this experiment, and in 1940 I had the privilege of being elected a member of the Committee. Since then I have taken a modest share in their efforts to keep the spirit of Q alive and to prepare for the time when it will again become possible to use its services for the work of reclamation.

There are a few questions to which the reader of the foregoing sections may still expect an answer: What are the distinguishing features of Q, as compared with other similar experiments, and where will be its place among future methods of dealing with a-social and anti-social behaviour?

As an unconventional attempt to re-educate young people of the 'behaviour problem' type—whether or not officially labelled as 'delinquents'—Q Camp might, at the first glance, be associated with such well-known experiments as Homer Lane's Little Commonwealth, the Caldecott Community, the George Junior Republic at Freeville, New York, the Californian Forestry Camps, August Aichhorn's Training School, and Anton Makarenko's Gorki Colony near Kharkov, the famous model of the 'Road to Life'. Yet, in spite of obvious similarities, among which might be ranked first the spirit of brotherly love and shared responsibility, many important differences leap to the eye. Only the most elementary of them can here be touched upon. Needless to say, to emphasize such differences implies no disparagement, and frequently even no criticism, of other systems. Q Camp principles are in no way intended as a panacea. Nothing is more needed in this field than manifoldness of methods to cope with the unending variety of individuals.'Homer Lane was the root and inspiration of all our work at Hawkspur Camp,' writes Mr. Wills in his book, and other founders of Q Camps may have had other models in mind, as for instance the Grith Pioneers or Aichhorn's work. Nevertheless, how many contrasts are there even in essentials: At Hawkspur Camp, ages ranged officially from sixteen and a half to twenty-five, and there were actually even several members up to the age of twenty-nine; fewer than one-third were under eighteen and two-fifths over twenty-one. The Little Commonwealth was intended for lower age groups, mainly between fourteen and eighteen, and, like the Gorki Colony, even admitted a number of young children. Still more is this true of the Caldecott

GROUP PROBLEMS

Community. As a consequence, all these institutions have, or had, to forgo those very primitive forms of living which were an essential characteristic of Hawkspur. Commonwealth citizens went to live at a farm with, it seems, adequate buildings; Makarenko established his colony in five delapidated brick barracks, and later on he managed to take possession of an unoccupied estate. No deserted farm happened to be in the neighbourhood of Hawkspur, and, as at the beginnings of North Sea Camp Borstal, for a considerable time members and staff had to live in tents. On the other hand, those bold and imaginative pioneer enterprises which would seem to bear the closest resemblance to Hawkspur in this particular aspect, North Sea Camp and the Californian Forestry Camps, are not only larger in size but have behind them all the material resources of the State, which provides an element of stability absent at Q Camps, although knowledge of the risk of closing through lack of funds was kept from the members. A remark like the one we find in one of the earlier Annual Reports of Q, that work was held up 'because there simply was not the money with which to buy materials for construction', almost reminds us of Makarenko's 'idiotic poverty of those early days'. Primitive conditions, accentuated by handicaps of this kind, may not only strengthen the bonds of affection between members and staff and the will to overcome difficulties and to achieve something positive, but may also go a long way to satisfy the need for punishment on the part of the individual and of Society. All this with the proviso, of course, which is sometimes forgotten, that even complete absence of the amenities of life is in itself no guarantee of success.

The Little Commonwealth had co-education, and so have the Caldecott Community, the George Junior Republic and Gorki, but there was none of it at Hawkspur. We appreciate its value and would wish to see it being used wherever possible, but we realize that, in the circumstances, it would have been premature. Considering the many opportunities of mixing with women outside the Camp, the voluntary character and the comparatively short duration of residence—19 inmates stayed for less than three months, another 18 for less than one year, and only 19 for more than one year, some of them with intervals—the matter was perhaps less burning than at long-term institutions. In view of the roughness of camp life and the absence of compulsion, even the above figures concerning length of stay are greatly to the credit of members and staff alike.

Students of institutional systems will be particularly interested to compare the scheme of shared responsibility as applied at Hawkspur with corresponding schemes in other places. It is a subject that, ever since the days of William George and Thomas Mott Osborne, has been regarded as one of the crucial tests of progressive institutional methods, though there exists much confused thinking as to the exact meaning of the term. 'Self-government' of inmates in its literal sense is to be found nowhere, and other more cautious terms, such as 'inmate participation' or 'shared responsibility' are therefore more appropriate. Such participation can apply to all or only one or two of the three traditional functions of government, the legislative, judicial and administrative. How far one may safely go in transferring some of these functions to inmates will largely depend upon their age, sex and character, on the size and spirit of the institution, and the ability of the staff to achieve their essential objectives without a formal show of authority. As a cautious form of inmate participation in the administrative sphere, in some of the Borstals and Approved Schools 'house captains', 'prefects' or 'leaders' are appointed by the head of the institution. The Californian Forestry Camps have developed a 'tribal' form of government with boy leaders, appointed by the Camp director, who have a voice in Camp affairs without any disciplinary authority over their fellows. In some American prisons, notably at the so-called ' Community Prison' at Norfolk, Massachusetts, and several American Reformatories and State Training Schools for delinquent children, Councils elected by the inmates are in operation with varying rights and duties, usually in respect to the running of kitchen, canteen, sport and other leisure-time activities. More elaborate are the methods reported from the Little Commonwealth, Gorki, Freeville, and at the Red Hill School, East Sutton, Kent, which is under the direction of a member of the Q Camps Committee, Mr. Otto L. Shaw.[1] Greatly as they differ from one another, they have in common the existence of an Inmates' Court, with more or less detailed rules of procedure and varying scope of jurisdiction. Apart from this, there was apparently not much self-government at Gorki, at least until

---

[1] Described in Mr. Shaw's interesting little book, *School Discipline. A Practical Application of Evolved Social-Legal Methods.*

GROUP PROBLEMS

1923, when Anton Makarenko's book ends. Not only did he believe in the need for discipline and the use of force 'until a community spirit is developed': the right of punishment and of expulsion rested in his hands, and he expressed some regret when the appointment of 'commanders' passed to the 'Soviet' of members. By far the most comprehensive scheme of all is the one evolved at the George Junior Republic, as it implies complete powers of legislation, jurisdiction and executive with full economic self-responsibility, supplemented by appeals for contributions from the public. To outside observers, this system may appear somewhat too artificial and ready-made in its willingness to adopt all the shortcomings of the world at large. One has to realize, however, that the present state of affairs has been reached after forty years of growth, the initial stages of which may not have been all plain sailing.

Seen in this setting, 'shared responsibility' at Hawkspur stands somewhere between the extremes. There was neither a 'leader' system nor a full-grown 'Republic'. As the chief characteristic may be regarded its experimenting spirit which, by a continuous process of trial and error, led the members through almost any conceivable form of government. Brief spells of anarchy or dictatorship were followed by various types of constitutionalism, the Camp Council exercising the usual three functions of government, with the over-ruling powers of the Camp Chief and the Q Camp Committee kept as discreetly as possible in the background. To a limited extent, the idea of economic self-responsibility of each member was adopted, including even, as at Freeville, the 'Poor Law' for those who 'did not want to work'. On the other hand, no exaggerated significance was attached to economic aspects at the expense of an all-round development of the personality. An ingenious combination was finally arrived at of the planned, paid and compulsory part of the work programme, performed in the morning and catering for the individual's need of security; and the unplanned, unpaid and voluntary activities of the afternoon, devoted chiefly to the spontaneous development of the personality. To regard the system as described in this pamphlet as the final word would be to misinterpret its spirit. 'Shared responsibility' was largely worked out in co-operation between members and staff, and any important change in personnel was bound to affect its practical working for good

GROUP FACTOR IN CRIME AND PUNISHMENT

or evil. Not rigidity but constant evolution must remain its essence.

What may be regarded as one of the most original and valuable features of Q Camp is its way of tackling the difficulties inherent in the psychological treatment of delinquents. In many institutions facilities for such treatment are either entirely absent or, where they exist, their incorporation into the whole system is usually on different lines. Two potential risks, it seems, have to be faced, though both of them can to some extent be neutralized by skilful handling. The one may be present in places where psychological treatment is given outside the institution or by a visiting specialist. Under this arrangement, the link between institution and psychologist may not be sufficiently strong and organic to provide the expert with that intimate knowledge of its communal life and spirit which he needs and to secure the sympathetic and efficient co-operation of the resident staff. Consequently, the patient's loyalties may become divided between psychologist and institution and his feeling of security and his confidence in the result may be undermined. The opposite difficulty may arise in places where treatment is given within the institution by a resident specialist. If the institution is small and the treatment intensive, the emotional temperature of the place may be raised to a permanent and unhealthy fever-pitch. The larger the institution, the shorter the average period of residence and the less intense the methods of treatment applied the easier will it be to avoid this danger. Under the system as applied at Hawkspur the advantages of these two methods seem to have been skilfully combined and their potential shortcomings eluded. In view of its smallness, the last mentioned risk had to be regarded as the greater; moreover, to secure the full-time services of a resident medico-psychologist would have been impracticable anyhow. Therefore, the other system was adopted, but with Camp Chief, Treatment Committee and treatment experts all working together as one organically united body, allowing for as much local separation between them as necessary to avoid tension. All this could be achieved only through well thought-out organization, through utter devotion and mutual understanding between those concerned; and, lastly, because of the smallness of numbers of inmates (never more than twenty at a time) in proportion to the available body of voluntary part-time experts, for all of which the credit was due

GROUP PROBLEMS

to the medical members of the Treatment Committee and to the I.S.T.D.

As the brief case histories in this booklet indicate, the human material, valuable and worth saving though it was, cannot throughout be regarded as promising from the treatment point of view. As stressed by Dr. Franklin, experimental units of the Q type, just as newly founded Child Guidance Clinics, are likely to receive 'other people's failures', who do not become any easier through their previous experiences. As compared with those of ordinary reformative institutions the members show certain deviations, not with regard to the frequency of 'broken homes' or similar family troubles among them (which are apparent in at least two-thirds of all cases), but in their mental, educational and emotional make-up: An I.Q. of more than 100 was ascertained by mental testing in about 44 per cent and estimated without test in about 16 per cent, both together comprising 60 per cent of the cases, which far exceeds the usual level in similar institutions, whereas only about 15 per cent had an I.Q. of under 86. About 40 per cent of the members had a secondary education, which again is entirely atypical (it may be recalled that in a group of 606 ex-Borstal boys whose records were examined by the writer, in his *Social Aspects of Crime*, the corresponding figure was 2·6 per cent). Moreover, the case histories show beyond doubt that a very high proportion of members were psychotics or borderline psychotics of a type generally regarded as unsuitable for Camp life and Q methods. In this respect, Hawkspur shared the fate of other adventurous enterprises in this field: in its desire to be of practical help in cases abandoned as hopeless by everybody else it had, occasionally, to act against its own regulations. This, among other factors, should be duly taken into account when the common yardstick of 'success' and 'failure' is applied. Our figures (out of 16 cases with unsatisfactory after-histories, 10 are psychotics and 5 show deep-seated symptoms) conform very closely to the general experience that recidivists are mainly recruited from the psychotic and psychopathic groups. It may suffice to quote from one of the follow-up studies made by Sheldon and Eleanor Glueck (*Later Criminal Careers*, 1937): out of about 500 young adult male offenders, followed up over a period of fifteen years after leaving the Massachusetts Reformatory, only 15 per cent of the successes, but no less than 90 per cent of the failures showed some psychiatric symptoms.

Whether, on the basis of such facts as here presented, Q Camp methods as such can be called an unqualified success is for others to decide. They will have to consider, above all, that the experiment was abruptly terminated by the war after only four years of practical work, which is not enough for any final judgement. Borstal can look back upon some decades of slow and steady development; the Californian Forestry Camps have now behind them about ten years of trial and error; and the George Junior Republic, too, seems to have needed an experimental period of considerable length. It is probable that Q methods will have to undergo certain changes if it should become possible to make a fresh start. Primitivity of life, for instance, though it should always remain an essential feature of Q, might not necessarily have to be adhered to for the whole period of an individual member's stay; with an expansion of the whole scheme it might become advisable to introduce a greater variety of methods, to be applied either simultaneously or one after the other, without destroying any vital characteristics. This would also facilitate the inclusion of younger age groups and closer co-operation with other branches of the reformatory system. Within the framework of the present system of dealing with behaviour problems in the young, Q might most fittingly be brought under sect. 80 of the Education Act 1921, and also under the category of Probation Homes and Hostels, and, given a certain relaxation of their regulations, it should not prove impossible to gain official recognition as such.

III. A REVIEW OF 'THE PRISON COMMUNITY' BY DONALD CLEMMER [1]

The author of this book is a sociologist who was employed as such for nearly a decade in a large prison in the State of Illinois, a prison which he regards as fairly typical of American penal institutions—the 'Middle-town' of American prisons, or 'just another place where men do time'. The book itself, however, is definitely *not* 'just another book about prisons'. It represents a new type. Up to now, we have had books on prison administration and prison life written either by ex-prisoners or prison officials, giving nothing but their personal views, or by outsiders with such limited

[1] Boston, U.S.A., The Christopher Publishing House, 1940. This review was first published in *The Modern Law Review*, Vol. V, Nos. 3 and 4, July 1942.

knowledge of the subject as can be gained by occasional brief visits. This is perhaps the first attempt on the part of a trained observer with a long and intimate first-hand experience to study prison life under sociological aspects, i.e. to analyze the 'culture', the social structure and the social relationships within the prison community. To judge from his methodological account, the author seems admirably equipped for his task, especially as his duties were not confined to the sociological side but included psychological work such as intelligence testing and many activities which brought him in close contact with every aspect of prison life. Years of experience in two other penal institutions and continued observation of discharged inmates provided additional insight. Of special value is the inclusion of a considerable number of essays, letters, and answers to questionnaires by the inmates themselves. The idea that prison has its social organization, quite independent of its official administration, is by no means new. It was, in fact, expressed fifty years ago by Raymond Saleilles and has been stressed by most of our ex-prisoner authors, but it was left to Mr. Clemmer to study it on scientific lines.

Clearly, the effect of imprisonment on the social behaviour of the inmates cannot be examined without adequate knowledge of their previous social histories. In his introductory chapters the author describes in detail the districts from where most of the 2,300 inmates come, age, race, nationality, physique, intelligence, occupational and marital status, previous convictions and the crimes for which they were sent to the institution. The data given are, generally speaking, in accord with the existing body of information on the characteristics of the American criminal. Those who may at first feel shocked at the high rate of mental deficiency (21·2 per cent below an I.Q. of 70) will soon arrive at a more balanced interpretation when they learn that the figure for the army draft was almost the same. There is the usual high percentage of individuals from broken homes, and the author, without offering an opinion as to the significance of the broken home as a causative factor in crime, definitely asserts that the resulting lack of family ties greatly affects the 'prison culture'. There follows a description of the prison itself which shows at least some of the characteristics of an American 'maximum security prison', as machine guns, tear and gas grenades, etc. The warden is appointed on a purely political basis, and most of the other members of the staff, too, reach their positions through political channels, in other words, an 'unbridled spoils system' is in force. As the author explains, this system seems to have done a lot of good in the years 1932–3 when, as a consequence of the economic depression, many young and efficient men could be appointed in place of the old type of job-holder who under a different system would have been irremovable. The prisoners' reactions to this method of appointment can be gathered from a remark in an inmate's essay on the work of the prison chaplain: 'His job is political, and like all political appointees he "passes the buck" to the other man who usually passes it on to the next.' The author recognizes, however, that besides the political one there are many other staff problems that have to be faced. 'The personality problems of employees in prison may be quite as serious as those of the inmates. . . . For the betterment of society both need to be controlled.' The training which these prison guards receive seems entirely inadequate. No wonder, then, that 'less than 5 per cent of the employees ever consider the reformative aspect'. Another distinctly bad feature is the overcrowding which necessitates the keeping of two prisoners in one cell, and this in an institution where the number of sexually abnormal or 'quasi-abnormal' men is estimated at 40 per cent (p. 257). In a chapter on 'Sexual Patterns in the Prison Culture' the effect of this system on individual inmates is clearly shown.

The prison receives men with fixed as well as men with indeterminate sentences, an important point to which perhaps too little attention is paid by the author. It might have been particularly revealing to collect some systematic observations on the effect of indeterminate sentences on the minds and behaviour of inmates; instead, we are allowed only a few occasional glimpses in this direction.

The central theme of the book is that 'prison is a highly complex community in which the social processes, to an extent, vary with those found in a free community'. This theme is discussed in a number of chapters on social relations, social groups, leadership phenomena, social controls, social implications of work and leisure. That criminals and prisoners are just as class-conscious as any other social group and show similar stratifications is well-known. There is hardly a single writer on these subjects who would fail to point out that professional thieves do not mix with amateurs or sexual offenders. Our author distinguishes the élite, the middle class and the 'hoosiers'; he admits, however, that the resulting social stratification is neither very strict nor very conscious. More important than this class division, and in fact second in importance only to the cleavage between officers and inmates, is the formation of social groups in prison, and it was the author's special aim to ascertain whether in a community of this kind the formation of primary groups is possible, i.e. of groups showing a highly integrated person to person relationship. To quote a few of his findings, it appeared that 18 per cent of the inmates belonged to such primary and another 40 per cent to 'semi-primary' groups, that with increasing length of stay in prison the desire to belong to a group tended to weaken, and that serious and highly 'criminalistic' offenders were more inclined to join a group than men imprisoned for either very trivial or very serious offences. An investigation of the leadership phenomenon showed that the type of leader to be found in prison differed from the leader type in free communities. None of the 'leaders' of these groups had, before their incarceration, been leaders in any kind of organization other than of a criminal character. On the other hand, to quote a remark by an inmate: 'Would any of these men (*sc*. historical heroes: Napoleon, Alexander, Washington, Cromwell) be recognized as a leader in one of our modern prisons? I think not. . . . The average prison leader has no vision, little wisdom, an insatiable desire for notoriety, enlarged adrenal glands and only a trace of thyroids.' Social ideals and purposes do exist among prisoners, but they are often different from those outside. That society and its representatives are the prisoner's natural enemies and that no prisoner should ever be helpful to an officer or talk to him, except on business, is an essential part of the unwritten Prison Code built up by generations of law-breakers. Again, this is common knowledge, but the author shows the considerable differences in responding to the Code that exist in actual practice, differences due partly to the conflict between the contents of the Code and previous standards of behaviour and partly to the fact that many prisoners are unable to be faithful even to their own Code. In prison, there is 'no consensus for a common goal', which helps to explain why prison riots are not much more frequent. Among the prisoners consulted by the author there was no unanimity, for instance, on such questions as whether stealing from inmates, which is of course strictly prohibited by the Code, was in fact of frequent occurrence. To make the confusion still worse, some rules of the Prison Code are rather complicated. It is allowed, for instance, to steal state property in prison, not, however, to sell the stolen articles.

Although the author states that in this prison idleness has not been so widespread as in other American prisons he admits that there has not been enough work to go round and that in important workshops the men are idle between 50 and 60 per cent of the time. He is, however, not particularly concerned about this state of affairs and the consequent lack of vocational training as—contrary to the predominant view—he does not believe in the reformative value of prison labour. Much more important is, in his opinion, the question of how the prisoner spends his leisure: 'One of the big problems in the future of America, as technocracy increases, will be the problem of leisure time. If we can teach our inmates enjoyable and socialized methods of spending their leisure time, it is possible that, as new values replace the old, ex-convicts will less frequently engage in crime. . . . Most of them must be taught that their basic satisfactions in life are not to be found in the field of work, but in the field of leisure-time activities. . . .' Surely, this is a rather unconventional theory with which many prison administrators will disagree, but it is worthy of serious consideration. It might even help to overcome the old fear, reiterated by recent writers, that educational progress will necessarily lead to a still more intense feeling of frustration among the masses for whom not enough skilled work will be available. At present, as the author shows in an instructive but rather depressing chapter on 'The Social Implications of Leisure Time', leisure-time facilities are still sadly inadequate in this prison. Efforts to improve them must of course be seriously handicapped by the evil 'leisure-time heritages' which the prisoners carry with them. The author calculates that 'leisure-time' occupies about 44 per cent of the prisoners' waking hours and that only 4 per cent of the total spare time is spent in ' collective recreation'. The latter is mainly of the 'spectatoritis' type only too common in English prisons as well, 'twenty men participate and the other 2,300 sit down and look on'. Equally gloomy is the account given of the state of the prison library; by comparison, English prisons seem to be distinctly superior in this respect. The prison school, as usual in U.S.A., has

GROUP PROBLEMS

its special superintendent and inmate teachers, the English system of using the services of honorary teachers from outside being unknown. The ideal might be a combination of both systems.

In the final chapter an attempt is made to assess the extent of assimilation or 'prisonization' that takes place among inmates, partly by drawing up a scheme of factors favouring such a process and partly by giving the histories of a number of prisoners. Nothing seems to be more conducive to high-grade prisonization than the loss of outside contacts and the imposition of a very long sentence. The whole question is of practical significance because those who show a high degree of prisonization are, as a rule, most likely to return to crime. Among the hundreds of prisoners with whom the author had become closely acquainted those who reformed were either men who should never have been sent to prison at all or men whose prisonization had been only very slight. There are, however, some exceptional individuals with long sentences who undergo a 'cycle of prisonization', experiencing a peak period during the intermediate stage of their term but recovering towards the end by extricating themselves from the harmful effect of group ties, by taking up new studies and making plans for a new life. This is not the place for a detailed comparison between the author's scheme of predictability, based upon the conception of prisonization, and that used by the Gluecks.

Simultaneously with Mr. Clemmer's study a fascinating book was published in this country whose author had just served more than twelve years in English prisons on a life sentence.[1] The writer, Jim Phelan, an intelligent observer and gifted novelist, suffers from an exceptionally strong contempt for 'penologists,' and an equally profound respect for 'psychologists'. His obsession prevents him from realizing that these two may occasionally be identical. How he would classify the author of *The Prison Community* is difficult to guess. One cannot, however, ignore the close harmony which exists between many of his findings and those of the American investigator. Space forbids to prove this in detail. All we can do is to express our satisfaction that modern penology, this strange ' "science" with no foundation of facts', this 'quasi-science which is unknown and uncategorized, e.g. in the British Museum Library', which is produced by men who 'do not even begin to comprehend a few elementary things about jails', some-

[1] Jim Phelan, *Jail Journey* (London, Secker & Warburg, 1940).

how contrives to obtain accurate results which bear out the statements of men with prolonged first-hand experience of prison life.

Note.—On the 'inmate social system' and on the importance of studying the 'small group' concept within the penal system see now also Lloyd W. McCorkle and Richard Korn, *Annals of the Am. academy of Political and Social Science*, Vol. 293, May 1954, pp. 89 et seq., and John James, *British Journal of Delinquency*, Vol. V, No. 4, April 1955.

CHAPTER 3

COLLECTIVE RESPONSIBILITY AND COLLECTIVE PUNISHMENT[1]

I. THE SCOPE OF THE PROBLEM

WHILE this paper, written as a contribution to a discussion by lawyers, philosophers and psychiatrists on *The Right to Punish*, is primarily concerned with collective responsibility in the field of criminal justice, the legal and criminological aspects of the problem are so closely related to others that no treatment of these aspects can altogether avoid trespassing upon neighbouring territories. The author has done his best, however, to limit such excursions to a minimum.

Collective criminal responsibility means responsibility of a group of individuals for crime committed by some, or perhaps even only one, of its members. It is an extension of individual responsibility to cover acts for which, without the conception of collective responsibility, the individual would not be held responsible. To some extent, it might be argued, the problem arises wherever the law establishes a link of this kind between a crime and a group of individuals some of whom seem to be less directly and less strongly implicated than others. If the aider and abetter, or the instigator, are punished together with and perhaps even with equal severity as the actual perpetrator, this might possibly also be regarded as an application of the idea of collective responsibility. However, whereas these legal forms of participation in another person's crime require, as a rule, more than mere passive acqui-

[1] A revised version of a contribution to *The Right to Punish*, published under the auspices of UNESCO and the Institut International de Philosophie in *Theoria* (Swedish Journal of Philosophy and Psychology), Vol. XIV, 1948, Part II, on the occasion of the Xth International Congress of Philosophy, Amsterdam, August, 1948.

COLLECTIVE RESPONSIBILITY

escence in the crime, the idea of collective responsibility applies even to cases where the individual, except for his membership of the group, has done nothing to further the commission of the crime. In other, less extreme cases, additional factors are present which strengthen the link between the actual culprit and his fellow-members; for example:

(a) the group as a whole has expressed its sympathy and solidarity with the perpetrator before or during the commission of the crime. This may not necessarily amount to instigating or aiding and abetting in the legal sense, for instance, where the crimes to be committed are defined only in the vaguest terms or the sympathy is expressed only tacitly and by implication, or where the person of the actual perpetrator of the crime remains entirely unknown to the group, or where the act of 'instigating' remains unknown to the perpetrator;

(b) or the group has done so after the commission of the crime;

(c) or it refuses to denounce the culprit and to hand him over for punishment, which may happen regardless of whether or not the group approves of the crime;

(d) or the group may in other ways, not definable in legal terms, have created the right atmosphere for the crime.

Finally, a factor of a technical, procedural character may arise and create a desire for collective responsibility: there may be a suspicion that each member of the group has been guilty of the crime, but actual evidence is available against none or only a few of them.

Needless to say, this list is by no means exhaustive.

The problem of collective responsibility, though closely related to, is not identical with that of the criminal responsibility of Corporations; it is wider since the unit whose responsibility is involved may be an unorganized group, such as a crowd, or a group such as a family, lacking many of the characteristics of the Corporation. On the other hand, some arguments pro and contra adduced in the case of Corporations apply equally to the problem in general.

If we now briefly consider the possible alternatives according to which the problem could be dealt with, they are:

(a) individual responsibility for individual crime, which is the system we have become used to regard as the normal one: every individual is held responsible exclusively for his actual share, enlarged only by legal conceptions such as instigating, aiding and abetting;

(*b*) individual responsibility for mass crime; for instance, in the case of the leader who is punished not only for his own share but also for criminal acts of his group;

(*c*) collective responsibility for individual crime: the group is held responsible for crime committed by one, or a few, of the members;

(*d*) collective responsibility for mass crime: the larger group is held responsible for crime committed by some considerable section of its members.

The reasons why collective responsibility is such a burning issue to-day are to be found partly in the practical field, in real life, and partly in the theoretical sphere, i.e. in the way in which our thinking tries to master reality. It is a commonplace to say that our age has become a mass age in which the sentiments, thoughts and actions of the individual are, much more profoundly than in other periods of modern history, dominated by those of the larger groups to which he belongs. The driving forces of our behaviour, social or anti-social, have often to be sought in the influence exercised by these large groups, such as the political party, the club, the Trade Union, rather than in the individual himself or in small primary groups such as a family. At the same time, the recent development of such comparatively new branches of scientific knowledge as Sociology and Social Psychology has greatly contributed towards a better understanding of the processes and mechanisms involved.

It goes without saying that collective responsibility and collective punishment, though closely bound together, are not entirely inseparable as responsibility may, rightly or wrongly, be assumed even in cases where no punishment is imposed. On the other hand, the question of collective punishment should not even arise where no collective responsibility is regarded as present.

II. HISTORICAL DEVELOPMENTS

It is a matter of great interest to reflect on the use which, at various stages of history, has been made of the idea of collective responsibility. The principle is rightly regarded as one of the basic characteristics of primitive society and, indeed, as one of the main points of contrast between primitive and modern thought. It

COLLECTIVE RESPONSIBILITY

would serve little purpose to give a list of references to illustrate this point. The whole of our anthropological literature abounds with examples taken from a great variety of primitive cultures.[1] The conception of blood vengeance, of vendetta, rests on the collective responsibility of the family; but, as Fauconnet has stressed,[2] even after the disappearance of blood vengeance the collective element sometimes survived at least in the field of pecuniary co-responsibility of the group. The same writer draws attention to the fact that, although collective responsibility has now become an exception in criminal law, wherever it has remained it shows the same common features, such as being confined to the most serious crimes against the State.

In recent years, an expert on the law of the Old Testament, David Daube,[3] has made an interesting attempt to clarify the conception of collective or, as he calls it, communal responsibility by distinguishing it from what he terms 'ruler punishment', and he also shows how these two conceptions are treated in the Bible: 'Briefly', he writes, 'in the case of communal responsibility proper, the community as a whole is deemed to be tainted by and answerable for the crime of any member (for example, a city may be answerable for a murder committed in its midst); while in the case of ruler punishment, the community suffers, not as answerable for the crime of a member, but as the property of a guilty ruler (for example, a sinful king may be punished by the plague decimating his people).' In his view, these two notions 'belong to very different religious and political settings (and) their history is not the same'. The first example of the working of the idea of communal responsibility which Daube uses for his discussion is, of course, Abraham's intercession for Sodom and Gomorrah. Abraham, he argues, though realizing the danger of grave injustice which may arise from the punishment of the whole group for the misdeeds of a

---

[1] 'Given the conception that the individual is merged in his group, it follows logically that his fellow-members are collectively responsible for his misdeeds. Though this is an archaic notion, it persists to the present day in the warfare of civilized nations' (Robert H. Lowie, *Primitive Society*, 2nd ed., 1929, p. 385). In *The material Culture and Social Institutions of the Simpler Peoples*, by L. T. Hobhouse, G. C. Wheeler and M. Ginsberg (1930), pp. 54 and 79, it is stressed that collective responsibility is by no means universal and that it tends to become more widespread with the growing use of a composition system.
[2] Paul Fauconnet, *La Responsabilité* (Paris, 2nd ed., 1928), p. 69.
[3] *Studies in Biblical Law* (Cambridge University Press, 1947), Chapter IV.

majority, did not see that justice ought to move in the direction towards purely individual responsibility. Instead, Abraham asks God to apply, in the place of the traditional principle, the idea of 'communal merit', i.e. the towns should be spared altogether if only a small minority of ten righteous citizens could be found. The collective element in dealing with groups of human beings, the idea that a group must be treated as a unit without any individual discrimination is to be retained, but only in favour, not to the disadvantage, of the group. 'Probably, communal thinking was so deep-rooted that Abraham could think in no other way. . . . So he criticized the results while, essentially, approving of the system.'[1] 'Why is there no doctrine of innocence by association?' asks Professor H. S. Commager in his brilliant chapter on 'Guilt by Association?'[2] Here it is!

However, as Daube shows, there are also distinct traces of the idea of individual, superseding collective, responsibility in the Old Testament, as, for example, in the story of Korah's revolt when Moses and Aaron pleaded with God to punish only the guilty, instead of the whole people; or in the commandment Deuteronomy xxiv. 16: 'The fathers shall not be put to death for the children, neither shall the children be put to death for the fathers: every man shall be put to death for his own sin'; or in the law Deuteronomy xxi. 1 that, if a murdered man is found near a town and the murderer cannot be discovered the elders of the town have at least to bring a sacrifice.[3]

Roman law, though on the whole accepting the principle of individual guilt, nevertheless knows collective responsibility with regard to the confiscation of the family fortune, and the *lex quisquis* of Arcadius (397 A.C.) has even been called by Fauconnet '*la plus célèbre de toutes les règles de responsabilite collective.*'[4] In the Germanic laws, it is mainly the penalty of outlawry that bears a collective character.[5]

In the treatment of the subject in medieval law, attention has mainly been focused on the criminal responsibility of Corporations.[6] The glossators, writes Ullmann, 'were bold enough to pro-

[1] Ibid., p. 157.
[2] H. S. Commager, *Freedom, Loyalty, Dissent* (Oxford University Press, 1954), p. 77.   [3] Daube, op cit., p. 160.
[4] Fauconnet, *La Responsabilité*, p. 78–9.   [5] Ibid., p. 80.
[6] See the study by Dr. Walter Ullmann, 'The Delictal Responsibility of Medieval Corporations', *The Law Quarterly Review*, Vol. 64, January, 1948.

COLLECTIVE RESPONSIBILITY

claim the corporate criminal liability, without however attempting to justify it on the strength of the sources available', with the only proviso that they required 'some vaguely conceived corporate will to commit a crime'.[1] Bassanius asks, for instance, in the case of some forest depredations jointly committed by the inhabitants of a village whether the village authorities had been with the crowd, whether there had been any ringing of bells, beating of drums or other external means of calling them together for corporate action, and if the answer was in the affirmative the village as such was to be held responsible. On the other hand, Pope Innocent IV is opposed to corporate punishment, mainly, it seems, because the penalty he had in mind was excommunication.[2] Bartolus, again, approves of it, even of such acts as the punitive destruction of entire communities for rebellion committed by their leaders. It is interesting to note, however, that he distinguishes according to the size of the guilty community: if it is small, the fine should be imposed only on those members who had given their explicit consent to the crime, whereas in the case of large groups, such as muncipalities or nations, distinctions according to guilt would be too difficult—a consideration which, in a modified sense, we shall later find again in the Nuremberg Judgement. Moreover, collective punishment is accepted by Bartolus only where the crime was committed in accordance with a communal resolution preceded by adequate deliberations.[3]

In England, William the Conqueror established the institution of 'murder-fine' which placed collective responsibility for the death of a Norman on the hundred, a small unit of local government: 'If a person were found dead, and there were no "presentment of Englishry", that is to say, if the body could not be proved to be that of an Englishman, it was presumed to be that of a Norman, and the hundred was rendered liable to pay a murder-fine'.[4] There was also the institution of Frank-pledge in early English law, which meant a group of adult men, sometimes all men living in a certain township, who were liable to a fine if they did not surrender those members of their group who had committed a crime. After the decay of this institution in the fourteenth

---

[1] Ibid., pp. 78–80, 84.   [2] Ibid., p. 82.
[3] Ibid., pp. 89–90.
[4] H. G. Hanbury, *English Courts of Law* (Oxford University Press, 1944), p. 28.

GROUP PROBLEMS

century, England, it has been said, 'possessed no effective machinery for arresting criminals or for preventing the commission of crime, until the creation, by Sir Robert Peel's energy, of the modern police force'.[1]

With regard to more recent periods of history, Fauconnet refers to certain provisions in the former Chinese law, according to which in cases of high treason and aggravated murder certain members of the culprit's family were liable to capital punishment or banishment for life.[2]

In some of the British Colonies, the Government has accepted the principle of collective responsibility as a living force and incorporated it in its own Ordinances. In Nigeria, for example, a Capital Punishment Ordinance provides that in certain cases punishment may be imposed on an entire group for an offence committed by one or more of its members. This Ordinance is, however, stated to have become a dead letter in actual practice.[3] In Transjordan under the British Mandate, a 'Board of Control' had power to arrest the relatives up to the fifth degree of the aggressors in tribal raids and to detain them until the aggressor had been handed over and the booty restored—a system which is said to have greatly increased the respect for law and order in that country.[4] Such examples could easily be multiplied.

Note.—Since this was written, with the intensification of political unrest particularly in Malaya and Kenya the use of collective penalties seems to have become more frequent. The following cases may be quoted from Press reports:

(a) 'After the murder of Sir Henry Gurney the entire population of one village was uprooted. However, prolonged police "screening" led to the release of all except a small fraction, but innocent as well as guilty had lost their village' (*The Observer*, 30th March, 1952).

(b) In Pekan Jabi, a village in Johore, where three policemen had been killed by terrorists, the rice ration was reduced for 4 weeks, a rigorous curfew imposed and the villagers were confined to their huts for 12 hours daily (*The Times*, 3rd November, 1952).

[1] C. S. Kenny, *Outlines of Criminal Law*, an entirely new edition by J. W. Cecil Turner (Cambridge University Press, 1952), paragraphs 429 and 690.
[2] Fauconnet, op cit., p. 71 et seq.
[3] C. K. Meek, *Law and Authority in a Nigerian Tribe* (1937), pp. 338-9.
[4] Meek, loc. cit.

COLLECTIVE RESPONSIBILITY

(c) After 12 men had been killed in an ambush on its outskirts Tanjong Malim, a town of about 5,000 inhabitants, was punished for non-cooperation. The High Commissioner for the Federation of Malaya (General Sir Gerald Templer) imposed a curfew of 22 hours per day, ordered shops to be closed except for 2 hours daily, forbade the townsfolk to leave, closed all schools, stopped all bus services and reduced the rice ration (*The Times*, 28th March, 1952). Shortly afterwards, questionnaires were distributed by the High Commissioner asking all householders for information which might be helpful in the fight against the terrorists. The correspondent of *The Times*, commenting on this, wrote: 'It is believed that the vast majority of the inhabitants cannot possibly have any positive information about the Communist organization' (*The Times*, 7th April, 1952). The case of Tanjong Malim was debated in both Houses of Parliament, and a motion signed by more than a hundred Labour members was tabled in the House of Commons deploring the imposition of collective punishment. In the House of Lords, the Secretary of State for Commonwealth Relations, while describing the rationing of rice as a non-punitive measure intended to deny the rice to the terrorists, admitted that the curfew and the closing of schools contained an element of punishment, 'designed to make clear to the villagers that they could not with impunity condone or assist cold-blooded murder' (*The Times*, 8th April, 1952).

(d) The whole population of Permatang Tinggi, a hamlet in northern Malaya, where a Chinese official had been murdered by terrorists was sent to a detention camp for failing to give information, and the hamlet was to be razed to the ground (*The Times*, 26th August 1952). This was described as 'the most drastic example of collective punishment during the campaign in Malaya' by Lord Listowel who also pointed out that it was not only contrary to British ideas of fair play and particularly hard on the children who lost their homes, but also bound to fail in its object since the population was more afraid of the terrorists than of the administration (*The Times*, 28th August, 1952). In his book on Malaya, Victor Purcell, after pointing out that 'the morality of collective punishment has been debated in Britain for centuries', reports that General Templer eventually abandoned the system as a failure. In Purcell's view measures of collective punishment are of no use whatsoever.[1]

(e) In Kenya, the African inhabitants of five sublocations of the Nyeri District were fined £2,500 under the Collective Punishment

---

[1] Victor Purcell, *Malaya: Communist or Free?* (London, Gollancz, 1954, p. 238.)

GROUP PROBLEMS

Ordinance for suppressing evidence of cases of arson in the area (*The Times*, 19th April, 1952). The policy of collective punishment in Kenya was fully debated in the House of Lords on the 26th November, 1952, and in the House of Commons on the 16th December, 1952, when the Government spokesmen, while defending the policy, admitted its weaknesses and stressed that collective penalties should be used only as the last resort and imposed on very small districts only (*The Times*, 27th November and 17th December, 1952).

In 1950, the Prime Ministers of India and Pakistan were reported to have concluded an agreement on the protection of minority rights which, among other measures, provided for the infliction of collective fines on localities where violations of the agreement would occur (*The Times*, 11th April, 1950).

Instances such as these show how difficult it is in this field to draw the line between legal, criminological and penological considerations, on the one hand, and political ones, on the other.

An interesting attempt to preserve the principle of collective responsibility in a form reconcilable with modern ideas is being made by the Commission at present working on the reform of the Ethiopian Penal Code of 1930. No collective punishment can be imposed according to art. 52 of the Draft Code where the majority of the group charged had neither approved of nor assisted in the commission of the crime, had explicitly advised against it and had delivered the culprits, or assisted in their delivery, to the organs of justice. Moreover, nobody will be punishable who can prove that he had taken no part whatsoever in the crime of the group. The sanction will be fines, confiscation, reparation, and, if there is danger of further collective crimes, confinement or removal from home.[1]

Under Nazi rule, the application of the principle of collective responsibility and punishment reached its hey-day, not only as a result of the system of hostages but also because of its use in Concentration Camps. In those numerous descriptions of life in such Camps which we owe to former inmates particular emphasis is laid on the fact that every inmate had to be a member of at least one collective unit within the Camp; that nearly every detail of

[1] See the informative article by Prof. Jean Graven-Geneva, at present consultant to the Ethiopian Ministry of Justice at Addis Ababa, 'Vers un nouveau droit penal Éthiopien' (*Revue internationale de Criminologie et de Police Technique*, Vol. VII, No. 4, Octobre-Decembre, 1954, pp. 271-2).

COLLECTIVE RESPONSIBILITY

Camp life was subject to collective regulation; and that collective responsibility and punishment was not the exception but the rule.[1] It was this aspect of Nazi penal technique—the infliction of suffering on whole groups of people regardless of individual guilt —perhaps more than any other of their outrages that eventually produced the widespread sentiment in favour of collective punishment of the German people as such. To such tendencies the Allied Powers did not yield; nor can it be maintained[2] that the Charter and Judgement of the Nuremberg Tribunal contain an application of the principle of collective responsibility.[3] The Charter, it is true, provided in addition to the punishment of individual persons the following possibility with regard to groups or organizations (art. 9):

'At the trial of any individual member of any group or organization the Tribunal may declare (in connection with any act of which the individual may be convicted) that the group or organization of which the individual was a member was a criminal organization.'

According to art. 10 of the Charter, the effect of such a declaration was that the competent national authority of any signatory of the Charter had the right to bring individuals to trial for membership of such a criminal organization, and that 'in any such case the criminal nature of the group or organization is considered proved and shall not be questioned'. Moreover, according to an Act passed by the Control Commission for Germany on 20th December, 1945, and quoted in the Judgement, membership of a group or organization declared criminal by the International Military Tribunal was recognized as a crime for which the usual penalties, including death and imprisonment for life, could be imposed. The Nuremberg Judgement stressed, however, that all these provisions should be applied

in accordance with well settled legal principles, one of the most important of which is that criminal guilt is personal and that mass

---

[1] See, for example, Benedikt Kautsky, *Teufel und Verdammte* (1946), p. 176; Bruno Bettelheim, 'Individual and Mass Behaviour in Extreme Situations' (*Journal of Abnormal and Social Psychology*, Vol. 38, October, 1943, pp. 417 et seq.)

[2] As done by Wolfgang Friedmann, *The Allied Military Government of Germany* (1947), p. 175.

[3] *Judgement of the International Military Tribunal for the Trial of German Major War Criminals* (London, H.M.S.O., Cmd. 6964, 1946), p. 80.

GROUP PROBLEMS

punishment should be avoided. If satisfied of the criminal guilt of any organization or group this Tribunal should not hesitate to declare it to be criminal because the theory of 'group criminality' is new, or because it might be unjustly applied by some subsequent Tribunals. On the other hand, the Tribunal should make such declaration of criminality so far as possible in a manner to insure that innocent persons will not be punished.[1]

In fact, the Tribunal restricted the scope of collective punishment in the case of every group or organization which it declared to be criminal to those members 'who became or remained members of the organization with knowledge that it was being used for the commission of acts declared criminal by art. 6 of the Charter, or who were personally implicated as members of the organization in the commission of such crimes'. Accordingly, the charge in the subsequent trials before Allied or German Tribunals was one of membership with knowledge that the organization was being used for the commission of crimes.[2] Moreover, the Judgement contains the further remark that persons 'who were drafted by the State for membership' should be excluded from responsibility unless personally implicated in crimes.[3] From this, it appears that the practical consequences of the special treatment meted out to criminal organizations by the Charter and the Nuremberg Judgement were twofold: First, the question whether a certain organization was a criminal organization was decided at Nuremberg finally and for all subsequent trials, and it was not open to individuals subsequently charged because of their membership to question this decision. This is a procedural device of a technical character, indispensable in a situation where the same point is of legal significance in an extremely large number of subsequent individual trials. To alleviate any undue hardship which might possibly have been caused to individual members if their organization was condemned, art. 9 of the Charter provided that they should be entitled to apply to the Tribunal for leave to be heard upon the question of the criminal character of the organization. In fact, such applications were received and dealt with in very large numbers. It should be noted in this connection that the Tribunal refused to declare the Reich Cabinet to be a criminal organization because, among other reasons, it was only a small

---

[1] Nuremberg Judgement, pp. 66–69.   [2] Friedmann, p. 175.
[3] Nuremberg Judgement, pp. 67, 79.

COLLECTIVE RESPONSIBILITY

group and there would therefore have been no technical advantage in dealing with it in a wholesale fashion.[1]

The second consequence of the provisions of art. 9 and 10 of the Charter as interpreted by the Nuremberg Tribunal was that a member of a criminal organization could be punished only if it could be proved against him that he had become or remained a member knowing that the organization was being used for the commission of crimes. Although opinion on this point may differ, it seems at least doubtful whether this has to be regarded as a deviation from the general principles of criminal law regarding complicity, in other words, whether complicity requires more than becoming or remaining a member of an organization knowing that it was engaged in crime. If this should be answered in the negative,[2] one would have to come to the conclusion that the principle of collective responsibility was not accepted in the War Crimes trials, in particular as all the individual defences such as insanity, mental deficiency, youth, could be freely argued in subsequent trials of each member. In his chapter 'Guilt by Association?'[3] Professor Commager, demonstrating the legal and moral perversity of the idea of collective guilt, refers to the statement of the Supreme Court of the United States in the Schneiderman case (320 U.S. 118) that 'men in adhering to a political party or other organization do not subscribe unqualifiedly to all of its platforms or asserted principles'. It seems that, in fact, all conceivable qualifications which the Supreme Court could have envisaged were allowed for in the Nuremberg trials.

III. SOCIO-PSYCHOLOGICAL AND PENOLOGICAL CONSIDERATIONS

Our historical sketch of the development of collective responsibility 'from Sodom to Nuremberg' would seem to indicate that this may be one of those ideas which correspond to certain deep-rooted emotional tendencies and can therefore never be completely destroyed in spite of the strongest efforts on the part of our conscious and rational thought. It is unwise, it might be argued, to shut our eyes to the unpleasant fact that Justice, as we conceive

[1] Nuremberg Judgement, p. 81.
[2] With regard to officers and members of governing bodies of corporations, modern English criminal statutes frequently even shift the burden of proof to the accused who has to disprove his knowledge or consent; see Glanville Williams, *Criminal Law: The General Part*, 1953, pp. 215 and 686 et seq.
[3] H. S. Commager, *Freedom, Loyalty, Dissent* (above note 2, p. 46), p. 82.

GROUP PROBLEMS

it, is not a natural but a highly artificial conception which only in exceptional cases bears any relation to what happens in real life. In this respect, the problem may bear some resemblance to that of Retribution which, much as we may dislike it, will probably have to be accepted for many years to come as one of the predominant features of our penal system. All the more is it the duty of penal philosophers and social psychologists to examine the various factors which may help to explain those tendencies.

Is there, to begin with, in the constitutional make-up of the human personality anything like an inborn, instinctive feeling that would demand collective rather than individual punishment for wrongdoing? If this were so, it would explain the prevalence of this institution in primitive communities. Could one assume, for instance, the existence of an innate tendency in the human mind towards generalization and simplification rather than a tendency towards individualization and discrimination in our judgements of other persons? No doubt, even when dealing with only one person, we are often inclined to use sweeping generalizations, to condemn an entire personality on the basis of one single case of misconduct which, perhaps too hastily, we regard as an expression of his true character: 'He has stolen once—he will steal again—he is a thief by nature.' Naturally, this way of thinking can easily be applied to the collective unit. If the man in the street has been cheated by his greengrocer he will be distrustful of greengrocers in general. This is one—though by no means the only—explanation of that phenomenon which supplies one of the oldest and most impressive illustrations of collective judgement, responsibility and punishment: Anti-semitism, and it also accounts for an exaggerated belief in the existence and strength of national character.[1] It is, moreover, closely related to the need for a scapegoat, though there is the difference between it and collective punishment that the scapegoat is not necessarily a collective unit and that, even where it is one, none of its members may in any way be responsible for the crime. The proneness to use generalizations and to pass collective judgements, which, as Bertrand Russell writes, is 'much

---

[1] From the very comprehensive literature on these two problems only two recent publications may be quoted: Morris Ginsberg, *Reason and Unreason in Society (Essays in Sociology and Social Philosophy)*, 1947, Chapters VII: 'National Character' and X: 'Anti-Semitism'; James Parkes, *An Enemy of the People: Anti-Semitism* (Penguin Books, 1945).

diminished by education',[1] is stronger with regard to groups such as the Jews where it is re-enforced by the presence of other psychological, sociological and historical factors; to some extent, however, it does exist everywhere. 'If the Tiber overflows into the city, if the Nile does not flow into the countryside, if the heavens remain unmoved, if the earth quakes, if there is famine or pestilence, at once the cry goes up: "To the lions with the Christians",' complained already Tertullian.[2] Cecil Roth[3] reports an episode which is said to have occurred in Oxford on Ascension Day, 1268, when for the alleged sacrilege of a Jew the whole Jewish community of the city were ordered to identify the culprit and, failing this, were thrown into jail until they had made reparation. To give a less extreme recent illustration of the tendency towards generalization from the daily life of a modern community: In 1942, a violent fire destroyed the 'Cocoanut Grove', a popular nightclub in Boston, Massachusetts, causing the death of nearly 500 people.[4] 'Through its news reports and featured articles, the press had directed its wrath against the public officials individually ... Significantly, however, ... the reaction of the public was essentially against the public officials *as a group or class*.' Their collective negligence, laxness and incompetence were blamed in 90 per cent of the 'letters to the Editor' published in one paper. The explanation for this 'blanket scapegoating' given in the article quoted below is: it was the desire for a simplification of legal and moral issues which had been obscured by the complexity of the building laws, with the consequent confusion as to the functions of various city officials, that made 'blaming them collectively much simpler than blaming them as individuals'.[5] Moreover, these officials were not usually known to the public as individuals; therefore, they were rather treated as a symbol for anything that was regarded as rotten in the local administration. Here again, one might conclude, certain special circumstances seemed to have

---

[1] Bertrand Russell, *Human Knowledge. Its Scope and Limits* (London, George Allen & Unwin, Ltd., 1948), p. 452.
[2] Parkes, p. 86.
[3] Cecil Roth, *The Jews of Medieval Oxford* (Clarendon Press, 1951), pp. 152 et seq.
[4] An interesting analysis of this case is given in an article by Helen Rank Veltfort and George E. Lee, 'The Cocoanut Grove Fire: a Study in Scapegoating' (*Clinical Supplement to the J. of Abnormal and Soc. Psychol.*, Vol. 38, April, 1943, pp. 138 et seq.).
[5] Veltfort and Lee, p. 146.

GROUP PROBLEMS

helped to bring into the open a tendency which might otherwise have remained hidden.

The fundamental question of the innate character of the desire for collective punishment has been experimentally examined by Professor Jean Piaget.[1] He asked children of various age groups to give their views as to whether they regarded punishment of a whole group as just, with regard to three different situations: (1) where no attempt was made by the adult to find out the actual culprit; (2) where the adults had tried in vain to discover the culprit, but he did not own up and the group refused to denounce him; (3) as under (2) but the group was not aware of the identity of the culprit. According to Piaget, the answers showed that the idea of collective responsibility evoked no spontaneous response in these children, i.e. collective responsibility in the sense of holding members of the group responsible merely because of their membership. If, however, the group declares its solidarity with the offender by refusing to denounce him, the children regard this as sufficient to justify collective punishment. The reasons for this attitude differ according to age: whereas the younger children simply think it wrong not to denounce the culprit and are inclined to take it for granted that, if a crime has been committed, somebody has to be punished for it at any cost, the older ones base their judgement on a feeling of solidarity not with the adult but with the group which, by refusing to co-operate with the adult, declares its willingness to bear the consequences for this refusal. There is, however, also a third category among these children: those who insist on treating each individual case according to its merits and, therefore, prefer punishment of nobody to that of an innocent. No undue importance should of course be attached to Piaget's results derived as they are from the study of one small group only, in particular as the reactions of children may well be different in different countries and cultural settings. To the knowledge of the present writer, only one other study based upon empirical material has been published after Piaget, using not children but adults: In that monumental piece of research, 'The American Soldier',[2] certain questions regarding the desirability of group

---

[1] Jean Piaget, *The Moral Judgment of the Child* (English translation, 1932), pp. 231 et seq. (London, Kegan Paul).

[2] Samuel A. Stouffer, *et al.*, *The American Soldier* (Princeton University Press, 1949), Vol. I, pp. 423 et seq.

COLLECTIVE RESPONSIBILITY

punishment for misconduct of individual soldiers are reported as having been put to a number of American officers. The majority of them, 58 per cent, expressed themselves unconditionally against the application of group punishment, whereas 42 per cent thought it might sometimes be useful. More detailed questioning showed that, in the experience of these officers, group punishment was regarded as likely to be more successful and more acceptable in certain situations and under certain conditions than in others. Conditions favourable to group punishment were, for example, that warnings regarding its imposition should persistently be given in advance and that it should be regarded as an established practice, not merely as the whim of an individual; that members of the group should be in a position to identify likely offenders in order to prevent their misconduct; and that the misconduct should be of a kind disapproved by the men themselves. As in the case of the children questioned by Piaget, these factors seem to be a not unreasonable combination of moral and practical considerations.

With regard to primitive communities, too, the evidence seems to indicate that it is by practical and rational considerations rather than by any constitutional factors characteristic of innate qualities of the human race that the prevalence of collective responsibility has to be explained. Collective punishment is useful as a means of preserving order and preventing crime. If the whole group has to expect punishment for misconduct of individual members, it will—this is the reasoning—do everything in its power to uphold order and discipline, and as the community spirit is particularly strong in primitive groups every member will endeavour to prevent the punishment of his group for individual crime. Where the group spirit is still a living force, the institution of collective responsibility is, therefore, the strongest possible deterrent, and it loses its effect where that spirit has disappeared.[1] There is the additional factor that pecuniary penalties have to be imposed upon the group because of the collective nature of the family property. From the point of view of penal philosophy, however, the principal argument in favour of collective punishment is that of deterrence and discipline, with the more constructive object of training for group life taking the second place. In Nazi

[1] See, for instance, Hans Kelsen, *Society and Nature* (first published in England, 1946), p. 361; David Daube, op. cit., pp. 180-1.

GROUP PROBLEMS

Concentration Camps, 'the idea was that every prisoner ought to feel responsible for any act committed by any other prisoner'.[1] The ultimate effect, however, it has been reported, was not only deterrence and better discipline but also some sort of acceptance of Gestapo ideals by the prisoners. Since a poor capacity for work was as much to the detriment of the group as misconduct and as weaklings were also more likely to become informers, even the prisoners sometimes adopted the Nazi ideology towards the extermination of unfit members. Again, it is stated that many of them did not want their escaped fellow prisoners to 'tell the story of the Camps' abroad.[2] In a way, such attitudes may, as Bettelheim indicates, show how collective punishment, by building up a strong feeling of group unity, can have the effect, whether intended or not, of forming a link between punisher and punished. On the other hand, the Nazi system was careful to prevent the growth of martyrdom, which would have unduly strengthened the feeling of a group unity limited to prisoners, by punishing the group more severely for actions by potential martyrs.[3]

It is largely in view of such penological, socio-psychological and educational mechanisms—the deterrent effect of fear and the disciplining, link-forming and community-building effect of collective treatment—that this form of punishment is so often used in schools and reformatory institutions for juvenile offenders, and occasionally also in prisons for adults. Training in group discipline frequently means collective privileges, rewards and punishments. To quote a few examples from the Press:

Five hundred schoolboys at . . . County Grammar School sat at their desks to-day when they should have been starting their Whitsun holiday. The headmaster saw that the Army Cadet Corps notice board had been slashed. Nobody owned up. So the boys were told they would have to go to school to-day.[4]

When a teacher at a secondary modern school was charged on five summonses brought by parents, alleging common assaults by caning thirteen-year-old boys in his class, the charges were dismissed by the Magistrates. Some boys in the class had 'stamped feet', and as they did not own up the teacher caned the whole

[1] Bettelheim, loc. cit. p. 434, note 16.
[2] Bettelheim, pp. 448–9.   [3] Bettelheim, p. 436.
[4] *Evening Standard* (London), 14th May, 1948.

COLLECTIVE RESPONSIBILITY

class. The Court took the view that he had acted reasonably in the interests of discipline.[1]

Experienced and enlightened educators insist that the instrument of collective penalties is an evil, though occasionally perhaps a necessary one, which should be applied only in carefully selected cases where the relationship between staff and pupils is good and the latter can be expected to appreciate the situation and to cooperate. In other words, it is an instrument to be used to strengthen an already existing spirit of loyalty and cooperation, not to create one where it did not exist before. In the 'Report of the Committee of Enquiry into the conduct of Standon Farm Approved School and the Circumstances connected with the Murder of a Master at the School on 15th February, 1947',[2] the dangers connected with collective punishments and even the mere threats of collective fines are strongly emphasized; and the latter are included in the list of the main causes of the murder by some of the boys of a master who was shot by mistake instead of the Headmaster whom they had actually intended to kill. It is pointed out in the Report that

The boys were firmly of opinion that collective punishment and collective fines were inflicted. The Headmaster and Staff told us that occasionally the boys were made to stand on the parade ground for periods of 15 to 40 minutes, but only for collective misconduct, disobedience and rowdiness ... Such forms of collective punishment inevitably caused deep resentment amongst innocent boys who felt they were being unjustly treated. Similarly the boys deeply resented the imposition of collective fines ... [which were, in fact, never actually imposed].

This feeling of injustice can easily become so strong that the deterrent and educative effects may be altogether lost. Moreover, although this has been doubted,[3] a group can as a rule better resist the pressure of punishment than an isolated individual. This in particular where the group is so large that the penalties to be inflicted can, for practical reasons, not be very severe. It is interesting to observe the various conflicting arguments concerning the impact of this factor—the size of the group—on the theory and practice of collective punishment: Bartolus and the Nuremberg Tribunal, as we have seen, use the argument that in the case of

[1] *The Times*, 6th November, 1954.
[2] London, H.M.S.O., Cmd. 7150, 1947, pp. 22 and 26.
[3] Bettelheim, loc. cit., p. 452.

GROUP PROBLEMS

small groups there is no need for collective punishment. Social psychologists stress that very large groups are often too successful in building up internal defence mechanisms for collective treatment to have much deterrent or re-educative effect. Criminologists may add that, according to the principles of mass psychology, the larger the group the slighter the individual guilt of each member is likely to be, especially in view of the strength of mass suggestibility which grows in proportion to the numbers involved. Politicians, as we have seen in the case of the attitude of British Government spokesmen dealing with the situation in Malaya and Kenya, are in favour of restricting the use of collective punishment to small areas, and educators, though perhaps for different reasons, agree with them. There seems therefore to exist a strong majority in support of the latter view.

Transferred from the sphere of penal to that of civil liability, entered into by voluntary agreement and combined with a system of 'shared responsibility', the idea of collective responsibility has with advantage been used in progressive institutions. Here, its dangers are much less pronounced. In a school for maladjusted children, it is reported,[1] the Governors insured the school property against wilful damage with the boys acting as a corporate body. Except with very disturbed children who could not be influenced by reasonable group pressure, this system worked well as the boys were anxious to prevent irresponsible behaviour. In all such cases, a system of 'shared responsibility'[2] which enables the group to exert its influence for good on individual members is the indispensable concomitant of collective responsibility; without it, the latter degenerates into tyranny.

In connection with the development of psychological warfare in the second world war, the psycho-sociological foundations of collective guilt and responsibility in Japan and the various ways in which they found their expression in Japanese society have been studied by American anthropologists, notably by Ruth Benedict[3] and Margaret Mead.[4] Here collective responsibility is shown as

[1] In a so far unpublished Ph.D. thesis, London, 1953, by Howard Jones.
[2] See above, Chapter 2, Sect. II.
[3] Ruth Benedict, *The Chrysanthemum and the Sword* (Boston, Houghton Mifflin & Co., 1947).
[4] Margaret Mead, 'Collective Guilt' (paper read at International Conference on Medical Psychotherapy, London, 1948), (*Proceedings of the International Congress on Mental Health*, London, H. K. Lewis, Vol. II).

COLLECTIVE RESPONSIBILITY

the natural outcome of a whole culture and of an atmosphere moulding the structure of society. Much more strongly than in other cultures, every member of the Japanese community is held responsible for the good name of his family and is punished not for the crime which he has committed but for the disgrace which he has brought over his family. It is a system closely connected with the idea of interchangeability of individual group members as found in primitive societies. As Margaret Mead points out, by allowing no individual choice or discrimination regarding the nature of the duties imposed upon the individual the Japanese system, while strengthening the child's feeling of group loyalty and respect for force, leaves no scope for the development of an individual conscience. As the group withdraws its support from members failing, for whatever reason, to carry out their duties towards it, the only way out open to the guilty individual is suicide.

IV. THE VARIOUS FORMS OF COLLECTIVE RESPONSIBILITY AND PUNISHMENT

The discriminating factors which have so far emerged have been mainly related to certain characteristics of the groups concerned and of the relationships existing between groups and members and between the latter and the crime. Factors found to be material are, for example, the size of the group, the existence of a feeling of group cohesion and loyalty among members, their disapproval of the crime, their ability to prevent it or at least to spot the offender; finally, any other factor revealing certain rudiments of individual guilt and thereby making collective responsibility less repulsive.

The problem now to be faced, though in many ways related to our previous discussion, nevertheless requires separate treatment: the existence of different forms of collective responsibility and, correspondingly, punishment. Although our illustrative material has been mainly taken from the field of the criminal law and its history, there have also been occasional cases of disciplinary, civil or administrative responsibility. Perhaps the most penetrating, and certainly the most widely discussed, attempt to classify the various forms of collective responsibility according to their nature and to the nature of the sanction attached to them has been made by the German philosopher and psychiatrist Karl Jaspers in his important book, *Die Schuldfrage*.[1] His argument, developed with special reference to the question of German guilt for Nazi outrages, can be reduced to the following basic ideas: There are four different types of guilt and of responsibility and of sanctions which have to be kept strictly separate; criminal-political-moral-metaphysical. Man is *criminally* responsible for certain clearly defined and proved acts against the criminal law, with consequent punishment inflicted by the Court. As citizen, he is *politically* responsible for actions of his Government; the crucial factor here is success or failure of that Government's policy, and the sanction is imposed by the victor on the vanquished. In the *moral* sphere, only the individual himself and his conscience are competent to judge, and in case of moral guilt repentance and heart-searching are required. *Metaphysical* guilt, finally, arises from the solidarity between human beings as such which makes everyone responsible for every wrong in the world, especially for crime committed with his knowledge, unless he has done everything in his power to prevent it. Others, however, are entitled to take the individual to task only in the criminal and political, not in the moral and metaphysical spheres. From this, it would follow that collective responsibility has its rightful place in each of these spheres except that of the criminal law, but in different forms. It is most tangible in the political field where it can be enforced by the victor; it may also exist in the moral and in particular in the metaphysical sphere, but here it can be neither proved nor enforced from outside.

In a more recent work,[2] Jaspers has expressed himself more briefly but perhaps also more clearly on the metaphysical side of the problem: The circle within which man says: '*mea culpa*' is growing wider. Every individual has from the very beginning, and before he realizes it, participated in the guilt of his ancestors as he founds his own life on theirs for good or bad. As an individual he becomes responsible for every wrong which is committed unless he risks his life to prevent it. However, Jaspers stresses again, though there can be a common feeling of guilt and responsibility among free men, nobody has the right to blame the other for this since everybody is equally guilty.

Crticism of Jaspers' line of argument will have to be directed

[1] Karl Jaspers, *Die Schuldfrage*, Zurich, 1946. English translation under the title: *The Question of Guilt*, by E. B. Ashton (New York, The Dial Press, 1947).
[2] *Philosophische Logik*. (Erster Band: Von der Wahrheit, 1947), p. 536.

COLLECTIVE RESPONSIBILITY

either against his fourfold distinction itself or against his way of drawing the lines of demarcation between those four categories. The distinction between legal, moral and political guilt is of course, one might almost say, one of the fundamental commonplaces of legal and political philosophy, and the additional category of metaphysical guilt, though perhaps not throughout clearly defined, is nevertheless equally indispensable. This metaphysical guilt comes probably nearest to Dostoevsky's idea of universal responsibility: 'Every one of us is guilty before all, for all, and for everything. . . . Even those who know nothing of crime are mysteriously accomplices in it',[1] although Jaspers' criticism of certain 'Eastern exaggerations' is probably directed against Dostoevsky. His criticism is justified since if every one is responsible for everything the practical consequence is that nobody is responsible.

In the discussions following the publication of Jaspers' book, his conception of metaphysical guilt has attracted more criticism than anything else. At the International Congress of Medical Psychotherapy, London 1948, where a special session was devoted to the subject of collective guilt, it was argued that Jaspers had confused the metaphysical concept of tragic guilt in ancient Greek philosophy and drama, and its idea of fate, with the Christian concept which recognizes neither fate nor collective guilt.[2] On the other hand, the theologian H. D. Lewis, while in principle strongly opposed to any extention of individual responsibility, nevertheless admits certain exceptions: first, the law 'cannot be scrupulously fair': a parent has to be held responsible for misconduct of his children even where he could not have prevented it (this apparently a reference to sect. 55 of the Children and Young Persons Act, 1933). Moreover, Lewis admits that, 'on account of the brotherhood of men' and also because we willingly take credit for the achievements of our children, compatriots and other group members we are to some extent involved in the sins of others.[3] In doing so he is in fact much nearer than he seems to think to views

---

[1] This aspect of Dostoevsky's philosophy is well brought out in Henry Troyat, *Firebrand. The Life of Dostoevsky* (English translation by Norbert Guterman, London, Heinemann, 1946), pp. 394, 405.
[2] D. Brinkmann—Zurich, Transactions of the International Congress of Mental Health, Vol. II, pp. 37 et seq.
[3] H. D. Lewis, *Morals and the New Theology* (London, Victor Gollancz, 1947), Chapter VI.

such as those of Jaspers. The idea of collective responsibility has found strong support from C. G. Jung and, more recently, from Sir Walter Moberly. C. G. Jung, it is true, prefers the term 'psychological' collective guilt,[1] and what he has in mind is in some way different from Jaspers' metaphysical conception. Sir Walter Moberly[2] (who refers to an address by Jaspers, not however to his book) also adduces reasons which are in part of a metaphysical and in part of a cultural character: on a higher plane, he feels, 'the thought "I am not guilty, though he is" is not so much untrue as unimportant and almost irrelevant. On this level no scheme of purely individual responsibility and justice will work. What a man is today, is due in large measure to all the persons and groups who have influenced him during his life'. This, we might say, is in part metaphysical and in part cultural co-responsibility. Here, and in the similar views of C. G. Jung, we seem to be approaching the truth. Jaspers' classification is in fact too narrow. There are more than only his four forms of collective responsibility. He not only ignores its existence in fields of the law other than criminal justice, in particular in the civil, administrative and disciplinary spheres. There is also collective responsibility and the collective social stigma of the family: even nowadays, all its members have to bear the stigma when one of them is sent to prison or sentenced to death, and Vyvyan Holland's recent book *Son of Oscar Wilde*[3] has been an impressive reminder of the fate suffered by the children of a lawbreaker sixty years ago. In fact, the members of every social group have to accept responsibility and sanctions for each of them in accordance with the peculiar character of their group; in accordance with the sphere where the behaviour occurs which happens to be disapproved; and in accordance with the character of the disapproving authority. There is, in particular, in addition to Jaspers' categories of political and metaphysical responsibility the cultural responsibility for which more is required than in the field of political or metaphysical responsibility: mere citizenship, which is sufficient to establish political responsibility, or being a member of the human race,

[1] C. G. Jung, *Essays on Contemporary Events* (London, Kegan Paul, 1948), pp. 46 et seq.
[2] Sir Walter Moberly, *Responsibility* (Oxford University Press, 1950), pp. 45-60.
[3] London, Rupert Hart-Davis, 1954.

COLLECTIVE RESPONSIBILITY

which justifies metaphysical responsibility, are not enough. The inheritance of a cultural tradition is required, but where it exists it may produce the feeling of collective responsibility and the willing acceptance of collective punishment even in those members of the group who have themselves been victims of the crime.

PART TWO

CRIMINOLOGY AND ITS METHODS

CHAPTER 4

LOMBROSO AND HIS PLACE IN MODERN CRIMINOLOGY[1]

IT would not be surprising if the centenary of Lombroso's birthday[2] were to provide, in many countries, an opportunity of reviewing his work. Together with the strange role played by Lombroso in the criminological science of to-day this event inevitably leads to the question: Are we at present entitled to speak of a Lombroso-Renaissance—are we really going 'back to Lombroso'? It is, therefore, intended in the present article—instead of merely adding to the large number of descriptions of Lombroso's theory already in existence—to examine the actual significance of his doctrines to modern Criminology. Let us for a moment recall to our minds the main stages of his scientific career. After an enthusiastic reception by admirers all over the world[3] his opponents very soon gained strength. The supporters of indeterminism[4] in philosophy and jurisprudence, feeling menaced by the aspects opened by the Positive School of Lombroso, joined hands with the inveterate adversaries of Criminal Anthropology, the leading crimino-sociologists, Franz von Liszt and others. But, it

[1] Reprinted from *The Sociological Review*, Vol. XXVIII, No. 1, January, 1936.
[2] There is apparently some difference of opinion as to this date. Lombroso's daughter, Gina Lombroso-Ferrero, and the *Enciclopedia Italiana* state, 6th November, 1835, Brockhaus' *Konversations Lexikon*, 18th November, 1836, Aschaffenburg (*Handwörterbuch der Kriminologie*—abbr. *Hdk.*—1, p. 833) even 1832. The first date is likely to be right.
[3] See, e.g., Havelock Ellis, *The Criminal* (1st ed., 1890); Hans Kurella, *Naturgeschichte des Verbrechers* (1893); Eugen Bleuler, *Der geborene Verbrecher* (1896).
[4] See, e.g., Enrico Ferri, *Criminal Sociology* (American ed., 1917), pp. 288 et seq., Ch. Goring, *The English Convict*, p. 13, Hans Gross, *Handbuch für Untersuchungsrichter* (7th ed., 1922), Vol. I, p. 153. Lombroso himself replied to the attacks in the preface to the later editions of his *L'Uomo Delinquente* (see, e.g., the German edition, *Der Verbrecher in anthropologischer, ärztlicher, und juristischer Beziehung*, translated by O. Fraenkel, 1887, Vol. I, pp. xxvi et seq.)

was, above all, the anthropologists themselves who rejected Lombroso's unscientific and uncritical methods and his perpetually changing formulations. In 1893 Adolf Baer, the Berlin prison surgeon, published his profound and unbiased work *Der Verbrecher in anthropologischer Beziehung*, and simultaneously Naecke, in several essays, tried to disprove Lombroso's statements.[1] In 1913 these works were followed by Charles Goring's *English Convict*, the most comprehensive and painstaking of all existing refutations of the conception of the born criminal. Relying on these researches criminologists of the early twentieth century became accustomed to disregard Lombroso's theories. 'If we ask how the Lombroso question stands to-day,' writes Hans Gross,[2] 'we may say that it is finished,' and 'the dream of the "born criminal", "the natural delinquent" as a special human type has been dreamed to a finish. Nothing remains of it except the sterile fact that a large number of criminals are in some way or another abnormal, just as are many other people who never come into conflict with the law at all.'[3] In view of such statements, it may perhaps seem rather superfluous to waste even a single line on Lombroso. But are they correct, and how far can they be reconciled with the fact that even in modern Criminology scarcely any other author is the subject of so many heated discussions and disputes as Lombroso? If his ideas are really dead, why not leave him in peace?

In the history of science it is essential to distinguish between the gist of a theory, i.e. its enduring principles, and its accidental and transient manifestations. Who, to-day, has the right to reproach the inventor of the steam-engine for not having produced at once a perfect model in the light of modern technology? It is Lombroso's lasting merit—and nobody should acknowledge it with deeper gratitude than the jurist—that he has saved criminal science from the shackles of merely academic abstractions and fertilized it with the rich treasures of the natural sciences. Previous to Lombroso's appearance criminal science, especially on the Continent, had been entirely dominated by the Classical School of

---

[1] See, moreover, Manouvrier, *Les Aptitudes et les Actes* (Paris, 1893); Jules Dallemagne, *Les stigmates anatomiques de la criminalité* (1896), and *Les stigmates biologiques et sociologiques de la criminalité* (1896).
[2] Op. cit., p. 158.
[3] Johannes Lange, *Verbrechen als Schicksal*, quoted from the English translation by Charlotte Haldane, *Crime as Destiny* (London, George Allen & Unwin, Ltd.), 1931, p. 30.

LOMBROSO'S PLACE IN MODERN CRIMINOLOGY

Beccaria, Feuerbach, etc. It contented itself with endless theoretical arguments and tried by means of sterile conceptions to fix the penalty which was supposed to 'fit the crime'. It was the criminal action alone that was examined as if it stood completely isolated from the other actions of its author. Consideration of the personality of the individual law-breaker was nobody's concern.[1] The criminal, it was thought, differed in no way from the average law-abiding citizen; he might just as easily have chosen an honest career if only he had wished to do so.[2] Typical in this respect was the attitude of the former Italian (Fr. Carrara) and German (Hegelian School) criminal science. Feuerbach, it is true, although himself a chief representative of the Classical School, had already in 1828–9 produced his *Aktenmässige Darstellung merkwürdiger Criminalrechtsfälle* (remarkable criminal cases, compiled from records of the courts), which was succeeded by several similar works. But these publications, meritorious as they were, suffered from the absence of direct observation of the criminal and were unable to change the fundamental attitude of that period towards the treatment of crime. Little wonder, then, that the figures of recidivism all over Europe in the second half of the nineteenth century increased alarmingly[3] and proved to be the best supporters of Lombroso. 'The principle that the criminal himself, and not an abstract idea of crime, should be punished was not invented by the Italian School,' wrote Franz von Liszt in his lecture on 'The tasks of Criminal Policy' (1889),[4] 'but the Italians recalled it to our minds at a time when Kant and Hegel, Fichte and Herbart, Schopenhauer and Ed. von Hartmann made us forget this fundamental aim of all criminal science. The Italians stirred us up from our metaphysical sleep and from our paralysing theoretical jurisprudence; somewhat rudely and with unnecessary noise, but with lasting success.' It is true that Lombroso had numerous forerunners, not only among the jurists interested in the psychological investigation of crime, but also in his original field of science. Apart from the obvious truth that Lombroso is almost unthinkable without Darwin, the fact remains that the special branch of

---

[1] See E. Ferri, *Criminal Sociology* (American ed.), pp. 4 and 43.
[2] See G. Daniel, *Zeitschrift für die gesamte Strafrechtswissenschaft*, Vol. L, p. 478.
[3] See, e.g., Lombroso's own figures, *L'Uomo delinquente* (German ed.), I, pp. 334 et seq.; Sir Evelyn Ruggles Brise, *The English Prison System* (1921), pp. 5, 221, etc.; v. Liszt, *Strafrechtliche Aufsätze und Vorträge*, Vol. II, pp. 238, 338.
[4] Op. cit., Vol. I, p. 307.

CRIMINOLOGY AND ITS METHODS

Criminal Anthropology, too, was not created by him out of nothing. In this connection it may suffice to mention the names of Broca and G. Wilson.[1] 'The science of Criminal Anthropology,' Ferri admits,[2] 'begins with the observations of English gaol surgeons and other learned men.' Nobody, however, was engaged in crimino-anthropological research with such energy and enthusiasm; nobody knew, as Lombroso did, how to popularize its facts and results. If Lombroso, to take only one instance, in a review of an essay on the '*vagabond-né*', writes:[3] '*Chaque jour on découvre quelques espèces nouvelles, quelque nouveau type de criminels*'; such words express a delight in the progress of his science which was certainly very naïve, but nevertheless apt to enrapture the uncritical public —a delight almost comparable to Ulrich von Hutten's 'O wonderful century, the minds awake—it is a joy to live!' Did Lombroso's enthusiasm, however, really succeed in discovering the *specific criminal types* which he sought, and are these types capable of definition according to *anthropological* characteristics? The almost unanimous opinion of to-day answers the second question in the negative. It is especially Lombroso's identification of the born criminal type with the conceptions of atavism and degeneration; the excessive importance which he attributed to epilepsy; his belief in an anthropological criminal type of even international uniformity[4] that are commonly rejected. The main features of his theory of the anthropological stigmata of the born criminal have been disproved by Baer and Goring, who examined the problem independently.[5] Many of the statements made by Lombroso in this respect are to-day at best no more than curiosities,[6] and even so far as they are partly confirmed by later researches[7] they cannot

---

[1] See the more detailed account given by Havelock Ellis, *The Criminal*, p. 37; K. Birnbaum, *Kriminalpsychopathologie* (1921), p. 142.

[2] *Criminal Sociology* (English ed., 1895), p. 3 (see p. 42 of the American edition).

[3] *Nouvelles Recherches de Psychiatrie et d'Anthropologie Criminelle* (Paris, 1892), p. 65.

[4] It should, however, not be overlooked that Lombroso recognized certain national and regional peculiarities (see, e.g., *L'Uomo delinquente*, Vol. I, pp. 152 and 213 of the German translation).

[5] Baer's investigations were apparently unknown to Goring.

[6] So when he stated that the amount of nitrogen in the urine of the born criminal was 0·38 in every kilogram, as compared with 0·82 in case of the occasional criminal (*L'Uomo delinquente*, German ed., II, p. 301).

[7] E.g. the frequency of epilepsy among criminals (Baer, pp. 300 et seq.; Goring, pp. 226 et seq.).

LOMBROSO'S PLACE IN MODERN CRIMINOLOGY

be regarded as sufficient foundations for his sweeping conclusions.

In spite of this rejection, however, there is a considerable change of tone perceptible in recent years. It is interesting to compare, for example, Goring's criticism with that of modern authoritative writers. Goring, it is true, also endeavoured to do justice to Lombroso, emphasizing that his struggle was directed not so much against Lombroso's results as against the methods by which they were achieved.[1] But, Goring stated, Lombroso's importance was not in his scientific work, but in his humanitarianism.[2] To a man of Goring's dispassionate objectivity, who approved of nothing but exact statistical data and measurements,[3] the fanciful anecdotical style of the Italian scholar could only be repulsive. Nothing is more characteristic in this respect than the sarcasm which he poured upon Lombroso's description of the birth of his theory: 'Newton must work by other laws than Victor Hugo.'[4] As a result of the Lombroso-Goring controversy, whoever has lost his belief in the reality of the born-criminal type should at least have become convinced of the existence of different types of scientists. To-day, one is slightly more inclined to tolerate the methods of Lombroso—in full acknowledgment of their shortcomings—as 'ingenious intuition'.[5] The deeper reasons for this reaction are to be found in the growing insight into the limitations of the method of 'measurements and measurements alone',[6] and in the fact that some previous critics had attacked many alleged statements of Lombroso which the latter had not made at all or made in a different sense.

At present, more emphasis is placed upon the important reservations by means of which Lombroso, in later years, tried to support his theory: his restriction (from the third edition of *L'Uomo delinquente*) of the conception of the born criminal to about 35 per cent of all criminals; his requirement of at least five stigmata for this

---

[1] *The English Convict*, p. 19.   [2] Op cit., p. 12.

[3] See, e.g., op. cit., p. 29: 'We must build upon measurements and upon measurements alone.'

[4] Op. cit., p. 13, note 2. See, on the other hand, the remarks by Leone Lattes (Pavia) in *La Giustizia Penale*, Vol. XL, Parte Prima (1934), p. 1: 'Onde si iniziò la grandiosa architettura scientifica che rese celebre ovunque il suo nome.'

[5] See, e.g., Aschaffenburg, *Handwörterbuch der Kriminologie*, I, p. 834. Also above, p. 14.

[6] Goring himself is subjected to the criticism that his methods, according to present conceptions, are inadequate (see Sutherland, *Principles of Criminology*, 1934, pp. 47, 55 et seq. and now E. A. Hooton, *The American Criminal*, Vol. I, 1939, Cambridge, Mass., Harvard University Press, pp. 18 et seq.).

type; his readiness to acknowledge the importance of mental, social, economic, and cosmic factors in addition to anthropological measurements;[1] finally, the practicability of some of his suggestions for penological reforms. And already at an earlier date Ferri,[2] rightly or wrongly, had emphasized that the contrast between the born and the occasional criminal, according to Lombroso's own statements, was to be regarded only as 'a difference of degree and modality'.

In his native country, the influence of Lombroso's ideas is very strong even to-day.[3] Among Italian scholars, the views of the well-known psychiatrist Benigno di Tullio (Rome) appear nowadays[4] to be very similar to those of Lombroso. 'If we sum up', he writes in a short study which summarizes his investigations,[5] the results of our examinations of pickpockets, burglars, hotel thieves, swindlers, sexual offenders, and juvenile delinquents, we venture to say that all genuine[6] criminals show constitutionally abnormal features, although in varying degrees. The genuine criminal always shows endogenous defects of development, the latter having been arrested at a past stage of mankind, and he thereby resembles primitive, even savage, tribes, etc.'[7]

Some of the fundamental ideas of Lombroso have gained admittance into the new Italian Penal Code of 1930. It is especially art. 108 of this Code[8] that is worth mentioning in this connection,

[1] See Birnbaum, op. cit., p. 146; O. Kinberg, *Basic Principles of Criminology* (1935), p. 166; Gruhle, *HdK.*, I, p. 910; Goring, op. cit., p. 263.
[2] *Criminal Sociology* (English ed.), p. 43.
[3] Very significant is in this respect Leone Lattes' article in *La Giustizia Penale*, Vol. XL, Parte Prima (1934), pp. 1 et seq. Thorsten Sellin (Philadelphia) gives an excellent survey of the position of Criminal Anthropology and especially Endocrinology in Italy ten years ago (*The Annals of the American Academy of Political and Social Science*, May 1926, pp. 233 et seq.). See, moreover, Q. Saldaña (Madrid), *Journal of Criminal Law and Criminology*, Vol. XXIV, pp. 333 et seq.
[4] Lattes, op. cit., p. 4, calls him 'più recente esponente della scuola lombrosiana'.
[5] *Zeitschrift für die gesamte Strafrechtswissenschaft*, Vol. L (1930), pp. 493-4.
[6] What does this expression mean? (The German original says 'echt'.)
[7] Nevertheless, as N. Cantor points out (*American Journal of Sociology*, Vol. XXXIX, p. 713), di Tullio's conception of the criminal type is dynamic, whilst that of Lombroso was static. The same contrast is stressed by Edmund Mezger, *Die Arbeitsmethoden der kriminalbiologischen Untersuchungsstellen*, *Der Gerichtssaal*, Vol. CIII, pp. 127 et seq.
[8] Di Tullio, *Monatsschrift für Kriminalpsychologie und Strafrechtsreform*, Vol. XXII (1931), p. 345, regards art. 108 as a direct approbation of Lombroso's theory. On the other hand, see Lattes, op. cit., p. 15.

because it deals with the so-called criminal by tendency as follows: 'A person who, although neither a relapser nor a habitual or professional delinquent, commits a crime, not without criminal intent, against individual life or safety ... which ... discloses a special inclination to crime, the cause of which is the particularly wicked nature of the guilty party, shall be declared a criminal by tendency.' Such a declaration 'shall entail the application of police measures' (art. 109) (official English translation[1]).

In Germany, Austria, and other Continental countries, Lombroso's school has been succeeded by the so-called Crimino-biological School, which has widely utilized the opportunities for research offered by the establishment of several Institutes for crimino-biological investigation. This School has its scientific centre in the *Kriminalbiologische Gesellschaft*, founded by Adolf Lenz in Graz,[2] and, since 1927, in the *Mitteilungen*, edited by this Society. Some of its members, it is true, are inclined to lay more stress upon the differences which separate them from Lombroso than upon the points in which they are in harmony with him. The Crimino-biological School owes—if not its origin—at any rate its attractive force mainly to the famous researches of Ernst Kretschmer.[3] The latter, as is well known, established his constitutional types regardless of the needs of Criminology; neither did he limit them to abnormal persons. As a psychiatrist, he endeavours to discover correlations with corresponding psychiatric types, especially with Kraepelin's distinction between *manic-depressive* or *circular* insanity, on the one hand, and *schizophrenia* or *dementia praecox* on the other. He extends, however, the main features of this contrast to two other pairs of types; First, the *cycloid* and the *schizoid* types

---

[1] Foreign Office, 1931 (H.M.S.O.).
[2] See his *Grundriss der Kriminalbiologie* (1927).
[3] *Körperbau und Charakter*, 9–10 ed., 1931. The English translation, under the title 'Physique and Character', was published in 1925 (International Library of Psychology, etc.). I am well aware of the fact that the Crimino-biological School by no means utilizes Kretschmer's typology alone. Nevertheless, it is impossible to deny the preponderating influence of the latter. As to the relations between Kretschmer's work and the Crimino-biological School, see esp. E. Mezger, *Kriminalpolitik* (1934), pp. 67–139; E. Mezger in *Der Gerichtssaal*, Vol. CIII, p. 127; W. Sauer, *Kriminalsoziologie*, Vol. I (1933), p. 26; Adolf Lenz, *Grundriss der Kriminalbiologie* (1927); W. Sauer, *Archiv der Rechts—und Wirtschaftsphilosophie*, Vol. XXIII (1929–30), p. 430; von Rohden, *Einführung in die kriminalbiologische Methodenlehre* (1933); Willemse, Constitution-Types in Delinquency (London, 1932); Reiter, *Monatsschrift für Kriminalpsychologie und Strafrechtsreform*, Vol. XXII, p. 78; Aschaffenburg, *HdK.*, I, pp. 834 et seq.

CRIMINOLOGY AND ITS METHODS

which consist of individuals standing between illness and health and exhibiting the symptoms of the distinctly abnormal circular and schizophrene types in a slighter degree.[1] Secondly: the *cyclothymes* and the *schizothymes*, i.e. the corresponding *normal* temperaments from which the pathological types are recruited.[2] Kretschmer, moreover, attempts to combine these psychological and pathological characteristics with certain bodily features, the asthenic,[3] the athletic and the pyknic types. His final results are commonly known. Among the schizophrenes, schizoids, and schizothymes, he states, the asthenic and athletic types prevail, as does, on the other hand, the pyknic type among the manic-depressives (circulars), the cycloids and cyclothymes. The next step was the correlation of these groups with criminal types. During the last twelve years, especially in Germany and Austria, many researches have been made with the object of discovering whether the types of Kretschmer are of any significance as regards Criminology. According to the prevailing opinion, this is in fact so. First, the members of the pyknic type, sociable and good-natured as they are, commit fewer and much less serious crimes, it is alleged, than do the other types (especially the athletic) whose characteristics are eccentricity, reserve, and unsociability.[4] Moreover, the question arose as to the relation of Kretschmer's types to *special types of crimes*. Here a difficulty exists which has already played its part in the controversies about Lombroso. How far is it possible to classify the concept of the criminal law, such as murder, manslaughter, larceny, etc., according to anthropological or biological types? Already Franz von Liszt[5] had rightly pointed out that it is impossible to regard the articles of the Penal Code as corresponding to anthropological types. Bleuler and others considered this objection as irrelevant, since Lombroso had not aimed at the legal

---

[1] See p. 122 of the English edition.
[2] See p. 208.
[3] In the later German editions, Kretschmer, in addition to the term 'asthenic', uses also the term 'leptosome', describing the asthenic type as the extreme form ('Kümmerform') of the lean leptosome type (see p. 19 of the 9th and 10th German edition, 1931).
[4] See, e.g., E. Mezger, *Kriminalpolitik*, pp. 93 et seq.; von Rohden, *Monatsschrift für Kriminalpsychologie*, etc., Vol. XXIV, p. 82; Riedl, *Monatsschrift*, Vol. XXIII, pp. 473 et seq.; moreover, several contributions to the *Mitteilungen der kriminalbiologischen Gesellschaft* and to the *HdK.* as, e.g., Aschaffenburg, *HdK.*, I, p. 835; Gruhle, I, pp. 559 and 910; Birnbaum, II, p. 271.
[5] *Strafrechtliche Aufsätze und Vorträge*, I, p. 309.

conceptions of crime and the criminal, but at the social ones which, it was argued, always remain the same. 'Every sane person who violates the existing social order is a criminal. This conception of crime never changes.'[1] Surely, it is self-evident that such an invariable sociological conception cannot exist. Not even Lombroso failed to recognize that crime in the sociological sense changes its contents just as much as does the legal conception.[2] Nevertheless, it is true that criminological types should not be based upon legal conceptions which take into account, instead of the personality of the wrongdoer, only the crime in question. This does not mean that Criminology may safely overstep all the limits set by the definitions of criminal law by treating a person as a criminal, although he has committed no crime.[3] But within the scope of actions punishable according to criminal law, Criminology must be free to establish classifications of its own. It is obvious that the legal distinctions between murder and manslaughter, between larceny and embezzlement, are unsatisfactory from the criminological point of view. The sexual murderer has usually more in common with other types of sexual offenders than with the political murderer who, on his part, may rather resemble the man who commits high treason. The legal conceptions of larceny, false pretences, etc., cover a great variety of criminological types.[4] These facts have not always been duly considered by Lombroso. On the one hand, it is true, his differentiation of born criminals, criminals by passion, occasional, habitual, juridical criminals and criminaloids forced him to take into account many aspects that were foreign to the law.[5] Often, however, he contented himself with the legal classifications as murderers, thieves,[6] or even spoke simply of 'criminals' in abstracto. Modern Criminology tries to

[1] Bleuler, *Der geborene Verbrecher*, p. 36.
[2] See, e.g., *Crime, its Causes and Remedies* (American ed.), pp. 57, 384, etc.; *L'Uomo delinquente* (German ed.), Vol. II, p. 278.
[3] See Sutherland, *Principles*, p. 19. From the above it does not follow that sociologically a man is not a criminal until he is caught by the law.
[4] See, e.g., Willemse, op. cit., p. 24. Now especially E. Seelig, *Lehrbuch der Kriminologie* (Jos. A. Kienreich, Graz, 1951), pp. 40 et seq.
[5] *L'Uomo delinquente* (German ed.), II, p. 266: some forms of larceny belong to the group of habitual crimes, others do not. Or II, p. 302: the frequency of tattooing varies among the different groups of thieves.
[6] 'The lips of violators of women and murderers are fleshy, swollen and protruding as in negroes. Swindlers have thin, straight lips' (Gina Lombroso-Ferrero, *The Criminal Man*, p. 16). Or see Lombroso's measurements of skulls (*L'Uomo deliquente*, I, p. 138).

avoid such mistakes. Moreover, it is recognized that the tripartition asthenic, athletic, and pyknic, does not cover the great variety of existing bodily types, so that it becomes necessary to introduce mixed forms. According to recent investigations carried out by members of the Crimino-biological School, it would appear that swindlers, for instance, belong mainly to the leptosome or kindred groups: among 300 swindlers examined by Riedl,[1] there were 124 = 41·3 per cent pure leptosomes, 34 = 11·3 per cent leptosome athletics, and 18 = 6 per cent leptosome pyknics, as contrasted with only 36 = 12 per cent pure athletics and 50 = 16·6 per cent pure pyknics. Among 200 prisoners convicted of malicious wounding, however, there were only 32 = 16 per cent pure leptosomes, 4 = 2 per cent leptosome pyknics, and 7 = 3·5 per cent pure pyknics, as compared with 87 = 43·5 per cent pure athletics, 40 = 20 per cent leptosome athletics and 30 = 15 per cent pyknic athletics. Among 300 thieves there were 105 = 35 per cent pure leptosomes, 37 = 12·3 per cent leptosome athletics, 9 = 3 per cent leptosome pyknics, 74 = 24·7 per cent athletics, 43 = 14·3 per cent pyknics. Expressed more simply by halving the figures for the mixed forms the proportions would be as follows:

(*a*) *Swindlers:* 50 per cent leptosomes, 24 per cent athletics, 26 per cent pyknics.

(*b*) *Men convicted of malicious wounding:* 27 per cent leptosomes, 61 per cent athletics,[2] 12 per cent pyknics.

(*c*) *Thieves:* 42·7 per cent leptosomes, 36·2 per cent athletics, 21·1 per cent pyknics.

Riedl gives no figures as to the prevalence of the three main types among the general population. According to von Rohden, the figures for the latter are: leptosomes, 60 per cent; athletics, 30 per cent; pyknics, 10 per cent.[3] If this should be true, the figures given by Riedl would not prove that the percentage of pyknics is strikingly low among criminals, as is claimed by the

[1] Riedl (above, p. 76) counts among the 'swindlers' prisoners with at least three convictions of false pretences (taken in the widest meaning).
[2] Riedl, p. 475, emphasizes that this high percentage cannot be explained merely by the stronger musculature of the athletics.
[3] See Mezger, *Kriminalpolitik*, p. 96. For Central Germany, the following figures are mentioned: Leptosomes, 50 per cent, athletics, 30 per cent, pyknics, 20 per cent (see Mezger, p. 97).

Crimino-biological School. There are other contradictions, too. Whilst Mezger states that among cyclothymes crimes of passion are comparatively frequent,[1] Riedl's investigations show the lowest figures for malicious wounding among the pyknics (from whom the cyclothymes are recruited). It appears that too much importance has still been attached to the legal classification of the crime, instead of to the particular methods of its performance.[2] Riedl's result, for example, that swindlers usually belong to the leptosome group may be true with regard to particular methods of swindling, whilst other methods that demand sociability and a behaviour calculated to inspire confidence are much more suitable for the pyknic type.

Another important statement frequently made by members of the Crimino-biological School is to the effect that criminals of the pyknic type usually are *occasional* and *corrigible* criminals, whilst among the leptosomes and especially among the athletics are found more *habitual* and *incorrigible* offenders.[3] One of the leading members of this School, Viernstein, makes very sweeping statements in this respect: 58 per cent of the schizothyme prisoners examined by him, he alleges, were incorrigible, whilst the corresponding figures for cyclothymes is only 12 per cent.[4]

In order to realize the practical consequences of these statements, one has to bear in mind that it has always been the explicit object of the Crimino-biological School to eliminate from the Progressive Stage System and other reformatory measures those prisoners who are regarded as incorrigible criminals.

The figures reached by Viernstein are, thus, far more pessimistic than the percentage claimed by Lombroso for his born-criminal type; but their reliability is probably of a similar character. It is, however, only fair to mention the fact that even among the

[1] Similarly von Rohden, *Monatsschrift*, Vol. XXIV, p. 83; Willemse, op. cit., p. 157.
[2] This is rightly stressed by Willemse, op cit., pp. 76, 87, et seq., who gives interesting examples of characteristic methods of thefts by leptosome criminals.
[3] Von Rohden, op. cit., pp. 86 et seq.; Mezger, p. 96.
[4] According to the same source, 40 per cent of the prisoners who committed crimes against property were corrigible, the corresponding figures for prisoners who had committed acts of violence and sexual offences being 84 per cent and 72 per cent respectively (see Hoffmann, *Monatsschrift*, Vol. XXIII, p. 385). These figures seem to be inconsistent with Riedl's statement that crimes of violence are committed mainly by athletics, combined with the thesis that among athletics there are more incorrigibles than among the other groups.

members of the Crimino-biological School considerable objections have been raised against Viernstein's views.[1] Above all, it has been urged that the sociological aspects of the problem should duly be examined. It seems, moreover, to be evident that the above reported doctrines are at present nothing more than generalizations of certain facts which apply only to special districts and special groups of the population. Many of the investigations hitherto carried out by members of the Crimino-biological School are concerned with inmates of Bavarian and Austrian prisons. That may explain, at least partly, the preponderance of the athletic type. Researches made among the prison population of Berlin, for instance, might perhaps have shown opposite results.

Another branch of Crimino-biological research that is closely connected with the fundamental ideas of Lombroso seems also to require a more critical attitude: the criminological investigations of *twins*. Johannes Lange's *Crime as Destiny* contains several valuable descriptions of criminal careers. It is, nevertheless, surprising that this book—in a much more dogmatical sense than was intended by the author himself—has been accepted by eminent criminologists as sufficiently conclusive to prove the preponderant significance of the endogenous factors of crime.[2] It is unnecessary here to repeat the objections already brought forward against Lange.[3] Suffice it to say that his case material is numerically much too limited to justify such important conclusions.[4] Moreover, the similarities between most of his monozygotic pairs of twins are, in fact, neither so close nor so significant as may appear at the first glance. Everyone familiar with a very great number of criminal records knows that such careers as those of the Heufelder, Lauterbach, etc., brothers are nothing extraordinary; their similarity, thus, loses a great deal of its significance. In fact, there are to be

[1] See, e.g., the considered opinion of Sieverts, *Monatsschrift*, Vol. XXIII, pp. 588 et seq.; Vol. XXIV, pp. 107 et seq. It is, moreover, the 'sceptic among German psychiatrists', Gruhle (Heidelberg), who has often asked for a more cautious attitude (see, e.g., *HdK.*, I, pp. 200 and 910).
[2] See, e.g., Aschaffenburg, *HdK.*, I, p. 831; Mezger, *Kriminalpolitik*, p. 111; Kinberg, *Basic Principles*, p. 303.
[3] See Sutherland, *Principles of Criminology*, pp. 80-1; Gruhle, *Zeitschrift für die gesamte Strafrechtswissenschaft*, Vol. L, pp. 433-4.
[4] Investigations on a wider scale are announced by Rosanoff, *Journal of Criminal Law and Criminology*, Vol. XXIV, p. 923. The researches carried out by the Russian Medicobiological Institute in Moscow (see S. G. Levit in *Character and Personality*, Vol. III, No. 3, March 1935, pp. 188 et seq.) are apparently not concerned with criminological problems as such.

found important differences even among many of the monozygotic pairs,[1] and several of the congruent traits are explainable by environmental influences.

If we attempt to sum up the main resemblances and contrasts existing between Lombroso and the Crimino-biological School, we may perhaps use the following formulations. Both aim at the discovery of criminal types, and both are inclined to stress the influence of internal factors of crime; they over-estimate, therefore, the incidence of incorrigibility. The majority of the members of the Crimino-biological School, however, warned by Lombroso's mistakes, content themselves with the allegation of certain inborn tendencies and predispositions towards criminal attitudes.[2] It is in this sense only that they acknowledge the existence of a born-criminal type, not, however, as an anthropological, but rather as a biological or even as a psychological type.[3] They try to improve upon Lombroso's inadequate classifications by the addition of several new groups—a method which, unavoidable as it is, may finally mean the end of any kind of classification.[4] They emphasize the many-sidedness of the 'biological' outlook as compared with Lombroso's one-sidedness (which, however, as already mentioned, was by no means so extreme as is often alleged). Bodily features are significant only so far as they are connected with corresponding mental traits, and social factors are not entirely ignored. Even among the different branches of the Crimino-biological School there are considerable variations of opinion and method.[5] The Belgian[6] and Latvian schemes, for instance, are mainly concerned with the psychiatric part of the problem, the Bavarian more with the biological. It is obvious that

---

[1] Willemse, op cit., pp. 162–3, suggests that one of the Heufelder twins belonged to the pyknic, the other to the athletic type.

[2] Lenz calls it '*kriminogene Disposition*' (*HdK.*, II, p. 62; *Grundriss der Kriminalbiologie*, p. 9, etc.).

[3] Von Rohden, op. cit., p. 77; Gruhle, *HdK.*, I, p. 911 (characterological-sociological type).

[4] Such a negative attitude is strongly supported by Saldaña, *Journal of Criminal Law and Criminology*, Vol. XXIV, pp. 333 et seq., and, according to him, by the Portuguese criminologist Mendes Correa. See, moreover, Saldaña's Biotipologia criminale in *La Giustizia Penale*, 1934, Parte Prima, pp. 326–74.

[5] See the survey given by Mezger, *Der Gerichtssaal*, Vol. CIII, and *Kriminalpolitik*, pp. 111 et seq.

[6] As to the Belgian system, see the report by its eminent exponent, Dr. Louis Vervaeck, *Journal of Criminal Law and Criminology*, Vol. XXIV, pp. 198 et seq.

these differences are closely connected with the fundamental outlook as regards crime and punishment that is dominating in the various countries. It is common opinion that Russian criminologists[1] represent the most sociologically minded and anti-Lombrosian wing; Bavarian, Austrian, and Italian criminologists the most strongly biologically orientated section. Kinberg[2] points out that the European School of Criminology, as a whole, is tending more towards the individual, endogenous theory of criminality, whilst Northern American criminologists are more interested in social aspects, and he finds the explanation of this contrast in the differences of social history and present social conditions. There is certainly some truth in this statement, and the example of Russia furnishes only a further corroboration of the rule. Nevertheless, it cannot be overlooked that, even apart from Russia, European Criminology is by no means unanimous. It would have been astonishing indeed if the occurrences of the Great War and of the post-war period had not brought home to European criminologists the importance of social factors. If we learn, for instance, that in Germany the index of criminality (calculated per 100,000 of the population) was as follows:[3]

(*a*) For petty theft, in 1913, 210; in 1920, 428; in 1923,[4] 633; in 1930, 156.

(*b*) For receiving of stolen goods: in 1913, 21; in 1920, 76; in 1923, 136; in 1930, 18.

(*c*) For murder: in 1913, 0·23; in 1920, 0·44; in 1923, 0·29; in 1930, 0·18.

(*d*) For malicious wounding: in 1913, 139; in 1920, 105; in 1923, 84; in 1930, 99.

we may find it impossible to explain such figures exclusively or even mainly on biological or pathological lines or by changes in law and procedure only.

On the other hand, the tendency to stress the importance of

---

[1] As to the attitude of the Criminological Institute in Moscow, see Kamenetzki, *Zeitschrift für die gesamte Strafrechtswissenschaft*, Vol. LI, pp. 597 et seq. A review in *La Giustizia Penale*, 1934, Parte Prima, p. 84, speaks of an 'antilombrosissimo' attitude of the reviewed Russian writer.

[2] Olof Kinberg, *Basic Principles of Criminology*, p. 167.

[3] The following figures are taken from Roesner, *HdK.*, II, pp. 44-5.

[4] I.e. when inflation had reached its highest level.

LOMBROSO'S PLACE IN MODERN CRIMINOLOGY

inborn factors is not entirely absent in modern American Criminology. In addition to what is called the 'Neo-Lombrosian theory' which replaces the physical type by a psychopathological one,[1] the doctrines of the endocrinologists are to be mentioned in this connection. One cannot regard them, as Saldaña does,[2] simply as a refutation of Lombroso. They are, of course, opposed to Lombroso's exaggerated views on the influence of heredity,[3] but they are not averse to his explanation of crime as mainly the result of other internal factors. According to the theory of some endocrinologists, the criminal individual who suffers from serious disturbances of the ductless glands is the typical born criminal.[4] The obvious advantage of this theory, as compared with the hereditarian doctrine, is that it is a more suitable explanation of the fact that so often only one child (or one pair of twins) is a criminal, whilst the other descendants are not.[5] On the whole, however, the endocrinological view shows shortcomings at least equivalent to those of the other successors of Lombroso.[6] When Schlapp and Smith, for instance, try to explain the criminal career of a girl by the hypothesis that she 'probably' suffered from a glandular defect from birth,[7] it is obvious that one might ascribe with equal justification the girl's downfall to the untimely loss of her parents. In fact, it is advisable to combine both factors and to dismiss finally all those theories which limit their considerations to one single side of the problem, instead of following the model set by Burt, Healy, the Gluecks, and others.

Only a few remarks have to be added on the *penological* views of Lombroso and their relation to modern Penology. Anthropological and hereditarian theories of crime always bear a somewhat negative character. Nevertheless, it is a mistake to believe that Lombroso's penological programme was entirely sterile

[1] Sutherland, *Principles*, pp. 94 et seq.
[2] *Journal of Criminal Law and Criminology*, Vol. XXIV.
[3] See, e.g., Lombroso, *Crime, its Causes and Remedies*, pp. 151, 174, 223, 376, and Parmelee's Introduction to the American edition, p. 31. As to the whole problem see M. Ginsberg, *Studies in Sociology* (1932): Inheritance of Mental Characters.
[4] See Schlapp and Smith, *The New Criminology* (1928). The third chapter of this books bears the title: 'Back to Lombroso.'
[5] Many of Lange's cases belong to this category.
[6] See the remarks by Sheldon and Eleanor Glueck, *One Thousand Juvenile Delinquents* (1934), p. 283.
[7] Op cit., p. 213.

and limited to a recommendation of the death penalty or preventive detention for born criminals. It is of little value to dwell upon the numerous lapses he committed in the field of Penology, too: his suggestion to render harmless dangerous criminal tendencies by supplying the individual with a profession which would enable him to indulge in his favourite occupations without breaking the law; his struggle against the better education and training of the prisoner, based upon the fear that education would promote criminal habits.[1] On the whole, however, he expressed very sound views on the fundamental principles of reformatory treatment of all prisoners except the born criminals. He was especially proud[2] of the fact that one of the chief founders of the Elmira Reformatory movement, Z. R. Brockway, had confessed that his work had been inspired by Lombroso's ideas.[3] Considering that Elmira was, to a certain extent, the model of the English Borstal system,[4] Lombroso may even claim the honour of being counted among the forefathers of this system. Moreover, whilst he was a convinced supporter of probation, he doubted the value of solitary confinement.[5]

These few indications may suffice to show that Lombroso's penological views have at least something in common with modern ideas. But even with regard to the criminological part of his work, it cannot be maintained that modern Crimino-biology has suddenly emerged as an entirely new science out of the complete breakdown of Lombrosianism. We are rather confronted with a gradual process of partial abandonment, partial retention and improvement of his methods and results—a process not infrequently encountered in the development of scientific doctrines.

[1] As to this problem see Lombroso, *Crime, its Causes and Remedies*, pp. 105 et seq., and, on the other hand, the excellent remarks in the *American Prison Handbook*, Introduction to the edition of 1933; Sutherland, *Principles*, pp. 452, et seq.; Roesner, *HdK.*, II, pp. 165 et seq.; Exner, *HdK.*, II, p. 21; Goring, op cit., pp. 267, 274 et seq.
[2] See Gina Lombroso-Ferrero, *The Criminal Man*, p. 192.
[3] Z. R. Brockway, *Fifty Years of Prison Service* (1912), p. 215.
[4] See Sir Evelyn Ruggles Brise, *The English Prison System* (1921), p. 91.
[5] See his *L'Anthropologie Criminelle* (2nd ed., 1891), pp. 145 et seq.

CHAPTER 5

THREE CONTRIBUTIONS TO THE HISTORY OF CRIME IN THE SECOND WORLD WAR AND AFTER

[These essays, slightly revised and with additional notes, have been included in the present volume mainly in order to show the scarcity of the material at the disposal of criminologists during the war and the immediate post-war period. Even at the time of editing this collection, however, no adequate historical treatment of the subject has been published. The I.P.P.C. symposium referred to in note 2, p. 86 below gives very little information on the criminological situation in this country during the various stages of the war and post-war years. Important subjects such as evacuation, shelter life, looting, crime among deserters, are barely mentioned. In the two volumes of the official War History dealing with social developments and social policy during the war, i.e. Richard M. Titmuss, *Problems of Social Policy*, 1950, and Sheila Ferguson and Hilde Fitzgerald, *Studies in the Social Services*, 1954 (in History of the Second World War, U.K. Civil Series, ed. by Sir Keith Hancock, H.M.S.O. and Longmans, Green & Co.), full details are given on evacuation and other factors disrupting family life during the war; there are only a few incidental references, however, to the impact of these factors on juvenile delinquency and hardly any on adult crime.]

I[1]

IN two previous investigations by the author an attempt was made to estimate the effect of the first World War and its aftermath upon crime, with special reference to England and Germany.[2] The

[1] Reprinted, with slight alterations, from *The Annals of the American Academy of Political and Social Science*, Vol. 217, September, 1941.
[2] *Social Aspects of Crime in England between the Wars* (London, George Allen & Unwin, 1940); *War and Crime* (London, Watts & Co., 1941).

CRIMINOLOGY AND ITS METHODS

present chapter will deal with such effects of the second world conflict upon crime in England as can so far be observed.[1] At the outset, however, it is important to note, first, that it is much too early to make anything but tentative statements, and second, that there is at present hardly any reliable information at our disposal with regard to countries outside the United Kingdom.[2]

Our previous studies have clearly brought out the fact that any generalizations on the subject are likely to be misleading, since, as a crime-producing factor, each war has its own characteristics. If this was true of pre-Hitlerian wars, it has surely become a commonplace to-day. To describe the criminological implications of totalitarian warfare, traditional conceptions will have to be either considerably modified or entirely abandoned.

POPULATION MOVEMENTS

The progressing adaptation of the United Kingdom to the needs of the war has necessitated population movements to an almost unprecedented extent. In addition to millions of men called up or volunteering for military service, probably even larger numbers of civilian workers, employees and officials, male and female, have had to be shifted from their homes to other places. Whereas even approximate figures for them cannot at present be given, statistics of persons moved under the Government Evacuation Scheme,[3] though permanently changing, are better known. The following

[1] The material concerning the United Kingdom was collected by the author in the course of an investigation carried out with the support of the Social Research Division of the London School of Economics and Political Science.

[2] This gap has now, to some extent, been filled by the special Bulletin of the International Penal and Penitentiary Commission (I.P.P.C.) on 'The Effects of the War on Criminality', Vol. XV, No. 4/11 of *Recueil de Documents en matière pénale et pénitentiaire*, Novembre, 1951, issued by Thorsten Sellin (Stämpfli & Co., Berne), with contributions from Austria, Belgium, Denmark, France, England and Wales with Northern Ireland, Norway, The Netherlands, Sweden, and U.S.A.

[3] On evacuation in general, see: (*a*) *Cambridge Evacuation Survey*, edited by Susan Isaacs assisted by Sibyl Clement Brown and Robert H. Thouless (London, 1941). (*b*) *Evacuation Survey:* A Report to the Fabian Society, edited by Richard Padley and Margaret Cole (London, 1940). The story is carried up to May, 1941, in Margaret Cole's Fabian Society pamphlet 'Wartime Billeting', Research Series No. 55 (London, 1941). (*c*) Ministry of Health, 'Report on Conditions in Reception Areas' by a committee under the chairmanship of Mr. Geoffrey Shakespeare, M.P. (London, H.M.S.O., 1941). In *War and Crime*, pp. 136 et seq., the author has briefly referred to certain possible analogies between evacuation in Great Britain and American immigration problems.

CRIME IN THE SECOND WORLD WAR

figures were published for 2nd November, 1939: unaccompanied schoolchildren, 750,000; mothers and young children, 542,000; expectant mothers, 12,000; other persons, 77,000; total, 1,381,000.[1] Many of these persons returned sooner or later or moved to still safer districts; other evacuation waves followed, and, in addition, very many persons evacuated themselves privately.[2]

This brief account may suffice to give an idea of the existing dislocation of home life. Moreover, it will illustrate the difficulties which confront any attempt to compare, for any given locality, pre-war with war-time statistics of crime. In the course of the war, a district may in turn have been a Reception Area, a Neutral Area, and an Evacuation Area, with corresponding changes in the numbers and composition of its inhabitants; and even if a district should have remained in one of these categories, the fluctuations of its population may have been as profound as they are difficult to assess.

For other reasons, too, statistical investigations into the effect upon crime of these population movements are unlikely to produce reliable results. With regard to juvenile offenders, for instance, local authorities and private persons in certain Reception Areas seem to have shown great reluctance to charge evacuee children. Not infrequently, such children have been sent home rather than brought before the local juvenile court.

The principal result of the population movements has been the breaking up, on a vast scale, of the family unit. Wives and children have had to be left behind, or the head of the household has had to stay at home with the older children when the wife was evacuated with the younger members of the family. In many cases the separation of husband and wife has led to matrimonial difficulties. As far as crime is concerned, the position should be examined separately for those who have remained at home and those who have left. Moreover, many of the latter have been brought into close contact with sections of the population with whom, from the regional, social, psychological, and perhaps even racial point of view, they have had very little in common. A third category of people has, thus, to be considered—the residents of the Reception Areas.

---

[1] *Evacuation Survey*, p. 42.
[2] The Geoffrey Shakespeare Committee, visiting seventeen reception counties at the end of 1940, found that the original population of 6,289,000 had been swollen by 1,566,000 evacuees. See Report, p. 3.

CRIMINOLOGY AND ITS METHODS

THOSE WHO STAYED HOME

No increase in crime due to the breaking up of normal family life has thus far become noticeable among adults. In some cases lonely husbands are said to have taken to drink, but drunkenness convictions in general have declined, mainly, of course, as a result of the reduction of the adult civilian population. Table 1 shows this decline.[1]

TABLE 1—Proceedings for Drunkenness

	In Liverpool	In London
1938	3,435	19,705
1939	2,772	18,062
1940	2,439	14,145

Much more have the lives of juveniles been affected by their separation from their elders. Probation officers in London and other cities refer to many cases of boys and girls of slightly over school age who, not falling under the government evacuation scheme, got into trouble because they had been left entirely on their own resources to 'run' the lonely home, or because they had to stay in unsuitable common lodging houses.

For the schoolchildren who remained at home, the closing of most of the schools in Evacuation Areas proved a source of the gravest danger. It was due partly to the requisitioning of school buildings for war purposes, to the lack of proper air-raid shelters, and to the absence of the teachers; but in part, schools were closed deliberately in order to provide a further stimulus for parents to send their children away or not to take them back. In this latter respect, the Government policy has not been wholly successful. At the end of 1940 there were still about eighty thousand children of school age in London, and in Manchester on 1st April, 1941, about sixty-eight thousand.[2] Thus, large numbers of city children were left to run wild with nothing to occupy them, and competent observers are unanimous in the belief that the increase in juvenile

---

[1] The London figures show subsequently a further steady decline until 1944 when they reached their lowest level with 8,032 cases. The figures per 1,000 of population were 2.265 in 1938 and 1.234 in 1944. In 1951 they had again reached the pre-war level with 19,605 cases = 2.348 per 1,000 (Report of Commissioner of Police for the Metropolis for the year 1951, p. 94).

[2] *The Times*, 4th December, 1940; *Times Educational Supplement*, 26th April, 1941.

CRIME IN THE SECOND WORLD WAR

delinquency in Evacuation Areas has been largely due to this factor.

In many districts the position has slowly improved, schools have been reopened, and very reluctantly steps have been taken against parents who tolerated persistent truancy.[1] Everywhere this has been followed by an immediate decline in juvenile delinquency, and in all probability the reputation of elementary schools as crime-preventing agencies will emerge from this war considerably strengthened. Likewise, the intimate relationship between truancy and juvenile delinquency has once more been established.

For adolescents of over school age, the closing of the majority of clubs, hostels, Sunday schools, evening institutes, and so forth, in Evacuation Areas has proved hardly less detrimental. In London at the end of February, 1941, out of 260 boys' clubs only 121, and of 220 girls' clubs only 60, had remained open, and even of them, not many were really active.[2] Moreover, a considerable percentage of playing fields had to be converted into allotments or used for military purposes.[3] Consequently, very few opportunities for constructive leisure-time occupation have remained. This has particularly aggravated the difficulties of the successful treatment of those juveniles who have already become delinquents. Moreover, the increase among boys of sixteen of drunkenness and of gang crime —both phenomena almost insignificant in pre-war England[4]— has largely been attributed to this curtailment of constructive leisure-time facilities.

THOSE WHO WENT AWAY

Little or no evidence is available to show that crime has noticeably increased among those masses of adults whom the war has forced to leave their homes and families. Almost exclusively, the general interest has therefore been focused upon the behaviour of evacuated children, and it is their experiences that, for a long time to come, will form a highly instructive subject of criminological studies. Statistical investigations into the problem, it is true, will, for reasons indicated above, be of little value. There is, however,

---

[1] See, for instance, the warning given by the President of the Board of Education, *The Times*, 13th December, 1940.
[2] *Times Educational Supplement*, 1st March, 1941.
[3] *Ibid*, 8th and 15th March, 1941.
[4] See the author's *Social Aspects of Crime*, pp. 183, 299.

gradually accumulating a wealth of individual case material, particularly from probation officers, wardens of homes for difficult evacuees, child guidance clinics, education authorities, and others, that will be of lasting significance. Among the principal causes of juvenile delinquency in Reception Areas have been the following: Having to leave home creates a feeling of insecurity and of being unjustly punished, especially for children from poor homes for whom the idea of being 'sent away' is closely connected with that of the penal institution. Having to live with strangers, moreover, gives a feeling of being an unwanted intruder, almost akin to being an illegitimate child. All the more has this been so when children have been repeatedly evacuated to different areas or even re-billeted within the same area. Sometimes matters have been made worse by wrong methods of billeting, especially in the earlier stages of evacuation when children were distributed among local people without much regard for individual needs. The billeting of children in private homes considerably above or below their own social class has largely proved a failure. Moreover, some children from well-to-do families could not get accustomed to their unwonted freedom from constant supervision. Boys from large orphanages or similar places, when billeted with private families, showed themselves unable to grasp the idea of personal property, of which they had hardly obtained any first-hand knowledge in their institutional lives.[1]

The contrast between city and country has constituted a further source of delinquency, children from city slums finding it difficult to give up long-established habits of picking up objects of little value which they find in the streets. On the whole, however, country people are said to have shown much understanding in this respect, and, generally speaking, it seems that the importance of the town-country contrast should not be over-estimated. Children brought to districts very similar to their own in size and social structure have, here and there, got into trouble just as much as have the city children sent to rural areas, which latter, of course, in view of the absence of the multiple store offer much less temptation.

[1] For further details on these points see the author's *Juvenile Delinquency in an English Middletown* (London, Routledge & Kegan Paul Ltd., 1948), pp. 59 et seq. The above was written several years before the publication of John Bowlby's psychiatric studies of the effect of early separation.

CRIME IN THE SECOND WORLD WAR

Conflicting views have been expressed as to whether it has mainly been the previously delinquent child that has appeared before juvenile courts in Reception Areas or whether evacuation has produced delinquency mainly among those who, in normal circumstances, would have kept straight.

With regard to methods of treatment, two factors have tended to produce a very interesting and complicated situation: the voluntary character of evacuation, and the influx of large numbers of juveniles from cities into rural counties with social and corrective services inadequate for their needs. On account of the first factor, parents of delinquent children, by threatening not to send them away or else to take them back, have sometimes been able to wield an unusually strong influence upon courts and probation officers. Moreover, evacuated children have not been slow to realize that to commit petty offences is one way of getting sent home. As a result of the second factor, the local services frequently have had to bear a burden which proved too heavy for them, and the consequent inadequacy of treatment may become an important source of recidivism. To relieve the strain on local resources and to secure the proper handling of delinquent evacuee children, the Home Office wisely sent out to Reception Areas some experienced London juvenile probation officers. In spite of their excellent work, however, the latter could hardly be expected to make good all deficiencies of local juvenile courts, remand homes, and hostels, and the lack of facilities for psychological treatment. It is only recently that the extreme shortage of accommodation in remand homes and approved schools is slowly being reduced and suitable homes for difficult evacuee children are being established in Reception Areas.[1]

LOCAL PEOPLE IN RECEPTION AREAS

In a few districts it has been stated that local children have occasionally been led astray by quick-witted evacuees. On the whole, however, no particular difficulties of this kind seem to have arisen from the mixing of the two categories.

[1] See Miss Evelyn Fox, 'Emergency Hostels for Difficult Children', *Mental Health*, Vol. I, No. 4, October 1940; Report on Conditions in Reception Areas (see note 3, p. 86 above), p. 10, note 3.

CRIMINOLOGY AND ITS METHODS

SHELTER LIFE

A further factor, also to some extent responsible for the breaking up of the home, has been the development of shelter life in Evacuation Areas. Since August, 1940, millions of people in these areas have had to spend most of their nights and, during winter months, their evenings in public or private shelters. While it is too early to foresee the ultimate effect of this modern cave dwelling, certain criminological facts can be tentatively stated.

The amount of crime against the person directly caused by shelter life does not seem to be excessive. It is true, in the earlier stages of the bombing there were frequent press reports of people who lost their tempers under the strain of danger plus discomfort and overcrowding. There have occurred assaults upon wardens and insulting words and behaviour among shelterers themselves. Shelters in certain districts were used as convenient meeting places by prostitutes and sexual offenders of all categories. With the gradual establishment of more efficient management and control, however, all these abuses have been largely suppressed. Greater difficulties are presented by offences of an economic character. Here, in fact, the opposite development appears to have taken place. The same evening paper which in the earliest days of the 'blitz' had triumphantly stated that on account of the raids there was nothing for the gaoler any more to do,[1] disclosed a bare fortnight later that pickpockets were again busy in London, exploiting conditions in crowded shelters.[2] Acts of wilful damage to public shelters are stated to be so frequent that, in one London district at least, they have to be kept closed in daytime, except during alerts.[3]

More pernicious has been the indirect effect of shelter life, particularly on juveniles. As the latter hardly ever choose to go to the same shelters as their own families, parental control at night has become largely a thing of the past, and even the police experience great difficulties in tracing juvenile delinquents. Professional young bicycle thieves or novices at shop-breaking who, under normal circumstances, would be arrested after their first few exploits, may now be able to continue their activities unhindered

[1] *Evening Standard*, 11th September, 1940, 'Crime takes Cover'.
[2] Ibid., 23rd September, 1940, 'Pickpockets Out as the Sirens Go'.
[3] Ibid., 6th May, 1941.

CRIME IN THE SECOND WORLD WAR

over a period of several months. Likewise, for girls the path of clandestine prostitution has become dangerously easy.

THE BLACKOUT

The blackout[1] has been responsible for two different types of law-breaking: blackout offences proper, and offences committed under the protection of the blackout.

No exact data of the first type have yet been published. In the available statistical returns, lighting offences are included among offences against the Emergency Legislation in general, which numbered, in Liverpool for instance, in 1939, 2,511; in 1940, 6,856. A London magistrate is quoted as having said in court: 'London is being bombed nightly and yet the courts are dealing with 1,000 cases a week of people who won't properly screen their lights.'[2] These cases range in gravity from the slightest negligence to deliberate illumination of windows or setting fire to haystacks during air raids.[3]

The second type of offences consists mainly of assaults on women, policemen, or air-raid wardens, burglaries, thieving from docks, the intentional giving of wrong change, and the like. No accurate information is available apart from numerous press reports which give the impression that there was a special outbreak of assaults on policemen in the autumn of 1940.[4]

On the other hand, air raids and the blackout, particularly during the initial stages of the latter, have substantially reduced certain categories of crime. It was even stated that confidence tricksters and other specialized crooks had completely disappeared during the three months August, September, and October, 1940,[5] probably because conditions had become too uncomfortable for their trade.

CHANGES IN WORK

The war has greatly diminished unemployment, changed the character of work and increased wages. All these factors have considerable bearing upon crime.

[1] See *War and Crime*, pp. 132 et seq.
[2] *Police Chronicle*, 29th November, 1940.
[3] A particularly bad case, for which a sentence of three years' penal servitude was imposed, is reported in the *Police Chronicle*, 20th September, 1940, p. 7.
[4] See *Police Chronicle*, 6th and 20th September, 1940.
[5] See *Daily Telegraph*, 1st November, 1940; *Police Chronicle*, 15th November, 1940, p. 1.

CRIMINOLOGY AND ITS METHODS

Table 2 shows the extent of the improvement in employment.

TABLE 2—Wholly or Temporarily Unemployed

	Men	Boys	Women	Girls	Total
August 14, 1939	908,752	38,347	245,209	39,384	1,231,692
August 12, 1940	409,651	29,862	308,739	51,200	799,452
April 21, 1941	200,494	13,844	197,105	28,658	440,101

As in the first World War, it took some time before women and girls could derive any benefit from the changes in the labour market.[1] Consequently, we may expect to find at least no decline in female crime for the first period of the present war. For men and boys, however, the position has become fundamentally different, and it is in particular one category of the men that has been thriving on the growing scarcity of labour—the old lag. Employers have had to abstain from asking awkward questions about the past, and even the newly established public services, as A.R.P. and similar ones, are sometimes only too glad to get men with first-aid certificates. On the whole, it seems that the old lag has admirably stood the test and is giving very little trouble. As far as he is concerned, recidivism, as happened during the last war, is likely to diminish considerably.[2]

Much more difficult, at least in the first year of the war, was the position of young men of slightly below military age who could secure none but very casual jobs. Consequently, many of them have drifted into crime while waiting to be called up. It seems that the relapse into crime of some ex-Borstal boys discharged at the outbreak of the war[3] has been largely due to this cause.

In exceptional cases, certain changes in habits of work, as night shifts, for instance, are said to have led to minor sexual delinquency, as indecent exposure.[4] Of far greater practical sig-

[1] See the author's *War and Crime*, pp. 109, 116.
[2] *War and Crime*, pp. 99 et seq.
[3] Ibid., p. 134. (Actually the effect of these early discharges does not seem to have been as serious as expected, in part because the waiting period was eliminated; see John Spencer, *Crime and the Services*, 1954, p. 168.)
[4] Some cases of this kind have been treated at the Institute for the Scientific Treatment of Delinquency, London (now the Institute for the Study and Treatment of Delinquency), to which the author is indebted for this information.

CRIME IN THE SECOND WORLD WAR

nificance, however, as a factor contributing to juvenile delinquency, has been the steadily increasing employment of married women outside the home, a tendency which does not appear in the unemployment statistics, as most of these women did not register in peace-time. In homes from which fathers and elder brothers are also absent, this has frequently resulted in a complete lack of supervision and care for schoolchildren.

INCREASED WAGES

The great scarcity of labour, together with the growing cost of living, has led to increases in wages which have been particularly conspicuous in the case of boys between fifteen and nineteen. Magistrates have frequently expressed their astonishment at the fact that such juveniles, in spite of their drawing wages of £3 to £6 instead of fifteen to thirty shillings before the war, over and over again appear in court charged with petty thefts. Social workers are unanimous in stressing the evil effect of such inflated earnings upon immature characters who neither save nor know how to spend their money wisely. It is after the war, however, that the real trouble will begin, when these young men will have to adapt themselves to low peace-time earnings.[1] Proposals to make saving compulsory, at least for the younger age groups, have so far proved unsuccessful.

LOOTING

Certainly not the most important but perhaps the most spectacular criminological feature of the war has been the advent of looting as a result of aid raids.

According to The Defence (General) Regulations, 1939, No. 38A, this offence can be committed 'in an area which has been subjected to attack by the enemy . . . or in any area to which this Regulation has been applied by order of the Minister of Home Security'; and it implies, apart from other less important cases, stealing from premises damaged by war operations or vacated by reason of attack by the enemy, or stealing articles which have been left exposed or unprotected as a consequence of war operations. The maximum penalty for looting is death or penal servitude for life,[2] and, by Order in Council of 4th October, 1940, courts of

[1] For the period after the first world war, see *Social Aspects of Crime*, op. cit., pp. 112, 293–4.
[2] Neither of these penalties has as yet been imposed.

summary jurisdiction have been given power to impose sentences of imprisonment up to twelve months, instead of the previous maximum of three months.

Looting cases began to come before the London courts very soon after the first air raids. In September, 1940, there were 539 cases, in October 1,662, in November 1,463, and in December 920 cases in the Metropolitan Area alone, and a special Anti-Loot Squad of detectives had to be formed by Scotland Yard.[1] At the beginning of February, 1941, a gas company inspector stated at a London juvenile court that there had been more than three thousand cases of thefts from gas meters, mainly in bombed houses.[2] At Leeds Assizes in March, 1941, the judge, referring to a 'perfect outburst of looting' at Sheffield after the raids in December, 1940, dealt with seventeen charges of looting.[3]

In the Metropolitan Area, 14 per cent of the offenders were schoolboys, and 45 per cent were under twenty-one. On the other hand, in only 2 per cent of the cases was the looted property valued at over £100; in about 50 per cent it was under £5. Accordingly, there has been comparatively little evidence of large-scale organized looting by professional criminals. Among 228 looting cases, collected from newspaper reports by the author with the assistance of the Howard League for Penal Reform, it was found that 211 had no known previous convictions. Although it is too early to make any definite statement, the old experience seems to be confirmed that in times of war the percentage of first offenders tends to increase. The offenders belonged to the following age groups:

Under 17: 6
17–21: 7
21–30: 20
30–40: 73
40–50: 27
Over 50: 20
Rest unknown

From a comparison of these figures with those given above it thus appears that most cases of juveniles have not been reported in the press. No fewer than 95 looters, i.e. 42 per cent, were in

[1] *Evening Standard*, 31st October, 1940; *Police Chronicle*, 16th May, 1941, p. 1.
[2] *The Times*, 4th February, 1941.
[3] Ibid., 4th March, 1941.

CRIME IN THE SECOND WORLD WAR

official positions or at least in positions of trust as air-raid wardens, auxiliary firemen or policemen, A.R.P. demolition or rescue workers, and so forth.

Although looting is an offence which, as a rule, can hardly be prevented by the police, under favourable conditions this has nevertheless proved possible. Not a single case, we are told, was reported after the big raid on the city of London in December, 1940, because the raid, though heavy, was confined to a small area, thus enabling the City Police Chief immediately to ring the whole district by detectives in plain clothes.[1]

ATTITUDES TOWARDS LOOTING

Most interesting has been the reaction of the courts and the public towards this new type of crime. As might be expected, the matter has become a favourite topic in the press, where the courts have often been strongly blamed for being either too lenient or too severe. Up to the time of writing, three stages can fairly clearly be distinguished in this development:

1. During the first stage, lasting approximately until the middle of October, 1940, magistrates, though almost invariably referring to the possibility of a death sentence, as a rule confined themselves to fines or short prison sentences. For this they came in for much criticism, especially as looting cases were increasing during October.

2. As a consequence, many courts resorted to more drastic measures, especially against men in official or semi-official positions. They were usually committed to assizes, where heavy sentences of penal servitude became not uncommon.

3. After a few months of vacillation, important sections of public opinion began to react unmistakably against draconic sentences of this kind.[2] It soon became apparent that it was, as a rule, by no means a particularly dangerous type of person who committed this offence, and stress was justly laid upon the great temptation for demolition workers, firemen, or juveniles to pick up damaged articles of little value which, apparently abandoned, might have been lying about for weeks. As one evening paper put it: 'If the bombs introduce a new crime into England, we do not

[1] *Police Chronicle*, 17th January, 1941, p. 1.
[2] See, for instance, articles and letters in the *New Statesman and Nation* of 30th November, 1940, 22nd February, and 8th March, 1941.

want them to introduce a new sort of justice.'[1] As a consequence, we may now sometimes find even auxiliary firemen simply bound over and taken back to their employment.[2] Reports from Nazi sources of courts-martial which had to be set up in raided districts to cope with 'plundering bands'[3] are without any foundation.

Nothing definite can as yet be said on the interesting problem whether the large-scale destruction of goods through bombing will ultimately lead to a general weakening of the sense of property, which, in its turn, may considerably affect the scale of values as it is reflected in the severity of the penalty.

PROFITEERING

There may be still another reason why the public and the courts are beginning to feel somewhat uneasy at the imposition of overharsh penalties for looting. It is the growing extent of profiteering in foodstuffs and other commodities—a menace which is slowly being recognized as no less serious than looting. 'They do not steal and they would call themselves traders or businessmen, but they are looters none the less.'[4] No statistics have as yet been published which would show the actual frequency of such offences. The figures are included in the 'prosecutions under the food control orders', of which 17,319 were successfully undertaken by the Ministry of Food between the outbreak of the war and the end of April, 1941.[5] There are now over two thousand such cases before the courts every month.

Whereas previously not much was said about it in public, the matter has become front-page news since the beginning of May, 1941, when a strongly worded statement was published by the Food Price Committee, North Midland Region, to the effect that 'speculation is rampant', that 'people who render no service in distribution are enriching themselves at the expense of the consumer', that 'prices have in consequence risen out of all reasonable proportion', and that the trivial fines imposed by some benches were 'a matter of ridicule'.[6]

[1] *Evening Standard*, 19th March, 1941.
[2] *The Times*, 5th and 8th May, 1941.
[3] See *The Times*, 6th May, 1941.
[4] The *Economist*, 3rd May, 1941, p. 584.
[5] *Sunday Times*, 25th May, 1941.
[6] *The Times*, 1st, 2nd, 8th, 10th, 16th May, 1941; Ritchie Calder, *New Statesman and Nation*, 26th April, 1941.

CRIME IN THE SECOND WORLD WAR

WAR-TIME CRIMINAL STATISTICS

The last published volume of English criminal statistics for the whole country is that of 1938. For the following years a certain amount of information has been made available through the press, in Parliamentary debates, and in annual reports of probation committees, clerks to justices, and chief constables. The last-mentioned material is, however, not accessible to the general public,[1] and, moreover, not all of it has yet been completed for the year 1940. Much more has become known about the statistical changes in juvenile delinquency than about those in adult crime. It cannot be too strongly emphasized that local figures are of very limited value because of the violent fluctuations in the child population due to evacuation. It can safely be assumed that at least in some cities the increase in numbers of juvenile court cases from 1939 to 1940 was partly due to the return of many evacuees. In Manchester, for instance, out of 89,000 schoolchildren 61,000 were evacuated in September, 1939, of whom 45,000 had returned by January, 1940. However, a comparison between the year 1938, when the figure was 914, and 1940, when in spite of evacuation it had risen to 1,323, shows that there is some cause for real alarm, though since the reopening of many schools the position has improved.

[*Note.*—Much of the further statistical material in this section has become out of date and has therefore been omitted. The reader is referred to *Criminal Statistics England and Wales* for the years 1939–45, published 1947, and to the I.P.P.C. report quoted in note 2, p. 86, above.

The scarcity of statistical information referred to in this paper continued, as shown below in sect. III, until August, 1947.]

II[2]

THE effect of war on crime and its treatment is a problem which may interest various categories of people for different reasons and in different ways. In time of war, the statesmen and the social reformer can be expected to pay close attention to the movement

---
[1] The only exception is the Annual Report of the Commissioner of Police for the Metropolis.
[2] Reprinted, with additional notes, from *The Fortnightly*, January, 1942.

CRIMINOLOGY AND ITS METHODS

of crime because mass violations of the criminal law may reveal hidden danger-spots which no community can afford to neglect in a period of external crisis. Professional students of crime will take advantage of the opportunity offered by sudden and profound changes in the social structure such as can be caused only by war or revolution in order to check the validity of their theories, and practical penologists and penal reformers will strive hard to save the badly knocked about penal system from complete shipwreck and to plan the outlines of its future reconstruction.

By now it has become a commonplace to say that this is a problem which can be successfully tackled only for each particular war separately, whereas comparatively little can be gained by theorizing about it on general lines. Though certain patterns of thought and of action seem to be inseparably connected with war as such, criminal behaviour in wartime must be understood less as a by-product of the international conflict itself than of the social and psychological conditions which it produces. As long as the latter remain in existence no improvement in the crime position is likely to take place even after the end of the actual fighting. There exist hardly more than perhaps half a dozen criminological 'laws' of apparently general validity on the effect of war on crime and for the very reason of their universal applicability none of them is particularly informative. For instance, we know that the total amount of crime, after declining during the initial stages of a war, usually increases towards the middle or the end; that the extent of the final deterioration mainly depends upon the course which the war has taken; that the increase is heaviest and begins almost at once among those categories of the population which remain outside the fighting services; that it is not so much, as is frequently assumed, crime against the person but economic crime that becomes more frequent; that the statistical sex ratio of crime becomes less favourable to the female sex; and, finally, that the penal system tends to deteriorate under the strain of war. All this, it must be admitted, is not very illuminating. As soon as we attempt, however, to supplement these general statements by more detailed observations for specific wars we find ourselves handicapped by the extreme dearth of the material available. There is some reason to hope that, at least in this country, the information which is being collected for the present war will be somewhat more comprehensive and systematic than for the war of

CRIME IN THE SECOND WORLD WAR

1914-18. Statistical investigations into the incidence of crime, it is true, are becoming more difficult than ever on account of the tremendous war-time changes in the local and occupational distribution of the population. Evacuation, the calling up of men and women and the shifting of industries have profoundly altered the population structure of the country. While this affects the total amount of crime only in so far as offences by members of the Forces are frequently dealt with by military courts and thereby excluded from ordinary Criminal Statistics, it renders almost impossible any comparison between pre-war and war-time figures for individual localities. To make matters worse, no Criminal Statistics for the whole country have as yet been published for the period after 1938, whereas during the last war the annual bluebooks came out much as usual, though on a greatly reduced scale. Such local figures as have so far been quoted in public seem to justify the conclusion that the total amount of 'crime known to the Police' has undergone no considerable changes since the outbreak of the war, the increase in some Reception Areas being balanced by the decline in a few Evacuation Areas. For London, by the way, the published figures of indictable offences show a reduction which is obviously less substantial than the decline in population would have justified (1938, 95,280; 1939, 94,852; 1940, 93,869).[1] On the other hand, we know from official publications that juvenile delinquency increased by approximately 41 per cent during the first twelve months of the war, and there are certain indications that delinquency among women is also, though less markedly, on the upgrade.[2] The conclusion is therefore that there must have been less crime among men over the age of seventeen. As the amount of 'crime known to the Police' remains unaffected by the calling up and the numbers of men serving overseas cannot be very large, this may indicate a real improvement. Nobody is likely to overestimate the value of such statistical considerations. Changes in Police activities, the creation of new offences, and many other factors may invalidate any conclusion based upon figures alone. There is in particular one aspect which seems to be

---

[1] In 1941 there was a sudden increase to 99,533, followed by a decline to 91,205 in 1943. The peak was reached in 1945 with 128,954 cases ('Report of Commissioner of Metropolitan Police for 1951', p. 42).
[2] This has been confirmed by the figures published after the war. See the I.P.P.C. publication referred to in note 2, p. 86, above, diagrams 5 and 8.

CRIMINOLOGY AND ITS METHODS

of the greatest importance for the study of war-time crime and to which so far but little attention has been paid, that is, the extent of habitual criminality and of recidivism.

Surely, neither to society at large nor to the practical penologist can it be indifferent whether 100,000 offences 'known to the Police' have been committed by 100,000 first offenders or by a small group of perhaps 2,000 habitual law-breakers, each of whom is responsible for an average of fifty offences. Whereas for the masses of first offenders social (including family) conditions may have to be regarded as the principal causes of crime, the habitual criminal is more likely to be the product of his psychological maladjustment or abnormality or of the unfair treatment he receives from state and society. In periods of war, the latter, absorbed as they are in their fight against the external enemy, become more indulgent in their attitude towards the criminal and are willing to give him a chance. On the other hand, the growing complexity of everyday life infects many more hitherto blameless individuals with the bacillus of lawlessness. Consequently, and this may be regarded as a further experience of universal validity, recidivism and habitual criminality tend to decline in time of war, and more newcomers begin to appear before the criminal courts, a development which may profoundly alter the practical problems involved. No large scale and systematic statistical information on the whole question of recidivism is available even for pre-war years, let alone for the present. The existing material, however, would largely seem to confirm our thesis, that is, the proportion of first offenders appears indeed to have increased at least among adults in general and among juveniles in Reception areas, whereas the opposite tendency is felt among juveniles in certain Evacuation areas. In support of this the following facts may be mentioned.[1]

According to press reports analysed by the author, out of a sample of 424 persons charged with looting 387, = 90 per cent, had

[1] Figures subsequently published by the Prison Commissioners show that during the war the percentage of persons received in prison who had no previous proved offences was considerably higher than before or after the war: 39·1 for men (45·5 for women) in 1940–4 against 32 in 1931–4, 27 in 1935–9 and 25·5 in 1951 for men (29·1 in 1931–4, 28·5 in 1935–9 and 30·4 in 1951 for women); see Report of Prison Commission for 1952, p. 43, and I.P.P.C. publication, Table 10. As it can hardly be assumed that the Courts were particularly inclined during the war years to send first offenders to prison, these figures would seem to confirm our thesis that there was a real increase in the proportion of first offenders.

CRIME IN THE SECOND WORLD WAR

no previous convictions recorded against them, which reveals an abnormally high proportion of first offenders. Of the remaining 37 only nine had more than three previous convictions and might therefore have been habitual offenders. In spite of the smallness of this sample there is no special reason to doubt its representative character, as far as looting is concerned. That habitual criminals are less easily caught is valid not only in war-time and can therefore hardly be stressed in this connection. Moreover, the same impression has been gained by many other observers, though it has not found expression in statistical figures. For other war-time offences such as violations of the Food Control regulations, profiteering, lighting offences, similar results are likely to emerge. The specific reasons for the prevalence of first offenders may be different for the different categories. Lighting offences are, as a rule, unintentional actions committed for no reason of financial gain, both factors characteristic of non-professional crime. Looting and the various types of profiteering are nothing but more pronounced forms of general patterns of anti-social behaviour which remain unpunished in times of peace, and their perpetrators, though public nuisances, do not therefore rank as professional lawbreakers. In other words, the juvenile looter may represent only a further stage in the normal development of the slum child who is used to picking up things lying about on the pavement, and the war profiteer is only the somewhat more unscrupulous war edition of the smart business man who, under normal conditions, manages to keep on the right side of the law.[1]

To the criminologist and the student of social psychology and ethics few other recent mass phenomena can have been more interesting than the outbreak of looting in the winter of 1940–1. Several thousand criminal proceedings for looting (there were 4,584 cases of this kind alone before Metropolitan courts during 1940) and the heated discussion which accompanied them may have proved that legislative action and increased penalties in themselves are unable to eradicate certain deep-rooted attitudes. In the popular mind, the idea of property cannot be altogether

[1] This view has now been confirmed by the material presented in Professor Marshall B. Clinard's book *The Black Market* (New York, Rinehart, 1952), pp. 293 et seq., where it is stated that only a very small proportion, less than one in ten, of American blackmarketeers brought before the criminal courts had a criminal record. The above figures refer to a slightly later stage of the war than those given on p. 96.

divorced from that of possession and of actual use, and in cases where this visible link between owner and property has been cut by temporary or permanent elimination of the former no threat of punishment can fully make up for it.[1] Robbing automatic machines and stealing by finding are the models which, better than anything else, can help to explain the background of looting. 'It is a thousand pities', a London magistrate was recently reported to have said, 'that the public does not always understand that stealing by finding is almost as bad as stealing in any other way.' When Professor T. H. Pear and Mr. E. C. Gates, J.P., Manchester, made an interesting attempt, on a small scale, to ascertain the attitude of young people to property they discovered that out of fifty adolescent boys thirty-one decided that they would keep a sum of ten shillings found in the street, and many others were not at all sure what to do.[2] Among the excuses offered in court by looters in the writer's collection of press cuttings are not only the common 'everybody is doing it' or 'it was a pity that the goods should be lying about unused', but also 'I didn't know that I was doing any harm, as I was told the lady was dead', whereas in another case the argument goes in the opposite direction: 'This is not looting—it would be different if he had taken it from the dead.' Such examples, which could easily be multiplied, indicate utter bewilderment and perplexity rather than moral wickedness, and the best cure for first offenders of this type will be education and guidance rather than severe punishment and stigmatization.

While looting and other war-time offences have widened the extent of criminality, the position of many men with pre-war criminal records has improved. Employers can no longer insist upon a spotless character and, as a consequence, not only manual labourers but even black-coated workers and professional men, in pre-war days the most difficult charges of After-Care organizations, have become easy to place. Their response seems, on the whole, to have been highly satisfactory, and they are said to be giving much less trouble than many young men with previously good characters. The Home Secretary's statement that there are in the Civil Defence Services 'a number of people whose records

[1] These points have subsequently been more fully discussed in the author's *Criminal Justice and Social Reconstruction*, Chapter 6, esp. pp. 100 et seq.
[2] See *Social Welfare*, published by the Manchester and Salford Council of Social Service, Vol. IV, No. 9, July, 1941.

CRIME IN THE SECOND WORLD WAR

are open to question, many even with criminal records, who have done a first-class job in civil defence', seems to be fully borne out by the facts. Thus the experience of the last war is repeating itself that even men with many previous sentences of penal servitude or imprisonment are likely to keep straight if they can obtain jobs with living wages and are not under a cloud of suspicion. It is to be hoped that this will not be forgotten when, after the war, work may again become less plentiful.

On the other hand, it will be asked why the present abundance of highly paid work so frequently fails to prevent young boys and even some mature men with hitherto unblemished characters from falling into crime. Recent discussions in the press and elsewhere have shown that, while most experts are inclined to regard the inflated earnings of to-day as direct incentives to delinquency, some others find it difficult to reconcile this interpretation with the traditional view that crime is largely due to poverty and should therefore disappear when economic conditions are improved. To this one might reply that the same factor can affect different types of people in a different way, and if other factors change, it may even affect individuals of the same type in a different manner. Although poverty and unemployment may rank high as crime-producing elements one should never forget that, in most cases, they can become effective only in co-operation with other unfavourable factors or may be neutralized by favourable ones. Likewise, events which, as a rule, have a crime-preventing effect may lose this character under special circumstances. And, finally, nothing is more dangerous than a sudden change in man's fortunes and even the most propitious happenings may require a long process of education and training before they are properly digested. These are platitudes, but their practical implications are sometimes overlooked. To shower inflated wages upon an adolescent entirely unaccustomed to them may easily upset his mental and moral balance, give him an equally inflated sense of his own importance and impair his relations with his family. It may well be true that, as has been stressed, these boys have to work very hard or that they are not the only ones who earn more than they deserve. To meet the latter objection it might be said that factors which are conducive to delinquency among adolescents are not less harmful because of the existence of others which render possible profiteering and similar forms of 'white-collar criminality', to use

CRIMINOLOGY AND ITS METHODS

a term popular with American criminologists. Nor is it the business of the theoretical criminologist to suggest any specific measures of an economic or social character, whether it may be compulsory saving or reduction of wages. All he can do is to sift the evidence, to interpret the working of the social and psychological mechanisms involved, and perhaps to recall certain analogous experiences made in most belligerent countries during the last war and after. In this country, the warnings of war-time prophets seem to have been fully confirmed during the years after 1918 by observations of prison and Borstal governors and social workers. The case may be quoted of a boy who, having earned £6 to £7 as a fitter's mate during the war, took to house- and shop-breaking when his earnings fell to less than £4. After his discharge from Borstal he was offered a job at thirty shillings which could hardly have been to his liking.

For children of school age, as already indicated, the situation seems to have developed on different lines in evacuation districts and in reception areas, the former having a larger share of persistent offenders, the latter more newcomers. At first, all those social and psychological factors which make for juvenile delinquency could easily be found assembled in reception areas, and it is therefore not surprising that many children had to appear before the juvenile courts who would normally not have become delinquent. After two years of practical experience many difficulties have been overcome by better organization and understanding. In particular, the sudden change from city to country life and the resulting 'culture conflict', which were responsible for many initial lapses, have in the long run frequently proved beneficial, and there is evidence from many quarters that the delinquency rates among evacuees are now lower than among local children. Although during the first year of the war court figures of juvenile delinquency and especially of recidivism may in some districts have been artificially reduced by the practice of sending offenders back to their homes instead of dealing with them in the reception area, the present improvement seems to be genuine.

In evacuation areas a selective process of an altogether different character is likely to have taken place. In the first instance, the proportion of bad homes and inefficient and neglected parents was almost certainly higher for those children who remained in bombed districts, and the proportion of children with delinquent tendencies who were sent back as 'unbilletable' after a brief

CRIME IN THE SECOND WORLD WAR

absence must also have been large. Conditions in such districts have, generally speaking, not been conducive to good behaviour, although the re-opening of many schools and clubs during the year 1941 has proved beneficial. In contrast to many reception areas there is but little to compensate non-evacuated children for the losses they have suffered. The consequences have become apparent in many juvenile courts, least of all perhaps in London, where the war-time increase in delinquency, according to the latest calculations of the L.C.C., appears almost negligible. It is only in conformity with the general picture that in some evacuation areas (noted in an interesting report by the Bristol Child Guidance Clinic issued in the summer of 1941) attention has been drawn to the alarming increase in delinquency and recidivism among feeble-minded and very dull children. Although the Bristol figures are too small to warrant any general conclusions, it is remarkable that 69 per cent of the children examined had been delinquent before and that 49 per cent of those who had previously been charged belonged to the very dull type (I.Q. 70–85) which represented only 31 per cent of the total.

Summing up the present crime situation one may be justified in saying that, in spite of the considerable proportion of first offenders who are coming before the courts, no signs of a truly alarming deterioration have so far become visible. Moreover, those observers who might feel inclined to deplore the absence of certain striking improvements which occurred during the last war should bear in mind that there was much less scope for them in 1939 than in 1914. To take but one example. Compared with the spectacular decline of drunkenness convictions from 183,000 in 1914 to 84,000 in 1916 and to 29,000 in 1918 the present improvement which may be no more than 12 per cent of the pre-war total of 50,000 to 55,000 is bound to appear less satisfactory than it actually is. It would seem essential, however, that the future development of the whole crime situation should be closely watched and that statistical material should be collected which might render possible, among other points, a more accurate estimate of how much of war-time crime is due to the activities of a small group of recidivists and how much to great masses of newcomers respectively.[1]

There can be little doubt that the growing strain on the penal

[1] Apart from the Prison Statistics referred to above, p. 102, n. 1, no information has subsequently been published on this point.

system will, as time goes on, result in a general increase of recidivism, especially among young people. While space forbids to deal in detail with the manifold problems of treatment, it may be pertinent briefly to analyse certain general trends. Is it simply a picture of wholesale deterioration that here meets the eye, or are there also visible certain changes for the better which might perhaps prepare the ground for a future reconstruction of the penal system? It is not only the crisis of this system itself that has to be considered but, first of all, the difficult position which confronts the criminal courts, including juvenile courts, in their sentencing policy. Even in peace-time criminal courts cannot perform their duties regardless of the general requirements of society at large. In time of war, these claims will grow in intensity and, within reasonable limits, it may become more important, for instance, to free man-power for essential war-work than to send offenders to prison. Special attention has to be paid to the changes in character and capacity which penal institutions and methods undergo in war-time. It is useless to commit juvenile delinquents to already overcrowded Remand Homes or Approved Schools. Probation Orders, appropriate as long as the offender remains in his usual surroundings, may become harmful when the probationer becomes an evacuee and has to live in a rural district with strangers who may regard a child on probation as an habitual criminal. Or, with the ordinary local prison in many respects thrown 'back to 1922' (*Howard Journal*, 1941, p. 7), a prison sentence to-day may mean something different from what it was in 1938. Moreover, the old experience has to be faced that in war-time the balance of power between the judiciary and the executive is altered in favour of the latter. It is not only in the case of Regulation 18b that this becomes apparent. When prisoners have to be transferred *en bloc* to Borstal Institutions or inmates of penal institutions are discharged much sooner than could be expected by the judges, the latter may well complain that their sentences are no longer carried out. But is this state of affairs not the logical conclusion of a process which, for good or evil, has been going on for a period much longer than these few years of war, a process which in the U.S.A. has culminated in a movement to take the power of sentencing, at least for adolescent offenders, altogether out of the hands of the judges and to entrust it to an administrative body, the 'Treatment Tribunal'?[1]

[1] See the details in *Criminal Justice and Social Reconstruction*, pp. 223 et seq.

CRIME IN THE SECOND WORLD WAR

With regard to the treatment of prisoners one of the most important experiences is that men transferred under the strain of wartime necessities to less oppressive conditions have responded well. The lesson to be learned is, as Mr. Alexander Paterson indicated some time ago, that oppressive conditions are, as a rule, unnecessary and should be replaced by a more constructive system of observation, classification and treatment.[1] If such facilities as observation centres, hostels, clinics for psychological treatment, and the like had been available on a sufficiently large scale at the beginning of the war, the overcrowding in penal institutions might have been avoided. That the present penal system is in need of greater differentiation on scientific lines rather than of mere expansion seems to be the chief lesson of war-time experience for the penal reformer.

III[2]

NOBODY in his senses could have failed to be prepared for a considerable rise in crime immediately after the war. The crime wave has in fact arrived, in England as in probably every other country, though perhaps not to the extent originally expected. The actual nature of this increase in terms of types of crime, local distribution, and similar factors, cannot as yet be stated because no Criminal Statistics have so far been published for the whole of England and Wales for the years since 1938.[3] We have to rely, therefore, mainly on figures given from time to time by the Home Secretary in replies to questions in the House of Commons, on local police reports and on the press. On the whole, more information for juveniles than for adults has been forthcoming from these sources and more for the London area than for provincial districts. The rise has been somewhat greater with regard to the numbers of 'crimes known to the Police' than of 'persons found guilty'. In the latter category, figures have even declined for some age groups since the end of the war, although there has been a considerable all-round increase as compared with 1938.

Murder.—The total of murders (England and Wales) known to

[1] *Howard Journal*, 1941, p. 12.
[2] Extracts from an article 'Crime and its Treatment in Post-war England', *Federal Probation*, Vol. XI, No. 4, October–December, 1947.
[3] Criminal Statistics for England and Wales, 1939–45, were published in August, 1947, i.e. too late to be referred to in the above article.

the Police, which used to be slightly more than a hundred before the war (114 in 1937 and 126 in 1938), reached its climax in 1942 with 209 murders and in 1945 with 218.[1]

A sensational case of murder occurred early in 1947 when ten Approved School boys, aged fourteen to sixteen, were charged with the murder of an assistant instructor on the staff of their school. They had planned to shoot the headmaster but actually shot the assistant who caught them stealing guns and ammunition from the stores of the school. Four of them were found guilty of murder and ordered to be detained during His Majesty's Pleasure, five others were found guilty only of conspiracy and committed to Borstal Institutions or Approved Schools, and one boy was sent to an institution for mental defectives.[2] Another murder case was interesting because the accused man was sentenced to death and his appeal dismissed by the Court of Criminal Appeal in spite of the fact that another man had, between conviction and appeal, confessed to be the murderer. After the dismissal, this confession was withdrawn in the course of an enquiry instituted by the Home Secretary,[3] and the convicted man was executed. It is not surprising that, true to the laws of imitation, a few months later, in another murder case history nearly repeated itself, with the difference that here the author of the 'confession' did not withdraw but was found to be insane.

Ill-Treatment and Neglect of Children.—Another type of crime against the person which, largely as the result of war-time conditions, has been much in the headlines in the later war years and the post-war period is ill-treatment and neglect of children. A total of 1,600 women are stated to have been sent to prison for offences of this kind in the three years 1943 to 1945. In one particularly bad case a man was sentenced to six years' penal servitude in 1945 for manslaughter of a boy boarded out to him by a local authority and his wife to six months' imprisonment for neglect, and as a consequence of the wide publicity given to the trial the whole

[1] See now the figures in the 'Report of the Royal Commission on Capital Punishment', 1953, Appendix 3, Table I, p. 300. Different figures are given in *Crim. Stat. for England and Wales*, 1939–45, p. 11.
[2] See the Report quoted on p. 59, note 2, above, and the Sixth Report on the work of the Children's Department, Home Office (London, H.M.S.O., May, 1951), pp. 72–3.
[3] See the Report by Mr. John Catterall Jolly, K.C. (London, H.M.S.O., 1947, Cmd. 7049).

CRIME IN THE SECOND WORLD WAR

subject of boarding out of children by local authorities was reviewed.[1] In another equally widely reported case a mother was sentenced to two years' imprisonment for cruel treatment of her eight-year-old daughter and the father to six months. A movement has recently been started to establish suitable training homes to which neglectful mothers could be sent as a condition of probation to receive training in mothercraft and domestic work, instead of unconstructive prison sentences.[2]

Crimes of Violence.—With regard to crimes of violence committed by juveniles, no detailed information is at present available except a statement by the Commissioner of Police for the Metropolis that in 1945, out of 209 persons arrested for robbery and assaults with intent to rob, 83, or about 40 per cent, were under twenty-one; 9 were twelve years of age or less.[3]

Crimes of an Economic Character.—Outstanding among crimes of an economic character are burglary, house and shop-breaking and receiving, Post Office Savings Bank frauds, smuggling, and currency offences. According to the Annual Report of the Liverpool Underwriters Association,[4] the number of claims for theft of cargo in transit also increased to an alarming extent in 1946. To judge from the frequency of press reports on such cases, jewellery, cigarettes, food, furs, carpets and clothing coupons seem to be particularly popular objects of large scale burglaries. On account of the increase in smuggling (16,000 cases of interception or seizure in the financial year April 1945–6 as against 6,000 cases before the war) a special training school for preventive officers has been established.[5] Obtaining money from the Post Office Savings Bank

---

[1] See Report by Sir Walter Monckton on the circumstances which led to the boarding out of Dennis and Terrence O'Neill, etc. (H.M.S.O., 1945, Cmd. 6636); *Memorandum on Boarding Out of Children and Young Persons* (Home Office and Ministry of Health, H.M.S.O., 1946).

[2] Although there has been no decline in the number of convictions for such offences, some progress in treatment has been made by establishing further Homes for neglectful mothers, by introducing special training courses for those sent to prison (see Report of Prison Commissioners for 1952, pp. 59 et seq.) and by undertaking research into the causes of cruelty and methods of treatment.

[3] More recent information shows that the number of crimes of violence against the person known to the Police has increased from 2,721 in 1938 and 4,743 in 1945 to 7,083 in 1953 and that the proportion of persons under twenty-one found guilty of such crimes has increased from 17 per cent in 1938 to 23 per cent in 1953 (*Crim. Stat. for England and Wales,* 1953, pp. vii and xvi).

[4] *The Times,* 20th January, 1947.

[5] *The Observer,* 18th May, 1947.

by means of forged documents has been widespread, but the breaking up in spring 1947 of two such gangs, each of which had been responsible for several hundred cases of this kind, is stated to have put an end to such practices for the time being.[1]

Perhaps the biggest headlines have been given in recent months to currency offences. There are, on the one hand, the illicit currency dealings by members of the Forces on the Continent, resulting in a loss of almost forty million pounds sterling to the Treasury in 1945-6,[2] and on the other hand, currency offences by visitors from Great Britain to the Continent who, being allowed to take with them no more than £75 each, in a number of cases resorted to the strictly prohibited practice of drawing cheques in favour of Continental firms. Heavy fines, and in a few cases prison sentences, have been imposed for such offences.

It would be altogether wrong to regard the rise in crime as something extraordinary or particularly alarming. It is nothing but the natural result of six years of total war with all its inevitable moral, psychological, and economic repercussions, and there is consequently nothing original in the many official and unofficial attempts to explain the present situation. The general cheapening of all values; loosening of family ties; weakened respect for the law, human life, and property, especially property of the State and of big firms; scarcity of all consumer goods, the black market and the resulting rise in prices; rationing and the well-justified austerity policy of the Government; easy accessibility of many bomb-damaged houses and ample supplies of guns and ammunition; lack of trained police officers and, finally, the activities of deserters are usually, maybe rightly, put forward. It was Mr. Chuter Ede, the Home Secretary, who said: 'No one would have thought of stealing a second-hand shirt in 1939; to-day the sight of a shirt on the clothes line has become a temptation.'[3]

There are only two factors in this list that would seem to require some further discussion: the understaffing of the police forces and the question of the deserters.

The English police, and in particular the Metropolitan Police Force, have always been counted among the most efficient Forces in the world, and they amply deserve all the praise bestowed upon them. It is characteristic that even at the height of the crime wave

[1] *The Times*, 7th, 14th May, 1947.   [2] *The Times*, 15th April, 1947.
[3] *The Observer*, 16th December, 1945.

CRIME IN THE SECOND WORLD WAR

there has never been the slightest criticism in this direction. On the contrary, even papers otherwise more likely to take an anti-Government line had headlines 'Don't blame the Police'.[1] The explanation is, apart from the general popularity of the London bobby, that it has become widely known through the press and the recruiting campaign of the authorities how seriously understaffed the Police Forces in this country at present are. According to the Home Secretary's statement,[2] the total male strength of the Metropolitan Police is 14,850 as compared with an authorized establishment of 19,740. For the whole country, the deficiency is 16,000. There had been no recruitment during the war, while the Police lost men to the services. Even if these 16,000 could be recruited at once they would still be in need of fairly long training. This question of training, especially for higher posts, has recently been investigated by an expert committee which recommended the establishment of a national Police College open to all forces of England and Wales, instead of the pre-war Hendon Police College which served the Metropolitan Police only.[3] Meanwhile nothing has been left undone to increase the efficiency of the available force by giving them better equipment and by enlisting the support of the public, the press and the wireless.

The Commissioner of the Metropolitan Police, Sir Harold Scott, has been personally instrumental for press conferences and for a series of popular broadcast discussions, 'It's your money they're after', and similar ones, with the object of enlightening the man in the street about the principal forms of confidence tricks, etc. Frequent appeals have been made to the public to make the widest use of the '999' telephone call emergency service which, in conjunction with the system of police patrols equipped with wireless, has been of considerable assistance to the force. In 1946, the number of such emergency calls by Londoners increased by 22,434 to 60,095, and arrests made by the crews of wireless cars increased by 1,126 to 5,588.[4]

The question of the deserters deserves in many ways the special attention of the criminologist. Very soon after the onset of the

[1] *Evening Standard*, 3rd May, 1947.
[2] *Hansard*, 8th May, 1947, col. 784. In this respect, the position has hardly improved (Report of Commissioner of Police for the Metropolis for 1952, pp. 7 and 20).
[3] See *Higher Training for the Police Service in England and Wales* (H.M.S.O., 1947, Cmd. 7070).   [4] *The Times*, 2nd January, 1947.

CRIMINOLOGY AND ITS METHODS

crime wave the view was expressed by the authorities and the press that the rise in crime was largely due to the activities of this group of outcasts of whom, according to official estimates, there were about 20,000 at large (as against 80,000 after World War I). Unable to get identity cards and ration books in the legal way, they were said to be living largely on their wits and always ready to commit even serious crimes. Widespread police searches were undertaken, without conspicuous success, and at the beginning of 1947 the Government began to realize that something more constructive was required to put an end to an unpleasant situation. An announcement was made by the then Minister of Defence in the House of Commons on 22nd January, 1947, that those deserters who would surrender voluntarily by 31st March, 1947, would have this fact and any other mitigating circumstances taken into account; their cases would be speedily dealt with and they would eventually be restored to normal civilian life and obtain those benefits to which their completed terms of service entitled them. In some sections of the press this concession was regarded as an unsatisfactory half measure, unlikely to yield results, and a complete amnesty was strongly recommended.[1] Events have proved this forecast to be largely correct as only a small minority of the deserters surrendered (842 up to the end of February; no later figures seem to have been published). It seems doubtful, however, whether the Government could have gone so far as to promise a full amnesty without giving serious offence to the general public and, in particular, to large bodies of ex-service men who are inclined to regard desertion as one of the worst crimes. To those interested in the possibilities and the inherent limitations of penal reform it was a valuable experience to see how this attempt of the Government to reduce the crime rate by bringing a large body of outlaws and actual potential criminals back to normal life in the community, i.e. by large-scale preventive action, was foredoomed to failure because of the limits to Government action imposed by the force of retributive tendencies among the population. Those who did surrender were dealt with speedily and on the whole with leniency, sentences ranging from a mere admonition to a maximum of two years' detention in a few very bad cases; but even these sentences were mostly suspended after one-third had been served.[2]

[1] *Evening Standard*, 24th January and 7th February, 1947.
[2] *The Times*, 12th March, 1947.

CHAPTER 6

METHODOLOGICAL PROBLEMS OF CRIMINOLOGY

I. METHODOLOGICAL PROBLEMS OF CRIMINOLOGY[1]

PROFESSOR ANDENAES' suggestion that one of my lectures at the University of Oslo might be devoted to methodological aspects was most welcome to me as, for many years, I have been increasingly aware of the crucial importance of methodological problems in criminological research. In my teaching at the University of London I feel obliged to spend more and more time on the matter which, with very few exceptions, is almost completely neglected in criminological textbooks. While a more detailed and comprehensive treatment of the subject has to wait for another occasion, I am therefore grateful for this opportunity of dealing briefly with a few selected topics.

First, what do we mean by methodology? It is, I submit, the critical study of the techniques of research employed by the investigator in his search for the factual material on which his conclusions and theories are based; a critical and conscious analysis of these techniques with the object of improving them and making deliberate planning possible. In the past, we criminologists have been notoriously uncritical in our methods, and all too often have we failed to realize that our 'facts', collected as they were by faulty techniques, were inaccurate and our conclusions and theories therefore untenable.

So far, Criminology has developed no specific methodology of

[1] A shortened and revised version of a lecture delivered on the 11th February, 1953, at the University of Oslo, arranged by the Faculty of Laws of the University in co-operation with the British Council under the Foreign Universities Interchange Scheme. Not previously published.

CRIMINOLOGY AND ITS METHODS

its own; its techniques of research are, on the whole, identical with those used in the other social sciences such as Psychology and Sociology, but to some extent also with those employed in Medicine, Biology and other natural sciences. Even so, however, the application of these techniques to criminological problems often presents very peculiar difficulties owing to the anomalous position of Criminology and the nature of its subject; in particular owing to the all-pervading influence of the criminal law and the exceptionally heavy stigma attached to crime and punishment. Human activities, if treated as criminal offences, are thereby driven underground and may get altogether out of reach of the investigator, while the material that can be reached may be wholly unrepresentative. To make matters worse, the traditional conception of justice may bar the application of certain techniques within the judicial system and to some extent even in the administrative field.

As rightly stressed by Edward Shils in his Foreword to the English translation of Max Weber's *Studies in the Methodology of the Social Sciences*,[1] methodological studies should be undertaken only by workers who are in close touch with actual research. Only they can be fully aware of the theoretical and practical problems to be mastered, and nobody else can be in possession of the material to which methodological principles have to be applied.

In a way, consciously or unconsciously the search for better techniques of criminological research has of course been going on for a fairly long time. Changes in our views on the nature and causes of crime have been due in part to changes in the general intellectual and cultural climate of the time and in part to improvements in methods of research. The former have been chiefly responsible for that long succession of general theories on the hereditary and environmental causes of crime which we have been witnessing in the course of the past hundred years. The latter, in their turn, have until recently been able to do little more than, by exposing the most obvious methodological fallacies, to hasten the changing over from one pet idea to the next following. Now, however, there seems to be a shifting of emphasis. We are becoming more and more sceptical of preconceived theories, and even if

[1] Max Weber, *The Methodology of the Social Sciences*, translated and edited by Edward A. Shils and Henry A. Finch, with a Foreword by Shils (Illinois, Glencoe Free Press, 1949).

METHODOLOGICAL PROBLEMS

we do not always know at the outset in what direction we may be carried off we are inclined to pin our faith on improved techniques rather than on ready-made formulae. Mere hypotheses which we are ready to abandon at any time take the place of those prejudices for which our predecessors used to fight to the last ditch.

A few examples, selected at random, may be quoted to show that methodological considerations did in fact play some part in previous research. Some of the mid-nineteenth century writers discussing the relation between economic conditions and crime were not unaware of the dangers arising from the injudicious use of statistics,[1] and the same applies to the Government Committees and private scholars who, more than a hundred years ago, tried to unravel the truth about the rise of juvenile delinquency in England.[2] In the course of the present century, the criticisms of Lombroso were mainly, though not exclusively, directed against his faulty techniques of anthropological measurement and his lack of a control group. Lombroso, however, has by no means been the only sinner in applying unscientific techniques. Some of his principal critics, including Charles Goring, as well as some of his defenders such as Ernest Hooton, have at least been guilty of employing badly selected control groups. The fashion which, after the decline of the Lombrosian School, regarded crime as primarily due to mental deficiency was largely discredited by the development of better techniques of measuring intelligence and greater awareness of the need for representative samples and for control groups matched according to cultural level and similar factors which had previously been ignored. This list could be prolonged almost *ad infinitum*, and at present it is a commonplace to say that progress in our field can come only through improved methods of research. Flashes of insight, imagination and genius will, of course, always remain indispensable, but they alone are not enough and as experience has shown they may have their dangers unless constantly checked by seemingly very drab and pedestrian investigations carried out in accordance with a strictly disciplined methodology and with meticulous attention to detail.

As the history of our discipline shows, we criminologists have

[1] See Thorsten Sellin, *Research Memorandum on Crime in the Depression* (New York, Social Research Council, Bulletin 27, 1937), pp. 21 et seq.
[2] See A. M. Carr-Saunders, Hermann Mannheim and E. C. Rhodes, *Young Offenders* (Cambridge University Press, 1942, and New York, The Macmillan Company, 1944), pp. 3 et seq.

indeed some special reasons to be particularly anxious to improve our instruments of scientific investigation. In hardly any other branch of knowledge has it happened so often as in our field that apparently firmly established theories had to be abandoned as fallacious or at least one-sided. It was for this reason that two American scholars, Jerome Michael and Mortimer J. Adler, in their book *Crime, Law and Social Science*,[1] after a devastatingly critical analysis of the researches so far carried out on the causes of crime, reached the conclusion that any attempt, with the techniques then at the disposal of research workers, to discover such causes was absurd and foredoomed to failure. Although this verdict has generally been regarded as going too far and being too negative, many other, more balanced writers such as the Gluecks, Paul W. Tappan, and Walter C. Reckless have expressed serious doubts as to the possibility of adequately isolating the many factors involved in any search for causes. Such scepticism has become a universal phenomenon nowadays in the social as well as in the physical sciences. 'Science', writes Sellin,[2] 'has abandoned the search for "final" causes. It has practically abandoned the concept of cause except to denote a functional relationship between or among elements or facts.' Causality, as Ernest Greenwood stresses in his masterly 'Experimental Sociology', 'is just one kind of order sought by science';[3] it is not the only one. Moreover, criminologists have recently, not without reason, been accused of being ignorant of the philosophical meaning of causation.[4] It is one thing, however, to warn—as these writers have done—against facile optimism in causal research, to insist on a better understanding of the meaning of causation, to show that valuable results can be achieved even without knowing the real causes of crime, and an entirely different thing to denounce any possibility of causal research wholesale and for ever. No doubt that reasonable scepticism has had some beneficial results in encouraging us to search for other objects of practically useful research within our immediate reach, regardless of the quest of causes. The most conspicuous example are the recent prediction

[1] New York, Harcourt, Brace & Co., 1933.
[2] Thorsten Sellin, *Culture Conflict and Crime* (Social Science Research Council, New York, Bulletin 41, 1938), p. 17.
[3] Ernest Greenwood, *Experimental Sociology* (New York, King's Crown Press, 1945), p. 19.
[4] Peter Lejins, *Social Forces*, Vol. 29, No. 3, March, 1951, pp. 318-19.

METHODOLOGICAL PROBLEMS

studies which aim at the discovery of predictive factors which may or may not be at the same time causative factors. Treatment, though more safely given on the basis of knowledge of causes, cannot be delayed until such knowledge has been obtained. As in medical practice, courts and penal administrators have, more often than not, to work on the basis of trial and error, and any assistance that can be provided through predictive devices should be welcomed. Of course, it should not be overlooked that even in such procedure by trial and error a certain minimum of knowledge regarding potential causes is indispensable.

In spite of such an obvious need for it, Methodology is not infrequently regarded with suspicion as something essentially sterile and impractical; and no doubt it can easily be overdone. 'There was a compelling persuasiveness', writes T. H. Marshall in his stimulating Inaugural Lecture on 'Sociology at the Crossroads',[1] 'about the famous cry, "Give us the tools, and we will finish the job." One may be forgiven for responding less eagerly to the scholar, be he sociologist or anything else, who says, "Give me a job, and I will spend the rest of my life polishing the tools."' This certainly is a warning much to be heeded in many fields, especially in Sociology proper, but in Criminology (with which Marshall was not concerned) we have hardly reached the stage where the study of Methodology is becoming a danger. On the contrary, rather foolhardily we have often been attempting to do jobs for which the tools had not yet been constructed.

Thirty years ago, the view—formulated already towards the end of the nineteenth century by Frederick Howard Wines and others[2] —that crime is always due to a multiplicity of causes was clearly re-stated and confirmed by Cyril Burt. The logical conclusion from this discovery that Criminology has to depend on the facts and theories produced by at least half a dozen different branches of knowledge is the doctrine of the multiplicity of research techniques and the need for team work. Ever since, we have been paying lip service to this doctrine, but have we always been willing

[1] Publication of The London School of Economics and Political Science, London, 1947 (Longmans, Green and Co., London, New York and Toronto), p. 19.
[2] Frederick Howard Wines, *Punishment and Reformation* (New York, 1895). See also Arthur E. Fink, *Causes of Crime. Biological Theories in the United States 1800–1915* (Philadelphia, University of Pennsylvania Press; London, Humphrey Milford, Oxford University Press), 1938, pp. 32 and 166.

CRIMINOLOGY AND ITS METHODS

and able to act in accordance with it? For a number of reasons, perhaps simply for lack of the necessary financial resources, criminological investigations have sometimes failed to tackle their problems from every possible angle. Even in two of the largest and most carefully planned and executed recent studies, important aspects of criminological research have not been as fully represented as some critics at least would have wished: in the Cambridge-Somerville study the inadequacy of the psychiatric services provided during the initial stages of the project has been criticized (see below, Section IIIb), whereas in the, in many ways exemplary, Glueck study *Unraveling Juvenile Delinquency* the sociological reviewers have almost unanimously regretted the absence of a sociologist from the research team.[1] The task before us is therefore not only to work out competent research techniques in each of the various special disciplines concerned in criminological research, but also to ensure the fullest co-operation between them.

To deal even superficially with the various techniques employed in criminological research a whole series of lectures would be required. All I can try to do here is to draw attention to some of the most commonly encountered difficulties and misconceptions.

In the field of *statistical techniques*, a few brief remarks may be made on some of the most important of them, in particular on control group studies and experimental techniques:[2]

Control groups are an indispensable tool in any kind of research, and in criminological investigations control groups of any description have been used ever since they were recognized as essential: control groups of non-delinquents to be compared with delinquents; of 'normal' boys to be compared with 'pre-delinquents' (Cambridge-Somerville); of recidivists for comparison with first offenders (Norwood East and others);[3] of 'affectionless' children and others also brought to a Child Guidance Clinic but not so labelled;[4] of non-delinquent brothers of delinquents and

[1] See, e.g., Frederick Trasher, *American Sociological Review*, Vol. 16, April, 1951, p. 264; Sol Rubin and Albert J. Reiss, *American Journal of Sociology*, Vol. LVII, No. 2, September, 1951.
[2] For some remarks on the use of statistics in Criminology see also M. Grünhut, *Journal of the Royal Statistical Society*, Series A (General), Vol. CXIV, Part II, 1951, pp. 139 et seq.
[3] W. Norwood East, P. Stocks and H. T. P. Young, *The Adolescent Criminal* (London, J. & A. Churchill, Ltd., 1942).
[4] John Bowlby, *Forty-four Juvenile Thieves* (London, Baillière, Tindall & Cox, Ltd., 1946).

METHODOLOGICAL PROBLEMS

criminals;[1] of identical and non-identical twins;[2] of murderers with understandable motives and others committing apparently 'motiveless' murders;[3] of sex offenders as compared with murderers and offenders against property.[4] In fact, the selection of the control group depends on the nature of the specific problem to be studied and on the availability of the material. Suitable control groups of non-delinquents, for example, are notoriously difficult to obtain as the latter are often disinclined to volunteer for purposes of research. Where they are available for criminological investigations they may yield valuable information on certain characteristics of the non-delinquent population not yet collected by research workers outside the field of Criminology. On the other hand, occasionally data already in existence for the general population can be used for purposes of control. Control group studies can be designed in two different ways, either by comparing two groups of individuals of whom at least one group is a delinquent one in order to ascertain the comparative frequency of certain characteristics; or by comparing two groups of individuals one of whom possesses a certain characteristic other than delinquency, not present in the control group, in order to find out which of the two groups shows the higher delinquency rate. For example, the relation between delinquency and illegitimacy can be studied either from the delinquency or from the illegitimacy angle by enquiring either how many illegitimate children are in a group of delinquents and in a control group of non-delinquents; or how many delinquents are in a group of illegitimate and in a control group of legitimate children. For practical reasons, the first method is usually preferred.

The following are the most obvious weaknesses of control group techniques as applied in most previous studies: First, the presence

[1] William Healy and Augusta Bronner, *New Light on Delinquency* (New Haven, Yale University Press, 1936); John Lewis Gillin, *The Wisconsin Prisoner. Studies in Criminogenesis* (Madison, Wisconsin, The University of Wisconsin Press, 1946).

[2] Johannes Lange, *Crime as Destiny* (English translation, London, George Allen & Unwin, 1931); Franz J. Kallmann, *Heredity in Health and Mental Disorder* (New York, W. W. Norton & Co., 1953), and many others.

[3] Denis Hill in 'Minutes of Evidence of the Royal Commission on Capital Punishment No. 13', p. 304 (London, H.M.S.O., 1950); the same, *Journal of Mental Science*, Vol. XCVIII, No. 410, January, 1952; D. Stafford-Clark and F. H. Taylor, 'Minutes of Evidence', p. 300.

[4] Gillin, see above, note 1.

or absence of the distinguishing criterion, whether it is delinquency or identity of twins or some other factor, is sometimes difficult to establish with absolute certainty. Secondly, even where control groups of non-delinquents are available it is usually more difficult to obtain detailed and reliable data on them than on delinquents; moreover, the knowledge of the investigators, in particular of inadequately trained field workers, that one of the groups is a delinquent group may easily bias their findings. While in some studies the danger of biased judgements has been avoided by keeping the workers concerned in ignorance as to which were the delinquents and which the non-delinquents,[1] this is not always feasible. A similar device of keeping members of a research team in ignorance about the findings of other sections of the whole project was adopted by the Gluecks in *Unraveling*.[2] Thirdly, control group studies as such are bound to be static, i.e. related to only one single moment in the lives of individuals without taking into consideration their development over a period of time. The research material itself may also become biased through the availability or otherwise of control cases. Where criminals are compared with their non-criminal brothers, it is not unlikely that those brothers who are ready to submit to interviews and tests are, for this very reason, particularly steady authoritarians and therefore in no way representative of the other non-criminal sibs.[3] Lastly, control group studies, by comparing the differential frequencies of various factors in the two groups, split the human personality into a large number of segments and may easily lose sight of the individual as a unit. Moreover, finding ourselves faced with a multitude of differences relating to various factors we do not know which of these differences refer to the same and which to different individuals. To some extent, however, these last-mentioned weaknesses can be overcome by skilful matching and holding constant of variables, leading to statistical intercorrelation of various factors and eventually to the working out of a typology. No special justification is needed for the requirement of matching the two groups by holding certain variables constant, as without it comparisons would be largely meaningless. There is no point in

[1] See, e.g., Sheldon and Eleanor Glueck, *Unraveling Juvenile Delinquency* (New York, The Commonwealth Fund, 1950), p. 363: 'blind' Rorschach analysis by Ernest G. and Anna H. Schachtel.
[2] *Unraveling Juvenile Delinquency*, pp. 17 and 25.
[3] This danger has been recognized by Gillin, p. 20.

METHODOLOGICAL PROBLEMS

comparing two entities which have nothing whatsoever in common. The greater the number of variables which are held constant the more do we move in the direction of typological research and, finally, towards the individual case study. The choice of the variables to be held constant depends on the special interests of the research worker and the objects of his research, but it can safely be said that certain basic factors such as age and, usually, sex will be among them. In *Unraveling Juvenile Delinquency* the Gluecks, for reasons which they were careful to explain in detail,[1] matched their groups for four factors: age, general intelligence, national (ethnico-racial) origin, residence in under-privileged neighbourhoods. Factors thus controlled are of course for all practical purposes thereby 'taken out of the picture', i.e. eliminated from the research. Nevertheless, they may remain of considerable significance not only by providing a typological basis, but also by colouring some of the seemingly uncontrolled factors. This is one of the weaknesses of the technique of holding certain factors constant which is sometimes overlooked. The fact that all the cases come from the same sort of neighbourhood can, for example, easily affect the family structure and atmosphere and similar factors which may be the very object of the investigation. In some recent research projects the technique of selecting the control group has been refined by a process of matching by sub-categories or by individual matching. The latter, which was used in *Unraveling Juvenile Delinquency*, leads to a 'terrible decimation' (Greenwood) of the available material.[2] Matching by sub-categories showing certain 'starred variables' has therefore sometimes been employed as a compromise, e.g. in the Cambridge-Somerville study.[3]

In control group studies as anywhere else we should be aware of the dangers of spurious correlations which may arise from faulty control group techniques. In an American investigation on the relationship between church membership and crime, referred to by M. J. Moroney,[4] a negative correlation was found between the

[1] *Unraveling Juvenile Delinquency*, p. 14.
[2] Ernest Greenwood, *Experimental Sociology*, p. 119.
[3] Edwin Powers and Helen Witmer, *An Experiment in the Prevention of Delinquency* (New York, Columbia University Press, 1951), Chapter VI (see also below, Section IIIb). Greenwood, p. 119.
[4] M. J. Moroney, *Facts from Figures* (Pelican Books No. A236, Harmondsworth, Middlesex, 1951), pp. 303-4.

number of offences per thousand of population and the percentage of church members among persons aged thirteen years and over, which seemed to indicate that church membership was a crime preventing factor. However, when the factors 'foreign immigrant' and 'large families' were eliminated from the enquiry, 'in the rest of the population church-going and crime seem to be positively associated'. (Is this good or bad?, asks Moroney, and he thinks it is good since 'a church that can only attract the respectable is failing to get at the people most in need of assistance'. This, however, only by the way as it has nothing to do with methodology.) Another illustration, taken from the field of recent prediction research:[1] A slightly higher rate of failure after discharge from Borstal has been found among lads who had been on probation before being committed to Borstal than among a control group of ex-Borstal lads who had not been on probation before. This might easily have been interpreted as indicating that a period on probation had had an unfavourable effect on these lads. The correct interpretation, however, may be this: First, boys who embark on their criminal careers at an early age are more likely to be placed on probation for their first offences than boys who commit their first offences somewhat later in adolescence.[2] Secondly, it is now the prevailing view among criminologists that those who are early starters in delinquency are more likely to develop criminal habits than those who start later.[3] The true (negative) correlation is therefore probably one between age at first crime and failure, not between probation and failure; and if the age factor is eliminated by being held constant for both groups, the one with and the one without previous probation, the differential failure rate may disappear.

With this last illustration we have already entered the field of research into the effect of methods of treatment. Here, adequate control group techniques are as indispensable as they are in our

[1] See H. Mannheim and Leslie T. Wilkins, *Prediction Methods in Relation to Borstal Training* (Vol. I of Home Office Studies in the Causes of Delinquency and the Treatment of Offenders, London, published for the Home Office by H.M.S.O., 1955), pp. 75-6.

[2] Although no direct evidence for this statement is provided by official Criminal Statistics, some conclusions might be drawn from the fact that the proportion of persons under seventeen placed on probation by the Magistrates is considerably higher than that of persons over seventeen. See, e.g., Criminal Stat. England and Wales for 1953, pp. XIX et seq.

[3] See below, pp. 139 and 159.

METHODOLOGICAL PROBLEMS

search for the 'causes' of crime or certain characteristics of criminals. The effect of specific forms of penal treatment can be established statistically, if at all, only by comparing a group of offenders who have undergone treatment of a certain kind with a matched group of those not so treated. In earlier investigations of this kind the obvious need for proper matching has often been ignored or only inadequately met. To give a few illustrations: In a 'Special Analysis of Records in the Criminal Record Office of New Scotland Yard for the Period 1932–37',[1] the records of 17,918 males and 2,749 females were examined who had been found guilty of 'substantial' offences for the first time in 1932. The object was to see how many of them had been found guilty again during the subsequent five years' period after undergoing one or the other of the principal methods of treatment. Age and sex were held constant, and as they had all been first offenders they were also matched according to their official criminal histories. The result was that those placed on probation showed a much higher failure rate than those imprisoned or fined, a result at the first glance greatly disappointing to all supporters of the idea of probation. However, as no distinction had been made according to type of offence, as probation and mere binding over without probation had been lumped together, and as the length of the prison sentence had not been taken into consideration (an offender might well have been in prison for the whole of the five years' period), the results could in fact not be regarded as conclusive.[2] In the Report of the Departmental Committee on Corporal Punishment of 1938 an attempt was made to ascertain the effect of this penalty on the subsequent criminal conduct of men flogged for robbery with violence. Realizing that subsequent conduct was likely to be correlated to previous criminal record it was arranged to compare two groups of men, one of them flogged and the other not, with similar criminal records. It was found that 'the higher proportion of success among those not flogged was not accounted for altogether by the fact that these included a larger proportion of persons with no previous convictions'.[3] Only among the group with the worst criminal records those flogged showed a slightly

[1] *Criminal Statistics for England and Wales for the year 1938* (H.M.S.O., Cmd. 6167, 1940), pp. XX et seq., in particular XXIII–XXVIII.
[2] See *The Howard Journal*, Vol. V, No. 4, p. 251.
[3] 'Report of the Departmental Committee on Corporal Punishment', Home Office (H.M.S.O., Cmd. 5684, 1938), App. III, pp. 133–4.

better subsequent record than those not flogged, but as the potential effect of the age factor had not been eliminated by keeping age constant here, too, the result was not altogether conclusive, in particular as no special attention had been paid to differences in mental stability which might well have been decisive in matters of the kind under investigation. Similar observations would seem to apply to the interesting Norwegian figures, published in the United Nations Report on Probation,[1] comparing the extent of recidivism in a group of male offenders who had been conditionally sentenced to imprisonment and in another group of first offenders who had actually served short periods of imprisonment. Although the extent of recidivism in the first group was found to be substantially lower than in the second, we are, rightly, warned not to attribute too much weight to this difference 'as offenders are selected as suitable for the award of conditional sentences on the basis of their favourable criminal prognosis and there is, therefore, no equality of initial criminal prognosis between the two groups in question'. In other words, the result would seem to prove, if anything, the efficiency of the selection made by the criminal courts rather than the greater efficiency of a conditional sentence in preventing recidivism. The question arises why penological investigations of this kind should always have to come to a premature end and remain inconclusive. In the prediction research on Borstal lads mentioned before where a similar difficulty arose, an attempt was made to carry the statistical work at least one stage further. In order to discover whether open Borstal institutions were more successful than closed ones, two groups of ex-Borstal lads were compared, one from open and the other from closed institutions, but both of them taken from the same statistical categories as established in the prediction tables. It was then found that lads belonging to the same 'risk' categories had a higher rate of success after treatment in open than after treatment in closed institutions.[2] In other words, the results of the prediction study were utilized for the purpose of checking the efficiency of different types of institutions. Only if the sentencing policy of the courts or the classification procedures of the administration should become so perfect that the same type of case would never be

[1] *Probation and Related Measures* (United Nations, Department of Social Affairs, 1951), p. 151.
[2] See the Report quoted in note 1, p. 124 above, on pp. 109-13, 211, 213.

METHODOLOGICAL PROBLEMS

differently treated—a degree of accuracy unattainable and perhaps not even desirable in real life—only then would such statistical operations become impossible as there would never be completely matched cases in different treatment groups.

In conclusion, a few words may be said on what I regard as one of the most important and fascinating aspects of the subject: the possibility of *experimental research* in Criminology. Obviously, there are many problems in our field which can be solved, if at all, only by experiment. How far is experimentation possible in Criminology? In a way, of course, one might be inclined to regard the whole administration of criminal justice and the whole penal system as nothing but one huge experiment, and in fact new penal methods, new prisons or reformatories are sometimes explicitly tried out as 'experimental'. However, this is not quite what the scientist would call an experiment since an experiment in the scientific sense requires rigid control and the holding constant of all variables except those forming the subject of the experiment—requirements which, as a rule, are beyond the possibilities of daily routine work. In addition to such technical difficulties there are, however, certain other, equally formidable, obstacles arising from the traditional conception of justice. As stated at the beginning of this lecture, in our methodological considerations in the field of Criminology we have throughout to be aware of certain limitations imposed upon our work by the philosophy of justice and of punishment on which the whole administration of criminal justice depends. Prediction research[1] makes sense only in a system of criminal justice which recognizes the importance of objectives other than retribution; only if we are interested in deterrence and reformation can we attach some weight to the possibility of predicting future behaviour. Corresponding considerations apply to the idea of experimental research. Experiment goes far beyond the simple application of control group techniques as used in our previous examples. Control group techniques take and compare their cases as they have, more or less by chance, already occurred and been subjected to certain forms of treatment. Experiments, however, mean exposing matched cases to different forms of treatment according to a planned and controlled scientific programme,

[1] The section of this lecture dealing with prediction research has been here omitted in view of the recent publication of the Borstal Prediction study referred to in note 1, p. 124, in which the whole subject is more fully treated.

and in doing so we are almost bound to clash with the idea of justice. Justice requires equal treatment of equal cases; experiment requires differential treatment of equal cases. Such differential treatment does already all too often occur by chance and mistake; but it must not happen on purpose unless we, and in particular the general public, are willing to make concessions for the sake of greater knowledge. Even in the field of medicine, which is not based upon the idea of justice, experiments are sometimes frowned upon, but on the whole it is recognized by the public that without them no progress is possible. If a criminal court, however, would in four equal cases—assuming that they are really equal—send offender A to prison, offender B to Borstal, place offender C on probation and fine offender D the public would revolt. The risk is smaller in the administrative field or in the work of private agencies not responsible to the public. The 'Cambridge-Somerville' experiment in the prevention of juvenile delinquency (see below, Section III*b*) could be carried out apparently without running into serious difficulties on this account.

Not only in experimental work but also in the application of research techniques in general clashes may occur between the needs of research, on the one hand, and legal and moral considerations, on the other. When it is a question of interviewing ex-prisoners or ex-Borstal boys or girls for purposes of a follow-up study, several years after their discharge, it has been strongly argued that such a 'raking up' of their past may be against the interests of the individuals concerned and therefore unethical. Studies of identical twins might considerably gain in scientific value if the twins could be separated from their families immediately after birth so as to make their environment as dissimilar as possible. But what about their rights as human beings and the rights of their parents to remain together as a united family? These are awkward questions which have to be faced by the research worker. Here as everywhere, ends and means have to be carefully balanced.

II. WHY DELINQUENCY? THE LIMITS OF PRESENT KNOWLEDGE

[On the 1st October, 1949, a Conference was held in London on 'The Scientific Study of Juvenile Delinquency', convened by the

METHODOLOGICAL PROBLEMS

following organizations: The British Sociological Society, The Howard League for Penal Reform, The Institute for the Scientific Treatment of Delinquency, The Institute of Sociology, The National Association for Mental Health, and the Royal Medico-Psychological Association. The subject of the Morning Session, as part of which the following paper was read, was 'The Limits of Present Knowledge', and the Proceedings were subsequently published by the National Association for Mental Health, London, under the title: *Why Delinquency? The Case for Operational Research*.]

I am neither a psychologist nor a psychiatrist or a statistician. I might perhaps describe myself as a cross between a lawyer and a crimino-sociologist (or sociological criminologist, if this should sound any better), and it is, of course, from this angle that you wish me to treat my subject.

I will divide my paper into two main sections: first, a brief survey of research done in recent years, and, secondly, some general reflections with special emphasis on the difficulties facing research in our field. You wish me to deal with the past and present rather than with the future which is reserved for the afternoon, but I am confident you will bear with me if I should occasionally say, 'this or that has not yet been done', implying that it should be done in the future. Again, although I take it that our discussions should be confined to this country, I trust that, in exceptional cases, a brief reference to work done abroad will be forgiven. And, if you allow me a last introductory remark, although we are to-day concerned with juvenile delinquency, I do not think we can exclude the adult altogether from our deliberations. Quite rightly, it has been said that in order to understand the adult criminal we must go back to his earliest childhood. But, on the other hand, is it not equally true that in order to understand the child we have to study the adult, especially the parent?

Very wisely, the organizers of this Conference have chosen as the title for our morning session, 'The Limits of Present Knowledge', and I am afraid when looking round to describe our knowledge and its limitations I shall probably find more limits than knowledge.

To the Americans, the modern scientific study of the delinquent begins with the publication of William Healy's book *The Individual Delinquent* in 1915. In this country, the corresponding date is 1925 when Cyril Burt's *The Young Delinquent* first appeared. Although its author is a psychologist, it is a landmark also with regard to the sociological side of criminological research, and I should like to stress already at this stage that, in my view, it has to be regarded as one of the greatest misfortunes that have befallen the scientific study of juvenile delinquency in this country that Sir Cyril Burt has never again devoted to our subject the full force of his wisdom and experience. As a consequence, such work as has been done in recent years has had to be done by others who had at their command neither his resources nor his authority.

Time is too short to give a complete survey of the research done since the appearance of *The Young Delinquent*. Nor do I regard such a survey as necessary for the period up to the publication in 1942 of the report on *Young Offenders* prepared for the Home Office at the London School of Economics because one of its chapters tries to summarize the work done on the subject up to the war.[1] Some remarks are, however, needed on that investigation itself and the main criticisms to which it has been subjected, and being one of the three authors, I will do my best to be accurate and impartial. I need hardly say that I am speaking only for myself. In order briefly to characterize the place which that study occupies, its achievements (if any) and its limitations, I might perhaps say this: We had the advantage of obtaining a case material sufficiently large to work out statistically significant correlations and an equally comprehensive control group material; moreover, our cases were drawn not only from London but also from six provincial cities believed to be in some respects representative. On the other hand, we had to be content with Court cases of boys only and with purely statistical enquiries without any broader sociological observations, nor was our work, as had originally been planned, supplemented by any psychological study. Where we tried to obtain information on certain subtler psychological issues, such as for example, 'leisure interests', 'ambitions or desire for change', we had some doubts (which are expressed in our report) whether our questions might not have been misinterpreted by some of the investigators. We had also to consider at least the possibility that some of the findings of our investigators might have been influenced by an unconscious bias in favour of control cases to the disadvantage of delinquent cases. Moreover, the

[1] A. M. Carr-Saunders, Hermann Mannheim and E. C. Rhodes, *Young Offenders* (Cambridge University Press, 1942).

METHODOLOGICAL PROBLEMS

manner in which the control group was selected (each delinquent boy was matched to a non-delinquent boy of the same age who, picked out by the head teacher of the school, could reasonably be regarded as his 'mate') excluded comparisons of certain factors connected with the neighbourhood and therefore common to nearly all boys of a particular school. The selection of the control group has also been criticized on the ground that, instead of leaving it to the discretion of the head teacher, it should have been done by some automatic device. The technique of holding certain factors constant was used in order to facilitate a progressive interpretation of the data obtained and to eliminate obviously irrelevant factors. It is true that, as has been stressed by prominent critics, the use of that technique was confined to one category of cases, the boys coming from normal, not 'broken', homes, but it is difficult to see why, as has been alleged, it would have been more illuminating to apply the same technique to the other category, the boys from broken homes.

Now, the last seven years period since the publication of *Young Offenders* is characterized mainly by the appearance, on the one hand of Dr. Bowlby's remarkable study which, except for the methodological points it raises is outside the scope of my present paper and, on the other hand, of a number of small-scale local surveys, distinguished neither by the techniques employed nor by the results obtained, all of them failing to give a really comprehensive sociological picture of the locality concerned, but nevertheless most of them useful beginnings in the direction towards a more scientific ecological study of the criminological situation, existing in different parts of the whole country. In my little book *Juvenile Delinquency in an English Middletown*, which may be regarded as just another of these small-scale local studies, a brief survey is given of its precursors in this field to which I may be permitted to refer.[1]

Special mention should be made, however, of a so far unpublished local survey carried out by a former postgraduate student and member of the teaching staff of the London School of Economics, Dr. May Ravden. Although concerned more with the sociological problems of the family as a whole than with the specific one of juvenile delinquency, Dr. Ravden's work, based

---

[1] Hermann Mannheim, *Juvenile Delinquency in an English Middletown* (Intern. Library of Sociology and Social Reconstruction, London, Routledge & Kegan Paul, 1948), pp. 4 et seq., where further references are given.

CRIMINOLOGY AND ITS METHODS

largely on home visits to a hundred Cambridge and a hundred Portsmouth families, forms an important contribution to the study of our problem because of its technique and its material.

Although mainly concerned with adolescent boys, the comprehensive enquiry into the personal characteristics—physical, psychological and sociological—of 4,000 Borstal lads from London and the surrounding counties, carried out by the Home Office under the direction of Sir Norwood East before the war, is also of considerable interest to us. Its object was, in addition to more practical ones such as better classification, the theoretical one 'to apply modern scientific methods to the elucidation of some of the causal factors which contribute to adolescent criminality'. No control group was employed, but by dividing the 4,000 cases in various ways many valuable internal comparisons became possible.[1]

In spite of its small size, an analysis made under the direction of Professor Pear (University of Manchester) by Dr. Gertrude Wagner of the attitude towards property of fifty boys aged fifteen to seventeen represents an interesting beginning which should have stimulated further research. A questionnaire was drawn up, containing questions related to various social situations, most of them closely connected with delinquency, and the boys were asked to state their views with regard to certain lines of action. The answers are very revealing and the technique should be applied, perhaps in a more discriminating way, to larger samples.[2]

Finally, such largely impressionistic studies as Marie Paneth's[3] *Branch Street* and David Wills' *Hawkspur Experiment* and *Barns Experiment*,[4] though not intended to be scientific, are much too interesting and important for the understanding of our subject to be ignored. On the treatment side, Miss Elkin's painstaking book on *English Juvenile Courts*[5] and Mr. Bagot's *Punitive Detention*,[6] Mr. Alec Rodger's well known *A Borstal Experiment in Vocational Guidance*,[7] Dr. Alexander Leitch's illuminating *Survey of Reformative*

[1] Norwood East, Percy Stocks and H. T. P. Young, *The Adolescent Criminal* (London, J. A. Churchill Ltd., 1942).
[2] *Social Welfare* (published by the Manchester and Salford Council of Social Service, July, 1941).
[3] London, George Allen & Unwin, Ltd., 1947.
[4] London, George Allen & Unwin Ltd., 1941 and 1945.
[5] Winifred A. Elkin, *English Juvenile Courts* (London, George Allen & Unwin Ltd., 1938).
[6] J. H. Bagot, 'Punitive Detention' (*English Studies in Criminal Science*, London, Cape, 1942). [7] British Medical Research Council, Report No. 78 (1937).

METHODOLOGICAL PROBLEMS

Influences in Borstal Training[1] and Mr. John Vardy's *Their Side of the Story*[2] should be mentioned. No competent follow-up studies have ever been made in this country which, needless to say, constitutes a particularly serious gap.[3] However, even on many points on which it would be much easier to obtain some factual information we are ignorant, for instance, on the extent to which certain conditions of probation are imposed by different courts.

It was one of my objects in giving you this very sketchy and by no means exhaustive survey to show that some research has in fact been done in this country since the publication of Cyril Burt's masterpiece. May I now turn to the second, equally important point and ask: What do we actually know about juvenile delinquency and its treatment as the result of these researches? As I said at the beginning, I see more limits than knowledge. There is, however, an attitude of mind which I find fairly often among students and others and which is usually expressed like this: We know already everything that is to be known about the causes of juvenile delinquency; let us waste no time and get on with the treatment! On the other hand, there are some distinguished American criminologists, such as Walter Reckless, Michael and Adler, and others, who maintain not only that we know next to nothing about those causes but also that we shall never know unless much more progress is made by psychology and sociology. I confess I am not particularly in favour of such a distinction between 'we', i.e., the criminologists, and 'they', i.e., the psychologists and sociologists. It reminds me too much of the old notorious 'they' which the man in the street uses when he means the Government. We criminologists, instead of sitting back and expecting 'them' to solve all our problems, might well take a more active part ourselves.

Now, the explanation of the difference of opinion is simple. As the result of the researches referred to before and, even more, of the much larger stream of semi-scientific or plainly unscientific publications that have appeared in the course of this century, the almost general impression has been created that everything is known in this field. Actually most of our 'knowledge' consists of

[1] Alexander Leitch, *The British Journal of Medical Psychology*, Vol. XX, Part I, 1944, pp. 77 et seq.
[2] John Vardy, *Their Side of the Story* (Guardian Press, Newton-le-Willows, 1942).
[3] This gap has now to some extent been filled.

CRIMINOLOGY AND ITS METHODS

half-baked truths and slogans, of unwarranted generalizations derived from a small body of observations and inadequate samples. Broken homes, neglectful parents, lack of playing fields and clubs, lack of discipline and religious instruction, and a few dozen other similarly effective headlines take the place of scientific knowledge, just as in the United States, in its pre-scientific age, the Negro or the foreign immigrant were made convenient scapegoats for the high American crime rate.

Without attempting to give a complete list of existing misconceptions, I might perhaps mention the following as the most frequent sources of error, apart from the only too well-known fact that the whole atmosphere is too highly charged with emotion.

First, there is the apparently ineradicable habit of confusing statistical correlations with causal explanations. If we find, as some American scholars, I believe, have found, that more children are born in districts where there are more storks, we are not likely to conclude, without further research, that the storks bring the children! If however we find, for example, more crime among unmarried than among married men we are inclined to conclude at once that marriage is a crime preventing factor for men. This confusion lies at the root of most of the erroneous ideas about the use of statistical methods in the social sciences. Statistical figures in themselves can provide no causal explanation, nor do they pretend to do so. Statistical figures and correlations are nothing but signposts; they show the direction where the problems and solutions may be found. Or, as MacIver says in his book on *Social Causation*: 'A correlation is a clue or a question mark.' 'Where there is causation there is also correlation, but where there is correlation there may be no corresponding causation. Many things are happening and many things are changing at the same time . . .'[1] Therefore, when we establish a fairly high correlation between juvenile delinquency and, say, broken homes we have proved nothing; we have found nothing but a clue, a signpost, and signposts *may* occasionally be misleading (I am not saying, of course, that this particular one is actually misleading!). Nevertheless, all those many positive or negative correlations between delinquency and other factors possess a considerable value for future research; they may, for example, help us to eliminate certain wrong conceptions and by that constant process of pro-

[1] *Social Causation* (Boston, Ginn, 1942).

METHODOLOGICAL PROBLEMS

gressive delimitation, so well described by MacIver, eventually come nearer and nearer to conclusions of a causal nature. Whereas the popular and optimistic view to which I referred before ignores the many pitfalls and limitations of statistical research, the pessimistic school in scientific Criminology underrates its potentialities.

The second weakness in our existing knowledge results from the use of unscientific conceptions, unscientific because much too broad and inadequately subdivided. Essentially different situations are lumped together without discrimination. One 'broken' home is often treated in our statistics exactly like another, regardless of the fact that the break may have been due to death in the one and to desertion in the other case; regardless of the age of the child at the time when the break occurred. 'Gang' means 'gang' to many investigators, although it may be nothing but a chance encounter, a casual collaboration in the commission of one isolated offence. Club membership is club membership, whether it refers to the real thing or only to a poor surrogate. Only in a very few investigations do we find an awareness of the danger of such over-simplifications and in still fewer a serious attempt to work out more scientific tools of research. As a consequence, if we ask ourselves "what do we actually know about the significance of such factors as club membership or living on new housing estates, or the part played by school, religious upbringing, the financial position of the family and dozens of others?" the answer—if given in a detached and scientific rather than in an emotional and partisan spirit—has to be: in spite of some indisputable progress, very little, in any case not enough to base any sweeping conclusions on it.

Sometimes, in our ignorance we stumble from one extreme to the other, e.g. with regard to the effect of films on juveniles where the old theory of imitation has been replaced by the hardly more discriminating theory of the 'healthy outlet'.

It is only one particularly striking feature of that tendency to use over-simplified, far too general and therefore unscientific terms that the fundamental difference between the occasional and the persistent offender has so frequently been ignored. It is generally believed that reformative efforts should mainly concentrate on the second category (the occasionals will usually be able to look after themselves). Nevertheless, in our research we often fail to pay sufficient attention to the essential points of contrast between these two categories, and as a consequence we may make statements of a general nature which may be true only for the one or for the other of them.

My third point of criticism refers to the well-known weakness of most of the investigations so far made—Cyril Burt's is an exception—that they are exclusively based on Court cases. Consequently—although Child Guidance Clinic material may fill some of the gaps—very little is known about delinquents who do not appear in Court and—with the exception of some of the care and protection and beyond control cases—about those non-delinquents who are in essential characteristics similar to delinquents. Clearly, this means an unscientific limitation of our material. We should include non-Court cases, but who shall decide whether they are actually delinquent if there is no finding of guilt by the Court? With regard to the second category, those who are not delinquents but have essential features in common with them, there is the difficulty of how to delimit this group. Thorsten Sellin, the distinguished American criminologist, suggests one should study not only the violators of legal norms but also those of certain non-legal 'conduct norms'. Dr. Bowlby has certain similar suggestions, and I agree in principle with him and with Sellin, but whatever we may suggest there will be differences of opinion as regards the exact definition of our concepts. In this country, in particular, the objections to such an extension of the scope of our researches are likely to be even stronger than in those countries where the line of demarcation between the juvenile who has committed an offence against the criminal law and the one who is for other reasons in need of social treatment is much less pronounced and where, in addition, a much higher proportion of juvenile delinquents is treated by non-judicial agencies. Consequently, I feel that even if we decide, as we should, to extend the scope of our enquiries beyond the delinquent Court case, we should nevertheless clearly distinguish between (*a*) Court cases of delinquents, (*b*) Court cases of non-delinquents, (*c*) non-Court cases of delinquents, (*d*) non-Court cases of non-delinquents who are social misfits.

Other gaps in our knowledge are due to the scarcity of local studies of a broad sociological and ecological character which would deal with the problem of juvenile delinquency in a more general setting, i.e. studies which would devote the same painstaking attention equally to all the many sociological aspects of the district and treat delinquency, as it should be treated, only as one

METHODOLOGICAL PROBLEMS

of them. Moreover, existing local investigations do not usually follow the same pattern, and their findings are therefore in most cases not comparable.

On the border between sociological and psychological methods in the study of crime lies the technique of the life history or the individual case story in general. It provides an important and interesting supplement to statistical and sociological-ecological investigations. Such individual case studies may be very different in character, and they may be autobiographies produced by the criminal himself or scientific or popular documents written by a third person. Whereas some countries possess a substantial literature of this kind, we have in this country only a limited number of autobiographies, and only a few of them dealing adequately with the childhood and adolescent age of the criminal. Mark Benney's *Low Company* is one of the exceptions. Moreover, there are hardly any scientific individual case studies written by impartial observers. One of the reasons may be the overstrict English law of libel, or perhaps even more the fear of an expensive libel action, which makes criminologists and their publishers as well as the authorities who are in charge of most of these documents hesitate to publish any description of an individual case detailed enough to be of scientific interest.

The scope of the controlled experiment in criminological research is obviously limited. Experiment usually means risk. While we are willing to risk even human lives for medical experiment, we are unwilling to do so in the field of social research. In a way, of course, any kind of consciously applied treatment is an experiment, and to some extent we are able to keep certain environmental factors under control during treatment, although this will naturally be more difficult for non-institutional than for institutional methods. Alec Rodger's work at Feltham is an excellent example of the use of the experimental technique in a limited field. We need more of it. Only recently, it has been stressed by Sir Cyril Burt in his remarkable paper in the *British Journal of Educational Psychology* that 'it would be perfectly practicable to take paired groups and subject them to planned experiments in alternative lines of treatment and training'.[1]

Reference may also be made to an experiment in the prevention

---

[1] Cyril Burt, *The British Journal of Educational Psychology*, Vol. XIX, Part I, February, 1949, pp. 32 et seq.

of delinquency which has recently been carried out over a period of eight years at Cambridge and Somerville, both in Massachusetts, with the object of finding out whether a group of boys, many of them regarded as pre-delinquents, assigned to a number of professional social workers, would do better than a carefully matched control group with the same proportion of pre-delinquents left to their own and the usual community resources. Although the results do not seem to be conclusive (in any case the control group boys did not show a substantially higher percentage of failures than the boys placed under supervision), the experiment is of value in showing the way in which the experimental method could be used.[1]

One of the real tragedies in the field of criminological research is the prevailing lack of co-operation and understanding between psychologists, psychiatrists, sociologists, statisticians and lawyers. Many examples could be quoted to substantiate this statement, but it will hardly be disputed. It is often mere ignorance of what others are doing or might be capable of contributing that creates the subjective feeling of one's own superiority and prevents real team work.

Having briefly sketched the many gaps in our knowledge and at least some of the factors responsible for them, I should like to put one question: has the research so far done been of any practical use to anybody? Has it been of any help to the legislator and administrator, and to the practical worker in the field, whether he be a magistrate, a probation officer or a worker in an institution? Has it given them a better understanding of the problems and how to deal with them or has it simply been so much waste of effort and of paper? Sixteen years ago, Sir Alexander Paterson wrote a paper under the title: *Should the Criminologist be encouraged?*[2] He was not too sure, apparently, what the answer to his question should be. The greatest encouragement the criminologist could wish for would be a favourable answer to the question I have put to you.

[1] See Section IIIb of this Chapter.
[2] Alexander Paterson, *Transactions of the Medico-Legal Society*, Vol. XVIX (1933).

METHODOLOGICAL PROBLEMS

III. THE STUDY OF THE YOUNG OFFENDER
Three Reviews

(a) A Critical Notice of DER FRÜHKRIMINELLE RÜCKFALLSVERBRECHER. CRIMINALITÉ PRÉCOCE ET RÉCIDIVISME, by Erwin Frey.[1]

Dr. Frey, for many years public prosecutor in the adult criminal court and juvenile court of the city of Basle and now professor of criminal law and criminology in the University of Zurich, has produced a study which might in some ways be regarded as the Continental European counterpart to the Glueck studies.

It is Dr. Frey's basic contention that there exists the closest inter-relation between juvenile delinquency and adult criminality and that the Swiss Penal Code and peno-correctional system, as those of many other countries, fail to recognize this fact and to draw the appropriate conclusions. There are, he argues, two categories of juvenile delinquents, the one, comprising at least 85 per cent of the total, where the delinquent phase is mainly due to environmental causes and reaches its natural end at the age of eighteen at the latest, and the remaining 15 per cent where delinquency is a symptom of a deep-rooted criminogenic disposition, leading, unless efficiently handled, to persistent and serious adult criminality. Given proper treatment, approximately three-quarters of the latter are likely to reform, whereas the other quarter, i.e., roughly 3 to 4 per cent of the total of juvenile delinquents, have to be written off as incorrigible. The earlier a juvenile embarks on criminal activities the more likely is he to become a persistent offender. Early delinquency as such, however, is not an infallible criterion unless accompanied by early '*Verwahrlosung*'. Moreover, no endogenous or environmental factors can by themselves produce persistent criminality; only a combination of the two categories can do so. Nevertheless the whole emphasis of the book is on the hereditary and constitutional side. It is in particular certain forms of psychopathy, and especially certain combinations of several forms, that lead to persistent criminality, whereas neither psychosis nor mental deficiency nor environmental factors are of any practical significance in this respect. Nature and nurture form a

[1] Basel, *Verlag für Recht und Gesellschaft* (Schweizerische Criminalistische Studien), Vol. 4, 1951.—This Critical Notice was first published in *The British Journal of Delinquency*, Vol. III No. 2, October 1952.

CRIMINOLOGY AND ITS METHODS

unit in that the milieu is determined by heredity and constitutional make-up. The individual does not simply drift into a certain milieu by accident; he chooses it in accordance with his personality type. Given adequate scientific examination, individuals thus tainted with psychopathic traits of a highly criminogenic nature can as a rule be recognized at the school-leaving age at the latest. This leads to one of the main topics of the study: the possibility of predicting recidivism.

The techniques employed by the author are statistical mass investigation, the more intensive observation of selected groups ('*Reihen-Untersuchung*'), and individual case studies. In his introductory statistical part he points out that on account of certain weaknesses of the Swiss Federal Criminal Statistics the material for his investigation had to be specially collected from cases dealt with by the authorities of the city of Basle. This material consists of eight groups, differing in size, age and criminality of population (see the list on p. 8). The first of the groups consists of 467 males (the whole study is limited to males), all of them '*verwahrlost*', who had been cared for by the authorities some time during the period 1912 to 1938 when they were between fourteen and eighteen years of age. Three hundred and three of them had been dealt with for delinquent behaviour, the others only as '*verwahrlost*', and it was found that, whereas the rate of persistent recidivism for the delinquent group was 26·7 per cent, that of subsequent criminal conduct of those without a history of early delinquency was only 3·7 per cent. It was also found that those early delinquents who had been sent to institutions had a higher rate of relapse (65·8 per cent) than those who had been boarded out or left with their own families (46·2 per cent). From this, the conclusion is drawn that the fact and the seriousness of early delinquency are highly predictive of subsequent recidivism. Similar results were obtained for a control group of 399 juveniles residing in various Swiss institutions between 1934 and 1936. The author has devised an interesting technique of measuring the intensity of recidivist activites after the individual's coming of age in terms of frequency, seriousness, and rhythm or tempo of reconvictions after discharge (pp. 77 et seq.) and also by means of a 'quotient of criminal intensity' (p. 263). However measured, those with a history of early delinquency (the '*frühkriminellen*') show a considerably higher intensity than the others. Already on the strength

METHODOLOGICAL PROBLEMS

of these statistical differences the author forms the view that there is no link between the two categories, the *'frühkriminellen'* being constitutionally different from the rest. The commonly held view that an occasional offender may, through adverse environmental circumstances, drift into habitual crime is, in his opinion, entirely unrealistic (p. 86). There is here a certain similarity between Dr. Frey's thesis and that, for example, expounded in the late Dr. Kate Friedlander's *The Psychoanalytical Approach to Juvenile Delinquency*, with the difference, however, that a psychological conception, the 'anti-social character formation' acquired in early childhood, occupies in Dr. Friedlander's system the place held by constitutional-biological factors in Dr. Frey's book. It may be noted already at this stage that Dr. Frey's own figures do not seem fully to support the theory to which he give so uncompromising expression. In a not inconsiderable number of his cases there is a fairly high intensity of recidivism even among those who are not *'frühkriminelle'* (see e.g., Tables 18, 19, 24), which would indicate quantitative rather than qualitative differences between the two categories (implicitly admitted by the author on p. 73, note 13). There is, moreover, no explicit definition of *'Verwahrlosung'* in Swiss law (p. 63, note 10), and it is left to the judge to make the best of this difficult term when applying Article 91 of the Penal Code. Without further enquiries the possibility cannot be excluded, therefore, that the degree of *'Verwahrlosung'* may have been more serious in the case of the *'frühkriminellen'*, and it can hardly be argued that the two categories had come from exactly the same kind of milieu.

The second part of the book is devoted to the more intensive study of smaller and more recent groups. There is in particular a group of 160 boys between fourteen and eighteen committed to reformatories in the years 1939 to 1948, for whom ample psychiatric reports and crimino-biological data were available. Cases where the information was regarded as incomplete were excluded. In the author's view it was a particular advantage that, with a few exceptions, he had personally conducted the preliminary investigations and kept in touch with these cases for long periods in his official capacity, and he is critical of studies where this personal link was absent. In his words, in each of these cases the possibility of future persistent criminality was considered right from the beginning, *'ab ovo'* (p. 96). This introduces two delicate

CRIMINOLOGY AND ITS METHODS

issues of methodology: the question of the potentially unrepresentative character of the sample and that of unconscious personal bias. Incompleteness of the available information is frequently due, and might possibly have been due in this case, to the fact that on the point in question there was nothing to report of special interest to the investigator concerned, which in the present connection might mean that no evidence of constitutional-biological abnormality could be found. Again, very close personal and official contacts between the investigator and his case material might unconsciously affect the objectivity of his observations and interpretations. This is a dilemma that has to be faced by many research workers in our field and elsewhere, and it explains why in recent American researches, such as the Cambridge-Somerville study, the final evaluation of the material was entrusted to experts not connected with its original collection. Obviously, such a device may mean heavy additional expenditure, and Dr. Frey cannot be blamed for not using it. All the more, however, should he and his readers be on their guard when interpreting and evaluating his material. There is no doubt, on the other hand, that Dr. Frey's official position gave him many invaluable facilities not open to outsiders.

This group of 160 cases was divided into two sub-groups: those who by the end of 1948 were at least twenty-three years of age and had already been discharged from the institution for at least four years (75 cases) and those who did not fulfil these two conditions (85 cases). For the second group, no final prognosis ('*Endprognose*' = EP) was regarded as possible, and only the preliminary prognosis made in the course of the proceedings ('*Vorprognose*' = VP) was used. The first group, however, was followed up to the end of 1949 when the average period after discharge was six and a half years and the average age almost twenty-six years. As control groups were used 83 non-criminal youths who had been sent to institutions in the same period on account of '*Verwahrlosung*' and also an unselected group of 70 serious recidivists. Further analysis of the material showed that of the 85 VP cases, 53, and of the 75 EP cases 39 were psychopaths, and that 27 of the 39 had become habitual and 10 occasional recidivists, whereas none of the 12 non-psychopaths had become habitual and only 5 occasional recidivists. From this the author concludes that whereas psychopathic offenders do not invariably become recidi-

METHODOLOGICAL PROBLEMS

vists, on the other hand, all habitual criminals are psychopaths (p. 113), and that not psychopathy as such but only certain forms of it are highly criminogenic. Here follows a detailed discussion of the meaning of psychopathy. While on the whole adopting Kurt Schneider's well-known typology, the author claims for the non-medical criminologist and criminal lawyer the right to have his own views on the subject. Eliminating some of Schneider's types and concentrating on those most strongly represented in his groups of psychopaths he points out that the cases exhibiting combinations of highly criminogenic forms of psychopathy had become recidivists of a more serious brand than the others. Dr. Frey admits that even his painstaking classification may still be too crude, and the reader may in fact occasionally get the, perhaps mistaken, impression that an individual is called 'normal' or a case of psychopathy classified as 'slight' mainly because of the absence of serious recidivism (see e.g., pp. 124 et seq., 225–231).

In his chapter on heredity the author criticizes, not without justification, the almost complete lack of scientific data on early childhood and hereditary factors in so many criminological investigations. For his own material of 160 cases he claims that the information at his disposal, though incomplete, was at least accurate and that it proves the very high positive correlation of bad heredity, especially of inherited psychopathy, and habitual recidivism. On the other hand, he utters a warning against undue pessimism which would ignore the dynamic elements of the human situation and the possibility of exceptions to the rule. It is of course hardly possible to criticize these sections of the book, entirely dependent as they are on the quality and interpretation of the case material. Compared with the treatment of psychopathy and hereditary factors, the chapters on environment, in spite of some good observations, seem to betray a certain lack of interest in the sociological aspects of the problem and a tendency to minimize the importance of unfavourable environmental factors or to deny their significance altogether.

In the third part of the book the author deals more specifically with the problem of early prognosis. He confirms the observation of other investigators that the common sense prognoses made by heads or staffs of institutions are correct usually in not more than 50 per cent and stresses the possibility of more reliable scientific techniques. In his brief review of the more important American and German prediction studies he stresses, perhaps somewhat too strongly, their disappointing results which he thinks, are due, to the inadequacy of their data on early childhood and also to what he regards as faulty techniques, i.e. the use of a number of isolated, in no way inter-related factors instead of a closely knit and logically coherent system. On account of the work of the former crimino-biological research centres he regards the German prediction studies, initiated by Exner, as superior to the American ones, though as inferior to his own material. In an elaborate footnote, added after the completion of the study, attention is drawn to a number of similarities between the main results of *Unraveling Juvenile Delinquency* and the author's findings. He criticizes, however, the quality of the biological and psychiatric data of the Glueck study, and the, in his view, unnecessary use of complicated statistical techniques; the device of keeping the psychiatrist in ignorance of the data collected by the other members of the team; and the attempt, which he regards as utopian, to predict on the strength of a bare six-factor scheme delinquent behaviour of so far non-delinquent children. Dr. Frey's own predictive technique is basically a combination of an assessment of the personality as a whole (*'Ganzheitsbewertung'*) and of the usual point system, with the requirement that there has to be a logical and criminological connection between each of the factors used. Two different forms of prediction are attempted: the one, of a preliminary nature (*'Vorprognose'*), as a rule worked out during the preliminary proceedings for offenders between sixteen and eighteen years of age (earlier prognoses are in Dr. Frey's view impracticable); and the second (*'Nachprognose'*), based mainly upon conduct and development during institutional life and while on licence, made not before the age of twenty-four has been reached and at least three years have elapsed since discharge. The author's prognostic table (pp. 326–8 and 341 et seq.) is in fact a systematic extract of the main contents of the records combined with a mathematical assessment according to good and bad points. The factors, or rather groups of factors, employed in this table are of a more general and less precise character than those used in most other schemes (e.g., 'type of personality', 'home milieu'), and the significance of each factor is assessed by the author in accordance with his views on its general criminogenic value, e.g., the factor 'leisure milieu' has a value (*'Basispunktwert'*) of only 5, early criminality, however, one of 35. The intensity which each factor shows in an individual case is also measured by coefficients ranging from 1 to 5 (a highly criminogenic form of psychopathy, for example, receives the coefficient 4·5, whereas in a simple case of mental deficiency the coefficient for the factor 'personality type' might be only 1 or 2). When the individual cases had been scored it was found that for the 75 cases referred to above the prognosis was correct in 84 per cent, which is certainly an impressive result. As a control, intuitive prognoses for the same group without reliance on his scheme of points were made by the author which were correct in only 74·6 per cent and showed more serious errors than those made under the points system. On the other hand, the author admits the presence of strong intuitive elements in his application of the point system (p. 335), and to the present reviewer the point prognosis as operated by Dr. Frey appears in fact only a somewhat less arbitrary and more systematic form of intuition. If a second research worker would have made an independent assessment of the same group of cases, a comparison of the results might have been of considerable interest as a test of the objectivity and 'repeatability' of the author's prognoses.

In an Appendix a number of detailed case histories is given which have been selected as typical and showing the characteristic traits of the recidivist. These histories are valuable and interesting, but in spite of the full material at the author's disposal he has occasionally to rely on what seems to be mere hearsay (e.g. p. 354: 'auch in der übrigen väterlichen Verwandtschaft soll es zahlreiche Sonderlinge und auffällige Charaktere geben'); and sometimes it is difficult to accept his evaluation of a case, e.g. when on p. 364 the conditions of upbringing are called 'very favourable' and the next following sentence reveals that the offender had hardly known his seriously psychopathic mother and that his father had remained entirely unknown to him.

To sum up: This is an important work which will take its place among the foremost publications of post-war Continental criminological literature. The author's determination and enthusiasm, his skill and ingenuity in handling a large body of facts, deserve the fullest admiration, and his material and techniques are likely to provide ample food for discussion in years to come. To the present reviewer, some of his conclusions would have been more convincing if the author had been more aware of his own bias and of the subjective nature of some of his interpretations.

(b) A Critical Notice of AN EXPERIMENT IN THE PREVENTION OF DELINQUENCY. THE CAMBRIDGE-SOMERVILLE YOUTH STUDY, by Edwin Powers and Helen Witmer with a Foreword by Gordon W. Allport.[1]

This is the second piece of large-scale criminological research published in the U.S.A. within the past few years. In the boldness of its design, in its liberal expenditure of money, time, and manpower it is the worthy counterpart of the Glueck study, *Unraveling Juvenile Delinquency*. Moreover, both investigations were carried out in Massachusetts and both are concerned with the causes, the prevention and prediction of juvenile delinquency; both make use of the control group technique, and both throw much light on the various aspects of the problem which they set out to study. Here, however, the list of similarities ends, and the critical reader has to turn to an analysis of a number of fundamental differences in their respective methods of research and in some of their basic assumptions. While the Glueck study was static, i.e. taking and comparing its two groups of boys as they had developed at a certain stage in their careers, the object of the Cambridge-Somverville Study was to observe the effect on its human material of environmental changes produced by the study itself—it was dynamic, an experiment, it was a piece of 'social engineering'.

The book under review consists of two major parts of which the first, mainly descriptive, is written by Edwin Powers who was connected with the Study from 1937, first as one of the 'counsellors' and from 1941 to 1948 as Director of Research. The second, evaluative, part is the work of an outside expert, Dr. Helen Witmer, Professor of Social Work at the University of California. There is in addition a detailed and searching Foreword by Professor Gordon W. Allport, the distinguished psychologist of Harvard University. The initiator and, until his death in 1939, the guiding spirit of the whole enterprise, however, was Dr. Richard Clarke Cabot, Professor of Social Ethics and of Clinical Medicine at Harvard who—another link with the work of the Gluecks—

---

[1] New York, Columbia University Press, 1951.—This Critical Notice was first published in *The British Journal of Delinquency*, Vol. III, No. 3, January, 1952.

METHODOLOGICAL PROBLEMS

had given strong encouragement to their initial researches and written the Foreword to their *500 Criminal Careers*. The somewhat unusual combination of these two University chairs characterizes the man and his way of thinking. 'He kept always before the profession the need for severe tests by which to judge the value of social service', we are told in the Obituary Note written by three of his Harvard colleagues (Appendix A). He believed in the redeeming value of friendship, of 'moral suasion'. 'A boy, he thought, should be early supplied with an ideal', for 'What is it that keeps any of us straight unless it is the contagion of the highest personalities whom we have known?', and 'fearful lest his preachment seem hollow', he devised and financed in 1935 the experiment described in the present volume. Its fundamental object was, on the practical side, to prevent juvenile delinquency and, on the theoretical side, to discover whether this could be done by providing a group of boys regarded by competent observers as 'pre-delinquent' over a period of ten years with all the aid, material and spiritual, which a resourceful and sympathetic 'counsellor' and friend could give. It may be mentioned in passing that an experimental design of this kind, which means exposing one of two matched groups to a stimulus withheld from the other, is, as Ernest Greenwood has reminded us in his *Experimental Sociology*, nothing new in social science, and it is somewhat surprising that no reference to experimental studies outside the field of delinquency research and to the valuable literature on the subject appears in a volume of the size of the present book. To carry out his plan, Cabot created a charitable corporation, the Ella Lyman Cabot Foundation, which was to take charge of the project. A large staff of directors, counsellors, research workers, and others was appointed, and two groups of boys were selected from two medium-sized Massachusetts towns, Cambridge and Somerville, one as the Treatment Group (T) and the other as a matched Control Group (C). The selection, which was left to a special Selection Committee of three experts, proved to be a lengthy and difficult process: In the first place, as the Study was looking for potential delinquents not yet known as such to the authorities the term 'pre-delinquent' had to be unmistakably defined. Moreover, as the boys were to be referred to the Committee mainly by their school teachers who were unwilling to label them as 'pre-delinquent', a list of less stigmatizing behaviour difficulties

CRIMINOLOGY AND ITS METHODS

had to be substituted for that term. Also, whereas the original programme foresaw only the inclusion of pre-delinquents, it soon became evident that such a restriction would lead to unhappy public relations as the boys would be generally regarded as actual delinquents. It was therefore decided to include a certain proportion of 'normal' boys, i.e. boys unlikely to become delinquents. Of a total of nearly 2,000 cases referred to the Study, 782 were eventually chosen, mostly aged between six and twelve, but with a median age considerably higher than envisaged by Dr. Cabot, of whom 46 per cent were thought to be pre-delinquent and 43 per cent 'normal', whereas the remaining 11 per cent were rated as 'zero'. These 782 cases, i.e. their files, were turned over to two staff psychologists, the 'matchers', for distribution into two equal groups. As in *Unraveling Juvenile Delinquency*, to those interested in methodological matters the chapter on matching is of particular value (pp. 61 et seq.). The matching was done partly for individuals and partly for sets of fairly homogeneous boys (p. 77). As 650 boys had to be paired to obtain the two groups of 325 each, which were regarded as suitable numbers, the reservoir of cases from which potential matches could be drawn was too small for any substantial arsenal of variables to be used, and a combination of subjective and statistical methods was worked out, with particular emphasis on six basic variables and certain typical inter-relationships existing between them. In spite of the undoubted ingenuity of this technique a certain feeling of apprehension cannot be altogether suppressed with regard to the accuracy of the results, especially when we read that for practical reasons actually only a small fraction of the 782 cases could be placed at the disposal of the matchers at any one time. As Edwin Powers rightly says, 'the implications of this limitation cannot be overlooked' (p. 75). While we are not at this stage concerned with the more fundamental criticisms of the control group method such as expressed in the second part by Dr. Witmer (see below), it is clear, and was only too well known to those in charge of the research, that even minor inaccuracies in the process of matching could greatly affect the final outcome. The allocation of the boys to the T and C groups was done by flipping coins.

The next step was the assignment of the boys to their counsellors, each of whom was to have approximately 35 cases, consisting of about 50 per cent pre-delinquents ('minus boys') and 50 per cent

METHODOLOGICAL PROBLEMS

'normal' ('plus boys') and 'zero' boys. A considerable amount of information is given about the characteristics of these counsellors, their ages, backgrounds, training, philosophy of social work and working techniques, and length of service for the study. In nearly every respect, these fifteen men and four women differed greatly from one another, and, all the more as closer co-ordination was not always attempted and 'each one was encouraged to use his own approach and his own techniques' (p. 136), these differences could not but affect the results. One of the main problems, however, was common to all these social workers: without any official standing, they were all expected to offer their help to people who had not asked for it and, in the case of the 'plus boys', did not even seem to need it. Nor were they supposed to terminate their friendly relations with those whose problems had disappeared. Was not all this at variance with the well established principles of social case work? As one of the counsellors put it, 'case work cannot artificially be imposed on the client like a blanket or a mustard plaster' (p. 97). However, in actual practice hardly any difficulties seem to have arisen from this; not only was there at the outset less resistance than expected, but in a special enquiry into the opinions of the boys made at the termination of the project the general tenor of the replies was still favourable to the study, and the unorthodox origin of the relationship seemed in many cases to be forgotten (p. 97). Nor was this surprising as, in addition to their primary object of establishing friendly relations, the counsellors had at their disposal a considerable variety of services, ranging from medical assistance and adjustment of family problems to summer camps, foster home placement and tutoring, or in the words of Edwin Powers, 'from removing nits from a boy's head to preparing him for higher education' (p. 154, see especially Chapters VIII, IX, and XXIII). The counsellors were not supposed, however, to initiate large-scale community projects such as the organization of new clubs or playgrounds (p. 99), nor to give financial aid except in rare cases (p. 100), and a newspaper report that 'the cream of civilization in the most modern and enlightened forms' was put at the feet of these boys aroused the understandable annoyance of the staff. A weakness in the technique of the study, at least in its first years, was inadequate group work and psychiatric service (p. 132).

The severest test encountered in carrying out the project came with the outbreak of the war which struck it during its third working year and took away first several of the counsellors and afterwards most of the older boys. As the result, only one third of the boys kept their original counsellor throughout their period of supervision, whereas approximately the same proportion had to be assigned successively to three or more counsellors (pp. 87 and 140). As a reduction in each counsellor's case load became imperative, in addition to the boys joining the Forces a few hundred other boys were gradually 'retired' from 1941 onwards, and in 1945 the counselling of the remaining 75 boys was terminated (pp. 136–152). Among those dropped at an early stage were many of the 'normal' boys who had in any case been included mainly in order to avoid stigmatization of the others.

One of the greatest merits of the experiment was the special attention paid to the need for continuous evaluation of its methods and results. In the Index of the book, the various aspects of evaluation take up more than two columns. While it lasted, 'the objectives of the study and the specific functions of the agency were constantly re-examined' by means of staff discussions and seminars (p. 128). Moreover, two special surveys were carried out, in 1941 and again in 1943, to make preliminary comparisons of the T and C groups and to discover whatever trend might be developing (Chapter XIX). Already then, the inevitable scarcity of the information available for the C boys proved a handicap. In the first survey, 14 tests were administered in addition to a series of interviews. Although no statistically significant differences emerged between the two groups, the result as a whole was slightly in favour of the T boys. In the second survey, when different tests were applied, a somewhat more distinct trend in the same direction became noticeable. After the termination of the Study, as already mentioned, a sample of 118 T boys were interviewed by six interviewers previously unconnected with the Study in order to obtain the boys' own judgements of it (Chapter XIII). Finally, and most important of all, there is Dr. Witmer's independent evaluation. Before dealing with her contribution, however, an aspect of the book has to be mentioned which, though dealing only with an offshoot of the study, is of considerable interest to criminologists: in Chapter XVIII, 'Can Delinquency be predicted?', some of the case material, a hundred T and a hundred C cases, is used to check, in the light of subsequent developments, the accuracy

METHODOLOGICAL PROBLEMS

of the predictions made nine or ten years before by the 'predictors'. 69 per cent of these 200 boys had originally been classified as probable future delinquents, 25 per cent as likely non-delinquents, and 6 per cent as doubtful. These predictions had been made on the strength of information rather inadequate with regard to heredity and early childhood and without a personal interview of the boy. Moreover, as it was not known at the time which of the boys would be placed in the T group, the predictions had to be made on the assumption that they would receive no such special assistance as that given to the T group later on by the study. A comparison of the original predictions and the final judgements showed that in both groups most of the boys who actually became delinquents had been correctly predicted, but that many others who had also been predicted delinquents had not become so. In other words, delinquency had been strongly over-predicted. What was more surprising was that the prediction for the C group was not significantly more accurate than for the T group where changes for the better might have been expected in view of the work of the counsellors. Similar results were obtained by using the predictions made by the boys' teachers; they, too, had largely been successful in predicting serious delinquency, but had otherwise been far too pessimistic.

Dr. Witmer, at the head of a research team engaged after the termination of the field work, has played her part as the independent arbiter supremely well. Her ten chapters, in which she leaves no possible technique untried in a critical evaluation of the significance of this experiment, will rank very high in the literature of the social sciences. The first, and all too legitimate, target of her criticisms is Dr. Cabot's basic hypothesis and the resulting design of the study: did he not start from the false medical analogy that delinquency was like a disease that might be cured by administering one specific drug? Moreover, could this drug, in the hands of so many individuals, doing more or less what each of them thought best, be regarded as having 'the unitary character of a specific medical remedy'? Was it not equally mistaken to select as the object of the study a long-term philanthropic goal such as the prevention of delinquency, instead of the short-term aim, with which social workers have to be content, of helping their clients through their current social and emotional difficulties? Again, was the control technique, though in many ways indispensable,

CRIMINOLOGY AND ITS METHODS

really adequate as the only method of evaluating clinical situations and changes in the behaviour of individuals? The clinical worker cannot be satisfied with statistical averages, and the over-all figures produced by the control group method had therefore to be supplemented by more detailed and searching case-by-case judgements of success and failure, compared with the boys' own opinions and other subjective assessments.

This methodological introduction is followed by a detailed analysis and classification of the individual cases according to type and degree of maladjustment, by an assessment of the personalities and work of the counsellors, and by a comparison of the adjustment made by the two groups. Naturally, to trace the C boys and to obtain information about them had become more difficult than before. Whereas Dr. Witmer's study was based on 254 of the 325 T boys (the others had to be discarded as 'retired' at too early a stage), only 148 C boys were available for evaluation, and the question arose whether they and their 'twins' among the T boys could be regarded as a representative sample of the total (p. 404). Moreover, the follow-up enquiries had, for understandable reasons, largely to be limited to interviews of the boys themselves and their families. The enquiries were made by two of the counsellors, but the adjustment ratings were reserved for Dr. Witmer alone, an arrangement which in her view neutralized the effect of possible bias in favour of the T boys (p. 406). The definition of 'adjustment' caused the well-known difficulties common to all follow-up studies. In Professor Allport's Foreword and in the Obituary Note, some illuminating reflections are made on this problem: an idealist like Dr. Cabot could not be content with such pedestrian and largely negative aims as 'delinquency-prevention' or 'adjustment'—'for him the test of every course of action was its capacity to add to human stature. Will it make for growth?' (p. 587). However, as Allport admits, spiritual growth can hardly be adequately defined and accurately measured, and no more satisfactory criterion has so far been found than Dr. Witmer's concept of 'social adjustment', the 'sociological counterpart to character' (p. 385), and her assessment of the value which the study services had to individual boys in removing handicaps to such adjustment. All these limitations have to be borne in mind when considering the significance of Dr. Witmer's final evaluation: although in about 40 per cent of the cases marked improve-

METHODOLOGICAL PROBLEMS

ments had taken place over the original situation, no significant differences could be established in this respect between the two groups (pp. 414 et seq.). Does this mean that in its practical and its theoretical objects the study has to be regarded as a failure? Dr. Witmer shows that this is not so. In a case-by-case analysis, less dependent on comparisons with the control group, she demonstrates that, and how, a good many T boys had actually benefited from the work of the counsellors. Clearly, this was a different criterion from 'adjustment' or 'improvement', as a boy might have improved for reasons unconnected with the study. The boys' own views, for what they were worth, were again elicited and compared with the investigator's judgement, and a considerable degree of conformity was found. About one fifth of the T boys seemed to have definitely, and another tenth slightly, benefited from the study (p. 450). An attempt was made to define more precisely the circumstances likely to produce this result or its opposite (Chapters XXVI–XXIX). In some of the cases belonging to the latter category, failure was due to the fact that the counsellor had become so involved in work with other members of the family that he had neglected the boy himself (p. 493). Perhaps the most definite impression which Dr. Witmer received from her analysis was the conviction that Dr. Cabot's hypothesis (that the help of an adult friend was all that was needed in preventive work) had, with a few exceptions, been disproved in cases of seriously maladjusted, delinquent or neurotic boys (pp. 506, 550, 553, 563, 573). The question poses itself whether this might not have been anticipated from the beginning so that such cases could have been excluded or be given very special attention. However, Dr. Witmer considers that it was a 'very worth while expenditure of funds to have demonstrated this not universally recognized truth'. One of the most important lessons she draws from this truth is the risk of encouraging too close a relationship between boys of this type and psychiatrically untrained workers (pp. 514, 518, 554), and she frankly admits the possibility that a few of these boys may have been harmed through their contacts with the study. Although her conclusion that failures were due to the personality of the boys and to the kind of work done with them (p. 565) and that more attention should in future be paid to closer co-ordination between type of boy and type of service (p. 555) is not particularly startling, her very able and scholarly analysis of the case material which leads to that conclusion represents a most valuable contribution to our knowledge. The various types of boys and of problems have been closely related to the various forms of treatment, and in many cases convincing explanations have been given for their success or failure.

There can be little doubt about our final assessment of the place of the Cambridge-Somerville Study in the history of criminological and sociological research. As an experiment, it has largely failed as it was perhaps bound to fail. In the first place, as Dr. Witmer has rightly indicated, Dr. Cabot, apparently misguided by a mixture of medical analogies and moral convictions, had been rather unfortunate in the choice of his hypothesis. 'Friendship' is not a drug to be applied for a period fixed in advance, and even if it were one it was, in this case, given in such varying strength over such varying periods by doctors of so diverse qualifications and creeds as to make it appear, in its effect, several hundred different medicines rather than a single one. The very scope, ambitiousness, and inexactitude of the scheme made it impossible adequately to control all the variables which should have been kept under control. Concessions which had to be made to the prejudices and susceptibilities of the public as well as to treatment needs constantly interfered with essential requirements of the research and may, imperceptibly but nevertheless very drastically, have influenced its results (see e.g. pp. 37 fn., 74, 97, 148, 150, 338 fn., and *passim*). In short, the matching of the two groups was far from perfect, the work of the counsellors inadequately co-ordinated, the effect of the ordinary social services on the control group, in spite of a special investigation subsequently made for Dr. Witmer (p. 575), insufficiently known. To make matters worse, war-time conditions made it impossible to maintain the element of stability and continuity which was of the very essence of Dr. Cabot's hypothesis. In the circumstances, no statistical assessment of the outcome of the experiment could be really meaningful. Moreover, one occasionally gets the impression that after Dr. Cabot's death the executors of his scheme may have too conscientiously and rigidly adhered to his original plan. Modifications were, apparently, made only where quite unavoidable. Mr. Churchill, in 1943, wrote of 'what happens when battles are governed by agreements made in all good faith months before and persisted in without regard for the ever-changing fortunes of war'.

METHODOLOGICAL PROBLEMS

True as it is that scientific experiments cannot be conducted like battles, there is nevertheless something of a battle in every piece of research.

The conclusion to be drawn from all this is not necessarily that experiments in the social sciences will always or, as Sorokin has suggested, in 99·9999 out of 100 cases be unsuccessful and inconclusive, but merely that they will have to be more modest and in keeping with the experiences of experimental social science rather than those of medicine. This in itself is already a useful lesson. Regardless of its value as an experiment and a piece of control group research, however, the Cambridge-Somerville Study has justified itself through the light it has shed on the requirements of successful rehabilitative work with difficult delinquents and on the possibilities of predicting future delinquency. It should be judged by what it has achieved rather than by what it has failed to achieve.

(*c*) A Review of JUVENILE DELINQUENTS GROWN UP, by Sheldon and Eleanor Glueck.[1]

Criminology—science or art? Although this old pseudo-problem is still alive, the controversy seems to have lost much of its former animosity, and even some of the most outspoken supporters of the 'art' theory are becoming increasingly willing to admit that the artistic approach does not necessarily exclude the application of scientific methods. What is in fact meant by that alternative, and does it reveal a difficulty which is peculiar to the understanding and treatment of crime? 'There is no anti-thesis between science and art,' wrote a great modern lawyer whose interest in the criminal law was admittedly but very slightly.[2] 'Every true work of science is a work of art. . . .' In a sense, this is true. What Ehrlich had in mind was the fact that receptivity of mind, imagination, 'power to give shape to one's material', to create an original method and technique, are just as much indispensable to the genuine scientist as they are to the artist. This does not, however, entirely answer our opening question. Those who doubt the character of Criminology as a science may be prepared to admit

---

[1] New York, The Commonwealth Fund, 1940.—This review was first published in *The Modern Law Review*, Vol. V, Nos 3 and 4, July, 1942.

[2] Eugen Ehrlich, *Fundamental Principles of the Sociology of Law*, translated by Walter L. Moll (Harvard University Press, 1936), p. 472.

CRIMINOLOGY AND ITS METHODS

that a given piece of criminological research shows those artistic qualities and is based upon an original method and technique. What they dispute is that even the most accomplished scientific research can substantially assist in the highly individualistic task of understanding and treating the law-breaker. Those in particular who are themselves masters in the art of dealing with offenders may feel somewhat uneasy about the possibility that dry statistical tables may, some day, take the place of human sympathy and understanding. If the criminologist wishes to overcome such residues of latent suspicion and antagonism he will have to do two things above all: First, to prove that, in his own person, he combines scientific knowledge with practical experience, sufficient to enable him to appreciate the actual problems of the judge, the administrator and the field-worker, and to be of real assistance to each of them; in short, to bridge the gap between theory and practice. Secondly, to draw attention to the fact that the process of transformation which is at present taking place in the field of Criminology and Penology is in no way peculiar to them, but has its counterpart in the spheres of Psychology, Education, and other branches of Social Science, all of which are equally concerned with the highly individualistic task of handling human material. One might perhaps also refer to the somewhat analogous process in the realm of pure art to which Dr. C. H. Waddington in his recent Pelican book *The Scientific Attitude*, has devoted an attractive though slightly rambling chapter 'Art Looks to Science'.

These brief remarks of a more general character seemed advisable to introduce a book of that somewhat uncompromising 'pure science' type which may easily provoke renewed attacks on the part of the 'art'-lovers. Since 1930, when they published their first volume in this remarkable series, Sheldon Glueck, the eminent criminologist of Harvard University, and Mrs. Glueck have patiently added particle after particle to their unique system of follow-up studies and Prediction Tables. These studies are neither easy to digest nor particularly entertaining. Their austere statistical tables, dry interpretations and dispassionate conclusions are only rarely enlivened by detailed individual case histories or other digressions of psychological interest. They show the way how to meet the legitimate criticisms of the deplorable deficiencies in the corresponding data available in this country. What we do know about the success or failure of our present ways of dealing

METHODOLOGICAL PROBLEMS

with the law-breaker is largely limited to personal impressions and to some interesting but inadequate official statistics. To indicate some of the principal weaknesses of the existing statistical data: First, they are unsystematic, almost each of them using different classifications, which makes any comparison of the various sets of figures impossible. Secondly, they are merely statistics of re-appearances in Court which do not take into account the possibility that a particular offender may have failed to reappear for reasons entirely unconnected with the success of the penal treatment received (as, for instance, death, emigration, residence in a penal or mental institution). Likewise, apart from the files of Probation Officers and After-care Organizations, no details of any kind are available which might indicate the causes of recidivism in individual cases.

The system of following-up as elaborated by the Gluecks tries to avoid such shortcomings by investigating the after-histories of individual offenders and by correlating their subsequent behaviour to their antecedents as well as to the type of penal treatment received. The present book is a continuation of an earlier enquiry, published in 1934 under the title *One Thousand Juvenile Delinquents*, which contained the results of a follow-up study of a thousand boy delinquents who had appeared before the Boston Juvenile Court during the years 1917 to 1922, when they were of an average age of thirteen and a half years. As these boys had, at the request of the Court, been examined in the Clinic of the Judge Baker Foundation, that first study was concerned not only with the subsequent behaviour of the boys during a five years period following the completion of their treatment, but also with the degree of co-ordination between Court and Clinic. The present work deals with the careers of the same boys during two further five years periods, thus giving the story for no less than fifteen years after penal treatment, up to a point when the average age of the group was approximately twenty-nine. The task of locating these men and of obtaining accurate information about their doings without giving offence to them or to their families must have been formidable. Thanks to the elaborate technique evolved by the authors and their trained staff of field-investigators it was successfully solved in the great majority of cases. After eliminating sixty who had died before the end of the third period, and a further ninety-two whose behaviour could not be adequately cleared up, the authors were able to collect the information they wanted for 848 men of the original army of a thousand, which seems to be a highly satisfactory achievement. Roughly speaking, the information refers to certain factors in their general histories, to changes in their criminal behaviour and to the 'peno-correctional' treatment which they had received during the follow-up period. Out of the wealth of interesting results which have emerged from this study, at least a few major findings may be quoted. There is, first, the fact that the percentage of offenders who could be regarded as 'reformed' increased from 15 at the end of the first five years to 26·8 at the end of the second, and to almost 40 at the end of the third five-year period. Moreover, even among those who continued to commit crimes the percentage of serious offenders decreased from 75 to 47. What may have been the reasons for these changes in behaviour? Improved environmental conditions? Efficient 'peno-correctional' treatment? Or simply settling down to normal life as a consequence of the process of growing older? Detailed comparisons between those who reformed and those who did not revealed that the former group, as was to be expected, enjoyed more favourable hereditary and environmental conditions. These differences, however, though significant, did not seem in themselves sufficient to explain the contrast in behaviour, and an additional explanation had therefore to be sought. Already in their previous study *Later Criminal Careers* (1937), which described the after-histories of 500 adult male offenders, the authors stressed the predominant importance of the simple process of ageing. Up to the age of thirty-five at least, maturation was found to be the strongest reformative factor, whereas those who had not reformed by then were much less likely to do so thereafter. This process of maturing, it was found, could be assisted and even accelerated by favourable environmental changes, and vice versa, whereas the various forms of mental instability proved the most formidable obstacle to reform. In the present volume this theory has undergone an interesting modification. The new material would seem to indicate that the cessation of criminal activities is related less to the arrival at a specific chronological age than to the distance from the onset of a criminal career. In this view the authors were confirmed by the results of a comparison of the group dealt with in the present volume and the group studied in *Later Criminal Careers*. In this comparison 'two series of offenders, quite different

METHODOLOGICAL PROBLEMS

in make-up and background and significantly different in the fact that one began to be delinquent (on the average) five years before the other, have been shown to resemble each other strikingly in conduct, *not at similar ages, but rather at a similar distance removed from the time they began to be delinquent.* This would seem to indicate that what may be called, after Quételet, the "propensity to criminality" has a more or less definite life span regardless of the age at which delinquent behaviour actually begins' (p. 105). This theory may seem to be at variance with the traditional view that delinquent tendencies which show themselves in early youth are usually symptomatic of some deep-rooted trouble and more difficult to cure than delinquent behaviour occurring during the later stages of adolescence. This latter view is, by the way, confirmed by one of the statistical tables in the present book, which the authors themselves interpret as indicating that '. . . where maladjustment known as "delinquency" begins early in life it is rooted more deeply . . . and more probably is related to the hereditary, biologic make-up of the individual than in cases where it does not begin to manifest itself until the adolescent years' (p. 114). On the other hand, the present reviewer may be permitted to quote his own finding that 'amongst the men who commenced their criminal activities after the age of forty there are comparatively many who at that late stage have become habituals with twenty or more convictions' (*Social Aspects of Crime*, p. 359). In short, the evidence hitherto available is too limited in scope and too conflicting to justify a final verdict. The authors can be relied upon, however, to check their discovery with their usual thoroughness.

Special attention is given to the nature and length of the penocorrectional treatment received by the group over the whole period, to the changes in penal methods, and to the behaviour of individual offenders during and after the various forms of treatment. One of the results emerging from this part of the study is the higher percentage of adjustment and success achieved by institutional treatment (Prisons, Reformatories) as compared with non-institutional methods (Probation, Parole, Foster-home placement). It may be worth remembering that similar results were obtained by corresponding investigations published by the Home Office in *Criminal Statistics* (for 1932 and 1938).[1] In both cases, however, it would be much too early for the supporters of probation and

[1] See above, p. 125.

similar non-institutional methods to accept defeat, and the authors themselves emphasize that much more detailed research into the working of the various methods of treatment is necessary, research which, as we are glad to hear, is already beginning. Nevertheless, even from the present study certain associations between personality types and the prospects of the various methods of treatment seem to emerge. It was found, for instance, that offenders of the solitary type responded better to probation than to institutional treatment, whereas the opposite was true of offenders with deep-rooted feelings of insecurity created by their early environment.

The numerous correlationships worked out between the personalities and environment of the offenders and their behaviour during and after peno-correctional treatment could be used for the construction of *Prediction Tables*. Ever since the publication of the earliest Glueck studies and the almost simultaneous investigations of Burgess, Vold, Monachesi and others, American penologists have realized the great practical significance of their work for the administration of criminal justice. As a consequence much time and thought have been devoted to the working out and improvement of predictive devices intended to assist the Courts in their task of finding the most suitable methods of treatment. The idea itself is simple enough and must appear convincing to everybody except the most extreme representative of the 'pure art' theory. If we know the individual and environmental conditions and the behaviour of a large body of offenders over a considerable span of time, we are able to select those factors which are most frequently related to certain types of behaviour and can devise Prediction Tables of a fairly general applicability. In the present study, out of sixty-three factors in the family and personal histories of the delinquents and their behaviour during each particular form of treatment five factors which showed the highest symptomatic value and about which information could be most easily obtained (birthplace of father, discipline by father, discipline by mother, school retardation, school misconduct) were chosen, for instance, in order to construct a Prediction Table for the likely behaviour of an offender during 'straight Probation'. Other factors showed the highest predictive value for institutional methods of treatment. In all, eleven different Prediction Tables had to be constructed. The total number of factors employed is, however,

METHODOLOGICAL PROBLEMS

not large, since some of them could be used in several tables. The authors claim, therefore, that the collection of the necessary information would not require more time than is at present needed for the usual report of a Probation Officer, and that on the basis of this information each offender could be scored in a few minutes, which may seem somewhat over-optimistic. In a special chapter it is shown how the Courts had actually dealt with certain offenders and how differently they might have been treated according to the Prediction Tables. In order to avoid possible misconceptions it should be mentioned, however, that the authors are particularly anxious to make it clear that their Tables are in no way intended to be used as the only basis of the sentencing policy of the Courts.

Sceptics may be inclined to say that, after all, every criminal Court, as a matter of course, pays attention to those factors upon which the Prediction Tables are based. They overlook the fundamental differences between casual, unsystematic, and unchecked personal observations and the accomplished machinery envisaged by the Gluecks. On the other hand, even those who unhesitatingly accept the need for more rational and scientific methods may have to admit that, in spite of the admirable pioneer work done by the authors, the factual material at their disposal does not yet seem throughout adequate. Their samples are still too small to be regarded as truly representative, and similar considerations apply to the facts upon which their judgement of success or failure of the various methods of treatment depends. Whether an individual offender will respond to probation rather than to one of the different types of institutional treatment can sometimes not be finally decided on the basis of one or even two experiments with these methods, because of the decisive influence of personal factors. Where one Probation Officer fails another may succeed. However, these are difficulties of which the authors themselves are no doubt fully aware (see, for instance, pp. 149–50), and which can in no way detract from the potential value of their work. The more clearly we realize these potentialities for the future administration of criminal justice the stronger will be our desire to see similar studies one day undertaken in this country.[1] That the methods and results of the authors will be applicable outside the U.S.A. only with certain modifications goes without saying.

[1] The day has now come; see above, note 1, p. 124.

PART THREE

AMERICAN IMPRESSIONS OF A CRIMINOLOGIST

CHAPTER 7

AMERICAN PRISONS [1]
with a note on British Columbia

I. INTRODUCTORY

TO deal with 'American Prisons' in one short paper, or even to deal with the subject at all, is in many ways a formidable undertaking. To begin with, one cannot but recall the long and distinguished line of European writers and penologists who have placed their impressions on record during the past 120 years—from Charles Dickens to Ruggles-Brise and Alexander Paterson in Britain, from Alexis de Tocqueville, Beaumont and Ducpétiaux to Paul Cornil in the French-speaking countries and from Dr. Julius to Moritz Liepmann and Franz Exner in Germany, to mention only a few of many famous names.

In the second place I am keenly aware of the limitations imposed on my survey by extrinsic circumstances. During most of my five months' stay in the United States I was largely occupied with two full-time teaching appointments as visiting professor in the Departments of Sociology of the Universities of Oregon and Pennsylvania, and my visits to Institutions were restricted to the one or two free days per week I had in term-time and a fortnight's interval between these two appointments—a period largely spent in California. Added to which, the United States is much too vast a country and too diversified for even one single aspect of it to be completely mastered in five months. I can tell you hardly anything

[1] Read at a Meeting of the Howard League for Penal Reform in London on the 1st December, 1953, and published in *The British Journal of Delinquency*, Vol. IV, No. 4, April, 1954.—My sincere thanks are due to all my American friends, University teachers, administrators, students, who not only made my visit possible, but did everything in their power to make it informative and pleasant. I am also much indebted to the staffs of Institutions, criminal and juvenile courts, probation officers, and many others, for their helpfulness and patience.

IMPRESSIONS OF A CRIMINOLOGIST

that you are not already familiar with, either from personal observation or from reading. All I can do is to underline a few general aspects and to add a few more specific, local features. If my visit has taught me anything it is to be utterly distrustful of any sentences beginning with the words: 'The United States' or 'The Americans' or 'The American Penal System'. Travelling from New York west to Oregon, with an all too short visit to Utah, and a longer one to California, and returning east by a different route to Pennsylvania, New Jersey and New York, the overwhelming impression one gets is one of diversity rather than of uniformity. What may be true of one locality may be entirely untrue of another a few hundred miles away. Many people outside the United States take it almost for granted that there is a vast unbridgeable and unpardonable cleavage between American theory and American practice, that what they find described and discussed in American penological literature bears no relation to the situation as it actually exists within the American penal system. Broadly speaking, this view, though to some extent understandable, is mistaken just because it ignores the vastness of the American scene. A progressive scheme of treatment, an ingenious piece of research carried out in one particular Institution, at one particular University or Clinic, will soon gain the widest publicity through the enormous network of American information services, and in the minds of those who regard the United States as one unit the impression may easily be created that the information provided with regard to happenings in one small corner gives an accurate picture of the general situation. In the same way, we are sometimes quite unreasonably surprised to meet Americans who are unaware of important developments taking place somewhere else in the United States. 'Americans are inveterate wanderers', 'the nation on wheels', writes John Gunther[1]; and this is certainly true up to a point. In no other country of the Western World are there so many people, by no means only members of the poorer classes, who live in trailers and are constantly on the move. At the same time I had not expected to meet so many people, again by no means only among the poorer classes or recent immigrants, who had, as they usually express it, 'never crossed the Mississippi'. To quote John Gunther again, 'probably not one per cent of the

[1] John Gunther, *Inside U.S.A.* Revised edition, 1951. (New York, Harper & Brothers), pp. 161 and 307.

AMERICAN PRISONS

people of the eight central states have ever seen New York or San Francisco' (p. 317).

Another mistake we are liable to make is to apply our own standards to what is after all a different world. We all know, for example, that most American prisons, reformatories and so on are much too large for our liking. American penologists are well aware of this; they, too, dislike monster institutions such as Jackson or San Quentin—which latter is in fact much better than its reputation—and almost unanimously regard their excessive size as one of the causes of the recent wave of prison riots—a topic with which I will deal later on. But size is a relative conception, and everything else, too, is very large in the United States. The individual American is used to larger distances, larger rivers, larger cities, factories, railways and buildings, and a prison with 3,000 inmates frightens him not quite as much as it might other people. One of the most progressive and enlightened penal administrations in the States, that of California, had just completed the construction of a new 'Vocational Training Institution' for young men near Tracy, not far from San Francisco, with a capacity of 1,200 inmates—much too big for our taste, but for a number of reasons perhaps the only solution. When inspecting the vast new structure I must confess I was, for a moment, a little flabbergasted, particularly in view of the universal condemnation of large institutions I had found in all my conversations with leading Californian administrators. But soon I began to realize that for technical reasons it will probably be impracticable in the near future to do away with all these overgrown monsters. I can, I think, safely say with Thomas Huxley in one of his 'American Addresses'—the one on 'University Education', delivered at the formal opening of the Johns Hopkins University, Baltimore, on the 12th September, 1876[1] 'I am not in the slightest degree impressed by your bigness, or your material resources, as such. Size is not grandeur, and territory does not make a nation. The great issue . . . is what are you going to do with all these things.' Although we may not be impressed by mere size it would be equally unreasonable to ignore its psychological effects and the technical difficulties produced by it. Nor should we ignore the penological implications of certain other fundamental differences

[1] Thomas H. Huxley, *American Addresses*, (London, Macmillan & Co., 1877), p. 125.

IMPRESSIONS OF A CRIMINOLOGIST

in national character and temperament. The inside cells of American prisons have been widely criticized as inhuman and depriving the inmate of the last tiny remnant of privacy. Can we be so sure, however, that Americans who, as a rule, do not fence in their homes and gardens, cherish privacy as much as we do as an essential commodity? I am not advocating the use of inside cells in this country, but we have to remember that privacy was the most dreaded penalty in the days of solitary confinement; and in their inside cells, cage-like as they certainly are, prisoners can still feel as part of the prison community.

As in this country and elsewhere, prison conditions have been rapidly changing in the United States, and perhaps at a particularly fast rate within the past twenty-five years. Sir Alexander Paterson was no doubt one of the shrewdest and most accurate observers, but even some of his findings of twenty years ago can no longer be regarded as truly reflecting the present position. For the understanding of the American penal system the most important factors are, I would suggest, *geography* and *mobility*, *politics* and *race*. While, for reasons of time, I have to leave for another occasion[1] the subject of race and certain other criminological problems, I should like to say a few words on the impact of the first three factors.

II. GEOGRAPHY AND MOBILITY

One has to see the vastness of so many States of the Union with their, in comparison, tiny populations to realize the impossible situation in which their administrators are placed. States with a territory of nearly 100,000 square miles (against the 58,000 of England and Wales) and a population with less than one million, or only a few hundred thousand, are not exceptional in some parts of U.S.A. In consequence, none of these States can afford more than one Central Penitentiary, perhaps one Reformatory, and one Training School for boys and one for girls. A State such as Utah, with a territory of 85,000 square miles and a population of approximately 700,000, possesses only one State Prison and one State Industrial School where boys and girls are kept together. However, I am not saying that such gaps in the institutional system are always and solely due to disproportion between territory and population. Oregon, a slightly larger State, with more

[1] See below, Chapter 8.

than twice the population of Utah and greater wealth, has indeed two separate Training Schools, one for boys and one for girls; but so far it possesses no Reformatory, with the result that many young people have to go to the County Jails which, of course, exist in each of the 36 counties of the State. No State-wide official statistics exist, but the Oregon Prison Association, a very active body, made a survey in 1950 of these 'Children behind Bars' and discovered that, in the five years' period 1944-8, what they rightly describe as 'a staggering total' of 9,853 boys and girls under the age of seventeen had passed through these Jails, 451 of them even under the age of fourteen. However, legislation has now been passed authorizing the establishment of an 'intermediate institution' for the sixteen to twenty-five-year-olds, and I had the privilege of being invited to address the Fiftieth Anniversary Meeting of the Oregon Prison Association in Portland on the English Borstal System which, naturally, was a very topical subject at this stage.

Only in exceptional cases does it apparently happen that neighbouring States, in one way or another, pool their resources. This has been done in particular with women prisoners who have occasionally been sent to prisons in other States to make up a group of adequate size, but similar developments are under consideration for other categories of prisoners.[1]

The complete independence of the individual States together with the small number of Institutions which so many of them possess explains why in American penology classification means so much more internal classification (i.e. classification within the Institution) than external classification (classification meaning, among other things, using different types of Institution for different types of offenders—a point which I hope to take up later on).

Migration on a large scale is another factor which makes prison administration unusually difficult in U.S.A. There are two main trends in these waves of internal mass migration: from east to west and from south to north. The population of California increased from one and a half million in 1900 and less than seven million in 1940 to nearly thirteen million in 1953. In the last decade or so

[1] See Richard A. McGee, *Contemporary Correction*, edited by Paul W. Tappan (New York, Toronto, London, McGraw-Hill Book Company, Inc., 1951), p. 88.

IMPRESSIONS OF A CRIMINOLOGIST

almost four million immigrants came from outside the State. 'The State of California', we read in the Biannual Report of the Department of Corrections for 1951–2, 'is unique in the United States in the amazing development and growth which is taking place. The decade of the 1950's will determine to a large degree whether or not the development and expansion in which we are now engaged will be constructive and far-sighted, or whether it will result in confusion and chaos'.[1] This growth in general population was accompanied by an increase of 128 per cent in the prison population in the eight and a half year period since the reorganization of the Californian Prison System in 1944—an increase which, described in the Californian Report as unique for the United States, has its counterpart in this country for the same period. However, for an administration which, as we know from the books by Scudder[2] and Duffy,[3] had in many ways to start from scratch, the strain must have been particularly heavy.

The migration from the Southern States to the North is almost entirely a mass movement of Southern Negroes to some of the big Northern States, Pennsylvania, Michigan, Illinois, etc.[4] The problems it has created for the prison administration of these States are perhaps even more baffling than those of California, although the latter, too, has its racial problem (*ca.* 15 per cent Mexicans and 20 per cent Negroes in Californian prisons in 1952); but, as I said before, I must leave a discussion of this most interesting and important subject for another occasion.

III. POLITICS (WHICH FOR MY PRESENT PURPOSES INCLUDES CERTAIN ASPECTS OF ADMINISTRATION)

We all know—and Americans are the first to deplore the fact—how much more deeply and openly than in most other countries the day-to-day administration of prisons, as of so many other institutions, has been invaded by politics in U.S.A. There is hardly any need to substantiate this statement—it is borne out by every modern American textbook and even by official pronouncements.[5]

---

[1] California Department of Corrections, Biennial Report, 1951–2, p. 30.
[2] Kenyon J. Scudder, *Prisoners are People* (New York, Doubleday & Co. 1952).
[3] Clinton T. Duffy, *San Quentin—The Story of a Prison.* (London, Peter Davies, 1951).
[4] John Gunther, op cit., pp. 312 *ff.*
[5] Mabel A. Elliott, *Crime in Modern Society* (New York, Harper & Brothers, 1952), pp. 612 and 715; Austin H. MacCormick, *The Annals of the American Academy of Political and Social Service*), Vol. 293, May, 1954, pp. 25 et seq.

AMERICAN PRISONS

In individual cases, however, it may be difficult to say where technical, professional considerations end and politics begin, and the outsider may occasionally ascribe to politics what is actually a non-political decision. If I may refer to a personal experience, my arrival in the State of Oregon coincided, almost to the day, with the sudden 'firing' of the warden of the Oregon State Penitentiary. This happened after an enquiry made in the Institution by a Commission appointed by the Governor and consisting of three Wardens from other States, lasting, it was alleged, only a few hours without giving the accused any opportunity of putting his case before the Commission. Throughout the two and a half months of my stay in Oregon this event was Subject No. 1 in the Press and in daily conversation. Public statements were made by the dismissed Warden and his successor, by some of the leading politicians, State officials and by private citizens. In view of the conflicting opinions presented and for other reasons it would be highly improper for me to express any personal views on the merits of the case, i.e. whether the official explanation of the dismissal, 'failure to maintain discipline', was the real and the only reason or whether political matters, too, played some part in it. The dismissed Warden himself seems to have never made any actual allegation that he had been dismissed for political reasons. The crucial element in the situation, however, appears to be that in many States Wardenships and other leading posts in the prison administration are not civil service appointments and can apparently be terminated without notice at the discretion of the controlling authority. According to the Attorney General's Survey, published in 1939,[1] in only four States (Colorado, New York, Ohio and Wisconsin), the entire prison personnel 'from the wardens to the last turnkey' enjoyed civil service status, while in most other States Wardenships were not civil service appointments. The view is expressed in the Survey that civil service appointments are not necessarily the ideal solution. 'Some of the prisons where permanence has long been the established policy are the least progressive, perhaps because there is so little change either in personnel or in penological ideas and ideals.' While this may often be true, the Survey has to admit that, on the other hand, 'prisons whose policies are the most enlightened are found among the States where a

[1] Attorney General's Survey of Release Procedures, Vol. V, 'Prisons'. (Washington, Department of Justice, 1939), pp. 64 et seq.

IMPRESSIONS OF A CRIMINOLOGIST

permanent personnel makes possible a continuing progress'. (In California, there are at present only 20 out of a total of 2,407 employees of the Department of Corrections exempt from civil service by statute.)[1] Without a certain measure of security of tenure no really independent, consistent and long-term policy can, as a rule, be expected.

Let us now turn to the controlling authority itself. Here we find an amazing variety of systems, as described in the Attorney General's Survey[2] and more recently and in greater detail by Richard A. McGee, the distinguished Chief of the Californian Department of Corrections.[3] In each of the States whose prison systems I was privileged to see at closer range I found a different structure. In Oregon supreme authority is vested in the Board of Control, consisting of the Governor, the Secretary of State and the State Treasurer, which is in full control not only of penal and reformatory Institutions but also of the various State Hospitals and the State Schools for the Blind and the Deaf. We may well question, with Mr. McGee, whether such a Board can ever effectively function since these high officials will be too busy with other equally important matters to spend much time on prison affairs; nor can they be expected to possess or acquire the necessary technical knowledge.

In Pennsylvania, the position is particularly interesting. Within the past ten years, it has been carefully reviewed and criticized in two elaborate Reports, known as the Ashe Report of 1944 and the Devers Report of 1953. At present, prison administration is one of the responsibilities of the State Department of Welfare, a very large Department which has also to deal with a great variety of other matters such as Homes and Hospitals, Mental Health, Child Welfare, and so on. As the inevitable consequence, the Bureaux of Penal Affairs and of Prison Industries which form one section of this 'sprawling body' and have to look after eight State Correctional Institutions, one House of Correction, one Workhouse, 68 County Prisons and 421 lock-ups, cannot get the attention and the funds required for progressive administration. A sum of eight million dollars, earmarked in 1945 for the modernization of the correctional system, 'got diverted into the mental hospital

---

[1] See p. 29 of the Report quoted in note 1, p. 170.
[2] See pp. 62 et seq. of the Survey in note 1, p. 171.
[3] See note 1, p. 169.

AMERICAN PRISONS

programme';[1] nor were other progressive provisions passed by the legislation in the same year carried out. To make the administration even more difficult, by an Act of 1826 the whole Commonwealth is divided into two prison districts, the eastern with the Eastern Penitentiary in Philadelphia as its most famous Institution, and the western with the Western Penitentiary in Pittsburgh, both with a large number of other less well-known Institutions. Each individual prison is a more or less independent unit, ruled by a Board of Trustees consisting of lay members, and apparently administered on such different lines that even the pay of the prison guards differs from one Institution to the other. Moreover, each of the two Penitentiaries has a large modern branch some distance away, the Eastern Penitentiary at Graterford and the Western Penitentiary at Rockview, sharing the Warden and the Board of Trustees with the parent Institution. The result of this administrative set-up is lack of co-ordination, integration, uniformity and consistency, and the principal recommendations of the 1953 Report are therefore: transfer of the Prison Administration from the Department of Welfare to the Department of Justice; the abolition of the two prison districts and of the autonomous character of individual prisons; and in particular the establishment of a Bureau of Correction headed by a Commissioner of Corrections responsible to the Attorney General, with the Boards of Trustees reduced to the rank of advisory bodies.

My criticisms of the present system in Pennsylvania are not intended to give the impression that the picture is one of complete gloom and stagnation without any redeeming features. In a State rightly famous as the cradle of American penology, and distinguished by the high quality of the penological work done in the theoretical field by its Universities and on the practical side by organizations such as The Pennsylvania Prison Society, The Philadelphia Advisory Commission on Commitment, Detention and Discharge of Prisoners, and The Crime Prevention Association of Philadelphia, such wholesale stagnation would be inconceivable. In fact, Pennsylvania does possess a number of first-class progressive Institutions. Of those which I have seen I would mention in particular Graterford, some 30 miles from Philadelphia,

[1] Edmund G. Burbank, *The Missing Keystone in Pennsylvania's Prison Programme* (a publication of the Pennsylvania Citizens Association for Health and Welfare, 1952), p. 10.

IMPRESSIONS OF A CRIMINOLOGIST
a modern medium security structure of the telegraph pole type, very bright and spacious, with large grounds, excellent workshops, full employment, outside cells, an adjacent farm, good educational facilities, no overcrowding (with a capacity of 2,000, it had only *ca.* 1,700 inmates at the time of my visit). The present Warden, or rather deputy Warden, as the Warden is shared with and resident in the Eastern Penitentiary, is the architect who designed and built the prison approximately twenty years ago. There are, however, no psychologists or social workers at Graterford, which receives its prisoners not direct from the Courts but from the Eastern Penitentiary where the work of classification is carried out. In spite of the absence of any real treatment programme and in spite of racial segregation—there are three wings for white and two for coloured prisoners—the atmosphere seemed to be healthy, and there have been no disturbances. On the debit side, however, there is the mother prison, the venerable old Eastern Penitentiary, opened in 1829 with 7 wings and a normal capacity of 923 inmates. There have been so many structural additions to the buildings in the past hundred years that it is difficult to discover the original design. The Penitentiary now houses 1,200 to 1,300 men in 12 or 13 wings, among them about 250 lifers. Life imprisonment may be for fifteen to twenty years, but sometimes for much longer. Some of the men have to sleep two or three in cells, some of which are dark with only small skylights, but good artificial lighting. The main industry, occupying approximately 65 men (5 per cent!), is printing; the others do maintenance work, cooking, or nothing. The classification and distribution of men between the Eastern Penitentiary and Graterford is done by the Senior Psychologist, who has been there for twenty-five years and is greatly respected: even he, however, cannot relieve the overcrowding of the Eastern Penitentiary in view of the rules which prevent the sending of certain categories of men to Graterford. It is stressed in the 1953 Report that only about 10 per cent of the male prison population require maximum security conditions, which for Pennsylvania would mean no more than 700 men who could be comfortably housed in the two State Penitentiaries. The overcrowding at the Eastern Penitentiary is due to the out-of-date belief that every long-term prisoner has to be kept under conditions of maximum security; and it is therefore one of the recommendations of the 1953 Report to reduce the

capacity of the Eastern Penitentiary to about 500 by dismantling some of its structures.

Far superior is the administrative set-up in New Jersey with its Department of Institutions and Agencies, headed by a Commissioner selected by a State Board of Control, until recently no less a person than that great international figure, Sanford Bates. The centralized thinking and planning, the co-operation and integration, so evident in New Jersey, show what can be done where an efficient system is operated by highly experienced and competent men.

Only nine States, of which California is one, possess what Mr. McGee calls 'the most refined administrative organization', i.e. a separate Department of Corrections. It is not altogether easy to understand the complicated set-up developed in California since the Prison Reorganization Act of 1944, but it is a development well worth the most careful study as it has transformed the Californian penal system from one of the most backward into one of the most advanced and centralized organizations in the United States. In the words of the centenary number of the *San Quentin News* (3rd July, 1952), the prison newspaper written by inmates, 'a completely new concept of penology in California came into being with the formation of the Department of Corrections eight years ago'. The Department consists of the following components.[1] (1) the actual Department, headed by the Director; (2) the Board of Corrections, which has 11 members and serves as a co-ordinating council for the Department; (3) the Adult Authority, with 5 members; (4) the Youth Authority, with three members, which is, however, not administratively responsible to the Director and whose activities are rather outside the scope of this paper; (5) the Board of Trustees of the Californian Institution for Women. In addition, there is a Correctional Industries Commission which will be discussed later on. While the functions of the first of these components, i.e. the Department of Corrections itself, would seem to require no further explanation, apart from the fact that it is not a collegiate body—the Reports which it issues are those of the Director, not those of a Commission—some additional details about the Board of Corrections and the Adult Authority seem to be called for. The Board acts mainly as an advisory, policy making

[1] McGee (see note 1, p. 169), p. 82; California Department of Corrections, Biennial Report, 1949–50, p. 4; Biennial Report, 1951–2, p. 6.

and correlating Agency for the Department. Under the Chairmanship of the Director, it consists of the five members of the Adult Authority, the three members of the Youth Authority, two members of the Board of Trustees of the California Institution for Women and two other 'qualified persons appointed by the Governor with the advice and consent of the Senate'. In addition, it has two further statutory functions: to advise cities and counties on jail and detention facilities and 'to make a study of the entire subject of crime, with particular reference to conditions in California'. An analogous body in this country would have to consist of members of the Prison Commission, the Children's Department, the Central After-Care Association, with the addition of a few private citizens, and there may be some similarity with the Home Office Advisory Council as far as the study of crime is concerned. The Governor appoints special Commissions charged with the study of specific subjects such as 'Organized Crime', 'Narcotics', and there is co-operation in this respect with the Universities. Of even greater interest are the functions of the Adult Authority. They are fixed by statute as follows:[1] (1) To serve as members of the Board of Corrections; (2) in collaboration with the Director of Corrections to study each prisoner committed to a State prison and to determine the institution or camp to which the individual is to be transferred; (3) to handle all matters concerned with the determination of length of sentence and release of prisoners; (4) to direct the administration of the State Bureau of Paroles; (5) to have other responsibilities, for example, the determination and forfeiture of credits or the forfeiture of earnings for misconduct in prison or camp, the restoration of civil rights of inmates and parolees; and (6) to serve as an advisory pardon board to the Governor on matters of executive clemency. From this, it becomes clear that the Adult Authority has been given certain very important functions exercised in this country by the Courts, the Prison Commission, the Central After-Care Association, and the Home Secretary respectively. First, as all prison sentences in California, except life sentences, are indeterminate, the actual length has to be fixed by the Adult Authority which regards the 'equalization of punishment' as one of its essential tasks. 'Wide variations in the sentencing policies of courts played a major role

[1] See *The Adult Authority. Principles, Policies and Programme*, fifth printing (Sacramento, June, 1952).

in transferring the fixing of terms from the courts to a single administrative board, such as the Adult Authority.' This is a very general problem on which so much has been written that no further discussion is called for on this particular occasion.[1] While the fixing of the length of sentence encroaches on the functions of the judges, several very important duties which, in this country, are the responsibility of the Prison Commission have been allocated to the Adult Authority, in particular the classification of the available Institutions, the study and classification of prisoners and their allocation to individual Institutions. Such so-called 'transfer approvals' alone numbered nearly 22,000 in the two-year period 1950 to 1952. Moreover, the Authority is competent to make rules concerning prison discipline. One might perhaps say that the Adult Authority is a quasi-judicial or quasi-legislative rather than an administrative agency, except for its work as the Board of Parole. It is only too obvious that in view of these overlapping responsibilities the closest and most harmonious co-operation is required between the authority and the Department of Corrections—co-operation which is regarded as safeguarded by the provisions of the Act of 1944.[2] In any case, the merits of any organization of this kind have to be judged by its achievements, and nobody can deny that they are outstanding. Apart from the rightly famous Forestry and similar Camps, an efficient classification system has been established with two Centres, San Quentin in the North and Chino in the South, under a Bureau of Classification and Treatment headed by that eminent scholar and administrator, Dr. Norman Fenton. The centre at San Quentin, it is true, has to work at present in very cramped conditions, but it will soon be more comfortably housed. Whereas, generally speaking, the distribution of professional staff, i.e. in particular psychologists, sociologists, counsellors, etc., is very uneven in American prisons, the Californian Classification Centres and corresponding Institutions in New Jersey and other States seem to be well supplied with them, and I should like to draw special attention to the advantages of having not only psychologists and social workers but also a sprinkling of sociologists in Classification Centres and some of the larger receiving Institutions. The outstanding work of sociologists

[1] See Hermann Mannheim, *Criminal Justice and Social Reconstruction* (London, Routledge & Kegan Paul Ltd. 1946), 227 et seq.
[2] See p. 3 of the publication in note 1, p. 176.

such as Donald Clemmer, author of *The Prison Community* and now Commissioner of Correction for Washington, D.C., of Dr. Lloyd E. Ohlin in Illinois, and others, bears witness of this.

IV. THE JAIL

One of the most mysterious sections of the American prison system is the Jail. In modern penological literature[1] it has received its generous share of condemnation which is no doubt amply deserved, although in recent times the regular inspections by the Federal Bureau of Prisons and other similar measures on the part of individual States should have done much to improve matters. My personal observations are far too limited to add anything of value to what is generally known. In view of the wealth of material on so many other subjects the absence of any accurate information on the number of such Jails and of their inmates is striking. The most reliable estimate seems to be that, as there are 3,100 counties in U.S.A. and as each county has at least one jail, there must be at least 3,100 County Jails in the whole of the States.[2] Many counties, of course, have more than one jail, and there are in addition City Jails, Workhouses, Police lock-ups, and so on. The number of persons serving short sentences in these Institutions in the course of one year is estimated at approximately threequarters of a million. 'An additional very large but unknown number is held in jail for a few hours or a few days and released without actual commitment'.[3] Much has in fact been done to improve physical conditions. The City and County Jail in Eugene (the seat of the State University of Oregon) for example, is a new and entirely adequate structure, and the only serious criticism one could make was the indiscriminate mixing, without any employment, of people of different ages and probably very different mental make-up. During my stay in Philadelphia one of the big local newspapers published an article headed 'Treat Inmates of County Prisons as Human Beings', maintaining that, in spite of repeated representa-

---

[1] See Barnes and Teeters, *New Horizons in Criminology* (New York, Prentice-Hall Inc., 1943), Chapter XXXV: Roberts J. Wright, 'The Jail and Misdemeanant Institutions' (Chapter XX of *Contemporary Correction*, see above note 1, p. 169); Roy Casey. 'Catchall Jails', *The Annals of the American Academy of Political and Social Service*, Vol. 293, May 1954, pp. 28 et seq.

[2] Wright, op cit., p. 312.

[3] Minimum Jail Standards recommended by the State of California Board of Corrections (revised edition, May, 1952), p. 5.

AMERICAN PRISONS

tions on the part of the Superintendent, conditions in one of the large Philadelphia County Prisons had 'approached the stockyard level.[1] It has to be noted that this particular prison receives a number of boys of sixteen and seventeen years of age and also mentally sick persons who have been difficult and for whom no other place can be found. (To the large numbers of juveniles passing through the Jails of Oregon attention was drawn earlier on.) I did not see this prison and cannot judge, but another similar Institution in Philadelphia, the Holmesburg County Prison—the scene of the so-called 'Holmesburg Tragedy' of 1938[2]—certainly deserved no such adverse criticism, interesting though it was in other respects. Built towards the end of the last century, Holmesburg looks like a fortress. Housing in its ten wings more than 700 Negroes and more than 300 white prisoners, it is a classical example of the star-fish type prison and can comfortably be overlooked from the centre. It receives by no means only short-termers as one might expect a County Jail to do. By an Act of 1860, the Courts have been given authority in the case of 112 different crimes to sentence an offender for long terms either to the Penitentiary or to the County Prison,[3] with the consequence that it depends on their discretion whether the State or the City has to bear the financial burden and also whether the case appears in the prison statistics or not. As pointed out in *Contemporary Correction*, this may to some extent explain the low official rate of the Pennsylvanian prison population.[4] In 1952 there were in fact nearly 800 prisoners in Holmesburg serving sentences of two years or longer, many of them for very serious crimes. There were even a number of condemned men at Holmesburg, one of them, I was told, awaiting the chair already for seven years, but all alike cheerfully mixing with the other prisoners and no doubt confidently expecting a reprieve. Most of the prisoners are there on indeterminate sentences, but some serve fixed terms, and in the Record Book I noticed two cases of false fire alarm, the one sentenced to 30 days, the other to two years. Altogether, Holmesburg seems to be not at all bad if used for short sentences, but for

[1] *The Philadelphia Inquirer*, 10th July, 1953.
[2] See Barnes and Teeters, op cit., p. 586.
[3] See also *The Court and Correctional System of the State of Pennsylvania* (published by the Penal Affairs Division of the Pennsylvania Citizens Association, Philadelphia 7, June, 1952), p. 16.
[4] Henry D. Sheldon, Correctional Statistics in *Contemporary Correction*, p. 30.

IMPRESSIONS OF A CRIMINOLOGIST

long-termers the absence of any educational and treatment programme and of adequate employment (on this see later) are serious handicaps.

V. THE EMPLOYMENT POSITION

On account of restrictive legislation, generally known as the Hawes-Cooper Act of 1929 and the Ashurst-Sumners Act of 1935 in the Federal field, and of narrowly conceived State Use laws, the employment position is, on the whole, highly unsatisfactory in American prisons. As I said before, in the Eastern Penitentiary real work is available only for about 5 per cent of the inmates. In Holmesburg there is work only for three hours per day; hundreds of men are doing 'maintenance', which usually means fifteen minutes daily scrubbing, and another three hours are spent in the Exercise Yard; there are, however, a Cannery and a Farm attached to the prison. San Quentin, which possesses good workshops but whose Jute Mill was destroyed by fire in 1951, has about 700 unemployed men spending the days idly in the Exercise Yard or in their cells. A new Textile Mill has been built, however, which will occupy 500 men. In Chino, the open prison or rather 'Institution for Men', in Southern California, justly famous for the splendid work of its Warden, Kenneth Scudder,[1] full employment is available on a large farm and in workshops and camps. This may be the place to comment on other aspects of this Institution. Notwithstanding its large size and the perhaps not altogether welcome presence on its grounds of a maximum security Reception-Guidance Centre, the atmosphere at Chino—mainly thanks to the remarkable personality of Warden Scudder—is relaxed and friendly; the excellent facilities for family visits on Saturdays and Sundays deserve special mention.

State Use laws may be formulated in different ways, some of them permitting the sale of prison goods only to State Institutions, others in addition to public bodies such as County or City Institutions; some of them backed by compulsory purchase legislation, others not.[2] Consequently, the amount of harm done by these statutes may vary considerably. In the face of such difficulties the persistent efforts made by various State Departments of Correc-

[1] See above note 2, p 170, and the shorter description of Chino by Scudder, *The Annals of the American Academy of Political and Social Science*, Vol. 293, p. 79).

[2] See Frank T. Flynn, Employment and Labour in *Contemporary Correction*, p. 244.

AMERICAN PRISONS

tions to secure at least a minimum of productive work deserve high praise. To give a few illustrations of this unending battle, the Governor of New Jersey has recently had to veto a bill which would have limited the printing work done in State Institutions to the use of hand-fed printing presses. 'If we were to depart from the freedom of prison management to select the manner in which prisoners are to be trained with respect to printing', the Governor writes, 'it would be perfectly logical to accept comparable restraints with respect to other products.'[1] In California, a Correctional Industries Commission was established by the legislature in 1947, consisting of the Director of Corrections as Chairman and six members appointed by the Governor, two representing organized labour, two representing industry, and one each for agriculture and the general public.[2] This Commission, apparently modelled on the lines of the Federal Prison Industries, Inc., seems to be doing excellent public relations work, for example, by publishing informative literature to sell to industry, labour and general public the idea that productive employment simply *has* to be found for prisoners.[3] No productive enterprise involving a gross annual production value of more than $25,000 can be established in prisons without the approval of this Commission after a public hearing. It is interesting to note that, according to calculations published by the Department of Corrections, the distribution of the Californian prison population with regard to employment is as follows: 30 per cent in productive enterprises; 35 per cent in maintenance and housekeeping services; 25 per cent in full-time, general and vocational education; and the remaining 10 per cent unemployable because of physical or mental handicaps.[4] Comparing this with the distribution published by the Prison Commission for England and Wales of the prison population in this country in 1952, we find certain similiarities and certain differences:[5] The

---

[1] See *The Welfare Reporter* (Official Publication, New Jersey Department of Institutions and Agencies, August–October, 1953), p. 3.
[2] Its activities are described in the Biennial Reports, e.g., 1951–2, pp. 21 et seq., and more fully now by Richard A. McGee, *The Annals of the American Academy of Political and Social Science*, Vol. 293.
[3] *How Prisoners can become Community Assets* (Sacramento, 1953), 'Why a Textile Mill at San Quentin State Prison'.
[4] Biennial Report 1951–2, p. 33, *How Prisoners can become Community Assets*, p. 10.
[5] 'Report of the Commissioners of Prisons for the year 1952' (H.M.S.O., 1953, Cmd. 8948), p. 49.

IMPRESSIONS OF A CRIMINOLOGIST

'non-effectives' number 11–12 per cent here against the 10 per cent in California; those engaged in 'domestic' work, which probably corresponds to 'maintenance and housekeeping', number 20 per cent (against 35 per cent), but no less than 68–69 per cent are productively employed in this country against only 30 per cent), whereas there is no counterpart here to the 25 per cent in full-time education. If we should have to include the Prison Commission's category 'Building Services' as 'maintenance' under 'domestic', the latter group would number 28 per cent instead of 20, while those in productive employment would be reduced from 68–69 to 60 or 61 per cent, which would still be twice as much as in California.

Earnings of those productively employed in American prisons are high. According to my notes, they ran to 15 dollars per month in San Quentin and the Eastern Penitentiary, somewhat lower at Graterford, but up to 30 dollars in some of the Forestry Camps. Tobacco is often provided free of charge and in unlimited quantities.

VI. EDUCATION

The figure just given of 25 per cent of Californian prisoners engaged in full-time education naturally turns our attention to this subject. Partly for its own sake, and partly because it is impossible in present circumstances to find work for all employable prisoners, education has gained a very prominent place in American prison administration, and a considerable volume of special literature, including a periodical, the Journal of Correctional Education, is devoted to the subject.[1] To a large extent, education not only supplements prison labour but has become a substitute for it. For illiterates or semi-illiterates, who are stated to number 10–25 per cent of the prison population,[2] it may even be compulsory in the sense that such prisoners are not paroled before they have learned to read and write. Some prisons, such as the Eastern Penitentiary and Graterford, rely on inmate teachers and correspondence courses; others, such as San Quentin, more on outside teachers. Personally, I regard the introduction of full-time or half-day

[1] Bulletin No. 3 of a useful new periodical *Correctional Research. A Publication of the United Prison Association of Massachusetts,* July, 1953, is a special number on Prison Education and surveys the whole development of the subject.
[2] *Correctional Research,* p. 4.

AMERICAN PRISONS

education as an extremely important development, and it may well be asked whether this might not be more valuable for many prisoners than, for example, 'domestic' work which in some cases is probably not much more than a high-sounding name for complete idleness. It is true that in prisons where well-paid work is available a prisoner may be torn between the attraction of educational classes and the lure of earning money; and it was admitted at Graterford that in such cases men sometimes drop their class studies to accept paid employment. The ideal compromise, recommended by the American Prison Association, would seem to be a 'split schedule' for prisoners likely to benefit from education as much as, or more than, from ordinary work, i.e. production or maintenance work for one half day and education for the other half. It would be a mistake, of course, to assume that the educational system has reached a high level everywhere in American prisons—'in the vast majority of penal institutions, especially the County and City Jails' it has recently been stated, 'there is little or nothing done that can be called education by any stretch of the imagination.'[1]

VII. PRISON RIOTS

The unprecedented wave of prison riots which the American Prison System has been experiencing since 1951—during the five months of my stay there were riots in at least three States, Oregon, Minnesota and New Mexico, and 24 riots have been counted in the course of one year—has led to a great deal of heart-searching and public discussion which will no doubt speed up many long-overdue reforms. It is one of the striking features of the situation that these riots have occurred not only in notoriously backward States but also in some of those possessing the most advanced prison systems and leadership in the whole of the United States, notably in New Jersey and to a minor degree even California. The matter has been considered with complete frankness by a special Committee of the American Prison Association, and also by some of the directly concerned administrators such as Sanford Bates, and in the official reports which I have seen there has been no attempt to do any white-washing. The two most specious attempts to explain these riots as happenings for which the prison system

[1] *Correctional Research*, p. 12, quoting from an article by Arthur L. Beeley (Utah).

IMPRESSIONS OF A CRIMINOLOGIST

was not really responsible have, it seems, largely been discarded. I am referring, in the first place, to the theory of imitation or contagion, meaning that once there is a riot somewhere others will necessarily follow in other prisons even where there are no real grounds for it. Contagion may well help to spread prison riots, but only as a contributory factor working on an already well-prepared soil. Secondly, there was the idea that there is now a new, and more dangerous, type of criminal in American prisons who is responsible for all the trouble. In former days, it was said, prisons were full of safe-crackers, bank robbers, and other reasonable men who could be relied upon not to do anything foolish; now, however, the era had come of sex offenders, psychopaths and similarly unstable people who do not know how to behave in prison. Occasionally, it was also pointed out that the period of the riotings coincided with the election campaign and that prisoners whose fate is so much dependent on party politics are more deeply interested in political changes than ordinary citizens.[1] It is now realized that even if there should be some truth in these two explanations it cannot be the whole truth and that the most important causal factors have to be found within the prison system itself.[2] To the European observer, one of the most striking features, especially in the big Jackson riot, is the presence of press representatives on the scene of the disturbances. While the Jackson riot was in progress and negotiations were taking place between

[1] 'Why did it happen? The Riot at Jackson Prison' by John Bartlaw Martin. *Saturday Evening Post*, 6th June, 1953, and following numbers. This is an exceptionally illuminating account of one of the most dangerous outbreaks. See now the same author's book *Break down the Walls* (London, Victor Gollancz Ltd., 1955). On the Jackson riot see also Vernon Fox, 'L'apaisement d'une revolte de prisonniers', *Revue de Science Criminelle et de Droit Penal Comparé*. July–September, 1953.

[2] Of the large literature on these riots the following publications deserve special attention: 'A Statement concerning Causes, Preventive Measures, and Methods of Controlling Prison Riots and Disturbances', prepared by the Committee on Riots under the Auspices of the American Prison Association, May, 1953, *The Prison Journal*, Vol. XXXIII, No. 1, April, 1953: 'Prison Riots . . . Why?' (containing contributions by James V. Bennett, Walter M. Wallack, Negley K. Teeters, and others); 'The Significance of Prison Riots': An address delivered at the general opening session of the National Probation and Parole Association in Cleveland by Commissioner Sanford Bates, 28th May, 1953; 'Behind the Prison Riots', by Frank T. Flynn, *The Social Service Review*, Vol. XXVII, No. 1, March, 1953; Austin H. MacCormick, *The Annals of the American Academy of Political and Social Science*, May, 1954; Paul Cornil, International Penal and Penitentiary Foundation, 2nd Bulletin, Melun, 1953, pp. 12–17.

members of the prison staff and the ringleaders several journalists and press photographers were present, asked questions and were requested by the ringleaders not only to give the widest possible publicity to their grievances but also to witness their solemn surrender. In fairness to American prison administrators one should, I suggest, give full credit to Sanford Bates's point that all these riots could happen mainly because of the exceptional freedom of movement enjoyed by American prisoners within the Institution and especially because of the system of feeding prisoners together in large mess halls. However, this can be merely a facilitating factor, not a causal one, as few people are likely to riot just because they have a chance of doing so. Is there any real danger, many observers will ask themselves, that as the penalty for these riots freedom of movement will be drastically curtailed? I do not think so—on the contrary, one can confidently expect that the principal result of the riots will be a speeding up of essential reform work.

In the Report issued by the American Prison Association the following are regarded as the fundamental factors in the genesis of these riots: '(1) inadequate financial support (i.e. of progressive prison administration), and official and public indifference; (2) sub-standard personnel; (3) enforced idleness; (4) lack of professional leadership and professional programmes; excessive size and over-crowding of institutions; (5) political domination and motivation of management; unwise sentencing and parole practices.' On most of these points I have already made some observations, but one or two brief comments may be needed on some of the others. 'Unwise sentencing and parole practices', for example: in spite of recent improvements, sentences are still too long and prisoners are still kept inside much too long. Sentences are too long in some cases because of the high minimum fixed by the law. In the State of Washington, e.g., the minimum sentence for an habitual criminal cannot be fixed at less than fifteen years, though the Board of Prison Terms and Paroles has power to reduce it after seven years have been served.[1] The length of the sentences imposed is, of course, no indication of the period actually served. When we read in the 'New York Times' of the 11th August, 1953, of the case of a man serving a 199-year sentence for aiding and

[1] State of Washington: Ninth Biennial Report of the Board of Prison Terms and Paroles', 1950–2, p. 13.

IMPRESSIONS OF A CRIMINOLOGIST

abetting another prisoner to escape from prison we strongly suspect that only part of it will be spent in jail, and the same will happen in the case of other slightly less extravagant sentences. Even so, when we read in the *New York Times* of the 5th August, 1953, of the death, of hardening of the arteries, of 'Sing Sing's forgotten man' who had spent 38 years there for homicide under the influence of drink, we feel—although we should not judge without knowing all the circumstances of the case—that the hardening of the arteries may not have been all on his side. Whereas in England and Wales in 1951 only 20 prisoners were received on *sentences* of more than 10 years, in the United States, in 1946, 1,219 felony prisoners were released after *serving* more than 10 years.[1]

A recently published official survey of the prison population of the State of New Jersey[2] gives, among others, the following interesting figures: In the period 1949-53 of a total of 3,653 prisoners, 21 per cent received, under the system of relatively indeterminate sentences, *minimum* sentences of five years and over. In England and Wales, in the years 1951 and 1952 the percentage of prisoners receiving fixed sentences of 5 years and over was 1·2.[3] It has to be borne in mind, though, that New Jersey prisoners classified as first offenders can be paroled after serving their minimum or one-third of the Court imposed maximum, whichever the lesser, which makes discharges possible in some cases even before the minimum (less good conduct time) has been served. As recidivists have to serve more than one-third of their maximum, it can safely be assumed, however, that sentences actually served, are, on an average, much longer in New Jersey than in England. Altogether, one feels that there are too many people in American prisons. Even leaving aside the Jail population, 167,374 persons were in American prisons at the end of 1952, as compared with 22,600 in England and Wales, which is approximately twice as many in proportion to population. The same applies even to California and New Jersey with roughly one per 1,000 of the population in prison against one per 2,000 in this country.

[1] 'Report of the Commissioners of Prisons for 1952', p. 183; Mabel Elliott, *Crime in Modern Society* (see note 5, p. 170, above); Paul Cornil, *Revue de Droit Penal et de Criminologie*, April, 1949, p. 5.

[2] *Two Thousand State Prisoners in New Jersey* (a statistical picture by Emil Frankel, Chief, Bureau of Social Research, May, 1954), p. 6.

[3] 'Report of the Commissioners of Prisons for 1951 (Cmd. 8692) and 1952 (Cmd. 8948), Table VIII.

AMERICAN PRISONS

Although the far more serious character of crime in U.S.A. should not be overlooked, one feels that, given an adequate supply of trained probation officers, probation might well be more widely applied.

'Sub-standard personnel' is also included in the American Prison Association's list as one of the factors responsible for the riots. While I am not competent to challenge this verdict of the most authoritative body on this subject, I am anxious to pay full tribute to the many fine and devoted members of the various administrations I have met in the course of my travels, from top-ranking executives down to simple guards and drivers, and also to the persistent efforts to develop suitable training schemes for prison personnel. The many 'Correctional Employees' Training Manuals' and similar publications issued in recent years by the Californian Department of Corrections bear witness to the competence and the spirit in which this difficult problem is being tackled. In his interesting recent book, *The Irony of American History*, Reinhold Niebuhr refers to Alexis de Tocqueville's scathing criticism of the 'troublesome and garrulous patriotism' of the Americans he had met in the course of his visit.[1] Every country produces people who are complacent and refuse to consider the possibility that they may be wrong. I have found no unduly high proportion of such persons in U.S.A., and on the other hand I have met many thoughtful and even diffident men who were most earnestly searching for the truth, men who were asking themselves, and others, whether they were on the right track or whether some radical re-thinking may be required in American prison administration. In some States, as I have tried to show, such radical re-thinking and re-making is already taking place. In due course, the other States will follow suit.[2]

This still leaves at least two regrettable gaps in my story: the Women's Prisons and the Federal Prison System. Of the former I will only say that those I have seen were good. Of Federal Prisons I have seen only Alcatraz which is in no way typical and will probably soon be closed—therefore I cannot judge. Even from the

[1] R. Niebuhr, *The Irony of American History* (London, Nisbet, 1952), p. 24.
[2] Particularly heart-searching is the recently published volume, to which repeated references have been made above, 'Prisons in Transformation', edited by Thorsten Sellin, *The Annals of the American Academy of Political and Social Science*, May, 1954. See especially the contributions by Austin H. Mac-Cormick, Richard A. McGee, and Lloyd W. McCorkle and Richard R. Korn.

IMPRESSIONS OF A CRIMINOLOGIST

distance, however, I have been impressed by the large number of leading administrators in the State Services who had gained their experience and reputation in the Federal Service. The progress made in the State Prison Systems is largely due to their inspiration. American experiences thus amply confirm the lesson learnt in this country since 1877, and before, that without a centralized régime no real progress is possible in prison administration.

NOTE ON BRITISH COLUMBIA

The foregoing account of my impressions of American Prisons would be incomplete without a few additional sentences on an all-too brief visit to Vancouver. An invitation from the John Howard Society of British Columbia to give a lecture on recent developments in the English penal and reformatory system provided a most welcome opportunity to see the principal institutions of that beautiful part of Canada. Under the expert guidance of Dr. C. W. Topping, Professor of Sociology in the University of British Columbia and well-known pioneer of penal reform in his country, the Federal Penitentiary at New Westminster, the Oakalla Prison Farm, with its Young Offenders' Unit, and the Borstal Institution New Haven were seen. The main impression received was one of slow, but steady and determined progress, recently accelerated by the publication of the Report of the Reform Commission of 1950. The most difficult problems of the British Columbian penal system, as presented in that Report and in the Annual Reports of the Inspector of Gaols and the John Howard Society,[1] are overcrowding, lack of classification, inadequate facilities for staff training, and drug addiction and alcoholism. The extent of these two last-mentioned evils may be seen from the following figures:[2] in 1950-1, of 4,930 prisoners, 3,108 were classified as 'intemperate' and 392 as 'drug addicts'; there were 3,032 breaches of the Liquor Control Act and 224 breaches of the Narcotic Drug Act, against only 2,230 offences

[1] 'Report of the Commission appointed by the Attorney-General to inquire into the State and Management of the Gaols of British Columbia, 1950,' Victoria B.C., 1951; Annual Report of the Inspector of Gaols for the year ended 31st March, 1952; 'The John Howard Society of British Columbia, Report for 1952, Vancouver.

[2] Annual Report of the Inspector of Gaols, p. 33.

against property. 'There is no special problem more under discussion in British Columbia than that of Narcotic Addiction and Drug distribution,' states the Report for 1952 of the John Howard Society. However, the particularly close collaboration existing between the Prison administration and the University, greatly stimulated by the John Howard Society, has now led, in addition to various administrative reforms, to the sponsoring by the Dominion Government of a Drug Addict Research Project and also to a grant by the Government of British Columbia to the University for the appointment of a full-time lecturer in Criminology and the introduction of a graduate training programme in the subject especially designed for the needs of institutional staffs.[1]

[1] Elmer K. Nelson, junr., 'A new Approach to Graduate Training in Criminology at the University of British Columbia, *The Journal of Criminal Law, Criminology and Police Science*, Vol. 44, No. 4, November–December, 1953, pp. 433–7; and on the whole subject of this Note C. W. Topping, 'The Rise of the New Penology in British Columbia', *The British Journal of Delinquency*, Vol. V, No. 3, January, 1955.

CHAPTER 8

AMERICAN CRIMINOLOGY [1]

A SUBJECT such as 'American Impressions' of a non-American, even if confined to the comparatively limited field of Criminology and to the short span of a five months' visit, can be tackled only by applying a very rigid selection. Having given some of my impressions of 'American Prisons' in an address to the Howard League for Penal Reform some time ago,[2] I now propose to concentrate on certain aspects of recent American criminological research. In view of the extremely strong influence which American Criminology has been exercising on its European counterpart, it is a matter of legitimate interest to us not only to enquire what have been, in the thirty years of its triumphant growth, the principal subjects of American criminological research, but also to consider whether any significant changes have occurred in the post-war period in its character and direction.

As far as I can see there have been in the main eight such topics, most of them of a predominantly sociological nature. As in this country, less effort than on the European Continent has been devoted in the United States to biological research in Criminology, and the crimino-biologists such as Ernest Hooton and William Sheldon, in spite of the considerable reputation acquired by the latter, have remained comparatively isolated figures. The psychiatrists, mostly psycho-analysts, and the psychologists have been concentrating on juvenile delinquency and sex crime. In the Universities, with the exception of Harvard University and of the School of Criminology of the University of California at Berkeley, most of the teaching in Criminology is done in the Departments of

[1] Based on a paper read on the 28th January, 1954, to the Scientific Group for the Discussion of Delinquency Problems, London, and published in the *British Journal of Sociology*, Vol. V, No. 4, December, 1954.
[2] See *The British Journal of Delinquency*, Vol. IV, No. 4, April, 1954; Chapter 7 above.

AMERICAN CRIMINOLOGY

Sociology. In the words of Thorsten Sellin,[1] 'advanced training in Criminology is practically limited to the Departments of Sociology in the postgraduate schools which prepare for higher degrees', and with reference to hardly any other country could Marshall B. Clinard's statement be made with equal justification that 'American criminology and sociology have developed together'.[2]

The eight main topics of American Criminology, it seems to me, have been, with some considerable overlapping between several of them, the following:

(1) The role of culture conflict, with special reference to the criminality of foreign immigrants and their children and of Negroes.
(2) The ecology of crime and the study of the delinquency area, with particular emphasis on the sociological factors in juvenile delinquency.
(3) Professional and white-collar crime.

(these three topics demonstrating the dominant part played by group factors in crime)

(4) Sexual crimes.
(5) Psychological and psychiatric factors in juvenile delinquency.
(6) Follow-up and prediction studies.
(7) The methodology of criminological research.
(8) In the field of Penology: prison reform.

To mention only a few of the most outstanding workers in these fields, it is to the contributions of sociologists such as Thorsten Sellin on culture conflict; of Clifford Shaw and the Chicago School on delinquency areas; of Edwin H. Sutherland and his associates, notably Marshall B. Clinard, on white-collar crime; to those of the sociologists Ernest Burgess and Lloyd E. Ohlin and in particular of the lawyer-sociologist Sheldon Glueck and the educationist Eleanor T. Glueck on prediction; and to the methodological spade work of the sociologists W. I. Thomas, Walter A. Reckless and

[1] Thorsten Sellin, *The Sociological Study of Criminality* (General Report for Sociology presented at the Second International Congress of Criminology in Paris, September, 1950); *The Journal of Criminal Law and Criminology*, Vol. 41, No. 4, November–December, 1950, p. 415.
[2] Marshall B. Clinard, 'Sociologists and American Criminology', *The Journal of Criminal Law and Criminology*, Vol. 41, No. 5, January–February, 1951, p. 550.

IMPRESSIONS OF A CRIMINOLOGIST

again Thorsten Sellin that we are primarily indebted. Most of the research on sex crime has been done by Kinsey and his collaborators, by psycho-analysts such as Ben Karpman; by various State Commissions and by the Langley Porter Clinic in San Francisco (see below); and on the sociological-legal side by Sutherland and Paul W. Tappan. The American literature on juvenile delinquency has become almost too vast for any individual names to be singled out for special praise, but William Healy and Augusta Bronner's pioneer studies have to be mentioned together with the more recent work of Maud A. Merrill, Tappan, Edwin Powers and Helen Witmer and in particular of the Gluecks. Lastly, American prison reform, apart from the publications of a number of brilliant practical administrators, owes perhaps more than to any other theorist to the always stimulating writings of Negley K. Teeters.

This short list can have as its object merely to recall to our minds some of the undisputed highlights of American crimonilogical literature, and it will also be appreciated that the pre-eminence given to sociological research, while reflecting the general trend of American Criminology and the personal bias of the writer, is in no way intended to detract from the value of the contributions made by representatives of other disciplines.

Most of these pioneer researches—with the only exception perhaps of certain highly theoretical methodological studies—had their origin in some very real, and in most instances justified, feeling of alarm, either on the part of the research workers concerned or on that of the American people as a whole; alarm at the excessive crime rate of the United States which was at first attributed to the foreign immigrant and the Negro; at the highly criminogenic conditions in the slum areas of their big cities; at the activities of boot-leggers, racketeers, gamblers and ordinary gangsters, and more recently of white-collar criminals; concern about the increase in sexual crime and about the failure of prisons and reformatories to deter or reform the criminal. To the superficial observer it might appear that all these researches were nothing but the natural repercussion in the scientific field of the feelings which had been agitating the man in the street, that in other words the scientific criminologist had throughout simply been carrying out the jobs he had been told to do by public opinion. Actually, the position has, in many instances, been different, and American criminologists have in fact been swimming more often against

AMERICAN CRIMINOLOGY

than with the current of public opinion, shaping it rather than sheepishly following in its wake. American criminologists, in these past thirty years, have shown a great deal of ingenuity and of courage in the selection of their subjects and in the way in which they have tackled them—courage of that remarkable and all too rare brand for which the German language has coined the term *'Civil-courage'*. In our admiration for the refinements of their methodology, in our envy of the lavish financial resources at the disposal of some of them we may have been ignoring this fact. It was not only laborious, it was also courageous and unpopular to prove that it was in fact not the immigrant but the American-born white who was largely responsible for the high crime rate; that American society rather than the Negro had to bear the blame for much of Negro crime; that the existence of 'delinquency areas' was inexcusable in the wealthiest of all countries; that the rate not, as had been commonly believed in the pre-Glueck period, of success but of failure in some American Reformatories after the first World War was around 80 per cent; that panic legislation of the kind passed by many States of U.S.A. against the 'psychopathic sex offender' was unwise and harmful. And, lastly, it may have required more than just ordinary courage to show, as the late Edwin H. Sutherland, did that some of the most powerful American business enterprises were in fact 'habitual criminals', persistently flouting the law of the land. Sutherland's 'White Collar Crime' did more than add just another piece of research to the pool of criminological knowledge—it made articulate the vague feeling of some of us that much of our work so far had been lop-sided and our conclusions misleading.[1]

This, roughly, is the background against which I wish to discuss the second of the two questions posed before: Has there been any fundamental change in the character and spirit of American Criminology, have those proud achievements of its pioneering epoch been lost in the turmoil of the post-war period? My answer is in the negative. While the heroic and pioneering age of American Criminology may have passed, while its pace of progress may have slowed down, there has been no fundamental change of

---

[1] See, e.g., Hermann Mannheim, *Social Aspects of Crime in England between the Wars* (London, George Allen & Unwin, Ltd., 1940), Chapter VII; *Criminal Justice and Social Reconstruction* (International Library of Sociology and Social Reconstruction, London, Routledge & Kegan Paul, 1946).

IMPRESSIONS OF A CRIMINOLOGIST

spirit, character, and direction. Naturally, in some instances what twenty or thirty years ago had been a novel undertaking calling for all the determination and originality of mind of the pioneer has become a routine procedure to which the public and even the administrator whose work may be subjected to searching criticism have grown accustomed. Following the example of Sanford Bates who, as Commissioner of Correction of the State of Massachusetts, in the nineteen-twenties purposely opened the door to the Trojan horse by inviting the Gluecks to make their follow-up study of inmates of the Concord Reformatory, American penal administrators and judges have shown remarkable open-mindedness in not only tolerating but actively encouraging scientific investigations which were likely to, and actually did, result in reports highly critical of their own work. As a reviewer of the recently published, officially sponsored, study of the New York City Children's Court by Professor Alfred J. Kahn of Columbia University aptly remarks,[1] this attitude is 'a good example of American democracy in action'. It might be added that there have been corresponding examples in this country of late.

Naturally, too, some of those old problems of the pioneering age have meanwhile been solved or in other ways disappeared or at least been deprived of their former significance. As space forbids here to deal with the whole range of the eight main topics listed above I will concentrate on two or three of them.

I. THE CRIMINALITY OF FOREIGN IMMIGRANTS AND OF NEGROES

With the decline in the rate of immigrants and even in the proportion of American-born children of foreign-born parents— within the period between 1915 and 1940 the percentage of such children went down from 41 to 5 of the total and from 1930 to 1940 that of foreign-born to the total white population declined from 22·7 to 9·7 per cent[2]—their crime problem was bound to lose much of its topical interest and urgency. In the State of New Jersey, for example, according to a recent official publication the percentage figure of foreign-born (white) prisoners has declined

---

[1] Dr. E. Preston Sharp, *The Annals of the American Academy of Political and Social Science*, Vol. 293, May, 1954, p. 187, in a review of Alfred J. Kahn, *A Court for Children* (New York, Columbia University Press, 1953).

[2] Mabel A. Elliott and Francis E. Merrill, *Social Disorganization* (New York, Harper & Brothers, 3rd ed., 1950), p. 587.

AMERICAN CRIMINOLOGY

from 42·7 in 1910–14 to 23·2 in 1930–4 and to 6·3 in 1950–3.[1] In 1941, Courtlandt C. van Vechten, in a widely noted paper,[2] drew attention to a resolution passed in 1845 by the 'Native American National Convention', assembled in Philadelphia, to the effect that, while the earlier immigrants had been people of superior quality, victims of political oppression, their successors were the most degraded of the European population. He thereby made it clear that the tendency to play off the older against the more recent immigrants had already been strong a century ago and had little to do with the actual changes that had occurred in the national and racial origin of the American people. It is significant that since 1941 the stream of publications in criminological journals on the seemingly inexhaustible subject of 'crime and the foreign immigrant' has almost completely dried up. Present-day writers, for example Mabel A. Elliott in her excellent textbook,[3] are rather inclined to underline the undesirable and far-reaching political repercussions of the rigid immigration laws passed after the first World War—repercussions which, as she writes, 'did not dawn upon those earnest and misguided congressmen of the post-war twenties'. Marshall B. Clinard, in his important study of the American Black Market during the second World War,[4] stresses that there is no evidence for MacIver's statement that recent immigrants had contributed more than their ordinary share to black market offences. In a study of juvenile delinquency in Baltimore, Bernard Lander shows that, while the Federal Slum Survey of 1903 had found concentrations of delinquency in sections mostly inhabited by foreign-born persons, in 1940 they had become a characteristic of areas of the native-born.[5] Although in recent official investigations of crime in the United States, such as that of the Kefauver Committee, gangster figures bearing non-English

---

[1] *Two Thousand State Prisoners in New Jersey. A Statistical Picture.* By Emil Frankel, Chief, Bureau of Social Research, State of New Jersey Department of Institutions and Agencies. Research Bulletin No. 118, May, 1954, p. 27.
[2] Courtlandt C. van Vechten, 'The Criminality of the Foreign-Born', *The Journal of Criminal Law and Criminology*, Vol. 32, No. 2, July–August, 1941, p. 138.
[3] Mabel A. Elliott, *Crime in Modern Society* (New York, Harper & Brothers, 1952), p. 295, n. 22.
[4] Marshall B. Clinard, *The Black Market* (New York, Rinehart & Co., Inc., 1952), p. 291.
[5] Bernard Lander, *Towards an Understanding of Juvenile Delinquency* (New York, Columbia University Press, 1954), pp. 35–6.

IMPRESSIONS OF A CRIMINOLOGIST

names are very conspicuous, their criminality is no longer, in the same way as it would have been as a matter of course twenty years ago, regarded as the natural and inevitable outcome of their foreign inheritance and of their failure to assimilate to American culture. In the light of its findings, the recommendations of the Kefauver Committee to tighten the Immigration Acts and facilitate denaturalization and deportation of criminals who had entered the country illegally and obtained citizenship papers on perjured applications appear to be nothing but a legitimate aspect of its campaign against big crime without any specific anti-immigrant bias,[1] and the moderate tone of these recommendations can safely be ascribed to the untiring efforts of American criminologists and their colleagues from allied disciplines to dispel erroneous conceptions and overcome old prejudices. The withholding of entry permits to scientists because of suspected communist leanings or for similar reasons lies in an entirely different sphere and outside the criminological field.

While immigration as a topic of criminological studies has retreated to the background, the position is different with regard to Negro crime. As we all know, the Negro Problem, the 'American Dilemma', is one of the most serious difficulties confronting the United States, and the view expressed by the Chicago Commission on Race Relations in their famous Report on the 1921 Race Riot that 'the relation of whites and Negroes in the United States is our most grave and perplexing domestic problem'[2] does not seem to have become out-of-date in the past thirty years. Here as everywhere, however, there is a difference between 'knowing' and seeing for oneself. One has to see and to live for some time in various parts of the States—not necessarily in the Black South—to understand what the Negro problem really means.

There is no need here to repeat all those facts and figures about Negro crime in general which can be found in every up-to-date American textbook on Criminology, not to mention the very comprehensive general sociological literature on the subject, cul-

[1] Senator Kefauver, *Crime in America*. Edited and with an Introduction by Sidney Shalett (London, Victor Gollancz, Ltd., 1952), pp. 25, 170 and in particular 249, where the recommendations of the Committee are reported.
[2] *The Negro in Chicago. A Study of Race Relations and a Race Riot*. By the Chicago Commission on Race Relations (The University of Chicago Press, 1922), p. xxiii.

AMERICAN CRIMINOLOGY

minating in Gunnar Myrdal's classic monograph.[1] Statistically, for most crimes the Negro crime rate is greatly in excess of that of the American white. While according to the Census for 1950 the number of whites in the U.S.A. was preliminarily estimated to be round 135 millions and that of Negroes slightly less than 15 millions, i.e. about 11 per cent,[2] the percentage of arrested Negroes is given in the Uniform Crime Reports for 1952 as slightly more than 25.[3] For certain categories of crime the position is even much more unfavourable for Negroes, for example, for murder and non-negligent manslaughter (829 Negroes arrested in 1952 against 444 whites) and aggravated assault (7,555 against 4,270).[4] It goes without saying that these figures have to be interpreted with more than the customary caution. If they are broken down according to age and sex and considered in the light of the differential rate of arrest and of differential treatment by the Courts and many other discriminating factors,[5] it is more than likely that the actual preponderance of Negro crime over white man's crime will prove to be much smaller than appears from these statistics. The excessively high number of Negroes in prison, to which I am going to refer below, is to some extent, it is officially admitted, due to the fact that they receive longer sentences and are less likely to be released on parole.[6] Another significant factor is that Negroes are greatly under-represented in the police forces.[7] In the case of

[1] Gunnar Myrdal, *The American Dilemma. The Negro Problem and Modern Democracy*, 2 vols. (New York and London, Harper & Brothers Publishers, 1944).
[2] 1950 Census of Population, Preliminary Reports, Series P 6–7, No. 1, quoted from Mabel A. Elliott, *Crime in Modern Society*, p. 297.
[3] Uniform Crime Reports for the United States and its Possessions, issued by the Federal Bureau of Investigation, U.S. Dept. of Justice, Vol. XXIII, No. 2, 1952, p. 117. See also *Encyclopædia of Criminology* (New York, The Philosophical Library, 1949), p. 269, where the arrest rate for 1946 per 100,000 of population is given as 1,938·7 for Negroes and 578·6 for whites.
[4] Uniform Crime Reports, Vol. XXIII, p. 117, Table 46.
[5] See, e.g., Myrdal, *American Dilemma*, Vol. II, pp. 966 et seq.; Guy B. Johnson, 'The Negro and Crime', *The Annals of the American Academy of Political and Social Science*, Vol. 217, September, 1941, pp. 94 et seq.; Mabel A. Elliott, p. 297; Teeters and Reinemann, *The Challenge of Delinquency* (New York, Prentice-Hall, Inc., 1950), p. 115; Hans von Hentig, 'The Criminality of the Negro', *The Journal of Criminal Law and Criminology*, Vol. 30, January–February, 1940, p. 662.
[6] Myrdal, Vol. I, p. 554, II, pp. 976 and 1433, n. 16; Johnson (above, note 5), p. 97. The Attorney General's Survey of Release Procedures, Vol. IV, *Parole* (Department of Justice, Washington), 1939, pp. 310, 319 et seq.
[7] See the comprehensive studies by William M. Kephart, 'The Negro

juveniles, it has also been pointed out that the relative paucity of other means of treatment makes referral to the Juvenile Courts more often imperative for Negro children than for others.[1] Nevertheless, it is probably true that the actual crime rate of Negroes is still higher than that of whites, in particular as it is maintained that crimes committed by Negroes against Negroes are frequently not reported and remain unpunished—a fact which, by the way, may further undermine the Negro's respect for law and order.[2] Much of the higher Negro crime rate has been and can no doubt be explained by reference to such familiar factors as culture conflict, the effect of mass migration of Negroes from the rural South to Northern cities, their lack of familiarity with city life, contamination by white criminals, overcrowding, slum-dwelling, inadequate schooling, and similar handicaps. The extent of this wave of Negro migration to Northern cities may be seen from the following figures: between 1930 and 1945 the Negro population of New York is said to have increased by 67 per cent, that of Chicago by 50 per cent.[3] 'Social organization is generally at a low level among Southern Negroes,' writes Myrdal,[4] 'but disorganization only reaches its extreme when Negroes migrate to cities and to the North.' It is a matter of considerable interest in this connection to learn from the writings of two Southern criminologists, Austin L. Porterfield and Robert H. Talbert, that in the twelve Southern States of U.S.A. the correlation between the proportion of Negroes in the population and the crime rate is strongly negative,[5] a fact from which these two writers rightly conclude that racial factors are not responsible for Negro crime. Their findings have now been confirmed for Baltimore by Bernard Lander who has shown that in areas of the city where the proportion of Negroes

Offender: An Urban Research Project', *American Journal of Sociology*, Vol. 60, July, 1954, pp. 76 et seq., and 'Negro Visibility', *American Sociological Review*, Vol. 19, August, 1954, pp. 462 et seq.

[1] Edward E. Schwartz, *The Annals of the American Academy of Political and Social Science*, Vol. 261, January, 1949, p. 17; Sidney Axelrad, 'Negro and White Male Institutionalized Delinquents', *American Journal of Sociology*, Vol. 57, 1951–2, pp. 569 et seq.

[2] Myrdal, Vol. II, p. 977.

[3] *Encyclopædia of Criminology* (above, note 3, p. 197), p. 274.

[4] Myrdal, Vol. II, p. 977.

[5] Austin L. Porterfield and Robert H. Talbert, *Crime, Suicide and Social Wellbeing* (1948), pp. 31 and 65; and *Mid-Century Crime in our Culture* (1954), pp. 32 and 82 (both publications of the Leo Potishman Foundation, Texas Christian University, Forth Worth, Texas).

is below 50 per cent there is comparatively more Negro delinquency than in areas with over 50 per cent Negroes, with the lowest delinquency rate in districts almost completely black. Tension and delinquency are highest where the two racial groups are nearly equal in strength, whereas the position is more favourable in areas where one of the groups possesses distinct numerical superiority. Lander's conclusion, which seems to be well-founded, is that Negro delinquency is not a function of race as such but a reflection of social instability.[1] John Gunther, in his *Inside U.S.A.*,[2] estimates that of the seven and a half million Negroes now on Southern farms only four will in future be needed—will the North be willing and able to digest the surplus? And how long is the process of social adaptation likely to take? Some years ago, the view was expressed by Walter C. Reckless that the Negro crime rate would probably remain high among the new arrivals from the South, but decline among the older settlers.[3] How far is this prognosis still valid?

In short, there is no lack of convincing explanations of the high Negro crime rate, but they can do very little to relieve the gravity of the situation. To illustrate what I have in mind I should like to present a few facts, most of them admittedly relating to only one of the Northern States, a State with a very high rate of Negro influx from the South, Pennsylvania. At the time of my stay there in 1953, one of the big Philadelphia prisons which I visited, the Eastern Penitentiary, had about 60 per cent Negroes (before the war only 30 per cent); its modern branch, Graterford, had about 50 per cent; a third prison, Holmesburg, about 70 per cent. The Negro population of Philadelphia numbers only 18·1 per cent of the total. The 'National Prisoner Statistics', published at frequent intervals by the Federal Bureau of Prisons, contains no information on colour, but the Census for 1940 gives the national percentage of non-white prisoners (which of course includes not only Negroes) aged 14 years and over as 29·8 per cent,[4] against a general population of 9·6 per cent. According to the New Jersey

[1] Bernard Lander, op. cit. (see note 5, p. 195), pp. 31, 60, 64, 82.
[2] John Gunther, *Inside U.S.A.*, (New York, Harper & Brothers, revised ed. 1951), p. 312.
[3] Walter C. Reckless, *The Etiology of Delinquent and Criminal Behaviour* (Social Science Research Council Bulletin No. 50, 1943), p. 43.
[4] *Contemporary Correction*, edited by Paul W. Tappan (New York, Toronto, London, McGraw-Hill Book Company, Inc., 1951), p. 20.

survey already referred to, while the general male population of the State aged twenty years and over consisted of 93·7 per cent whites and 6·3 per cent non-whites, court commitments to prison of non-whites numbered 44 per cent in the period 1950–3.[1] With regard to the younger generation, when I visited the Philadelphia Juvenile Court, about 80 per cent or more of the juveniles dealt with were Negroes. This may have been accidental, but the following more moderate figures collected from the very informative Annual Report of the Philadelphia Municipal Court for 1951 are bad enough:[2]

Delinquency cases:
Boys—whites 2,723
negroes 2,556 (48 per cent)
Girls—whites 502
negroes 716 (59 per cent)

The juvenile delinquency figures, which show an overall rate of 51 per cent Negro delinquents, have to be read in connection with the figure of 22 per cent Negroes among the population of Juvenile Court age in Philadelphia. This means that of 1,000 white boys only 18 were delinquent, but of 1,000 Negro boys 62. The percentage of recidivists was 36 among white boys and 50 among Negroes, of broken homes 30 against 57, of delinquents 'living with both own parents married to each other and living together' 67 among whites and 42 among Negroes.

To turn to another aspect of the matter, I found racial segregation of some kind or other in all the Pennsylvanian prisons which I visited. Only scanty information on this subject is available for the United States as a whole and, as Professor Teeters found in his survey of fifty-eight Institutions a few years ago, the position differs from State to State.[3] According to Teeters, segregation is the rule with regard to eating and accommodation, but in several large prisons in the North with a high rate of Negroes there is no segregation whatsoever. In Pennsylvanian prisons there are separate wings and separate feeding arrangements for Negro prisoners, but as a rule they mix with the others for work and

[1] See the New Jersey Survey (above, note 1, p. 195), p. 16.
[2] Thirty-eighth Annual Report of the Municipal Court of Philadelphia for the year 1951, pp. 30, 39, 43, 75–6.
[3] Negley K. Teeters in *The Prison World*, May–June, 1952, and May–June, 1953, reprinted in *Criminology. A Book of Readings*. By Clyde B. Vedder, Samuel Koenig, Robert E. Clark (New York, The Dryden Press, 1953), p. 584.

AMERICAN CRIMINOLOGY

exercise. From my observations, for what they are worth, relations between the races seemed to be friendly, but, as an experienced prison psychologist said, 'the situation has to be carefully watched'.

The same need for careful watching also exists with regard to the possibility of race riots outside prisons. They have undoubtedly become much less frequent since that notorious period during and after the first World War, and Gunnar Myrdal, writing about ten years ago, regarded the future outlook as fairly hopeful, at least for the North. Actually, it is reported by the Tuskegee Institute in Alabama that no lynchings have occurred in the United States during the year 1952, though other forms of violence have not declined.[1] That untiring vigilance is the price of progress in this field as in any other may be shown by reference to a report published towards the end of my visit in the *New York Herald Tribune*.[2] According to this report, for the accuracy of which the responsibility has to be left to the newspaper, one-tenth of Chicago's police force had to be ordered out 'to squelch potential racial rioting' at a Federal housing project on the southern edge of Chicago. '750 policemen went on riot duty as roving white mobs, estimated at 1,000, stoned windows, cursed and jeered at the police patrolling the vicinity . . . During the rioting at least five persons were hurt.' And what was the cause of all this turmoil? The arrival on this new housing estate of a Negro family who had been moved in as highly eligible by the Chicago Housing Authority. As a rule, the Housing Authority stated, they moved in several coloured families at a time for safety's sake, but in this case they had not known that the family was coloured. This Chicago incident, by the way, had occurred approximately a month before Professor Brogan, the eminent authority on American matters, in a broadcast talk on 'The Negro in the United States', maintained that nowadays in fact nobody in the United States really minded having a Negro family next door.[3] This coincidence does not of course altogether disprove Brogan's statement. Detailed studies made in recent years by American sociologists of the position in certain Northern cities, such as Minneapolis, have shown that, as the result of the persistent struggle against racial prejudice in conjunction with the

---

[1] *The Times*, 2nd January, 1953. It has now been reported that there have been no lynchings for the past three years in succession (Report of the Fed. Bureau of Investigation, *The Times*, 6th Jan. 1955).

[2] *New York Herald Tribune*, 12th August, 1953.

[3] *The Listener*, 24th September, 1953, p. 491.

IMPRESSIONS OF A CRIMINOLOGIST

housing shortage and a helpful decision of the Supreme Court in 1948, many Americans are becoming less reluctant to accept Negro families as their next-door neighbours.[1] Generalizations, however, will probably remain hazardous for some considerable time. This difficulty, often even impossibility, of obtaining decent accommodation for Negroes was one of the complaints made in very strong and emotional language by a Negro student in a paper on 'Negro Criminality' which he submitted to me at his own initiative. Better housing, as John Gunther and many other American writers have repeated time and again, is one of the most urgent needs of the Negro.[2]

All this does in no way mean that responsible Americans are not deeply concerned about the situation or that nothing is done to reduce its iniquities and dangers. On the contrary, in addition to the truly enormous and most valuable literature to which I have already referred and to the great amount of educational work done by American Universities and Colleges, where courses on race relations are an integral part of sociological teaching, there are many important nation-wide inter-racial organizations such as the N.A.A.C.P., i.e. National Association for the Advancement of Coloured People, and the National Urban League whose aim, among many other objects, is to fight crime among Negroes as well as against Negroes.[3] There are also very active local agencies such as the Philadelphia Fellowship Commission which concerns itself not only with the colour problem but with any kind of racial tension and prejudice. In its monthly Bulletins this Commission publishes lists of individual cases of violence, vandalism, anonymous hate letters, and so on, briefly indicating the kind of action taken. It is a crime-preventing agency in the truest sense of this phrase. On the other hand, it is interesting to note that, according to Professor Mabel A. Elliott, well-intentioned pressure exerted by some of these organizations makes it occasionally impossible for research workers to obtain useful data on minority problems.[4]

[1] Arnold M. Rose, Frank J. Atelsek and Lawrence R. McDonald, 'Neighborhood Reactions to Isolated Negro Residents: an Alternative to Invasion and Succession', *American Sociological Review*, Vol. 18, No. 5, October, 1953, pp. 497 et seq. [2] John Gunther (above, note 2, p. 199), p. 314.
[3] See Myrdal, Vol. II, p. 838; Elliott and Merrill (above, note 2, p. 194), p. 660.
[4] See *Social Problems* (published by the Society for the Study of Social Problems), Vol. I, No. 3, January, 1954.

AMERICAN CRIMINOLOGY

Summing up this part of my observations, I would say that American criminologists and sociologists have done a first-rate job in elucidating the truth regarding the extent and causes of Negro crime; and as recent writings such as those by Porterfield and Talbert show there has been no slackening in this respect. American humanitarians and educationists have been doing their very best to establish a network of preventive agencies to improve race relations and reduce the rate of crime committed by and against Negroes. It is mainly in the penological field, with regard to the institutional treatment of Negro offenders, that not only practical but also theoretical achievement seems to lag somewhat behind. In the first place very little factual information has been published on the treatment of Negroes in Institutions. Apart from the well-known section on the colour problem in Moreno's *Who shall survive?*, apart from Professor Teeters' brief statement on segregation and a few equally brief occasional references to the inadequacy or complete absence of institutional facilities for Negro juvenile delinquents, the subject of segregation in prisons is hardly mentioned in American penological literature. As so little has been done to clarify the facts of the situation it is not surprising that their evaluation should have been equally neglected. A striking contrast seems here to exist between the penological field and other aspects of the American Negro problem. As has been stressed by Frank F. Lee, 'the race relations pattern is not uniform, but varies from one institutional area to another',[1] racial discrimination in his view being strongest in housing and least marked in education. In both these fields much research has been done in recent years and remarkable progress has been achieved in drawing the practical consequences from theoretical clarification—progress culminating in the fundamental decision of the Supreme Court of the United States of the 17th May, 1954, declaring racial segregation in Schools unconstitutional.[2] With regard to segregation in the Armed Forces, there has been the pioneer work of Samuel A.

[1] Frank F. Lee, 'The Race Relations Pattern by Areas of Behaviour in a Small New England Town', *American Sociological Review*, Vol. 19, No. 2, April, 1954, pp. 138 et seq. See also the useful survey of the different levels of 'Discrimination against the Negro' in Elliott and Merrill (above, note 2, p. 194), pp. 642–61; and 'Civic Rights in the Nation's Capital' (Report of a Committee on Civil Rights, 1947), reproduced in H. S. Commager, *Living Ideas in America* (Harper & Brothers, 1951), pp. 424 et seq.

[2] *The Times*, 17th, 18th, 21st and 25th May, 1954; Alastair Buchan in *The Observer*, 23rd May, 1954.

IMPRESSIONS OF A CRIMINOLOGIST

Stouffer and his team,[1] followed by David G. Mandelbaum's monograph[2] and other careful studies showing not only that segregation was wasteful and produced poor fighting qualities, but also that it could be dispensed with without leading to inter-racial friction. As the result, it is stated, separate Negro units are becoming less frequent and Negroes may be assigned to any unit.[3] Corresponding changes may well be taking place in many parts of the United States in prisons, reformatories and institutions for children, but there is no adequate information, and in some States no radical reforms seem to be contemplated. Nobody will be rash enough to maintain that the evidence presented for other institutional fields can, as a matter of course, be applied to racial segregation in prisons where the human material is likely to be inferior and friction more intense than outside. The need for 'careful watching' will certainly remain. It can be argued, however, that research and experiment, based upon the experience of States without segregation, might help to clarify the situation and show how far the others could safely go. Although numerically the problem is very small as compared with that in housing, education, or the Armed Forces, it is the principle that matters rather than the scope of discrimination. At a time when so much emphasis is rightly placed upon improved techniques of classification in penal and reformatory Institutions, segregation on a purely racial basis seems to be the very negation of all the progressive work done in this field. 'American Negroes', writes the distinguished Negro sociologist E. Franklin Frazier in his recent article in *The British Journal of Sociology*,[4] 'have been amalgamated to a large degree with whites and they are acculturated in respect to European culture. But they are not assimilated in American society, since they are regarded as American *Negroes*, seldom even as Negro *Americans*, and they think of themselves as Negroes first and only secondarily as Americans.' Surely, segregation in penal and reformatory Institutions is one of the safest methods not only of preventing assimilation of those who need it most, but also of per-

[1] Samuel A. Stouffer *et al.*, *The American Soldier* (Princeton University Press), Vol. I, 1949, Chapter 10: 'Negro Soldiers'.
[2] David G. Mandelbaum, *Soldier Groups and Negro Soldiers* (University of California Press, 1952).
[3] Mandelbaum, p. 116.
[4] E. Franklin Frazier, 'Theoretical Structure of Sociology and Sociological Research', *British Journal of Sociology*, Vol. IV, No. 4, December, 1953, p. 300.

petuating the feeling of injustice among social groups much larger than those directly concerned.

II. SEXUAL CRIMES AND THE 'PSYCHOPATHIC SEX OFFENDERS LAWS'

A complicated situation has arisen in recent years in the United States with regard to the treatment of sexual offenders—not merely through the inherent complexity of the subject itself, intensified by the baffling diversity and antiquated character of the traditional type of criminal legislation dealing with individual sex offences, but even more, since 1937, through the passing in a considerable number of States of the notorious 'psychopathic sex offenders laws'. Some of this exceptional legislation, enacted under strong public pressure, is ill-considered and, if actually applied, capable of doing serious harm. The nature and intensity of this pressure may be illustrated by the following quotation from Professor Karl M. Bowman's *Review of Sex Legislation and Control of Sex Offenders in the United States*, undertaken as part of the 'California Sexual Deviation Research' (see below):

There is considerable evidence that a substantial change has occurred in public opinion in the United States. Where formerly people agreed that it was better for a hundred guilty persons to escape than for one innocent person to be convicted, now an increasing number of persons say that it is better for one innocent man to be convicted than for one guilty man to escape.[1]

There is no need to go into the details of this widely discussed topic as we are here concerned merely with the attitude of American criminologists towards this change in climate as expressed in certain aspects of the Psychopathic Sex Offenders Laws. Ignoring technical points of detail, the principal criticisms directed against this type of legislation have been: (*a*) their unsuccessful attempts, or complete failure, to provide a practicable legal definition of their basic term 'sexual psychopath'; (*b*) their inability to distinguish between the really dangerous sex criminal and the petty offender who is a nuisance rather than a danger to society; (*c*) their tendency to relax, or completely abandon, certain essential procedural safeguards of individual liberty; (*d*) their failure to provide effective

[1] Karl M. Bowman, *Final Report on Californian Sexual Deviation Research*, March, 1954, p. 34.

IMPRESSIONS OF A CRIMINOLOGIST

facilities for treatment of those detained for indefinite periods; and (*e*) the fact that in a number of States far-reaching measures have been legalized against 'sexual psychopaths' without the requirement of a conviction, or occasionally even a charge, of a criminal offence. This latter device of diverting such measures from the field of the criminal to that of the civil law, by which it had apparently been hoped to make these extraordinary departures from the traditional principles of criminal justice more palatable, has, however, failed to assuage scientific opinion. A determined war has been waged for some years by lawyers and psychiatrists alike against these statutes and the popular misconceptions behind them, with two criminologists, Sutherland and Tappan, among their earliest and most outspoken critics.[1] To their efforts more than to anything else has it probably been due that unprejudiced fact-finding investigation is more and more replacing panic legislation and administration. In a few States, notably Wisconsin,[2] the principle of indefinite detention without conviction of crime has lately been abandoned, and the future seems to belong to State-sponsored researches such as the California Sexual Deviation Research rather than to further panic legislation. As comparatively little seems to be known in this country about the Californian project, carried out by the Langley Porter Clinic in San Francisco and now nearly completed after four years of work, a brief outline of its structure may not be out of place. Headed by a psychiatrist, Professor Bowman, and a sociologist, Professor A. R. Mangus, its chief characteristic is the team approach which has enabled the Clinic to tackle the problem of sex crime from many different angles. The result has been: a largely statistical

---

[1] Edwin H. Sutherland, 'The Diffusion of Sexual Psychopath Laws', *American Journal of Sociology*, Vol. 56, No. 2, September, 1950, pp. 142 et seq.; and 'The Sexual Psychopath Laws', *The Journal of Criminal Law and Criminology*, Vol. 40, January–February, 1950, pp. 443 et seq. Paul W. Tappan, *The Habitual Sex Offender*. Report and Recommendations of the (New Jersey) Commission on the Habitual Sex Offender as formulated by Paul W. Tappan, *Technical Consultant*, 1950. See also Morris Ploscowe, *Sex and the Law*, Chapter VIII (New York, Prentice-Hall, Inc., 1951); T. C. N. Gibbens, 'Recent Trends in the Management of Psychopathic Offenders', *British Journal of Delinquency*, Vol. II, No. 2, October, 1951, pp. 103 et seq.

[2] See Anton Motz, 'Wisconsin's Sexual Deviate Act', *Wisconsin Law Review*, Vol. 1954, No. 2, pp. 324–35, where it is pointed out that the Act of 1947 has now been greatly improved and made workable by requiring a conviction, making the proceedings part of criminal instead of civil or administrative procedure and by eliminating the term 'sexual psychopath'.

and sociological study of sex crime in California, especially in San Francisco; a pioneer study of the child victim of sex offences; psycho-physiological studies of sex deviates; a survey of the existing Psychopathic Sex Offenders Laws and of castration legislation; and an analysis of research techniques in sexual deviation studies.[1] In thus attacking the problem on the broadest possible front these studies have been able to demonstrate its true nature and proportions against the exaggerated and distorted views held by the public.

While it has been the main object of these brief remarks to show that in the field of sexual offences, as in that of Negro crime, the persistently unprejudiced and scientific attitude of American criminologists, in conjunction with their colleagues from neighbouring disciplines, has cleared the air and produced a more wholesome atmosphere, there still remains a point of general significance which seems to me to touch upon certain fundamental weaknesses in the present position of Criminology as a discipline claiming to be of a truly international character. I will take as my starting point the only too well-founded criticisms of the device, employed in some of the Psychopathic Sex Offenders Acts, of providing drastic, though ostensibly non-criminal, measures such as indefinite detention without conviction or charge of a crime (see above). The logic of such legislation can hardly be disputed—if an individual is likely to commit serious crime in future why should the State have to wait until he has actually done so? Why not take preventive measures in time, and if they do not fit into the traditional penal system why not divert them to the field of civil or administrative proceedings? The only valid opposition against the logic of such legislation can come from the criminologist and from the defender of individual liberty. While the former will argue that, in spite of the progress made in crime prediction techniques, criminological knowledge has not yet reached the stage required to predict with any confidence that a certain individual, if left at large, will actually commit a serious crime, and in particular that he will do so, say, within the next year or

---

[1] The following are the principal publications of this project: Reports of March, 1952, and of January, 1953, and the Final Report referred to above (note 1, p. 205), all of them printed by the Assembly of the State of California. See also the Report of the Sub-Committee on Sex Crimes of the Assembly Interim Committee on Judicial Systems and Judicial Processes, August, 1952.

IMPRESSIONS OF A CRIMINOLOGIST

two or three years,[1] the latter will draw from this state of affairs the conclusion that the risk to society through the possibility of future crime is less serious than the harm done to the individual concerned through indefinite detention. A distinction might possibly be made between the person who has already demonstrated his dangerousness, his '*état dangereux*', through the commission of several crimes and the person who has so far never fallen foul of the law. However, we are all aware of the hazardous nature of the 'once a thief always a thief'.

Clearly, we are here faced with one of the fundamental problems of penal policy and it is not surprising that it has been heatedly discussed in Continental European literature for at least half a century, if not for much longer. Although, as a legislative matter, it is in the first place the concern of the politician and the lawyer, the criminologist is in fact no less directly involved since it is his responsibility to supply the information needed for legislative purposes and for the administration of criminal justice. After the period of silence imposed by the last war, the controversy has been revived in recent years in particular through the foundation of an 'International Society of Social Defence', with headquarters in Genoa, with its international congresses and its own journal, the *Revue Internationale de Défense sociale* (formerly *Rivista di difese sociale*). Its adherents are found mainly, but by no means exclusively, in the latin-speaking countries where its programme has been explained and defended in numerous publications. Its most outspoken critic has so far been the Swiss criminologist and former juvenile court judge Professor Erwin Frey-Zurich.[2] Whether this Society, with its slogan '*Il faut non plus une peine pour chaque délit, mais une mesure pour chaque personne*',[3] would actually go so far as to approve of measures such as provided in some of the Psychopathic Sex Offenders Laws without requiring conviction of a crime may

---

[1] See Etienne de Greeff, 'Les Indices de l'Etat dangereux', in *L'Examen medico-psychologique et social des Delinquants* (Premier Cours International de Criminologie, Paris 15th September–24th October, 1952), pp. 639–56.

[2] Erwin Frey, *Strafrecht oder Sociale Verteidigung?*, *Schweizerische Zeitschrift für Strafrecht*, Vol. 68, No. 4, 1953, pp. 405–40.

[3] See Frey, p. 408; Filippo Gramatica, *Revue Internationale de Défense Sociale*, Vol. 6, No. 1–2, January–June, 1952, p. 4; Vol. 7, No. 3–4, July–December, 1953, p. 125. Marc Ancel, 'Les doctrines nouvelles de la défense sociale', *Revue de Droit pénal et de Criminologie*, October, 1951; Marc Ancel, 'Droit pénal et défense sociale', *Revue Internationale de Défense Sociale*, Vol. 7, No. 1–2, January–June, 1953, pp. 1 et seq.

here be left open as this is in any case not the place for a comprehensive critical review of the programme of the 'International Society of Social Defence'. Its literary output, though largely repetitive, has been very extensive, and there seem to be differences of opinion within the Society itself. The point which I wish to make is that, apart from a passing remark by Sutherland,[1] American discussions of the Psychopathic Sex Offenders Laws seem to contain no reference to, and show no awareness of, that much older and more general European controversy. This is an omission characteristic of a certain cleavage between North American Criminology, on the one hand, and its Continental European and South American counterparts, on the other. At the beginning of the present century, the American Institute of Criminal Law and Criminology at North-Western University in Chicago, in order to stimulate interest in criminological ideas in the United States, promoted the translation and publication of the most important works of leading European criminologists. The success of this act surpassed all expectations, and whatever international flavour American Criminology still possesses is largely derived from it. Whether or not there is any need to-day for a repetition of that pioneer enterprise,[2] closer attention might well be paid by American criminologists to the general trends of scientific movements abroad, if only on account of the dangers they might reveal. On the other hand, it has to be admitted that there are comparatively few criminologists in latin-speaking countries to-day whose writings betray more than superficial familiarity with modern Anglo-American criminological thought. This mutual isolationism is to some extent no doubt due to difficulties of language; to an even larger extent, however, it has to be ascribed to certain fundamental differences in approach and emphasis: theoretical discussions of penal policy only distantly related to realities, which are so dear to the hearts of many criminologists on the European Continent, seem to evoke less response in the United States now than they did fifty years ago when still possessing the charm of novelty. In American Criminology, theoretical interest has become

[1] Edwin H. Sutherland, *American Journal of Sociology*, Vol. 56, September, 1950, p. 148.
[2] In the meantime, the *Journal of Criminology, Criminal Law and Police Science* has arranged the publication of a new series of articles on the work of a number of eminent European criminologists, beginning with Margaret S. Wilson's article on 'Gabriel Tarde' in Vol. 45, No. 1, May-June, 1954.

IMPRESSIONS OF A CRIMINOLOGIST

largely concentrated on sociological and methodological issues rather than on those legal and philosophical aspects dominating the European scene. In a way, this may simply reflect the difference between the legal mind of the European and the sociological training of the American criminologist. Whatever the reasons, the impression remains that, instead of a unified discipline, there are at present in existence several national, or perhaps regional, Criminologies for different parts of the civilized world. Let us hope that the work of international bodies such as UNO, UNESCO, and the International Society of Criminology, with their International Congresses, will in due course produce a common language and, if not a greater uniformity of outlook, at least a joint discussion of the common problems.

CHAPTER 9

MISCELLANEOUS TOPICS

I. AMERICAN JUVENILE COURTS [1]

COURTS and other agencies competent to deal with juvenile offenders are of one of the following four types, each with its specific merits and corresponding weaknesses:

England	European Continent except Scandinavia	United States	Scandinavian Countries

The special merit of the English system is its meticulous consideration of the offence and the guilt of the offenders with corresponding formality and observance of rules of evidence. Its principal weakness is that it is merely a 'modified criminal court', with too much of its stigma and (limited) publicity, and that its minimum age of criminal responsibility (eight years) is too low. The opposite extreme is that of the Scandinavian Child Welfare Councils which are not courts at all and have no formality, no rules of evidence, no publicity, and little stigma attached to them, with a corresponding weakening of judicial safeguards and a certain tendency to leave important questions of fact and guilt unanswered. The two other systems stand somewhere between these extremes in that they share with England the juvenile court idea and some of its rigidity and with Scandinavian Child Welfare Councils some of their greater informality and the absence of any kind of publicity. There remain certain important differences between the rest of the European Continent and the United States: whereas European countries have a dual system, Chancery Courts for the younger and 'modified criminal courts' for the older juvenile offenders, American juvenile courts are throughout on the lines of Chancery Courts, dealing with delinquency not as an

[1] Based on a lecture given to the Fourth International Course in Criminology, London, on the 6th April, 1954. Not previously published.

IMPRESSIONS OF A CRIMINOLOGIST

offence with which children are 'charged' but as a 'condition' which has to be treated, with little differentiation between the delinquent and the neglected or dependent child.

It will be appreciated that this, as any such attempt to reduce the great variety of existing laws to a scheme, is an over-simplification. With such a proviso, however, we may say that it is at least the theory; and when I went to the United States I took with me this picture of 'ideal types' and also a certain prejudice in favour of the American and the Scandinavian systems, which latter I had been privileged to observe in the course of a lecture tour to Oslo in February, 1953—a prejudice above all due to their more intimate atmosphere, their exclusion of publicity and lack of rigid rules, and their refusal to bring very young children before a 'modified criminal court'.[1] I have changed none of my convictions, but as the result of whatever impressions I have been able to collect through my few personal contacts with American Juvenile Courts I am inclined to stress, as in the case of American prisons, their diversity rather than their uniformity of systems. While, in theory, the division, given above, into four types of agencies may be correct, in actual practice there seems to be more similarity between, say, the Philadelphia Juvenile Court and its counterpart in a large English city than between the former and the Juvenile Court in a small American town such as, for example, Eugene in Oregon. In other words, the hard facts of daily life may easily defy the best intentions of the ideologist. In Eugene, I attended a meeting of the Juvenile Court in the judge's private room, with only the judge himself, the probation officer and the juvenile and his mother present. In the Philadelphia Juvenile Court, on the other hand, I found the same pressure of work, an average of 40 to 45 cases per sitting, the same very large Court room with its completely impersonal atmosphere as in some busy English Courts, with the judge high up on a raised bench and a large crowd of persons present. In many States of U.S.A. the position differs from county to county.

Even so, however, there are many important differences between the two systems. American Juvenile Court judges are mostly professional lawyers, many of whom have to share their time be-

[1] See Hermann Mannheim, *The Dilemma of Penal Reform* (London, Allen & Unwin, Ltd., 1939), pp. 178–98; *Juvenile Delinquency in an English Middletown* (London, Routledge & Kegan Paul, Ltd., 1948), p. 118.

MISCELLANEOUS TOPICS

tween the Juvenile and the Adult Courts. In Philadelphia, for example, only one of the judges sits in the Juvenile Court fulltime, and in the State of New Jersey only four, of twenty-one, counties have a full-time judge. It is interesting that in New Jersey the full-time Juvenile Court judges are much less inclined than their part-time colleagues to commit juveniles to institutions.[1] The extreme pressure of work in large Courts makes an intake and also a referee system often indispensable, which means that all cases except those requiring 'extensive treatment and judicial disposal' can, at some stage or other, be informally adjusted without being brought before the judge.[2] In Philadelphia the decision is taken at the Juvenile Detention Centre by persons authorized by the presiding Judge of the Court, i.e. the Superintendent of the Centre, or his assistant and a psychiatrist, after a personal interview of the child, prosecutor, the parents and witnesses, and it has to be confirmed by the judge. In 1951, 47 per cent of the cases passing through the Detention Centre were in this way adjusted without formal court hearing, and it is stressed that the procedure has the advantage of sparing the first offender who has committed a trivial offence the shock of a formal court appearance and of enabling the judge to give more time to serious cases.[3] In San Francisco, where there is only one part-time Juvenile Court judge for a city of approximately 800,000 people, in 1952 out of a total of 4,756 referrals 3,256 were 'dismissed in intake'.[4] 'Adult matters are assigned to probation departments as the result of court actions; the volume of juvenile work, however, is largely dependant upon intake policies and procedures.'[5] Professor Alfred J. Kahn of Columbia University, in his recent exhaustive and illuminating study of the New York City Children's Court,[6]

[1] State of New Jersey Department of Institutions and Agencies. *Children in New Jersey Juvenile Courts* (Trenton, N. J., December, 1950).
[2] See the excellent Annual Reports of the Municipal Court of Philadelphia (Thirty-eighth Report for the year 1951, pp. 12 et seq.). On the Referee system and informal adjustment in general see Teeters and Reinemann, *The Challenge of Delinquency* (New York, Prentice-Hall, Inc., 1950), pp. 317 and 319; Paul W. Tappan, *Juvenile Delinquency* (New York, Toronto, London, McGraw-Hill Book Company, Inc., 1949), pp. 329–32 and *passim*; Frederick W. Killian, *The Annals of the American Academy of Political and Social Science*, Vol. 261, January, 1949, pp. 96 et seq.
[3] Annual Report for 1951, p. 14.
[4] San Francisco Youth Guidance Centre, Annual Report, 1952, p. 20.
[5] *Probation Services in California*, 1948–9 (Sacramento), p. 10.
[6] On p. 302 of the book quoted above, Chapter II, note 1, p. 194.

dismisses the referee system as 'inappropriate where there is no lack of judges', which seems to be a very important proviso depriving the dismissal of most of its practical significance. The present writer has found no evidence in the United States to force him to modify his view that some sort of a clearing house, referee system or otherwise, is needed for Juvenile Courts with large caseloads.[1] Whether this clearing house should be part of the Juvenile Court itself or an outside agency and what should be its compositon and function will be a matter for discussion. In recent years, for lack of something better, the old system of Police cautioning has been revived, apparently in a greatly improved form, in the 'Liverpool City Police Juvenile Liaison Scheme', which aims at preventing recidivism by dealing with suitable cases of first offenders outside the Juvenile Court.[2] While such local Police schemes have their undisputed merits they cannot, in the long run, take the place of a clearing house more in line with modern ideas of social work.

The opportunity afforded by the referee system and similar official schemes of inofficial adjustment without a formal court hearing greatly enhance the importance and status of the American Probation Service. In the absence of an office of Clerk to the Justices, the principal probation officer, often called 'Director of Probation' or 'Director of Juvenile Department', appears to be the most important figure in Court after the judge, and it is stated that the probation officer's recommendations are accepted by the judge in at least 80 per cent of all cases. Whether such a concentration of powers and responsibilities is good or bad depends on the quality of the probation officers, and in this respect there has been some occasional criticism in recent years in American literature and in unpublished reports of political appointments, inadequate salaries and lack of training prevalent in some areas. The position here does not substantially differ from that in the prison service (above, p. 171). According to Tappan, writing in 1949, less than one-sixth of the United States jurisdictions apply the civil service system to probation officers,[3] and he realizes that even this system is no

[1] See *Lawless Youth*, by Margery Fry and others (London, George Allen & Unwin Ltd., 1947), p. 53. Also *Juvenile Delinquency in an English Middletown* p. 48.
[2] See note in *The British Journal of Delinquency*, Vol. II, No. 2, October, 1951, p. 160.
[3] Paul W. Tappan, op cit., pp. 341 et seq.

MISCELLANEOUS TOPICS

adequate safeguard of effective selection. The Domestic Relations Court of New York City, whose work Tappan regards as of considerably higher quality than that of most other American Courts, and the Childrens' Court which forms one of its two Divisions, have in fact been repeatedly the subject of severe criticisms, mainly because lack of funds, it is said, makes it impossible to appoint enough trained probation officers, psychiatrists, and well qualified judges to carry out the intentions of the new Youth Act.[1]

In Philadelphia, 'it is an established rule of the court that every child whose case is to be heard by the court must have a thorough physical and mental examination, including an intelligence test', and as the rules of criminal procedure are not applicable to American Juvenile Courts these as any other preliminary investigations, may well be carried out before the first court hearing.[2] Psychiatric examinations of juveniles, undertaken by the Neuropsychiatric Division of the Court, numbered 5,763 in 1951, which, together with equally extensive work on adults and medical examinations of a non-psychiatric character, makes an impressive caseload. As the otherwise so detailed Annual Report of the Court gives no information, however, on the staff of psychiatrists, psychologists, and other workers available for these examinations, it is impossible to form any opinion about their thoroughness and actual value to the Court.[3] In the New York City Juvenile Court, the number of psychiatric examinations is much smaller, only 1,445 in 1951, and even here some doubts have been expressed as to the adequacy of existing services.[4]

However justified these and other strictures made in recent years by American writers of their Juvenile Courts may be, the outsider cannot fail to be impressed by the spirit of honest self-criticism and the desire for improvement which alone make such searching enquiries possible.

---

[1] See letter to the *New York Times* of 19th March, 1954, by the President of the New York County Lawyers Association; also the Reports quoted by Tappan and more recently Alfred J. Kahn.
[2] See Teeters and Reinemann, op. cit., pp. 263, 327; Tappan, pp. 187 and 212.
[3] Annual Report for 1951, pp. 298 et seq.
[4] Alfred J. Kahn, pp. 228 et seq., Tappan, p. 213.

IMPRESSIONS OF A CRIMINOLOGIST

II. PREVENTIVE WORK

FOLLOWING the example of the Gluecks in *Preventing Crime*, most American textbooks very appropriately list existing schemes of preventing juvenile delinquency under the headings of Family, School, Church, Police, Child Guidance Clinic, Club, Community, and special Agencies.[1] While this is not the place to give a comprehensive view of all these schemes, a few words may be said about one or two of them with which the writer came into personal contact during his stay.

Preventive schemes based upon the Police, of which the New York Juvenile Aid Bureau of the Police Department of New York City with its Police Athletic League[2] is the most outstanding, have perhaps more than any other scheme been exposed to criticism on the ground that the Police, in view of their training and general status within the community, are not really suitable for preventive work. The spokesmen of the New York Department, on the other hand, maintain that the Police embark upon such work only when it is not done by other social agencies and that it is not their intention to monopolize it. In 1952, Dr. James J. Brennan, himself closely connected with the New York Police Athletic League, conducted by means of questionnaires and personal observation an interesting enquiry to ascertain the present nature and extent of Police Prevention Programmes. It was found that of 177 cities with populations of 25,000 and over who replied to the questionnaire 133 reported having Police Preventive Programmes.[3] There are, however, considerable variations within this group, the most important difference being that between New York where, with an annual case load of 20,000 and a Juvenile Aid Bureau personnel of 230, recreational youth activities are directly sponsored by the Police, and Philadelphia where the programme is conducted by another specialized agency, though with close partici-

---

[1] See, e.g., Tappan, Chapters XVIII and XIX; Teeters and Reinemann, Chapters XV and XVI; Mabel A. Elliott (above Chapter 7, note 5, p. 170), Chapter 28. Sheldon and Eleanor Glueck (ed.), *Preventing Crime* (New York, McGraw-Hill Book Company, Inc., 1936).

[2] See Teeters and Reinemann, p. 581.

[3] James J. Brennan, *The Prevention and Control of Juvenile Delinquency by Police Departments* (New York, 1952 (mimeographed)). Also the same author, *International Child Welfare Review*, Vol. VIII No. 2, 1954, pp. 57 et seq.

MISCELLANEOUS TOPICS

pation of the Police. Under the 'Philadelphia Plan',[1] the very efficiently organized Crime Prevention Association of Philadelphia, with a staff of 80, operates in addition to its elaborate recreational and research activities a 'Referral System' under which juveniles passing through the Association and the Police Juvenile Aid Bureau are referred to Neighbourhood Committees for special attention. In 1953, more than 5,000 cases were so referred, but before referral each case is carefully screened and only cases not serious enough to warrant arrest and Juvenile Court intervention are referred for preventive work. The details of this organization would repay serious further study as it may well be that, while avoiding the dangers of complete identification with the Police, it has been able to reap all the benefits of close liaison with the latter.

III. RESEARCH PROJECTS

HERE again, mention can be made of only two research projects to which my attention was especially drawn during my stay in the United States and which, on account of their objects and techniques, should be of particular interest in this country and elsewhere: the Highfields Project, New Jersey, and the California Intensive Parole Supervision Project.

(1) The object of the Highfields Project[2] is to ascertain how far long-term institutionalization of adolescent offenders may safely be replaced by probation with short-term group therapy, or 'guided group interaction' as it is officially called, in a place roughly corresponding to an English Probation Home. The Project was inaugurated in 1950 jointly by the New Jersey Department of Institutions and Agencies and the New York Foundation, with an independent Scientific Advisory Committee established by the Vincent Astor Foundation. It operates at Highfields in New Jersey, the former home of Col. Charles Lindbergh which had been donated to the State. In essence it is a comparison of the

---

[1] Teeters and Reinemann, pp. 661–2, and Annual Reports of the Crime Prevention Association of Philadelphia.

[2] See H. Ashley Weeks, 'Preliminary Evaluation of the Highfields Project, *American Sociological Review*, Vol. 18, No. 3, June, 1953, pp. 280 et seq.—Acknowledgment is made to the New Jersey authorities for giving access to the unpublished Annual Reports issued by the New Jersey State Board of Control and to a paper by Dr. F. Lovell Bixby, read at the National Probation and Parole Association Conference at Atlantic City on 27th April, 1950.

IMPRESSIONS OF A CRIMINOLOGIST

success or failure rates of two matched groups of boys aged sixteen, one of them placed on probation and sent to Highfields for up to four months and the other committed to the State Reformatory at Annandale for periods of up to eighteen months, with an average stay of a year. Obviously, the selection of these two groups has its difficulties as, although Annandale is used only for first offenders, the Courts would naturally tend to take the view that to Annandale a type of boy should be sent who differs from the one to be placed on probation with a condition of short-term residential treatment. An agreement was reached with the judges, however, according to which matched groups were indiscriminately selected for the two institutions. The Project can therefore be regarded as a controlled experiment of an operational character. So far only preliminary results have been released which seem to show that 'Highfields accomplishes as much, if not more, in four months of stay as Annandale in more than a year'.

In initiating this Project, the New Jersey Department of Institutions and Agencies and the supporting Foundations have no doubt taken an important step in the right direction. There has been no lack of experimentation in recent years in the treatment of offenders in institutions and at large, but only rarely has there been any systematic attempt by means of a scientifically controlled experiment to compare the results of different kinds of such treatment.[1] We all have certain preconceived views in the matter—we may prefer, for example, probation to institutional treatment, small open to large closed institutions, Borstals to Prisons, short-term to long-term Approved Schools, and so forth, but as a rule we have no real evidence to support our claims. It is only very recently that the superiority of the open over the closed Borstal Institution, for the same type of lad, has been statistically established in this country,[2] but at the time of writing, the other of these claims are still awaiting confirmation. Seen in this wider setting, the Highfields Project assumes a very special significance. On the other hand, the technical difficulties of this, and similar,

---

[1] Similar experiments have recently been initiated in Sweden: see Torsten Eriksson in *The Annuals of the American Academy of Political and Social Science*, Vol. 293, May, 1954, p. 158.

[2] See *Studies in the Causes of Delinquency and the Treatment of Offenders*, Vol. I; 'Prediction Methods in Relation to Borstal Training', by Hermann Mannheim and Leslie T. Wilkins (London, published for the Home Office by H.M.S.O., 1954), pp. 109 et seq., 120.

MISCELLANEOUS TOPICS

experiments can hardly be over-estimated. In the case of Highfields, the Project has been fortunate, it seems, in overcoming the traditional objections of the judiciary to any form of experimenting with different sentences for the same type of offender.[1] Whether complete identity of the two groups has in fact been achieved cannot, however, be said with certainty from the information so far released. Boys with previous institutional experience, sexual deviants and 'pronounced pathological offenders' have, it is stated, been excluded from both groups, but no criteria have so far been given of the manner in which these highly subjective concepts have been defined, nor have any particulars been published of the working of the selection process. Moreover, as Annandale receives young men between sixteen and twenty-five years of age the possible influence of the older men on the boys, compared with the more homogeneous Highfields group, has to be taken into consideration, which means that any lack of better results in the Annandale group might to some extent have to be interpreted as demonstrating the effect of contagion rather than of length of stay or of the group treatment at Highfields. It is to be hoped that in the final evaluation of this promising research full details might be published regarding selection and other features, in order to enable the outsider to judge whether the two groups have been strictly comparable.

(2) *The California Intensive Parole Supervision Project*[2] is also a controlled experiment of operational character with an equally definite practical object. As in the Highfields Project, it is the intention of the experimenting body, which is here the Californian Department of Corrections and the Adult Authority, to ascertain whether greater intensity of treatment or supervision can compensate for, or may even be more effective than mere length. In both instances, 'quality or quantity?' is the slogan behind the research. The major hypothesis underlying the Californian Project is that, as most relapses of released prisoners occur during the first three months after discharge,[3] the provision of more intensive

[1] See above, p. 127.
[2] See the Note in *The British Journal of Delinquency*, Vol. V, No. 1, July, 1954, p. 67. The author is obliged to the Californian authorities for being given access to various unpublished Memoranda on the subject and to a paper by Mr. Walter A. Gordon, Chairman, California Adult Authority.
[3] See also the publication referred to on p. 218, note 2, pp. 127 et seq.

IMPRESSIONS OF A CRIMINOLOGIST

supervision for this crucial period will reduce the proportion of parole violations and make earlier discharges possible. These are the main objects of the Project which was put into operation in the course of the year 1953 by selecting fourteen parole officers (P.O.I) to give intensive supervision to batches of fifteen parolees each for three months after release. After this initial period the men are transferred to normal caseload supervision, i.e. to parole officers (P.O.II) having to supervise ninety men each at a time. This scheme, therefore, provides for an intensive supervision of sixty men per officer annually, or altogether for 840 men per year, enjoying the benefit of better after-care. Some of these men are granted parole dates advanced by approximately three months, while the others are released as usual. There is also a control group of the same size throughout placed under ordinary supervision. In the selection for both, the experimental and the control groups, only cases with definite handicaps such as serious physical or mental illnesses, are excluded; otherwise the selection is made at random. The Parole Officers I, though experienced men, are also selected in such a way as to make them representative of the Californian Parole Service. Special emphasis is placed on the closest co-operation between the Departments concerned and on improved parole recording. To co-ordinate and integrate the Intensive Training Unit a new post of Senior Sociologist has been created, and an Advisory Committee has been established on which the University of California in Los Angelos and the School of Criminology in Berkeley are represented.

PART FOUR

TWO PENOLOGICAL PROBLEMS

CHAPTER 10

CAPITAL PUNISHMENT: WHAT NEXT?

I. BEFORE THE REPORT OF THE ROYAL COMMISSION OF 1953[1]

THERE are three aspects to the question of capital punishment: first the moral-humanitarian-religious; secondly, the popular, i.e. the views, prejudices and superstitions of the man in the street; and, lastly, the scientific, i.e. the penological, psychiatric, sociological—in short, the accumulated knowledge and experience of the experts of various brands. To ask for complete integration and reconciliation of all three viewpoints would mean crying for the moon, but without at least a certain minimum of support from each of them no lasting solution will be possible.

As events of recent months have shown, the abolitionists have been relying mostly on humanitarian and, to some extent, on scientific considerations, whereas the strength of the antiabolitionist camp is almost wholly derived from popular arguments. As far as the Government is concerned, it has been vacillating between the two extremes, while the voice of the penologist has only occasionally and dimly been heard crying in the wilderness.

In brief, the abolitionist argument is this: capital punishment is a barbarous anomaly in an otherwise humane penal system; as experiences of many other countries have shown, it is unnecessary as a deterrent; moreover, it is in many respects dangerous and harmful, in particular because of the possibility of miscarriages of justice. The anti-abolitionists reply that capital punishment is less inhuman than the proposed alternative of life imprisonment; that

[1] This article was published, without the footnotes, in *The Fortnightly Review*, October, 1948, approximately six months before the setting up of the Royal Commission on Capital Punishment, and subsequently re-published as a pamphlet of the Howard League for Penal Reform, London.

TWO PENOLOGICAL PROBLEMS

it is indispensable as a deterrent (foreign experiences, so they argue, are inapplicable to conditions in this country) and because the man in the street, alarmed by the recent increase in crimes of violence, insists on its continuance; and that the danger of miscarriages of justice is negligible under a well-ordered administration of criminal law.

The Government, apparently with no particularly strong convictions on either of these points, hits on the most obvious compromise of distinguishing between different types of murder. The formula chosen is easily demolished by the forensic skill of the anti-abolitionist camp; the Government is defeated in the House of Lords, and this, for the time being, has put an end to the matter.

To carry through a great piece of law reform on a controversial issue, bound to arouse the profoundest emotions and prejudices of the masses, one needs both strong personal convictions and the most thorough scientific preparation. This applies to legislative no less than to tank battles. While strong personal convictions cannot be requisitioned at will, research can be instigated by Government action. When the new national insurance scheme reached its first preparatory stage during the war, Sir William (now Lord) Beveridge was asked by the Minister concerned to submit a report. On our problem, no research worth mentioning was set in motion by the Government in connection with the introduction of the Criminal Justice Bill although it was clear from the beginning that the question of capital punishment would become a burning issue in the course of the parliamentary proceedings. It might be retorted that a considerable amount of valuable information had already been collected by the Select Committee on Capital Punishment which reported in 1930. However, this material has inevitably become out of date in many respects. Nor were the methods employed by the Committee of the standard required for scientific purposes. Particularly unsatisfactory is, at least as far as conditions abroad are concerned, the technique of relying almost exclusively on oral or written evidence by *ad hoc* witnesses, instead of studying first and foremost the vast amount of printed material already in existence in most countries—a procedure which, though more laborious and time-consuming, is more likely to yield reliable results. This does not mean that the traditional technique employed by Royal Commissions and Departmental Committees is

CAPITAL PUNISHMENT: WHAT NEXT?

valueless. It has no doubt very considerable merits, in particular because of the opportunity which it affords of personally examining and cross-examining lay witnesses and expert witnesses. On the other hand, the weaknesses of that technique have been so clearly exposed in more recent years that, as a matter of course, it should at least be supplemented by other research methods.

It was significant that during the recent debates in the House of Commons one of the speakers who had been a member of the departmental committee of 1930 indicated that of the two American expert witnesses at the disposal of the committee the one who had appeared in person and subjected himself to cross-examination had impressed him more than the one who had merely submitted a written memorandum. (Hansard, 14th April, 1948, col. 1058.) Although, from the layman's point of view, this is easily understandable, it remains nevertheless true that such chance factors should not be decisive in scientific investigations, and it should also be clear that an impressive presence and quickness in repartee are not necessarily the most valuable equipment of the successful research worker who needs patience, imagination and knowledge of his material and research techniques more than anything else.

Finally, it has to be remembered that on certain important points the committee of 1930, though apparently well aware of what was needed, proved to be incapable of obtaining the desired information. For example, with reference to an analysis, published in the Criminal Statistics for 1905, of the 'motives or causes of murders committed by all persons convicted of murder in England and Wales during the twenty years ending 1905' the Report of 1930 states (p. 21): 'We should have desired that the Home Office analysis had been brought up to date, but their witnesses explained to us that the various forms and causes of murder interlaced and overlapped one another and that it had not been thought useful to continue the analysis beyond 1905.'[1]

Surely, this is a most important point. It is hardly more than a commonplace to say that any reasonable debate on the punishment for murder should be preceded by a painstaking enquiry into the

[1] An indication of motives or causes of certain categories of murder for the period 1900 to 1949 is now given in Appendix 3, Table 4, to the Report of the Royal Commission on Capital Punishment 1953 (Cmd. 8932), pp. 304 et seq.

psychological, physical and social characteristics of an adequate sample (at least a few hundred cases) of persons who have committed murder and into the causes and motives of their crimes. This sample should include not only an adequate proportion of murderers found insane but, as far as possible, also data about those who committed suicide (in 1946, the last year for which figures have been published, in thirty-one of a total of 113 cases of murder of persons aged one year and over, the murderer or suspected murderer committed suicide).[1] Only by means of such an analysis can we expect to obtain some objective data on such points as the frequency of premeditated, 'cold-blooded' murder, the degree of 'moral wickedness' involved, perhaps even on the potential deterrent effect of the death penalty, and many others. Illustrative cases supplied by those distinguished speakers who took part in the recent parliamentary debates, either from their own judicial experiences or from second-hand sources such as press reports, useful and impressive as no doubt they are, can in no way take the place of the comprehensive study which we have in mind.

The present writer knows from his own practical work, covering not only trials but also prosecutions and preliminary investigations on charges of murder, how much the information obtained during the trial itself is usually limited to the mere 'facts' of the crime itself—facts which may tell comparatively little of the real story. This view is further confirmed by the impression gained from a study of the very carefully edited volumes of the 'Notable British Trials Series' or 'The Old Bailey Trial Series' and from the published recollections of eminent high court judges. Nobody would, of course, be content nowadays with an analysis on the lines of that published in 1905 with its crude psychological and sociological armoury. Between then and now we have had some outstanding developments, including Freud and his followers, which have not only shed new light on the psychology of crime in general but also given us a small number of illuminating case studies of murderers, such as Robert Lindner's *Rebel Without Cause* and Frederic Wertham's *Dark Legend*. We have had Andreas Bjerre's careful, though perhaps less penetrating observations on the

---

[1] For the fifty years from 1900 to 1949 the number of cases in which the suspect committed suicide is now given as 1,674 out of 7,454 murders known to the Police (Report of the Royal Commission, Appendix 3, Table 1, England and Wales).

CAPITAL PUNISHMENT: WHAT NEXT?

Psychology of Murder, based on Adlerian ideas; and on the sociological side H. C. Brearley's *Homicide in the United States* and some detailed statistical investigations carried out in Germany.

I do not, for a moment, claim that these researches have solved all the problems which the legislator has to face when he tackles the thorny subject of capital punishment; nevertheless, familiarity with their methods and results will reduce the danger of merely repeating all the old and long exploded slogans. There is no doubt much truth in the contention, for example, that foreign experiences cannot be applied indiscriminately to conditions in this country. Nevertheless, simply to contend that conditions are totally different here from those existing in abolitionist countries without taking the trouble carefully to study these differences seems unsatisfactory. It has repeatedly been asserted—by Sir John Anderson, for instance (Hansard, 14th April, 1948, col. 1002)— that the absence of an increase in the frequency of murder in abolitionist States such as the Scandinavian countries proves nothing as they possess no great cities comparable in size to London or Glasgow, the tacit assumption being that the very big city has necessarily the highest murder rate and presents the most difficult problem for the preventive efforts of the legislator. How far is this actually borne out by the available information? The volumes of Criminal Statistics for England and Wales have become so incomplete since the beginning of the 1939–45 war that no information regarding the local distribution of crime can be extracted from them. But in the period 1936–8 altogether 375 cases of murder had become known to the Police in England and Wales (estimated population, forty millions). Of these 375 cases, 104 had been committed in the Metropolitan Police District, Liverpool, Manchester and Birmingham (estimated population together ten and three-quarter millions), which is only slightly more than their proportionate share.[1] This may be surprising in view of the generally accepted fact that there is more crime in urban than in rural districts. Professor Brearley, in the book already referred to,[2] shows that in the great majority of states of the

[1] In 1953, according to unpublished Home Office Statistics which are available to research workers, 143 cases of murder became known to the Police in England and Wales, of which only 38 occurred in the Metropolitan Police District, Liverpool, Manchester, and Birmingham.

[2] H. C. Brearley, *Homicide in the United States* (University of North Carolina Press, 1932).

TWO PENOLOGICAL PROBLEMS

U.S.A. the homicide rate is higher in towns than in the country. On the other hand, these differences are much less significant than those between the different states in proportion to population density. For example, whereas according to Professor Brearley the homicide rate per 100,000 of population was 8·26 for the whole of the U.S.A. for the period 1919–27, it was only 1·43 in Vermont and 4·82 in New York State as against 29·55 in Florida. The difference between New York State and the Southern far less densely populated and industrialized, states is considerably greater than that between the urban and rural districts of New York State.[1] This is borne out for the immediate pre-war years by figures supplied by the National Council for the Abolition of the Death Penalty. The abolitionist states of the U.S.A., as Mr. John Paton has recently reminded us (Hansard, 14th April, 1948, col. 1015) include Michigan with Detroit, one of the most highly industrialized cities of the world, but its murder rate is not only substantially lower than that of Illinois or California but also incomparably lower than that of the agricultural Southern states. The frequency of homicide in the U.S.A. seems to depend on racial tension rather than on the degree of industrialization.[2]

Needless to say, the bare figures of crime statistics can never give a completely reliable picture of the actual position. One would have to know much more of the conditions of each locality and of individual cases to form a definite opinion about the actual effect of very complex social factors such as life in big cities, and I have selected the question of population density and extent of industrialization merely as an illustration to show that we are still too easily inclined to take matters for granted and to base our arguments on points which are in fact still greatly in need of further investigation. One cannot but agree with one of the speakers in the House of Commons debate of 14th April, 1948 (Mr. Donovan, Hansard, col. 1028) who said: 'I listened in order to detect, if I could, that differentiating factor in other countries which would make even the trial of this experiment unsafe in this country. I am bound to say that I did not hear it . . .' Not one of the subsequent speakers, including those participating in the

[1] See now also the books by Austin L. Porterfield and Robert H. Talbert referred to in Chapter 8.
[2] See now the material presented in the Report of the Royal Commission, Appendix 6, pp. 345 et seq., and p. 365 et seq. Also *Uniform Crime Reports for the United States and its Possessions*, Vol. XXIII, No. 2, 1952, Tables 33–7.

CAPITAL PUNISHMENT: WHAT NEXT?

House of Lords debate, even attempted to provide the missing evidence that, in the words of the Attorney-General, 'the result of abolition would be different in, say, Dundee to what it was in Detroit or different in Birmingham to what it was in Brussels' (Hansard, 15th July, 1948, col. 1425).

In view of the conspicuous part which the question of grading has played in the parliamentary debates it must be dealt with briefly here. What has so far been said about the absence of any systematic collection of scientific data applies to the question of grading only with some modification. Efforts of some kind or other to establish various degrees of murder have of course been made in many countries for a very long time. They form only one part of the more comprehensive problem of how to distinguish degrees of killing, that is to define the difference between murder, voluntary and involuntary manslaughter, and accident. This is a problem which exists, quite independently of that of capital punishment, just as much in abolitionist countries. There are limitless varieties and combinations in the art of killing, some of them fundamentally affecting the severity of our judgement. It is a matter of legislative technique, involving issues of much greater complexity than purely technical ones, how far these distinctions should be embodied in a statute or left to the discretion of some judicial or administrative authority. Moreover, if the matter is dealt with, wholly or in part, by statutory definition, it is again the task of the legislator to determine the character of his definitions, whether the statute should attempt to settle in rigid terms any conceivable point of detail, leaving as little as possible to judicial interpretation, or whether the legislator should be content to indicate, by means of broad and elastic conceptions, the general policy to be pursued.

In a way, we are here concerned only with two different aspects of the one question of how to distribute power between legislature, judiciary, and executive. Power can be delegated by the legislator either by refusing to settle certain issues altogether or by settling them in such a way as to leave the decision of important points to the courts or the administration. Where trial is by jury further complications arise from the necessity to define the respective competence of judge and jury. In addition to such questions of competence, the legislator has to choose whether his definitions

TWO PENOLOGICAL PROBLEMS

should be based on objective or on subjective criteria or whether they should be mixtures of both.

The comparative history of the law of homicide shows an immense variety of techniques, and to give an idea of the different systems employed a comprehensive volume would be needed. Speaking generally, however, one finds a tendency in modern Continental legislation to employ wide and elastic terms instead of making attempts, regarded as more or less futile, to limit judicial discretion. Occasionally, this means the use of words capable of very different interpretation in the hands of different judges, for example, in the Swiss Federal Penal Code of 1937 which defines murder as 'killing under circumstances or with a premeditation revealing a particularly wicked state of mind or particular dangerousness', whereas manslaughter is characterized by a 'strong emotion which appears excusable in the circumstances'. In Swiss law, the difference is, however, not one of life or death but merely one between life imprisonment for murder and a maximum of ten years penal servitude for manslaughter. In addition, the Swiss Code has a general provision for homicide falling under neither of these extreme categories, with a minimum penalty of five and a maximum of twenty years penal servitude. A Nazi statute of 1941 defined the murderer as a person who kills 'for the sake of killing, or to satisfy his sexual lust, or out of greed or from other base motives, or with special malice or cruelty or in a manner dangerous to the whole community or in order to facilitate or to cover the commission of another offence'.[1]

U.S.A. legislative technique favours a combination of both objective and subjective elements, and it is in this connection in particular that the various definitions of first degree murder in American statutes are of immediate practical interest to us at the present stage. The Select Committee of 1930 secured some information on the American system of grading; it appears doubtful, however, whether an adequate picture of the extremely complicated legal position was in fact obtained.[2]

[1] The question of grading has now been fully treated in the Report of the Royal Commission, pp. 167 et seq. and Appendix 12. In addition to the eight countries of Western Europe referred to in the Report, reference may be made to the Czechoslovak Penal Code of 1950, art. 216, and the Jugoslav Penal Code of 1951, art. 135.
[2] See now the detailed discussion of American Law in the Report of the Royal Commission, pp. 181 et seq.

CAPITAL PUNISHMENT: WHAT NEXT?

The first American state to introduce statutory degrees of murder was Pennsylvania in 1794. Since then, most other states have followed suit, while in a small minority capital punishment has been retained absolutely or the choice between capital punishment and life imprisonment is left to the discretion of the courts. Some states have several degrees not only of murder but of manslaughter as well; and Wisconsin is stated to hold the record with three degrees of murder and four of manslaughter. The general pattern used in twenty-six of the states which distinguish degrees of murder reserves capital punishment for murder 'perpetrated by means of poison, or lying in wait, or any other kind of wilful, deliberate and premeditated killing, or committed in the perpetration, or attempt to perpetrate any arson, rape, robbery or burglary.' Although important states such as New York and Massachusetts use other patterns, they all have in common the emphasis on deliberation and premeditation and they all single out for special attention murder perpetrated in the course of committing some other serious crime. The general impression conveyed by a study of the statutes and the writings of American experts is one of confusion rather than of clarity, and it can hardly be said that American legislation on the subject could provide us with a suitable model. It should, nevertheless, be carefully examined as demonstrating, more convincingly perhaps than the law of any other country, certain inherent limitations of legislative technique. In any case, it is not surprising that the Report of 1930 expressed itself against the grading of murder although it concluded that in spite of existing difficulties grading 'may possibly have a place in the future of the Penal Code of our country'.

There is one further point to which attention might be drawn in this connection as it has some special bearing on the English law of homicide: the general dissatisfaction with what is regarded as the essential psychological criterion of murder, deliberation and premeditation. The meaning of these two words has been watered down by the courts so much that it no longer requires even the two elements of 'cold blood' and the lapse of some appreciable time between planning and execution. The result is that, in the words of Mr. Justice Cardozo in a famous address to the New York Academy of Medicine in 1928, the distinction has become 'so obscure that no jury hearing it for the first time can fairly be expected to assimilate and understand it. I am not at all sure that

TWO PENOLOGICAL PROBLEMS

I understand it myself.... Upon the basis of this fine distinction with its obscure and mystifying psychology, scores of men have gone to their death.... I think the distinction is much too vague to be continued in our law.'[1]

The corresponding phrase in English law is 'malice aforethought'. As Lord Simonds said in the House of Lords (20th July, 1948, col. 1045), these words 'have from time to time received a varying interpretation to satisfy the changing conditions and the changing conscience of the people'. With great respect, is this not simply an eloquent way of saying that the phrase can always be made to mean what the judges of the day believe it should mean? As Kenny, the great textbook writer of modern English criminal law, puts it, the words have become a 'mere arbitrary symbol. For the "malice" may have in it nothing really malicious; and need never be really "aforethought".'[2] Can such an 'arbitrary symbol', particularly in the hands of untrained jurors, be regarded as a secure basis for a judgement on life or death?

If we now turn to the recent Government proposals, defeated in the House of Lords, there is first the surprising fact that, according to the explanation given by the Attorney-General (Hansard, 15th July, 1948, col. 1430), the intention of the Government was not 'to define degrees of murder, to classify cases according to the heinousness or moral gravity of the offence ... The purpose of the new Clause is to include those cases in which public opinion feels that the suspension of the existing arrangements in regard to the death penalty might involve risks which ought not to be taken at this time.' Or, as the Lord Chancellor explained (House of Lords, 20th July, 1948, col. 1010), the object was to select 'those particular categories of murder in which the death penalty definitely has a deterrent effect'.

It is difficult to maintain that there is any real difference between these Government proposals and the old idea of grading. There is hardly any evidence to show that the object of establishing degrees of murder has been to introduce moral distinctions at the expense

---

[1] *Law and Literature* (1931), pp. 96 et seq.
[2] Kenny, *Outlines of Criminal Law* (Cambridge University Press). See, e.g., 14th ed. 1933, p. 135. In the 'entirely new edition' of 1952, the editor, Mr. J. W. Cecil Turner, calls it 'the archaic and now misleading phrase ...' (p. 117). According to Professor Glanville L. Williams, *Criminal Law: The General Part* (London, Stevens, 1953), p. 65, the word 'malice' in 'malice aforethought' does not bear its usual technical meaning.

CAPITAL PUNISHMENT: WHAT NEXT?

of considerations of deterrence. However, whether or not the Government scheme may be called one of grading, the decisive arguments against any scheme based explicitly on considerations of deterrence to the exclusion of those of morality are, first, that we have no real knowledge of the deterrent effect of capital punishment on specific categories of murderers, and, secondly, that such differences as do no doubt exist in this respect are more likely to be connected with types of personality than with types of action, whereas the distinctions proposed by the Government were largely distinctions on the basis of types of activity (the systematic poisoner, the recidivist murderer, the murderer in prison or about to commit some other offence, and so on) which are not necessarily identical with personality types. Thirdly, a differentiation based on considerations of deterrence instead of morality may well appeal to the scientific mind; it will be entirely unsuitable for a jury whose moral feelings may be outraged by it. Moreover, as has been so cogently stressed in the House of Lords, the proposed categories would have burdened the trial with excessive complications, reminiscent of French trials of 150 years ago with sometimes several hundred separate 'questions' to be put to the jury.

The conclusions to be drawn are these. As long as capital punishment remains, it will be futile to pin one's faith upon new legislative formulæ and distinctions between degrees of murder. With one exception: the 'constructive' murder of English law which can, and should be, abolished by legislative action regardless of the question of the death penalty. The Government proposals (sub-section 4) attempted this by introducing the new conception of 'express malice' but, apart from other minor blemishes, the attempt, as the Lord Chief Justice has pointed out in the House of Lords, was limited to capital cases instead of applying to murder in general.[1]

Apart from this one point of constructive murder, no improvements can be expected from new definitions of murder since no formulæ will be strong enough to provide a basis for decisions on life and death. Without capital punishment, fairly satisfactory definitions, as the Swiss example shows, can be found, and hardships can always be adjusted by the court. As long as the death

[1] The abolition of the doctrine of constructive malice has now been recommended by the Report of the Royal Commission, p. 45.

penalty remains, the legislator will have to continue to delegate the supreme responsibility. To whom, however, should it be delegated? To leave the decision to the jurors is clearly impossible as it would be entirely beyond the capacity of their untrained minds.[1] The public prosecutor would be an equally impossible choice as his impartiality might be questioned by the public. The principal objection to leaving it to the judge is that the responsibility is too heavy for one man whoever he may be, and that different judges might have different policies. The former, though not the latter, consideration applies equally to the present system; although the Home Secretary is, of course, greatly assisted by his advisers the ultimate result rests on his decision alone. A special tribunal, under the chairmanship of the Home Secretary, of which the trial judge would be a member, might be a better solution.

However that may be, it should be borne in mind that, in any case, the days of capital punishment are limited. What matters most is that the present interval should be used to prepare the ground by adequate scientific investigation of the kind referred to at the beginning of this article. Too much has so far been left in this respect to private initiative, though the National Council for the Abolition of the Death Penalty has done excellent spade work within the narrow limits of its resources. It is now for the Government, which has just been granted the power under the Criminal Justice Act to spend money on research, to take over and greatly to expand the research activities of that body, as distinct from its propaganda work. If, by the time the results of the investigation are available, the crime situation should have improved, abolition may become practical politics.

II. AFTER THE PUBLICATION OF THE REPORT OF 1953 [2]

Although concentrating on the legal and psychiatric aspects of

[1] See below, p. 239.
[2] This paper was published in *The British Journal of Delinquency*, Vol. IV, January, 1954, pp. 168 et seq., under the heading 'concluding Remarks', as part of a symposium in which the legal aspects of the Report and of the Royal Commission of 1953 were treated by Mr. Gerald Gardiner, Q.C., and the psychiatric aspects by Dr. Edward Glover. The symposium was subsequently republished as a separate pamphlet by the I.S.T.D. (Institute for the Study and Treatment of Delinquency) in collaboration with the Howard League for Penal Reform, London.

CAPITAL PUNISHMENT: WHAT NEXT?

the Report my colleagues, quite inevitably, have had to touch upon certain other matters as well. No clear-cut dividing line is possible in this field, and I may occasionally have to trespass beyond the province of the crimino-sociologist and penologist. My principal limitation will be that of space.

The Report, not being allowed to make any pronouncement on the advisability of total abolition of capital punishment, has been compared to a 'Hamlet without the Prince'. It might be tempting to speculate whether 'Hamlet' might not be just as fascinating a play without the Prince bodily on the scene. In fact, the case for abolition seems to be stronger now than it might have been if the Royal Commission had been permitted explicitly to deal with it and had actually done so. In a 'Hamlet' without the Prince every word and every gesture of the actors would have borne witness to his existence and would have argued his case. So it is here with abolition. Nothing the Commission could have done could have prevented this effect. Which, of course, does not alter the fact that the position in which the Commission was placed by their terms of reference was both awkward and unenviable.

Before discussing some of the findings and recommendations it might be pertinent to dwell briefly on certain questions of method, some of them already adumbrated by Dr. Glover. In an article published several months before the setting up of the Commission[1] the present writer argued that an investigation by a scientific body might possibly be preferable to one by a Royal Commission, that a scientific study of a sample of murderers was needed, and that, in any case, the techniques employed by the Select Committee of 1930 could no longer be regarded as adequate. No doubt, a Royal Commission has functions additional to those of a research body, but this is no reason why, in so far as they are identical with those of the latter, their methods should not also be the same and their work be measured by the same standards. The question can hardly be evaded, therefore, whether from the methodological point of view the present Report represents a step forward. In some ways it certainly does. Patiently and conscientiously, and armed with powers greatly superior to those of any private research body, the Commission has collected and ably analysed a vast amount of valuable material; and it is no reflection on its work to say that to the serious student of the problems of Capital Punishment the

[1] Here reproduced under I.

TWO PENOLOGICAL PROBLEMS

Minutes of Evidence are probably more important than the Report itself. The techniques employed by the Commission, however, are largely conventional techniques. Witnesses were heard, invited and uninvited, official and private; some of them representing organizations, others only themselves; some giving only oral evidence, others also submitting elaborate written statements. Prisons and other institutions were visited in this country and abroad. In compliance with the Terms of Reference, special attention was devoted to the position in a number of Commonwealth and foreign countries. Questionnaires were addressed to their Governments; personal visits were paid to the United States and several European countries, and many distinguished experts were heard. As already observed most of these techniques are traditional techniques; any progress that has been made lies only in the greater thoroughness displayed in the collection of evidence and in the superior interpretation and evaluation of that evidence. With regard to scientific issues, including the interpretation of foreign laws, the Commission seems to have relied mainly on the answers received to the Questionnaire and on the evidence given by witnesses. There are two exceptions, however. In Appendix 6 on 'The deterrent value of Capital Punishment' the results of some original research, largely statistical, are presented, although even here most references to foreign literature are secondhand, i.e. taken from Professor Thorsten Sellin's Memorandum.

The second exception is to be found in those parts of the Report dealing with the English and Scottish law of murder and of insanity, which are scholarly pieces of legal research. Less satisfactory, however, is the treatment of the position in some Continental countries. Although the Commission had at their disposal the excellent Memoranda supplied in reply to their Questionnaire by the Governments and eminent legal authorities of these countries, in at least one essential point one gets the impression that the summary given in the Report (p. 164) and in Appendix 11 (p. 437) is based upon a misinterpretation. Nor is there any evidence of independent research through which this misunderstanding might have been avoided. The point we have in mind is the subjective element in the definition of murder. According to the Report, in most, if not all, European countries about which the Commission made enquiries, the requirement of 'intent' in the conception of murder is substantially the same as in this country,

CAPITAL PUNISHMENT: WHAT NEXT?

with the exception of the doctrine of constructive murder which does not exist on the Continent. According to Danish law, it is added, 'where a person ought to have been able to foresee the result of his action, an intention to produce that result may be presumed'. With great respect, this does not seem to the present writer to follow from the material at the disposal of the Commission. Nor is it the view prevailing in the very comprehensive Continental literature on the subject of *mens rea* in general and of *dolus eventualis* in particular, which stresses that there is no 'intent' where the offender did not actually approve of the fatal result of his action. A mere 'ought to have been able to foresee' is not enough.[1]

The question arises whether, apart from the need for more independent research into certain fundamental principles of Continental Criminal law, the work of the Commission might not have gained in value by the use of additional techniques of research. The Balfour Committee on the Procedure of Royal Commissions which reported in 1910, recognizing the infinite variety of problems to be faced by different Commissions, rightly refused to recommend a rigid set of rules of procedure. Extravagant and revolutionary innovations in research techniques would clearly be out of place in the work of Royal Commissions. This, however, does not necessarily exclude the use of techniques which, though unknown or not yet adequately developed twenty or thirty years ago, are now fairly generally accepted. It might be asked, for example, whether a public opinion poll of the kind conducted in Sweden some years ago and referred to in the Memorandum submitted by Professor Strahl-Uppsala could not have been safely initiated by the Commission instead of leaving this powerful weapon altogether to the Press. Attention might also be drawn to the survey of 'Social Attitudes as related to Social Class and Political Party' published a few years ago by Dr. H. J. Eysenck in which attitudes to capital punishment of samples of conservative, liberal, socialist and communist middle class and working class people were studied by means of questionnaires.[2] Similar research on matters of detail might have been done

[1] See also Glanville Williams, op. cit., pp. 47–8.
[2] H. J. Eysenck, *The British Journal of Sociology*, Vol. II, No. 3, September, 1951, pp. 199 et seq.—Similar criticisms of the technique employed by a recent Departmental Committee have been made by A. G. Rose, *Five Hundred Borstal Boys* (Oxford, Basil Blackwell, 1954), pp. 173–4.

extremely well by a Government Department (the Social Survey), and would have helped to ascertain the views of various sections of the community on certain important problems raised in the Report. To mention only one that concerns what is perhaps the principal recommendation of the Committee, i.e. to leave the crucial decisions to the jury, the objection was expressed before the Commission 'that the duties of the jury are already onerous and arduous enough, and that it would be unfair to require citizens selected at random to bear the heavy responsibility of deciding whether the death sentence should be imposed . . .' (paragraph 572). The Commission itself regards this, rightly, as 'a matter of opinion', but makes no attempt to find out what the opinion of the public may be on this point. Similar considerations apply to the statement 'we received no evidence that the public regards as inadequate the periods at present served by life sentence prisoners' (paragraph 649). The statement is probably correct, but it would have been better to supply the missing evidence. The possibility cannot be altogether excluded, of course, that the results of such studies of public opinion might be embarrassing to penal reformers, but it is a possibility that has to be faced in accordance with the general principle that the devil we know can be tackled more easily than the devil we don't know.

In other fields of scientific method, no trace can be found in the Report of any consideration given to the suggestions for research into the possibility of spotting potential murderers and of treating aggressive psychopaths put forward in the evidence of the *Institute for the Study and Treatment of Delinquency*.[1] Nor does the list of fifty very brief case histories in Appendix 4, though not without interest, do full justice to the legitimate claims of the case history technique. This is characteristic of the general weakness of the Report in the field of Criminology proper. It has made hardly any contribution to our knowledge of the crime of murder. There are repeated references to the well-known fact that 'there is perhaps no single class of offences that varies so widely both in character and in culpability as the class comprising those which may fall within the comprehensive common law definition of murder' (paragraph 21, see also 617). The opportunity has been missed, however, to make a thorough sociological study of a representative sample of persons found guilty of murder in this

[1] *The British Journal of Delinquency*, Vol. II, October, 1951, pp. 144 et seq.

CAPITAL PUNISHMENT: WHAT NEXT?

country, and apart from the fifty case histories covering a bare five and a quarter pages all we have got are some statistical tables showing the age and sex distribution of murderers and the kind of victims involved.[1]

To return to the recommendation to leave the question of life or death to the jury, to the present writer this does not seem to be quite as absurd as assumed by many eminent critics. No doubt the Commission might have been on safer ground if it could have shown that its proposal was in accord with a substantial body of public opinion. Apart from this, however, it has to be stressed that the recommendation, although a 'radical departure from the traditional conception of the functions of a jury' (paragraph 571), is a step in the right direction towards closer co-operation between judge and jury. As the Report states, there is nothing new in the idea of giving the jury some share in the choice of sentence, and apart from the countries studied by the Commission, i.e. Belgium, South Africa, and the United States, experiments in this direction have in fact been made in other lands.[2] The recommendations of the Commission suffer, however, from two fundamental weaknesses: first, the requirement that the decision of the jury on the sentence should be unanimous, which may well deprive the whole proposal of most of its practical value; and, secondly, the refusal to admit the presiding judge to this stage of the deliberations. This, together with a rule of unanimity, would make any consistent sentencing policy impossible. The latter danger is admitted by the Report (paragraph 575), but in view of the remaining Prerogative of Mercy not regarded as serious. To the present writer, any system which would open the door to a vacillating sentencing policy of the Courts in murder cases or be devoid of principles seems to be intolerable.[3]

[1] Appendix 3, Tables 1, 4, 6 and 7.
[2] In particular in France. See François Gorphe, *Les Décisions de Justice* (Paris, Recueil Sirey, 1952), p. 82. On Jury discretion see also J. E. Hall Williams, *Modern Law Review*, July, 1954.
[3] The view expressed above that the recommendation of the Royal Commission to leave the decision to the Jury is not quite as absurd as assumed by many critics should of course not be understood as implying the writer's general approval of trial by Jury (on this, see *Criminal Justice and Social Reconstruction*, pp. 246-9). It merely means that, *if* trial by Jury is retained in English law, any such attempt to bridge the present gap between Judge and Jury by giving the former some share in the guilt finding and the latter some share in the sentencing process seems to be welcome. The Royal Commission is in favour of the second, not however of the first idea.

TWO PENOLOGICAL PROBLEMS

In its discussion of the deterrent effect of Capital Punishment the Report shows a remarkably independent attitude and refuses to be swayed by sweeping generalizations based on subjective impressions of a few individual cases. It is good to have it officially confirmed, for example, that 'what an offender says on his arrest . . . is not necessarily a valid indication of what was in his mind when he committed it (the crime)' (paragraph 61) and that one should not 'base a penal policy in relation to murder on exaggerated estimates of the uniquely deterrent force of the death penalty' (paragraph 68).

The same independence of mind is shown in penological matters where the Report, while giving praise where praise is due, does not hesitate to criticize certain aspects of the present penal system. How far these criticisms are justified may be a matter of opinion, and it would be interesting to have the views of the Prison Commissioners on the paragraphs of the Report dealing with work and earnings of prisoners (63 and 636). Most important of all, however, are the conclusions arrived at by the Commission, after careful study of the evidence from this country and abroad, with regard to the treatment of those murderers who have so far been executed but would, in view of the discretion to be given to the jury, in future have to serve life sentences. Are they likely to present insuperable difficulties in prison or are existing arrangements adequate? The answer is that under present conditions a normal prisoner could, if necessary for the protection of society, serve a longer term than previously thought possible without undue risk of moral and physical deterioration, and that the presence of such prisoners would therefore constitute no insuperable difficulties to the prison administration. For mentally abnormal prisoners the Commission lends its support to the Prison Commissioners' well-known project of a new specialized institution for psychopathic or otherwise abnormal prisoners. While all this seems to call for no special comment, it is to be regretted that with regard to the after-care of prisoners discharged after serving very long sentences the Report refuses to accept the view of experts in this field that all such prisoners should be required to keep in touch with an After-Care Association after release. In spite of the low rate of recidivism of murderers it seems to be unduly optimistic to assume that, with the exception of prisoners with a bad criminal record or mentally abnormal prisoners, the decision can safely be left to them whether

CAPITAL PUNISHMENT: WHAT NEXT?

or not they should be under the supervision of an after-care agency.

Whether the recommendations of the Report will be accepted or not, there can be no doubt that the work of the Royal Commission has produced fresh evidence in favour of total abolition and represents nothing but another step towards this final goal.

POSTSCRIPT

The Report of the Royal Commission was debated in the House of Commons on the 10th February, 1955 (Hansard, cols. 2070-2190), when a motion to suspend capital punishment for a period of five years was defeated by 245 to 214 votes. Although the matter had been left to a free vote, the supporters of the motion came mainly from the Labour benches, the opponents mainly from the ranks of the Conservative Party; but a considerable number of members, mainly Labour, abstained. The Home Secretary, Major Lloyd George, while stressing that no final decision had as yet been taken by the Government, made it clear that no major alterations in the present law and practice could be expected for the time being. With regard to the drastic changes in the law of insanity and mental deficiency as recommended by the Royal Commission he even went so far as to say: that 'no advantage would be gained by disturbing the present position' and that it was better 'to leave matters as they are' (col. 2078). In spite of this negative result the debate was not without its remarkable episodes, in particular when a former Home Secretary, Mr. Chuter Ede, who in 1950 had refused to reprieve Timothy John Evans frankly admitted that 'Evans' case shows . . . that a mistake was possible, and that, in the form in which the verdict was actually given on a particular case, a mistake was made. I hope that no future Home Secretary . . . will ever have to feel that although he did his best . . . he sent a man to the gallows who was not "guilty as charged" ' (col. 2090). As long as the death penalty remains such irremediable errors of justice can never be altogether excluded.[1]

[1] As will be recalled, the Evans case was closely connected with the famous case of J. R. H. Christie who, in 1953, after Evans' execution, made a confession that he, not Evans, had killed Mrs. Evans. See the two Reports by Mr. J. Scott Henderson, Q.C., on the Evans case (H.M.S.O., Cmd. 8896 and 8946, 1953) and the criticism in *The Observer*, 20th September, 1953.

CHAPTER 11

SHORT TERM IMPRISONMENT AND ITS ALTERNATIVES [1]

I. INTRODUCTORY

THE meaning of the phrase 'short term imprisonment' may be in need of some clarification. 'Short' is a relative conception, and even a sentence of one week may seem long to some prisoners. What we have in mind when using the term as penologists is probably 'too short to achieve the modern objects of imprisonment', i.e. to be of any constructive value. In the remarkable memorandum in which the Prison Commission for England and Wales outlined their 'proposals for the development of the Prison system for adults during the immediate post-war years',[2] it is pointed out that for the purposes of that memorandum a 'short' sentence means a sentence of less than four years, taking into account the period of remission of one third of the sentence. It was also stressed there that in order to derive the full benefit of the training provided at a Training Prison, such as Wakefield or Maidstone, a minimum sentence of twelve months would as a rule be required. Allowing for remission and the inevitable delay arising through the selection for, and transfer to, the Training Prison, such a sentence would be just adequate to provide the necessary minimum training period of six months. Similarly, in the semi-official 'Report on the Psychological Treatment of Crime' by W. Norwood East and W. H. de B. Hubert[3] a sentence of less than six months is regarded as generally insufficient for psychotherapeutic treatment in prison and sentences of between six and

[1] Report presented to the Twelfth International Penal and Penitentiary Congress (The Hague, 1950), and brought up to date in the note and references.
[2] 'Annual Report of the Prison Commission for the year 1945', (1947), pp. 64 et seq.
[3] H.M.S.O., 1939, p. 158.

SHORT TERM IMPRISONMENT

twelve months are recommended for offenders likely to benefit from such treatment. Without going more deeply into the matter, one might therefore conclude that sentences which do not provide for the offender an undisturbed period in prison of at least six months for vocational and character training, general education, and in suitable cases for psycho-therapeutic treatment have to be regarded as too short from any constructive point of view. Such sentences can therefore be justified, if at all, only for the purposes of retribution and deterrence. It cannot be the task of this paper to enter into a discussion as to whether or how far these two objectives can in fact be achieved through short term imprisonment. In conformity with the prevailing tendency in modern Penology we take it for granted that sentences which do not provide that undisturbed period of at least six months are harmful.[1]

II. THE PRESENT POSITION IN GREAT BRITAIN REGARDING SHORT PRISON SENTENCES

(1) *England and Wales.* For many years, there has been a certain tendency of the Courts to avoid the imposition of very short sentences. This may be shown in the following Table:[2]

TABLE 1

Sentences of not more than one month

	1913	1938	1947
Men	81,986 = 78·2%	13,865 = 51·0%	6,511 = 23·3%
Women	29,334 = 87·7%	2,430 = 70·7%	1,279 = 39·2%

[1] In the Resolution of the I.P.P.C. of 1946, endorsed in 1948 (*Recueil de documents en matière pénale et pénitentiaire*, Novembre, 1948, p. 343, note 1), only sentences not exceeding three months are classified as too short.

[2] Computed from the 'Report of the Prison Commissioners for the year 1948', p. 17. The percentage figures are percentages of total receptions in prison.—In recent years, the tables have been slightly modified, and separate figures are now given not for 'sentences of not more than one month' but for 'sentences not exceeding five weeks'. The percentage figures for the latter category were 26 in 1949 and 25·3 in 1951 for men and 41·7 in 1949 and 40·2 in 1951 for women. This indicates that no substantial changes in the proportion of these very short sentences have occurred since this paper was written. The same applies to sentences of not more than 6 months, at least with regard to men where the percentage figures are 70·2 in 1949 and 70·5 in 1951. For women, however, the proportion of such sentences has even further increased to 96·8 in 1949 and 95·6 in 1951.

TWO PENOLOGICAL PROBLEMS
Sentences of not more than six months

	1913	1938	1947
Men	100,122 = 95·5%	25,017 = 88·3%	19,528 = 70·0%
Women	33,130 = 99·1%	3,268 = 95·1%	2,863 = 87·8%

On the other hand, the percentage of sentences of between one month and six months has not only not declined but in fact greatly increased (from 17·3 per cent in 1913 to 37·3 per cent in 1938 and to 46·7 per cent in 1947 for men; from 11·4 per cent in 1913 to 24·4 per cent in 1938 and 48·6 per cent in 1947 for women). Even the absolute figures have considerably risen in this category between 1938 and 1947, i.e. from 10,152 to 13,017 for men and from 838 to 1,293 for women.

It should be noted that these figures refer only to persons sentenced to imprisonment, excluding those committed to prison for non-payment of fines (see below III, 2a). On the other hand, they do not necessarily mean as many different individuals since in some cases the same individual may serve several short prison sentences within the course of one year.

Separate figures are available for young prisoners between the ages of sixteen and twenty-one. In 1947, out of 2,589 boys and 323 girls of this category sentenced to imprisonment, 731 boys and 111 girls served sentences of not more than one month, and 1,919 boys and 269 girls sentences of not more than six months.[1]

(2) *Scotland.* In Scotland, the average length of sentences of imprisonment has risen from 33·5 days in 1939 to 81·4 days in 1948. This rise is attributed, however, not to any drastic change in the sentencing policy of the criminal courts but to the transfer to Scotland from England and abroad of Court Martial cases from the services with long sentences.[2] The actual length of sentences of imprisonment imposed within these ten years is shown in

[1] Annual Report, pp. 21–2. As a consequence of the Criminal Justice Act, 1948, sect. 17, the frequency of such sentences has considerably declined. Further material on the subject of short prison sentences for young offenders has meanwhile been published by Sir Leo Page, *The Young Lag* (London, Faber and Faber, Ltd., 1950) and by John Spencer, *Crime and the Services* (London, Routledge & Kegan Paul, Ltd., 1954), especially pp. 233 et seq.; also by W. F. Roper, *The British Journal of Delinquency*, Vol. I, No. 1, 1950, p. 20.

[2] 'Report on Prisons in Scotland for the years 1939–1948' (Edinburgh, H.M.S.O. 1949), p. 6. Before the war, reports on Prison Administration were published annually, and the practice has now been resumed.

SHORT TERM IMPRISONMENT

another Table,[1] from which the following figures are taken:

TABLE 2

	Under one month	One month and under 3 months	3 months and under 6 months	6 months and under 12 months	Total of all Sentences of Imprisonment
1939	8,142	2,892	626	306	12,097
1948	2,499	3,730	1,232	884	8,769

It appears, therefore, that in Scotland, too, only sentences under one month have become less frequent, whereas otherwise there has been a considerable increase in short prison sentences. The figures are not strictly comparable to those for England and Wales as the first category in the Table excludes sentences of one month which are included in the first category of the corresponding statistics for England and Wales.

III. THE AVAILABLE ALTERNATIVES AND THEIR LIMITATIONS

The alternatives to the short prison sentence may be institutional, non-institutional or semi-institutional.

(1) *Institutional alternatives.* (a) Detention in police cells under section 13 of the Criminal Justice Administration Act, 1914, and Section 4 of the Money Payments (Justices Procedure) Act, 1935. The maximum period of such detention is four days, but of the 454 male and 71 female adult offenders dealt with in this way in 1948, 452 males and 70 females were actually detained for not longer than the one day of conviction.[2] This measure is obviously in no way constructive, and its only advantage over the short prison sentence is that it is less expensive and avoids the stigma and possible contamination of the prison. The proposals made in the Criminal Justice Bill, 1938, for the improvement and extension of this measure have, rightly, not been embodied in the Criminal Justice Act, 1948.

(b) Borstal training. This is probably the best institutional

---

[1] pp. 33.
[2] *Criminal Statistics England and Wales 1948*, Table V. The corresponding figures for 1953 are 233(222) males and 29(27) females: *Criminal Statistics for 1953*, Table VII.

alternative to prison available in Great Britain, but its scope is limited by the law and the capacity of the existing Borstal Institutions. The Criminal Justice Act, 1948, has at the same time widened and narrowed the categories of offenders to whom this training may be applied. While it can now be used even for young people showing no definite criminal tendencies, the age range which had before been from sixteen to twenty-three years has now been reduced to a maximum of twenty-one years. It remains to be seen whether the net result will be an increase or a fall in numbers. So far, many more boys and girls of Borstal age have been sent to prison in recent years than to Borstal,[1] and as shown above (II) most of them on sentences of not more than 6 months. It has also been stressed by the Prison Commissioners year after year that too many first offenders of this age category are sentenced to imprisonment and that even for many of those with several previous convictions a Borstal sentence might have been preferable to imprisonment.

(c) Approved schools. These Institutions can only in a few cases be regarded as alternatives to short term imprisonment since only persons under the age of seventeen can be committed to them and the number of such persons sent to prison is very small. As the Criminal Justice Act, 1948, sect. 17, contains further restrictions on imprisonment of young persons the number is likely to decline even more in future.

2. *Non-Institutional alternatives.* (a) Fines. Ever since the beginning of the fight against short term imprisonment, the fine has been regarded as one of the most important weapons in that struggle. To achieve its object, however, it has to be backed by suitable legal provisions and court practice to avoid, wherever possible, imprisonment for non-payment of fines. In modern English criminal law, particularly since the Criminal Justice Administration Act, 1914, it has been the tendency not only to enable the courts to make wider use of this penalty but also to

---

[1] See 'Annual Report of the Prison Commission for 1948,' p. 19. Since 1948, the position has changed, and in 1951 receptions of persons of this age group numbered 1,977 males and 112 females to Borstal and only 1,155 males and 88 females to prison. As rightly stressed by the Prison Commissioners (Report for 1952, p. 21), even the latter figures are still too high, considering that 324 of these boys and 22 of these girls had not before been found guilty of offences.

SHORT TERM IMPRISONMENT

make it easier for the offender to pay the fine instead of having to go to prison. The duty was imposed on the Magistrates to accept instalments of fines, to allow time for payment and also, when fixing the amount of a fine, to take into consideration, among other things, the means of the offender. This, in connection with improved economic conditions and a reduction in drunkenness offences, led to a fall of the annual average number of cases of imprisonment in default of payment of fines from about 83,000 before the first World War to about 13,000 in the years after. Another important step in the right direction was taken by the Money Payments (Justices Procedure) Act, 1935, which provides that magistrates shall not, as used to be done before, when imposing the fine simultaneously fix the period of imprisonment in case of default, unless they have some special reason for doing so, e.g. the gravity of the offence. This ensures that the offender has to be heard again in court and that an enquiry has to be held into his ability to pay before he can be committed to prison.[1] Under another provision of the Act of 1935 the magistrates have power to place an offender under supervision until the fine has been paid, and in the case of offenders under the age of twenty-one they have to do so unless it is impracticable or undesirable. Partly as the result of this Act, the number of cases of imprisonment in default of fines has now fallen to about 3,000 per year).[2] There are other reasons for this improvement, too: higher wages and the fact that, on the whole, the level of fines actually imposed has not kept up with the changes in the value of money which have occurred in the past ten years or so. No statistics are available to show the developments in the average amounts of fines for different categories of offences. There have been frequent complaints, however, that fines have been too small. In the past, this may often have been due to the failure of the legislator to increase the legal maximum which, in many nineteenth-century statutes, was only forty shillings. Nowadays, especially in wartime Acts dealing with profiteering, black market offences and the like, the permitted maximum is usually high enough to ensure that the offender at

[1] To some extent, the powers of the magistrates under this Act are still doubtful; see e.g. *The Magistrate*, July–August, 1942.
[2] More than one-third of these had been sentenced for drunkenness and more than one-sixth for larceny, whereas the number of prostitutes is very small ('Annual Report of Prison Commission for 1948', pp. 103 et seq.). The total has now risen again to approximately 5,000 cases in 1953.

TWO PENOLOGICAL PROBLEMS

least derives no prefix from the offence. This may have made courts more inclined to impose fines instead of imprisonment. The provision in sect. 13 of the Criminal Justice Act, 1948, which extends to Assizes and Quarter Sessions the power, so far exercised only by magistrates, to impose a fine for a felony may have a similar effect.

Recent *Criminal Statistics* show a strong tendency of criminal courts to make even more use of the fine than before. Between 1938 and 1948 the percentage of persons of all ages found guilty of indictable offences who were dealt with in this way increased from 17 to 29 for males and from 22 to 33 for females. For boys under 14 years the increase was from 5 to 13 per cent. Of persons found guilty of non-indictable, i.e. the less serious, offences 94·7 per cent were fined in 1948, and of persons found guilty of black market operations and similar offences against still valid Defence Regulations about 90 per cent.[1]

In spite of this tendency, it can hardly be expected that fines will in the future altogether take the place of short prison sentences. Many cases will remain where magistrates will be unwilling to impose fines because they are not regarded as punitive enough or because the offender is not likely to pay a substantial sum and the imposition of a fine therefore seems unnecessarily to complicate proceedings.

(*b*) Probation. This is an alternative more in line with modern penological thought than the fine, but it is regrettable to see that probation, too, has failed to eliminate the short prison sentence. After a period of slow but steady growth from the passing of the Probation of Offenders Act, 1907, up to the last war, the percentage of offenders placed on probation has in recent years greatly declined. Although the absolute figures for indictable offences (all age groups) show an increase from 21,820 in 1938 to 24,386 in 1948 (males) and from 3,525 to 5,027 (females), in view of the considerable post-war rise in crime this means in fact a fall in the use of probation from 32 to 22 and from 36 to 29 per cent, respectively, and for some of the younger age categories the reduction has been even more drastic.[2] There can be little doubt that the

---

[1] *Criminal Statistics for 1948*, pp. X to XVI.—These figures have remained substantially unchanged.

[2] *Criminal Statistics for 1948*, pp. X and XI.—These figures, too have remained substantially unchanged.

SHORT TERM IMPRISONMENT

territory lost by probation has to some extent been occupied by short prison sentences. It would exceed the scope of this paper to discuss all those developments which explain why probation has recently been receiving less than its due share. One of these factors, however, seems to be obvious: a hardening in the attitude of judges and magistrates, not unexpected in view of widespread public anxiety, which makes them less willing to replace prison by probation. Another factor may be the better understanding on the part of the Courts of the limitations of probation, resulting in a more discriminating selection of cases.

(c) Dismissal and Binding over without Probation. Dismissal means that although the accused has been found guilty and convicted of the offence no further action is taken against him. (This is now called 'absolute discharge' under the Criminal Justice Act, 1948, sect. 7). 'Binding over', now called 'conditional discharge', means that the offender, without being placed on probation, may be sentenced for the original offence if he commits another offence during the period of conditional discharge, which is now for a maximum of one year. Both these methods are extensively used, for example, in 1947 for 18 per cent of all adult offenders and for 22 per cent of adolescents between seventeen and twenty-one dealt with by Magistrates Courts; for 38 per cent of all juveniles under fourteen years and 26 per cent of those between fourteen and seventeen).[1] Neither of them can be regarded as constructive, but they are probably indispensable for certain minor offences, many of which might otherwise be punished by short term imprisonment. They take the place of the judicial reprimand used in some countries.

(3) The Criminal Justice Act of 1948 provides two further alternatives to short term imprisonment which have, however, not yet been put into operation: Detention Centres and Attendance Centres.[2] Detention Centres (sect. 18) are intended for persons

[1] *Criminal Statistics for 1947*, pp. IX and X.
[2] This paragraph has now become largely out of date. There are at present more than twenty Attendance Centres and two Detention Centres for boys in existence in England and Wales, and the numbers of juveniles committed to them in 1953 are as follows (*Criminal Statistics for 1953*, Tables IX and X): Attendance Centres: age 14-17 : 418; under 14 : 336. Detention Centres: age 14-17 : 186. For details see, on Attendance Centres, R. M. Braithwaite, *The British Journal of Delinquency*, Vol. II, January 1952, pp. 242 et seq.; on Detention Centres Max Grünhut, Vol. V, January, 1955, pp. 191 et seq., and Annual Report of the Magistrates' Association for 1953-4.

between fourteen and twenty-one for periods of detention up to three or, in certain cases, six months. Attendance Centres (sect. 19) for persons between twelve and twenty-one, are meant only for limited periods of attendance, not exceeding altogether twelve hours. As it cannot be foreseen how much these new types of Institutions will be used by the courts it is impossible to say whether they will produce a substantial fall in short prison sentences for persons under twenty-one. With regard to Detention Centres it is even difficult to express any views whether they are likely to constitute an advance over short term imprisonment as everything will depend on the manner in which such a sentence will be carried out.

While the Attendance Centre constitutes a semi-institutional alternative just beginning to function, probation with the requirement of residence (now Criminal Justice Act, 1948, sect. 3 subsection 4) is another alternative belonging to this category which has been available for many years. It is used mainly for young offenders whose homes are bad or at least unsuitable for them but who are not regarded as in need of institutional treatment in the fullest sense. They may be placed on probation and required to reside, for a period not exceeding one year, either with relatives or in a foster home or in an approved probation home or hostel or in another institution, remaining meanwhile under the supervision of the probation officer. Adults may also be required to live wherever directed. It has to be borne in mind that, as a probation order can be made only with the consent of the offender (unless he is under fourteen years of age), such requirements cannot be imposed against his will. Although very little information has been published to show the extent, nature, and success of this system,[1] it is generally regarded as efficient and may save many offenders from imprisonment who would have but little chance of being placed on probation if the requirement of residence were not available. The suggestion has recently been made that the system should be made compulsory, extended beyond the present maximum of one year and become independent of probation.

[1] See now John C. Spencer and Tadeusz Grygier, 'The Probation Hostel in England' (*Focus*, November, 1952; re-published by the I.S.T.D., London).

SHORT TERM IMPRISONMENT

IV. SUGGESTIONS

(1) Perhaps the most obvious remedy seems to be the legal prohibition of all prison sentences under three or even six months.[1] Although we are in favour of it, certain dangers likely to arise from it should not be overlooked. Unless such a prohibition is backed by a sympathetic and enlightened judiciary and supplemented by the provision of adequate alternatives it may lead to undesirable consequences: In cases where they regard a prison term as indispensable the courts may, instead of choosing one of the alternatives, resort to unnecessarily heavy sentences. Moreover, they may send accused persons to prison on remand for a few weeks even in cases where there is no real need for a remand to prison and where it is clear from the beginning that the sentence eventually to be imposed will not be one of imprisonment. A period of imprisonment on remand may therefore become the substitute for a short prison sentence with the added disadvantage that the accused is deprived of his right to appeal against the prison sentence. There can be little doubt that, to some extent, this happens already now,[2] but it would become even more frequent if the minimum length of imprisonment permissible would be substantially raised. The Criminal Justice Act, 1948, sects. 27 and 48, by providing for the establishment of Remand Centres for persons under twenty-one, will reduce at least the number of young offenders sent to prison on remand as soon as such Remand Centres will be established on an adequate scale.[3]

Another difficulty arises from certain technical provisions of English criminal law which may however be encountered in other legislations as well. For some offences, for example indecent exposure, the maximum term of imprisonment that can at present be summarily imposed is three months; more than 300 sentences of under three months were passed for this offence in 1947. If the maximum were to be substantially raised, the accused would have

---

[1] See the comparative material in *Recueil*, Novembre, 1948, pp. 339 and 355-6 (see note 1, p. 243 above).
[2] See F. T. Giles, *The Magistrates Courts* (1949), p. 69 and the address by the Hon. Ewen E. S. Montagu, *The Magistrate*, November, 1953, p. 74.
[3] No such Centres have so far been established, and the number of persons between fourteen and twenty-one committed to prison in 1951 on remand, but not subsequently sent to prison on conviction was 2,683 males and 413 females (*Prison Commissioners' Report for 1952*, p. 23).

TWO PENOLOGICAL PROBLEMS

the right to be tried, or the magistrates might feel that he should be tried, by a jury, which is not suitable, however, for cases where children may have to appear as witnesses.[1] Moreover, longer prison sentences should be imposed for such offences only if they can be served in special institutions or at least combined with therapeutic treatment. As such institutions or adequate facilities for treatment in prison are often not available, the raising of the minimum term would simply mean that such sexual offenders would receive longer sentences without the constructive treatment which alone could justify the greater length. This example may illustrate the complexity of the technical problems which might result if the minimum term of imprisonment were raised without a simultaneous revision of criminal procedure and of the whole penal system.

(2) Devices such as conditional suspension of prosecution or abstention from punishment,[2] while useful in themselves, seem to serve mainly other purposes than as alternatives to short prison sentences. Where an efficient probation service exists, it is more likely that the Court will use probation as the substitute for prison than any of those measures which have little constructive value. In particular, abstaining from prosecution or 'deferred prosecution' for juvenile offenders, widely used in some districts of the U.S.A.,[3] owes its existence to the wish of the authorities to avoid Court appearance and conviction. It is more lenient even than probation and will hardly be used in cases where imprisonment, instead of probation, is contemplated.[4]

(3) Of greater practical importance is the establishment of special institutions where specific types of offenders such as chronic alcoholics, psychopathic sex offenders, etc., can receive, instead of the present short prison sentence, the prolonged scientific treatment which they require. For those who are in need of such

[1] See on this *The Criminal Law and the Sexual Offenders* (London, British Medical Association, 1949), p. 12.
[2] See *Recueil*, November, 1948, pp. 357-8.
[3] See Conrad P. Printzlien, *Federal Probation*, March, 1948.
[4] After this was written, some interesting material has been published for various European countries, notably Norway, showing the wide scope of the application of conditional suspension of prosecution and its potentialities, in particular for young offenders (see *Probation and Related Measures*, United Nations, Department of Social Affairs, New York, 1951, pp. 140 et seq.). See also *Yearbook of the Northern Association of Criminalists*, 1951-2, pp. XVIII et seq.

SHORT TERM IMPRISONMENT

specialist treatment open Colonies on Swedish lines[1] may be one of the solutions.

In this connection, an interesting experiment recently initiated by the Prison Commission for England and Wales should be mentioned.[2] It is concerned with prisoners in need of psychotherapeutic treatment who cannot receive it at one of the prison psychological centres because their sentences are too short (see I). Arrangements are being made for some of them to be treated at their local prison by outside psycho-therapists employed by the National Health Service in the hope that, once contact has been established in prison, the prisoner will be more likely to continue treatment after discharge. Some of the obstacles to psychological treatment for short term prisoners may in this way be overcome until special institutions will be provided which will justify the imposition of longer sentences on offenders in need of prolonged treatment.

(4) The conversion of fines into labour for the State or the local community, or the imposition of a sentence of compulsory labour without the preliminary device of a fine, has for many years been regarded as one of the most attractive alternatives. Unfortunately, the information so far obtainable from countries where it has been tried is too scanty to form any definite opinion,[3] but the hope may be expressed that this gap will be filled by the Reports submitted to the Congress of 1950. The Soviet system has become the target of so much political controversy[4] that it can hardly be used for scientific purposes even by way of illustration.

(5) In view of the inadequacy of our present-day knowledge, our principal recommendation has to be of a preliminary character: Before any more definite proposals can be made, research is needed in at least two directions:

(a) In a number of countries the records of an unselected sample of a few hundred short-term prisoners should be examined. Among the factors to be analysed should be the following: age, sex, occupation, personal and family history, mental capacity,

[1] Göransson, *Recueil*, November, 1948, p. 341; also p. 344.
[2] 'Annual Report for 1948', p. 62, also 'Report for 1952', pp. 105–6.
[3] *Recueil*, pp. 361, 355–6. See, however, the interesting references to the Finnish labour colonies in the Yearbook of the Northern Associations of Criminalists, 1948–9, pp. xviii and xxx.
[4] See especially David J. Dallin and Boris I. Nicolaevsky, *Forced Labour in Soviet Russia* (London, Hollis & Carter, 1948).

education, offence, length of sentence, previous convictions and punishment received, loss of employment through imprisonment, treatment in prison (including vocational training, educational classes, privileges, psychological treatment), description of the prison concerned, after-conduct over a few years. The object of this study should be to determine in how many cases another, more suitable, method of treatment might have been available to the courts. If possible, the after-conduct of a control group of offenders, showing the same characteristics as the first sample but treated differently (for example, by probation, fines, etc.) might be examined in order to ascertain whether they show any marked differences in their after-histories. In addition, another sample of remand prisoners should be examined to see to what extent remand is used as a substitute for prison sentences.

(b) Some of the material on alternatives which is likely to be submitted to the Congress should be studied at greater detail in a number of countries with a view to collecting further information on alternatives already successfully applied.

POSTSCRIPT

I. The Hague Congress, for which this paper was written, resulted in the following compromise Resolution: [1]

'(1) Short term imprisonment presents serious inconveniences, from a social, economic and domestic point of view.

(2) The conditional sentence is without doubt one of the most effective alternatives to short term imprisonment. Probation conceived as suspended pronouncement of sentence or as suspension of execution of sentence, appears also to be one of the solutions much to be recommended. The granting of suspended sentence or of probation to the offender should not necessarily prevent a later grant of a similar measure.

(3) Fines are quite properly suggested as a suitable substitute for short prison terms. In order to reduce the number of those imprisoned in default of fines it seems necessary that:
  (a) the fine be adjusted to the financial status of the defendant;
  (b) he be permitted, if need be, to pay the fine in instalments and

[1] See Proceedings of the Congress, published by the Secretary-General of the Congress, Dr. Thorsten Sellin, (Bern, International Penal and Penitentiary Commission, 1951), Vol. II, pp. 222-46, 285-91, and the final text of the Resolution, p. 436.

SHORT TERM IMPRISONMENT

be granted a suspension of payments for periods when his income is inadequate;

(c) unpaid fines be converted into imprisonment not automatically but by a court decision in each individual case.

(4) It is suggested also that recourse should be had to judicial reprimand, compulsory labour in liberty, the abstention from prosecution, or a ban in certain cases against exercising certain professions or activities.

(5) In the exceptional cases when a short term imprisonment is pronounced, it should be served under conditions that minimize the possibility of recidivism.'

While there can hardly be any serious disagreement with these recommendations, it cannot be said that they represent a very substantial advance over the opinions expressed by the First International Congress, London, 1872,[1] or the resolution of 1946. The following interesting features of the deliberations may be mentioned: The general rapporteur, Mr. Göransson-Sweden, as also the national rapporteur for Norway, Professor Andenaes in his preparatory report, uttered a warning against the misconception that short-term imprisonment should be avoided at all cost. There is some force in his argument that in Sweden 90 per cent of short-term first offenders did not recidivate within five years after release, but it has to be borne in mind that prison conditions in Sweden are exceptionally favourable and that, according to Göransson, about two-thirds of these short-termers are sent to open colonies where they can do productive work and are paid approximately the equivalent of one dollar a day. Another of his arguments, that long-term imprisonment also has its unfavourable consequences for the prisoner, is no doubt true but somewhat besides the point as offenders are not sentenced to long-term imprisonment solely because of its beneficial results to the individual concerned, but for other cogent reasons as well.

The most radical motion submitted to the Congress (by Mr. Cannat-France) but finally withdrawn, proposed a recommendation to the governments to prohibit sentences of one year or less. This, although it was mentioned neither by the supporters nor by the opponents of the motion, is in line with the state of affairs in the Soviet Union where imprisonment up to one year has been replaced by other forms of forced labour.[2]

[1] See Negley K. Teeters, 'Deliberations of the International Penal and Penitentiary Congresses'. Sponsored by the American Prison Association, Philadelphia, 1949, p. 32: Question 10). The resolution of 1946 is reproduced in the *Proceedings* of 1950, Vol. II, p. 223.

[2] See my *Dilemma of Penal Reform* (London, George Allen & Unwin, Ltd., 1939), p. 133.

TWO PENOLOGICAL PROBLEMS

The need for further research on the lines suggested in this paper was referred to by one single speaker [1] and completely ignored in the Resolution.

II. In France, where a term not exceeding one year is regarded as 'short', an interesting scheme has recently been initiated according to which in such cases the state prosecutor has been authorized, after consulting the trial judge and the magistrate chairman of the Aftercare Society, to defer execution of the sentence indefinitely. For those who have to serve their sentence various modes of execution exist, including solitary confinement, placement in a workshop outside the institution, or semi-freedom, i.e. working outside without supervision and staying in the institution at night. See Charles Germain, *The Annals of the American Academy of Political and Social Science*, Vol. 293, May, 1954, p. 143.

III. In an investigation recently carried out in Denmark the conclusion was reached that, for a sample of 126 prisoners serving terms of not more than five months, the imposition of a short prison sentence seemed to be the most appropriate way of disposal in only 14 cases, whereas for the great majority of them other measures provided by Danish law were regarded as more appropriate by the investigators. See Karen Berntsen and Karl O. Christiansen in *International Review of Criminal Policy*, No. 6, July, 1954, pp.24 et seq.

[1] Professor Hurwitz-Denmark, p. 289.

PART FIVE
CRIMINAL LAW

CHAPTER 12

THE SOCIOLOGICAL ASPECTS OF THE CRIMINAL LAW [1]

A Methodological Study

I

WHILE a paper on some sociological problems of Criminology might have been a relatively easy undertaking—though perhaps slightly marred by the feeling that it is almost impossible to say anything original on so hackneyed a subject in a single lecture—the position seems to be entirely different with regard to the sociological aspects of the Criminal Law. This is not only a comparatively neglected topic; it is also a field of study where, before anything useful can be said about its actual problems, an attempt has to be made to define its meaning and scope. The sociological aspects of the Criminal Law cannot profitably be discussed without an examination of the whole conception of the Sociology of Law of which they are part and parcel. The various attempts to define this conception, made by great sociologists and legal philosophers such as Max Weber, Durkheim, Ehrlich, Kantorowicz, Roscoe Pound, Sinzheimer, and more recently by Gurvitch, Timasheff, Julius Stone, Jerome Hall, Michael and Adler, and others, have no doubt been important milestones towards that goal, although occasionally one might have longed for some more

[1] This paper reproduces, with some alterations, the substance of a lecture delivered in May, 1949, at the University of Utrecht as part of a series, arranged by its Criminological Institute, on the juridical, sociological, psychological, and moral aspects of the Criminal Law. The lecture was subsequently repeated at the Universities of Leiden and Amsterdam.
A Dutch translation was published in the Dutch sociological journal *Mens en Maatschappij*, Amsterdam, Vol. 25, January, 1950, under the title: *De sociologische Aspecten van de Strafwet*. The English version has not been previously published.

practical guidance instead of ample theoretical hair-splitting. Nevertheless, much still remains to be done in this field in general and with regard to the Sociology of the Criminal Law in particular. Attention was paid, though not always by lawyers, to sociological problems in the Criminal Law perhaps earlier than in most other branches of the law. However, the coming into existence of Criminology, and especially of its sociological section, Crimino-Sociology, has somewhat obscured the position, and as the main topic of this paper is neither Crimino-Sociology nor its twin brother, the sociological aspects of Penology, it is essential that a clear line of demarcation should be drawn between these two disciplines, on the one hand, and the Sociology of the Criminal Law, on the other.

Can we be sure, however, that a distinction of this kind can be made at all? In the opinion of a distinguished Russo-American writer, Professor Timasheff, Criminology is in fact identical with the Sociology of Criminal Law.[1] Surely, such an identification is unjustified already for the reason that Sociology—even in its widest sense—is not the only scientific discipline which supplies Criminology with its material and its methods of study. The psychological aspects of Criminology, in particular, are equally important as the sociological ones although, as pointed out elsewhere in this volume, in American Criminology the sociological approach prevails. There are, however, some further arguments against Timasheff's view which will be discussed later on.

According to Professor E. H. Sutherland, the American criminologist, Criminology consists of three main divisions: the Sociology of Law, Criminal Aetiology, and Penology, and he defines the Sociology of Law as 'an attempt at scientific analysis of the conditions under which criminal laws develop'.[2] This view, as will also become clear in the course of this paper, is just as unacceptable as that of Timasheff. While it is no doubt one of the functions of the Sociology of the Criminal Law to examine the conditions under which criminal laws develop, such an examination cannot be regarded as coming under the scope of Criminology.

[1] See N. S. Timasheff, *An Introduction to the Sociology of Law* (Harvard Sociological Studies, Vol. 3, Cambridge, 1939), pp. 27 et seq.
[2] E. H. Sutherland, *Principles of Criminology* (Lippincott, Chicago) 4th ed., 1947, p. 1.

THE SOCIOLOGICAL ASPECTS

One of the principal legal authors in the field of the Sociology of the Criminal Law, Professor Jerome Hall, draws the following distinction between Criminology and the Sociology of the Criminal Law: Basing himself upon the supposition that the Sociology of Law can be distinguished as a separate branch of Sociology only if its close relationship to actual legal rules is preserved, he uses the term Sociology of Criminal Law for the body of sociological knowledge specifically related to rules of the Criminal Law, whereas Criminology to him means the study of certain social phenomena independent of such rules.[1]

From this variety of views it becomes clear, as indeed it may have been obvious from the beginning, that we cannot expect to arrive at a satisfactory definition of our basic conception without a simultaneous discussion of the scope of Criminology, that of Sociology and, perhaps, even of some other kindred disciplines.

It is a well-known fact that, in spite of many efforts, no universal agreement has so far been reached as to the exact meaning and scope of the term Criminology.[2] Quite apart from the purely terminological question of whether the term should include matters of treatment as well or whether for the latter a special term, Penology, should be used, there is still a considerable amount of controversy. It is generally accepted that it is the object of Criminology to study criminal behaviour and the physical, psychological and socio-economic factors behind it; how and why people commit crimes; the kind of crime they commit and the kind of people they are; and whether they, or at least some of them, can be grouped together in types. Beyond that, there is controversy. In particular, is Criminology concerned exclusively with *criminal* behaviour in the legal sense or rather with the much wider conception of *anti-social* behaviour? And should it be confined, as an 'idiographic' discipline, to the study of facts and causal relations or probabilities and, as Penology, to that of the

---

[1] See Jerome Hall, 'Criminology and a modern Penal Code', *Journal of Criminal Law and Criminology*, 1936, Vol. 27, p. 1 (reprinted in his *Readings in Jurisprudence*, p. 1070); Hall, *General Principles of Criminal Law* (Bobbs-Merrill, Indianapolis 1947), pp. 558-9.

[2] Definitions such as those given by Mabel A. Elliott, *Crime in Modern Society* (above, Chapter 8, note 3, p. 195), p. 24 ('the scientific study of crime and its treatment') or H. v. Hentig, *Crime: Causes and Conditions* (New York and London, McGraw-Hill, 1947, p. 1 ('the facts known about crime and crime control') are too general to assist us in overcoming the specific difficulties with which we are here concerned.

effects of treatment in individual cases; or is it also a 'nomothetic' discipline, aiming at the discovery of scientific laws and uniformities of a general nature?[1]

With regard to the first question, I agree with Professor Thorsten Sellin's view, brilliantly expounded in his *Culture Conflict and Crime*,[2] that the subject matter of Criminology can be limited to the study of criminal behaviour as defined by the Criminal Law just as little as Psychiatry can be confined to a study of types of mental disease defined in legal terms, and that it should rather be extended to the study of what Sellin calls 'conduct norms', i.e. norms of behaviour laid down by all the various social groups to which the individual belongs and of which the State with its law is only one. As Beth has expressed it,[3] Criminology tends to become the 'science of undesirable social behaviour'. This means, for example, that the study of drunkenness, prostitution, gambling, sharp business practices, 'white collar crime', and the like, or of conditions such as pathological lying, truancy, and social maladjustment in general is a proper subject for Criminology, whether or not these forms of anti-social behaviour or conditions happen to be covered by the Criminal Law. It has to be admitted that the substitution of the 'conduct norm' for the legal norm as the object of study of Criminology means greater vagueness, but it makes at least sure that important forms of anti-social behaviour can receive the careful examination which they require.

This wider use of the term Criminology seems to be in accordance with Jerome Hall's distinction, referred to before, between Criminology as the study of certain social phenomena regardless of the Criminal Law and the Sociology of Criminal Law as the branch of Sociology especially related to the latter. As Hall rightly points out,[4] this distinction is likely to be reduced to almost nil

[1] On this difference see, e.g., Timasheff, op. cit., p. 19. G. W. Allport, *Personality* (1937), p. 22, rightly regards the two categories as potentially overlapping. See also G. W. Allport, 'The Use of Personal Documents in Psychological Science', Social Science Research Council, New York *Bulletin 49* (1942), pp. 53 et seq. and *passim*; T. H. Pear, 'Perspectives in modern Psychology,' *British Journal of Psychology* (General Section), Vol. XXXVIII, Part 3, March, 1948.
[2] *Culture Conflict and Crime* (1938), (New York, Social Science Research Council), Bulletin 41, pp. 19 et seq., 30 et seq.
[3] Marianne W. Beth, *Journal of Criminal Law and Criminology*, Vol. 32, no. 1, May–June, 1941, pp. 67 et seq.
[4] *Journal of Criminal Law and Criminology*, 1936, Vol. 27.

THE SOCIOLOGICAL ASPECTS

in the case of all major offences since the legislator has to penalize most anti-social acts of a really serious character, but it remains a matter of considerable importance with regard to anti-social behaviour of a somewhat less serious nature where it may depend on a number of factors and considerations whether or not the legislator may decide to make use of the machinery of the Criminal Law.[1] It is only by making Criminology in this way independent of the Criminal Law that it can be used to prepare the ground for changes in the law by collecting material which may show that forms of anti-social behaviour so far ignored by the legislator should in fact be treated as offences.[2]

A corresponding process is now taking place in the field of Penology which latter is no longer exclusively confined to the study of the various methods of legal punishment. Probation, for example, as has to be concluded from the Criminal Justice Act, 1948, sect. 7, is no longer punishment in the legal sense. Nevertheless, it will, perfectly legitimately, remain an important subject of study for the penologist. The same applies to the various techniques in the field of psychological treatment of offenders. Although legally outside the scope of punishment, their implications and results have to be carefully studied by penologists. There is, in short, a belt of territory surrounding the legal conceptions of crime and punishment which cannot be allowed to remain outside the fields of study of Criminology and Penology.

With regard to the second question posed above, there can be no doubt that Criminology is both an idiographic and a nomothetic science; idiographic in so far as it aims at the observation and systematic classification of facts about human behaviour in individual cases, nomothetic in so far as its object is the discovery of uniformities and general laws. The same seems to apply to

---

[1] See the analysis given in my *Criminal Justice and Social Reconstruction* (1946), pp. 5-6, and *passim*. Also Marshall B. Clinard, *The Black Market* (New York, Rinehart & Company, Inc., 1952), Chapters 9-11.

[2] In one of the discussions following the lecture it was objected that if the study of behaviour which was not criminal in the legal sense would become the domain of the criminologist, instead of being left to the sociologist or psychologist, this might unduly influence the legislator to make such conduct punishable. There is no evidence, however, to show that criminologists are, as a class, unduly in favour of penalizing certain forms of conduct only because they happen to study them; so far they have rather shown the opposite tendency. Nor is it likely that legislators will be more inclined to accept the advice of criminologists than that of other experts.

the Sociology of Criminal Law which also has these two aspects, the idiographic and the nomothetic, although the second is here the more important of the two.

Needless to say, the difference so far stressed between the Sociology of Criminal Law as always related to the Criminal Law and Criminology as not necessarily related to it is not the only difference. As already mentioned, Criminology has other foundations besides Sociology, especially Psychology, Anthropology, Biology.

II

After these introductory remarks on certain points of difference between Criminology and the Sociology of the Criminal Law it has to be stressed, however, that in order to give an adequate definition of the latter we have to look at it not only in its relation to Criminology. There are in fact four different disciplines required to cover adequately the scientific study of crime in all its aspects. Leaving the fourth of them for later discussion, the first three are:

(1) *Criminology* (including Penology), as already defined.

(2) The scientific study of the *Criminal Law*, which is a branch of Jurisprudence and is either (*a*) *analytical*, i.e. concerned with the logical and linguistic—but, as we shall immediately see, by no means only with the logical and linguistic—interpretation of specific legal provisions and of their relation to one another; or (*b*) *historical*;[1] or (*c*) *comparative*. Its main function is to describe what kind of behaviour is, or was in the past, or still is in other countries, an offence and how it is punishable.

(3) *The Sociology of the Criminal Law*, which examines the structure of Society and its various groups and institutions, their position and influence; the values and attitudes of different groups within a given population—all this in relation to the Criminal Law as a whole and to its individual provisions. How far, for example, are the structure, position and strength of a particular group within Society responsible for the legislation relating to this or, may be, to another group? And what is the effect of such legislation on these groups? This, however, can be regarded as a provisional definition only, and, before attempting to produce a

[1] It is, of course, true that, as Stone has stressed, there can be an analytical historical jurisprudence (*Modern Law Review*, July, 1944, p. 107).

final formula, it might be advisable to compare it with some of the definitions so far attempted by representative sociologists.

Professor Ginsberg, in an interesting review of the English translation of Eugen Ehrlich's *Grundlegung der Soziologie des Rechts*,[1] selects the following four as the most important problems of the Sociology of Law:

'(1) What is the nature of legal norms, and how are they to be distinguished from other special norms, such as those of morals, religion, convention and fashion; (2) What are the conditions, social, economic and political, under which legal rules arise and become differentiated from the other forms of social regulation; (3) What influences are exerted by the various forms of social rules upon one another; to what extent, for example, is law affected in its historical evolution by changes in moral outlook; (4) how is actual law related to ideal justice and are there valid methods for studying this relationship?'

It is obvious that the first two of these points bear some relation to the distinction, mentioned before, between legal rules and 'conduct norms' and that the second and third points are concerned with what is included in our provisional definition of the Sociology of the Criminal Law; and the same may apply, though somewhat more remotely, to Ginsberg's last point.

More complicated are the various attempts made by Professor Gurvitch to define the Sociology of Law. If we select, for example, the following comparatively simple, but apparently only provisional, definition our criticism would be that it seems to include the sociological aspects of Criminology as well: 'The Sociology of Law is that part of the sociology of the human spirit which studies the full social reality of law, beginning with its tangible and externally observable expressions, in effective collective behaviours. . . .'[2] This impression that for Gurvitch Criminology, or at least Crimino-Sociology, is part of the Sociology of Law, is strongly confirmed by his subsequent remarks and in particular by his detailed references to Ferri's work on the sociological factors in the causation of crime as 'valuable contributions to the genetic sociology of penal law' (pp. 80 et seq.).

On the other hand, Professor Sutherland's definition, referred

---

[1] *Modern Law Review*, 1937, Vol. I, p. 169.
[2] George Gurvitch, *Sociology of Law* (English ed., Routledge and Kegan Paul, 1947), p. 48.

CRIMINAL LAW

to above, of the Sociology of Law as an attempt at scientific analysis of the conditions under which criminal laws develop would seem to be too narrow as it does not include the study of the effect of criminal legislation on the various groups in Society. In any case, however, such an analysis can be regarded as part of Criminology not, as Sutherland does, without any qualifications, but only in the limited sense that certain criminological facts, such as the growth of crime of a certain type, may produce a certain type of criminal legislation. It seems preferable, however, to leave problems of this kind to the Sociology of the Criminal Law.

An illustration may be useful at this stage to show where the line of demarcation should be drawn between the sociological part of Criminology and the Sociology of Criminal Law. Taking, for example, the subject of female delinquency, as far as its sociological aspects are concerned the following division seems to exist: The *criminologist* is interested in questions such as the numerical size of the problem, its statistical fluctuations, the ratio of female to male offenders in different countries; ages and types of women involved; types of offences committed; sex differences in participation in crime (as instigator or actual perpetrator or aider and abetter) and whether offences are committed mainly singly or in groups; apparent causes of female delinquency; marital, social and economic status of offenders; relation between female delinquency and prostitution; the methods of punishment applied to women as compared with those applied to men, and the effect of these methods; possibly also the role of women as the victims of crime. The *criminal lawyer's* contribution would be the legal interpretation and analysis of those provisions of the Penal Code which have a special bearing on the matter, in particular, of those offences which are mainly or exclusively committed by women or where the law is different for men and women; as, for example, infanticide, child destruction, abortion, homosexual acts, prostitution; or of legal provisions in the field of punishment relating only to women as, for example, the exemption of a pregnant woman from the death penalty. Lastly, the points to be studied by the *Sociology of the Criminal Law* would be the general position of women, married and unmarried, in different societies and periods and its effect, *not* on the criminal *behaviour* of women, which would be an examination of potential causes of female delinquency and therefore the task of the criminologist, but on the criminal law itself,

THE SOCIOLOGICAL ASPECTS

i.e. how far the sociological position of women in a given society is responsible for the state of the law of abortion, infanticide, homosexuality, or prostitution, in that society. Moreover, the study of the attitudes prevailing within different groups of the population to such legal provision affecting women would come under the scope of the Sociology of Law, as distinct from the study of individual attitudes which is the domain of Social Psychology.[1] In addition, the Sociology of the Criminal Law may have to consider a number of other broader subjects such as, for example, the population trends in a given community, its economic condition, the moral and religious views of the various social groups within that community and their bearing on the criminal law of abortion, infanticide, and so on.

While all this may provide some indication of the relation between Criminology and the Sociology of the Criminal Law, it cannot, as we have just said, be regarded as the final answer because of another stumbling block which is still barring our way. When previously referring to the Jurisprudence of the Criminal Law (above II, 2) we mentioned only three of its branches: the analytical, the historical, and the comparative. There is, however, what may be provisionally called a fourth branch, *Sociological Jurisprudence*, and its relationship to the Sociology of Law still remains to be examined. Are they perhaps the same thing under a different name or are they two disciplines to be kept strictly separate? The latter view is strongly defended by Timasheff[2] and also by no less a person than Dean Pound who, in his Preface to Gurvitch's *Sociology of Law*, stresses: 'Sociology of Law is not sociological jurisprudence any more than the latter can claim to be an adequate Sociology of Law'.[3] On the other hand, Professor Stone in his important book *The Province and Function of Law*[4] declares himself still unconvinced that 'a distinct science ("Sociology of Law") exists or can exist side by side with an applied study of law in society ("Sociological Jurisprudence")'. I believe

---

[1] On the difference in the objects and methods of Sociology and Social Psychology see G. Murphy, L. B. Murphy and Theodore M. Newcomb, *Experimental Social Psychology* (New York and London, Harper & Brothers, revised ed., 1937), pp. 15 et seq., 890 et seq.

[2] Op cit., pp. 15 et seq.

[3] Op cit., p. xv.

[4] London, Stevens & Sons, Limited, 1947, Chapter XVII: 'Scope and Nature of Sociological Jurisprudence', especially pp. 393-4.

CRIMINAL LAW

with Roscoe Pound and Timasheff that we are here indeed concerned with two different branches of scientific study, although I am not sure whether my way of drawing the line of demarcation is the same as theirs. Sociological Jurisprudence, as Timasheff rightly recognizes, is 'not a new branch of Jurisprudence which could be added to analytical, historical and comparative Jurisprudence; it is rather a new method, or a new viewpoint, to be used within every branch.[1] It means, in particular, the use of sociological techniques and material in the interpretation of specific legal provisions. Legal terms can be reasonably interpreted only in the light of the views and attitudes and mores of the community. To give a few illustrations: What constitutes 'obscene literature' or 'indecent assault'; what the law understands by a 'thing' that can be the object of theft; what is 'excessive', and therefore prohibited, punishment ('cruelty') administered by parents or teachers; when a denying of the Christian religion is done in a 'scandalous' manner and therefore constitutes the offence of blasphemy; when the behaviour of a common prostitute who loiters and importunes for the purpose of prostitution may be regarded as an 'annoyance' of residents or passers-by; whether a document is a 'defamatory libel', i.e. one 'calculated to bring another person into hatred, ridicule or contempt, or to lower him in the estimation of right thinking men'; whether defamation of a whole group renders the publisher liable to a criminal prosecution because it is calculated 'to promote ill-will and hostility between different classes of H.M. subjects' or 'to stir up ill-will towards the class as a whole';[2] what constitutes 'unlawful' and therefore criminal abortion; what is 'provocation' sufficiently 'gross' to transform murder into manslaughter—obviously, all these and a hundred similar questions cannot be satisfactorily dealt with by the Courts by means of purely legal analysis, i.e. without taking into account the attitudes and needs of contemporary society and of the different groups within it.[3] Judicial decisions of this kind require a thorough sociological study, for

[1] Timasheff, op cit., p. 28, note 7.
[2] See 'Report of the Committee on the Law of Defamation' (London, H.M.S.O., Cmd. 7536, 1948), p. 11; Rupert Cross and P. Asterley Jones, *An Introduction to Criminal Law* (London, Butterworth & Co., Ltd., 1947), p. 255.
[3] Although the foregoing illustrations are taken from English criminal law they are, I believe, with suitable modifications also applicable to other legal systems.

THE SOCIOLOGICAL ASPECTS

example, of the sex behaviour approved or at least tolerated in a given society at a given time; of the kind of parental discipline which this society and the various social classes in it regard as appropriate in ordinary family life; of the latitude which they are willing to grant to atheists and free-thinkers and to political controversy in general; of the population policy to be pursued in view of the economic position of the country; of the right of minority groups to be protected; and so on.

An admirable illustration of such reflections, at the same time legal and sociological, may be found in the following remarks recently made by Mr. Justice Stable when addressing the jury in a case against a London firm of publishers charged with publishing obscene literature:[1]

'Your verdict will have great bearing on where the line is drawn between liberty and licence,' he said. 'We are not sitting here as judges of taste. We are not here to say whether we like a book of that kind. We are not here to say whether we think it would be a good thing if books like that were never written.' The test laid down in 1868 of whether a book was obscene was whether the tendency was to deprave those into whose hands the publication might fall and whose minds were open to such immoral influence. The book had to be judged on today's standards. ... 'Are we going to say in England that our contemporary literature is to be measured by what is suitable for a fourteen-year-old schoolgirl to read? ... in our desire for a healthy society, if we drive criminal law too far—farther than it ought to go—is there not a risk that there will be a revolt and a demand for a change in the law? Might not the pendulum swing too far the other way and allow to creep in things we can at the moment keep out? ... At a time like to-day when ideas, creeds and processes of thought seem to some extent to be in the melting pot and people are bewildered to know in what direction humanity is heading, into what column we propose to march, if we are to understand how life is lived in the United States, for example, in France, Germany, or elsewhere, the contemporary novel of those nations may afford us some guide—it may be the only guide to many.'

These examples will suffice to demonstrate the nature of the problems which sociological Jurisprudence may have to solve in the interpretation of the Criminal Law. Sociological Jurisprudence

[1] *The Times*, 3rd July, 1954. See also a similar American view in *Cornell Law Quarterly*, Vol. 34, Spring 1949, p. 442, et seq.: 'Inadequacy of present Tests as to what constitutes Obscene Literature'.

CRIMINAL LAW

as a special method or technique to be used in the analysis of specific legal enactments is, however, inevitably limited to the interpretation of existing provisions in the light of the sociological situation. The task of the Sociology of the Criminal Law, on the other hand, is more comprehensive; it begins earlier and ends later than that of Sociological Jurisprudence, and it covers a wider field. It has to study the whole of that sociological situation as it might, or should, have been taken into consideration by the legislator even where it is clear that it has actually not been considered or that it has no bearing on the interpretation of a specific legal provision. Assuming for the sake of argument that, for example, the sociological analysis of the total situation may show that the present attitude of English Criminal Law towards abortion has no support any more among large sections of the population and also that abortions are no longer regarded as harmful by the medical profession and as undesirable by population experts. These findings would belong to the sphere of Sociology of the Criminal Law because they would show that certain important arguments in favour of the prohibition of abortion have ceased to exist. But if, in spite of this, the law would still declare abortion a crime and if it would go so far as explicitly to prohibit the making of any exceptions, those sociological facts would be of no use to the technique of Sociological Jurisprudence in its interpretation of the law. They would be of great importance, however, to the last of the four branches of scientific knowledge referred to before, which will be discussed below, i.e. *'Kriminalpolitik'*.

Very often there will be overlapping between the resp. spheres of Sociological Jurisprudence and the Sociology of Law. For example, an analysis of the attitude of the community towards religion may be of importance not only for the interpretation of the offence of blasphemy, i.e. part of the positive criminal law, but also for an understanding of the reasons for and against the abolition of this offence. In a 'Study in popular attitudes to religion, ethics, progress and politics in a London Borough', undertaken some years ago by 'Mass-Observation', one of the conclusions was this:[1] 'Not more than one person in ten in Metrop is at all closely associated with any of the Churches, and about two-thirds never, or practically never, go to Church. The majority,

[1] *Puzzled People* (London, Victor Gollancz Ltd., 1948), p. 156.

THE SOCIOLOGICAL ASPECTS

however,—four out of five women and two out of three men—give at least verbal assent to the possibility of there being a God and most of the rest express doubt rather than disbelief. . . . Irrespective of their own religious beliefs, the majority of people in Metrop consider that religion should be taught in schools . . . Throughout the Survey an attitude of "good-will" towards the *idea* of religion and religious faith is apparent. . . .' If we accept this statement as truly reflecting the views of the majority of the English people (Mass-Observation makes no claim of this kind), it would furnish an important argument against the abolition of the offence of blasphemy and at the same time show the direction in which the Courts should move in their interpretation of the law, i.e. it would provide at the same time material for the Sociology of Law and for Sociological Jurisprudence, as well as of course for *Kriminalpolitik*.

The relations between the three different approaches which have so far been discussed might perhaps be expressed as follows: *Criminology* is *independent* of the Criminal Law; *Sociological Jurisprudence* is *entirely dependent* upon the existence of *specific legal provisions* which have to be interpreted in dealing with individual cases; *Sociology of Criminal Law* is *related* to the Criminal Law *in its entirety*, but not necessarily related to specific legal provisions.

(4) Turning now to the last of the four categories to be considered, there seems to exist no appropriate English term for the German *Kriminalpolitik* or the French *'politique criminelle'*. In its general outlines, its meaning is clear, although there are differences of opinion as to its exact scope. The essence of *Kriminalpolitik*—a term which, according to Robert von Hippel,[1] goes back approximately to the year 1800—is that it is concerned with the *reform* of criminal justice and of the penal system. However, there are writers such as Michael and Adler, who claim for the Criminal Law all questions of what *should* be done in this field.[2] Others fail to draw any distinction between *Kriminalpolitik* and Criminology.[3]

[1] *Deutsches Strafrecht*, Vol. I (1925), p. 535, note 1.
[2] Jerome Michael and Mortimer J. Adler, *Crime, Law and Social Science* (1933), pp. 42 and 338.
[3] Edmund Mezger's book *Kriminalpolitik* (1934), for example, is largely a textbook on Criminology, although towards the end he stresses that the mere exploration of causes is no substitute for evaluation (p. 203). In his article 'Kriminalpolitik' in the *Handwörterbuch der Kriminologie*, Vol. II (1933), pp. 861 et seq., he seems to regard Criminology sometimes as part of *Kriminalpolitik*, sometimes as its indispensable pre-requisite. Only the second view is correct.

CRIMINAL LAW

Again others[1] take the view, which has something in its favour, that *Kriminalpolitik* is no real self-contained unit and that it should rather be divided into two sections, each of which would form part of another discipline: as far as it means considerations *de lege ferenda* for the reform of the positive law it should be treated as part of the scientific study of the Criminal Law (as suggested by Michael and Adler); as far as it means penal reform in the narrower sense, such as improvements in the administration of the prison system which can be carried out without any changes in the law, it should be part of Penology. An argument against this view is that it makes the scope of the subject too much dependent upon the techniques employed by the legislators of different countries. In some countries, the essential principles and even details of prison reform, for example, are embodied in the law (e.g. the Swedish Prison Act of 1945), whereas in others, e.g. Great Britain, the matter is almost entirely left to administrative rules and regulations.[2] It would, therefore, seem to be preferable to keep the whole subject together as a separate discipline of *Kriminalpolitik*, i.e. 'the discipline dealing with the policy of reforming the Criminal Law and the penal system', drawing the practical —political conclusions from the material collected by the sociology of Criminal Law and by Criminology and Penology in all their aspects, sociological as well as psychological; and from the experiences gathered in the process of administering the Criminal Law with the assistance of (analytical, historical, comparative and sociological) Jurisprudence.

Although emphasis has been placed upon the existence of four different branches of scientific endeavour related to the subject of crime and punishment this should not be misunderstood as meaning that they correspond to four different academic disciplines, each of them requiring different academic chairs and textbooks. We may well be satisfied with the present bipartition into Criminal Law and Criminology, provided we are clear in our own minds what it implies.

[1] Ernst Seelig, article, 'Kriminalpolitik', *Handwörterbuch der Kriminologie*, Vol. II (1933), p. 75; more recently in his *Lehrbuch der Kriminologie* (Verlag Jos. A. Kienreich, Graz, 1951), p. 17.
[2] See, e.g., The Criminal Justice Act, 1948, sect. 52, and Lionel W. Fox, 'The Swedish Prison Act 1945 and the English Criminal Justice Act 1948', in *Festskrift Tillagnad Karl Schlyter* (Stockholm, Isaac Marcus Boktryckeri—Aktiebolag, 1949), pp. 102 et seq.

THE SOCIOLOGICAL ASPECTS

This being so, the practical usefulness of the distinctions so far drawn might possibly be doubted. As has been shown, they are distinctions regarding the kind of questions to be asked and the objects to be pursued by the various disciplines. There are also certain differences in the techniques employed. While, with the exception of *Kriminalpolitik*, they are at the same time both idiographic and nomothetic, the Sociology of the Criminal Law is more concerned with the general, and Criminology more with the particular. Criminology studies conditions leading to crime, the Sociology of Law conditions leading to criminal legislation. The dissection of the various operations required is helpful, or even indispensable, as it leads to a better understanding of each of them and facilitates the best possible division of labour between the sociologist and the lawyer. Whereas knowledge of the law is not required of the criminologist but indispensable in the field of Sociological Jurisprudence, both legal and sociological training seem to be needed to deal with the problems of the Sociology of the Criminal Law. *Kriminalpolitik*, in its turn, is exclusively normative. It pre-supposes certain standards and values and is closely connected with ethics and religion. Neither Criminology nor Sociology or Jurisprudence can determine these values: they are not policy-making disciplines. All they can do is to assist the policy-makers by supplying the knowledge without which the process of building up these values and the final decision regarding the order in which they should be placed are inevitably ill-informed and one-sided. To take a reasonable decision on the subject of reforming the law of abortion, for example, it is, as already pointed out, essential to know as much as possible about the state of public opinion, divided according to sex, social and religious groups, and about the views held by the medical profession and population experts. The final decision, however, is a political and ethical one; it means making up our minds as to which of these, probably conflicting, views should be given preference—it is a matter of evaluation. As in the case of the politician in general, we do not expect the *Kriminalpolitiker* to be a scientifically trained expert—all we expect him to do is to make the most conscientious use of the information provided by experts.

CRIMINAL LAW

III

Enough has probably been said to clear the way for a slightly more detailed discussion of some specific problems of the Sociology of the Criminal Law. Such problems, of course, do arise in connection with nearly every section of the Criminal Law. With some of these problems I have attempted to deal in my book *Criminal Justice and Social Reconstruction* which is essentially an essay in the Sociology of Criminal Law and also in Sociological Jurisprudence. Even within the short period of time which has elapsed since that book was completed new problems have arisen, whereas some of the older ones may appear in a slightly different light.

There is, first, the problem of the collaborators—a subject of paramount importance in the post-war administration of justice of formerly occupied countries. For my knowledge of the facts and problems involved, which is naturally second-hand and incomplete, I am indebted to such authoritative sources as Professor van Bemmelen for the Netherlands,[1] Mr. Givskov and Mr. Christiansen for Denmark,[2] and the Association of Scandinavian Criminologists who have repeatedly discussed the matter in their *Yearbook of the Northern Associations of Criminalists*.[3] While it would be presumptuous for me to deal with questions of policy such as how collaborators should be treated, I may be permitted to use the subject for an analysis of certain points of legal and sociological methodology. As Professor van Bemmelen has shown in his interesting paper, it is extremely difficult to draw the right line between punishable and non-punishable collaboration. According to Givskov, the Danish Penal Statute of 1945 dealing with 'Collaboration in Work and Trade' punished not indiscriminately any kind of collaboration but only 'offensive' collaboration since, as Givskov says, 'it was absolutely necessary for the economy of the country to a certain degree to collaborate in work and trade

[1] J. M. van Bemmelen, 'The Treatment of Political Delinquents in some European Countries', *Journal of Criminal Science*, Vol. I, 1948, pp. 110 et seq.
[2] Carl Christian Givskov, 'The Danish "Purge-Laws",' *Journal of Criminal Law and Criminology*, Vol. 39, November–December, 1948. Karl O. Christiansen, *Mandlige Landssvigere i Danmark under Besaettelsen* (Male Collaborators with the Germans in Denmark during the Occupation), (København, G.E.C. Gads Forlag—1950 and *Landssvigerkriminaliteten*, Gads Forlag, 1955).
[3] See Yearbooks for 1944–5 and for 1946–7 (Ivar Haeggstroms Boktryckeri A.B., Stockholm).

THE SOCIOLOGICAL ASPECTS

with the Germans'. The Danish 'Purge Law' did not, and perhaps even could not, provide a precise definition of this term 'offensive collaboration', but confined itself to a list of examples not intended to be exhaustive.[1] As a consequence, the Danish Courts had to assume the whole responsibility of interpreting that vague term, and this could obviously be done only in the light of a full examination of the many political, economic, sociological and moral factors involved. There can hardly ever have been before Criminal Courts a more difficult task of *Interessen-Abwägung* in the sense of Ehrlich and other members of the School of Sociological Jurisprudence. Similarly, the Belgian Law of 1945 quoted by Professor van Bemmelen contains many complicated terms requiring analysis and interpretation of a political, social and economic rather than of a strictly legal character. Nevertheless, such an analysis still remains within the scope of analytical and sociological Jurisprudence. Where, however, it is no longer a question of interpreting specific legal provisions but rather of examining the total sociological, political, economic situation of collaboration, specifically related to the problem of punishing collaborators, there we enter the field of the Sociology of Criminal Law. Then we would have to deal with such matters as the following: Was, as Givskov states, economic collaboration necessary in order to save the national economy, and to what extent, or would passive resistance or a 'scorched earth' policy or perhaps a policy of 'Satyagraha' in Gandhi's sense[2] have been, objectively speaking, more useful; and, quite apart from objective arguments of this kind, what were the views of different sections of the population; were they predominantly in favour of scorched earth policy at any cost or rather of the more prudent course of restricted collaboration to avoid complete economic collapse; and what were the risks to be run in case of non-collaboration, and so on? Information on all these points was needed to prepare the ground for the legislator who, on the basis of this material, had to make his political and moral evaluation and to pass his laws (*Kriminalpolitik*), and the decision might well have been different in different countries and in relation to different stages of the war.

[1] See also Stephan Hurwitz, *Zeitschrift für die gesamte Strafrechtswissenschaft*, Vol. 63 (Berlin, 1950), pp. 132-4.
[2] M. K. Gandhi, *An Autobiography or The Story of my Experiments with Truth*. Translated by Mahadev Desai (Ahmedabad, Navajivan Publishing House, 1945 ed.), p. 389.

CRIMINAL LAW

Another interesting example of the expansion of the field of Sociological Jurisprudence, taken from recent international criminal law, is the newly created crime of *Genocide*, as accepted by the General Assembly of the United Nations on 11th December, 1946. It means the systematic and deliberate extermination of whole national, racial, or religious groups, not necessarily destruction in the physical and biological sense, but sometimes perhaps rather in the cultural and political sense.[1] Although the so-called 'cultural genocide' has been omitted from the final version of the Convention, the view has been expressed that the destruction of a group as social unit, for example, by the extermination of its leaders, is covered by it.[2] It is clear that, in view of the ambiguity of such concepts as race, nation, etc., the interpretation of the phrase 'national, racial and religious groups' may involve a sociological study of great complexity.

In *Criminal Justice and Social Reconstruction* an attempt was made to show that, in view of the changed conception of property and changes in the economic and social structure of our society large sections of the present criminal law, especially in the economic sphere, have lost touch with contemporary developments. While this is not the place to go into the details of this problem, I might perhaps briefly refer to the case of an offence of an economic character to which attention was drawn in England and abroad through the investigation carried out by a special Tribunal sitting under the chairmanship of Mr. Justice Lynskey.[3] Although this was in no way a criminal trial and the findings of that Tribunal have nothing in common with the finding of guilt and the sentence of a criminal court, the basic problem was the same, i.e. the interpretation of the concept of corruption. According to English law, to be guilty of an offence under the Prevention of Corruption

[1] See on it especially Raphael Lemkin, *Axis Rule in Occupied Europe* (Washington, Carnegie Endowment for International Peace, 1944), Chapter IX; *History of the United Nations War Crimes Commission and the Development of the Laws of War*, compiled by the U.N. War Crimes Commission (London, 1948), pp. 196 et seq. See now also Arthur Wegner in *Materialien zur Strafrechtsreform*, Vol. I (Bonn 1954, Dr. Hans Heger, Bad Godesberg), pp. 391 et seq.

[2] See Hans Heinrich Jescheck, *Zeitschrift für die gesamte Strafrechtswissenschaft*. Vol. 66, 1954, pp. 193 et seq., especially p. 213.

[3] 'Report of the Tribunal appointed to inquire into Allegations reflecting on the Official Conduct of Ministers of the Crown and other Public Servants' (London, H.M.S.O., Cmd. 7616, 1949).

THE SOCIOLOGICAL ASPECTS

Acts[1] it is not enough for an official to accept, for example, a consideration from a person seeking to obtain a contract from the Government. It must be done 'corruptly', and the onus is on the accused to prove that the gift was made innocently. To interpret this word 'corruptly' a sociological study may be required of the economic and social structure of the community concerned and its legal 'super-structure'. Special attention will have to be paid to the economic, social and legal relationships between Government bodies and officials, on the one hand, and the representatives of private enterprise, on the other, in an economic system which tries to combine the advantages of a planned economy with those of a system of *laissez faire*. With reference to the proceedings before the Tribunal it was pointed out by the then Prime Minister, Mr. Attlee,[2] that 'it would be a great mistake to think that Ministers should live cloistered lives. It is essential that they should have close acquaintance both with the people and with the problems with which they have to deal.' And it was stressed by responsible organs of the Press that there was a 'danger that the pressure of public opinion, as a result of the Tribunal's revelations, may make necessary liaison between Government and industry more difficult and defective in the future than it is now'.[3] While I am in no way here concerned with the merits of the cases with which the Lynskey Tribunal had to deal, it is my object to show that a reasonable interpretation of the term 'corruption' is impossible without a sociological analysis of the facts and needs of present-day society, especially of the standards of conduct generally accepted in business and Government circles regarding the mutual relationships between their respective representatives, and of how far such standards are justified in view of the legitimate requirements of the community. It is then the task of the scientific interpretation of the Criminal Law to examine how far these standards are compatible with the letter and spirit of the law; and it is, finally, the task of *Kriminalpolitik* to decide on changes in the law if it should be regarded as desirable, for example, to lay down explicitly a standard of conduct different from the one accepted by some sections of the community.

[1] An Act for the better Prevention of Corruption of 4th August, 1906 (6 Edw. 7 Ch. 34) and an Act to amend the law relating to the Prevention of Corruption of 22nd December, 1916 (6 & 7 Geo. 5 Ch. 64).
[2] House of Commons Debate of 3rd February, 1949 (*Hansard*, cols. 1855–6).
[3] Mr. Alan Campbell-Johnson in *The Observer*, 5th December, 1948.

CRIMINAL LAW

Equally far-reaching have been the changes in values and attitudes concerning the family and their repercussions in the interpretation of offences protecting family life. In former years, a husband who killed his wife after her confession of adultery was treated by English courts as having acted under gross provocation and therefore as guilty not of murder but only of manslaughter. In 1949, however, the House of Lords in Holmes *v.* Director of Public Prosecutions repudiated this rule on the grounds that, in Lord Simon's words, 'the application of common law principles in matters such as this must to some extent be controlled by the evolution of society . . . as society advances, it ought to call for a higher measure of self-control in all cases. . . .'[1] The crucial points seem to be not only that modern society disapproves of the law of the jungle and demands more self-control, but also that it regards the wife no longer as the absolute property of her husband. Moreover, as adultery has become more frequent and is often nothing but a convenient device to supply the legal requirements of a divorce its social condemnation is no longer as strong as it used to be. Sociological Jurisprudence and *Kriminalpolitik* have to be aware of such developments, and the results of such awareness are visible in the decision of the House of Lords and in the tendency of modern Continental penal legislation to abolish the offence of adultery.[2] It is not surprising that in the United States, where some of the State legislations provide fairly substantial penalties for this offence these provisions have become dead letters.[3]

The growing habit of artificial insemination by a donor other than the woman's husband has also presented entirely new problems to the interpretation of statutes penalizing adultery and even incest or rape. As in some legal systems the husband's consent to his wife's adultery is immaterial wife and donor would be guilty of an offence, if artificial insemination should be regarded in law as an equivalent to the normal sexual intercourse which legislators probably had in mind when creating the offence of

---

[1] Holmes v. Director of Public Prosecution (1949) 1 K.B. 405. See also Report of Royal Commission on Capital Punishment, 1953 (Cmd. 8932), p. 50. Kenny's *Outlines of Criminal Law* (new ed. by J. W. C. Turner, Cambridge University Press, 1952), p. 137.
[2] See, e.g., The Finnish Statute of the 23rd September, 1948, and the Jugoslav Criminal Code of the 2nd March, 1951.
[3] Morris Ploscowe, *Sex and the Law* (New York, Prentice-Hall, Inc., 1951), pp. 155 and 281.

adultery. In an often quoted Canadian case of more than thirty years ago this was in fact the conclusion drawn by the Court.[1] Sociological Jurisprudence of to-day will have to examine, however, whether such an interpretation is not in fact a distortion of the true *Gestalt* of the conception of adultery. It will have to be considered, in particular, what is the real object of penalizing adultery: what is the law supposed to protect? the purity of the offspring or the religious bond of marriage or the confidence of one partner in the loyalty of the other? If it is the latter, surely, consent should matter. Again, this is not the place to provide an answer to these highly disputed questions, but only to show that no satisfactory answer can be given without a sociological analysis of the values and attitudes of present-day society.[2]

One of the impressions one may get from the material so far presented is, I think, the growing tendency of the legislative technique of present-day Criminal Law to use very vague and general terms, leaving more and more scope to judicial interpretation. This is the inevitable consequence of the growing complexity of the problems to be mastered and perhaps also of the ever increasing tempo of modern legislation. As a result, the technique to be employed in the interpretation and application of such legal enactments seems to be more and more in line with what might be called *Gestalt* Jurisprudence, i.e. the replacement of the 'traditional study of single segments of behaviour abstracted from their natural setting' by the study of behaviour as a whole functional organism.[3] Moreover, as the problems are becoming too big and the legal conceptions required in dealing with them too complicated to be mastered by a mere technique, it will, I believe, also mean the growing replacement of the technique of Sociological Jurisprudence by a real science of the Sociology of Law.

[1] Orford v. Orford, 1921, 49 Ont. L.R. 15, quoted by Ploscowe, *Sex and the Law*, p. 115, and in *Minnesota Law Review*, Vol. 33, January, 1949, p. 151.
[2] The whole problem is fully discussed in *Artificial (Human) Insemination* (London, Heinemann, 1947), the report on a conference held on 11th April, 1946.
[3] G. W. Allport, *Personality* (1937), pp. 16 et seq. Problems of legislative technique are more fully discussed in *Criminal Justice and Social Reconstruction*, pp. 203 et seq. and *passim*.

CRIMINAL LAW

IV

So far, I have been dealing mainly in general terms with the meaning of, and the need for, a sociological approach to the Criminal Law. May I now, in conclusion, draw attention to a few more specific lessons which the criminal lawyer may do well to learn from the sociologist? They might be summed up as follows:

(1) The work of the sociologist, as that of the anthropologist, has made it clear that the law is only one form of social control, and that there are other, equally powerful or perhaps even more effective, forms of social control besides legal punishment and the threat of punishment, such as reward, pressure of public opinion, and others.

(2) It has also shown that the study of the individual in Society and in his relations to other individuals is at least as important and indispensable to the lawyer as the study of the individual in isolation and that the sociological changes in the structure of Society require corresponding changes in the Criminal Law.

(3) Finally, the Criminal Law has to pay more attention to the mass character of modern Society and to the fact that most human effort is nowadays dependent upon team work or at least greatly influenced by the mass atmosphere.

With regard to this last aspect of the matter, the Criminal Law has so far only inadequately grasped the significance of the mass element in criminal behaviour. Its provisions concerning complicity, conspiracy, and so on have been mainly concerned with political offences, and their object has largely been to distinguish between leaders and masses and to increase the penalties in case of mass crime. It is not enough, however, to regard the dangers arising from the mass factor in crime merely as a justification for the infliction of heavier sentences or for an extension or reduction of the scope of criminal responsibility. We have to realize that this factor may influence the whole atmosphere even where it is not a matter of several individuals participating in the commission of the same crime or of several crimes. It may be equally important where, legally, we have to deal with a number of separate crimes, each of them independently committed by different individuals. I have in mind, for example, problems such as that of mass stealing from factories, docks, etc. which have recently attracted much

THE SOCIOLOGICAL ASPECTS

attention. In such cases, the common sociological and psychological background is largely ignored by the law. The law of criminal procedure, for example, as far as I am aware, permits joint charges and joint trials only where several persons have participated in the same offence. The common sociological and psychological background would become much clearer and the real significance of such epidemics of crime would be much better grasped by the public if, with all due safeguards, such cases could be tried together—or at least dealt with together after the finding of guilt—even where no joint participation in the commission of the same offence in the legal sense is involved. Not only the criminal law but also the law of criminal procedure has important sociological problems awaiting solution.

Again, it is usually better understood by sociologists than by lawyers that 'the group as a whole is often the best of disciplinarians . . . the group itself is frequently able to exert more effective control over the conduct of its members than can an outside individual charged with special authority'.[1] I am much in sympathy, therefore, with the experiments recently made by eminent Dutch judges in enlisting the co-operation of the whole group of workers to which the offenders belong.[2] These experiments seem to be promising, provided we know enough of the inner structure and life of these groups to tackle them in the right manner, and provided these groups possess sufficient homogeneity, coherence, stability and sufficiently strong and lasting common interests. 'In a large community, like a modern city, contacts tend to be impersonal and escape into anonymity is possible.'[3] If there is a steady coming and going among the workers of a factory, and they have nothing in common with one another, the group approach is likely to fail. In any case, however, experiments such as these show how much the criminal court judge of to-day is on the point of becoming not only an educationist—this he has in fact been already for a long time—but also a sociologist.

[1] Ogburn and Nimkoff, *Handbook of Sociology* (1947, Routledge & Kegan Paul, Ltd, London), p. 182.
[2] See Chapter 2, Section I above.
[3] Ogburn-Nimkoff, p. 183.

CHAPTER 13

THE TREATMENT OF MENTAL DISORDERS IN CONTINENTAL CRIMINAL LAW [1]

BETWEEN English law and most of the continental criminal codes there is an essential difference as to the legal definition of 'insanity'—a difference all the more important as it concerns the most disputed part of the English law of insanity. According to the McNaghten rules of 1843, which dominate the law in England, as well as in the majority of the United States [2] at least in theory, 'to establish a defence on the ground of insanity it must be clearly proved that at the time of the committing of the act the accused party was labouring under such a defect of reason, from disease of the mind, as not to know the nature and quality of the act he was doing; or, if he did know it, that he did not know he was doing what was wrong'. The struggle against these McNaghten rules, which started in this country as early as the middle of the nineteenth century, is based upon the opinion that the rules are too narrow, since they take into account only the knowledge, the conscious part of the intellect of the individual, not his subconscious mind or his emotional life or will power. As early as 1864 Maudsley wrote: 'The fundamental defect in the legal test of responsibility is that it is founded upon the consciousness of the individual—the most important part of our mental operations takes place unconsciously.' [3] And sixty years later Lord Atkin's Committee proposed that, in addition to the McNaghten rules, 'it should be recognized that a person charged criminally with an

---

[1] A shortened and revised version, with an additional note, of a paper read to the Institute for the Scientific Treatment of Delinquency, London, and published in *The Journal of Mental Science*, Vol. 84, May–July, 1938.

[2] See, e.g., the account given in *Michigan Law Review*, Vol. 34, 1936, p. 569.

[3] *Insanity and Crime* (1864), p. 39.

THE TREATMENT OF MENTAL DISORDERS

offence is irresponsible for his act when the act is committed under an impulse which the prisoner was by mental disease in substance deprived of any power to resist'.

Most of the continental Codes acknowledge this irresistible impulse test either explicitly or by implication. Let me begin with the German Code of 1871. Until 1933, its famous sect. 51—the only section of the Code the number of which is almost generally known to old and young in Germany—contained the following provision: 'There is no punishable act if at the time of commission the actor was in a state of unconsciousness or of morbid disturbance of the mental faculties which excluded the free determination of the will.' The Code thus adopted the so-called mixed, or biological-psychological, method shared by the majority of the continental Codes (except the French Code)[1] as well as by the McNaghten rules; there must be a mental disease, and this disease must produce certain psychological consequences. This mixed method does not imply that the psychiatrist may decide the question of mental disease independently and that, on the other hand, he has nothing to do with the question of what psychological consequences the disease had produced. In German as in English law the court is never bound to follow the opinion of the expert, even in purely medical questions, but, on the other hand, the German expert had further to answer the question whether the mental disease had reached such a degree as to exclude the free determination of the will.[2] Now this latter question is really a little odd when put to a psychiatrist whose belief in the existence of freedom of will, even among mentally normal people, is perhaps not very strong. As has been said: 'In choosing a criterion which involves the most abstruse problems concerning the human soul, the Teutonic genius has but proved faithful to itself; no other eye could look into the metaphysical abyss without turning dizzy.'[3] The volitional element, excluded in the McNaghten rules, was here introduced in a form the crudeness of which could not fail to evoke opposition. Interpreted literally, the law might have become wholly impracticable. A few distinguished psychiatrists

---

[1] In Sweden, a purely biological definition was introduced in 1945, according to which it does not matter whether the offender did or did not understand the nature of his act; see Gösta Rylander, *British Journal of Delinquency*, Vol. V, No. 4, April 1955.
[2] See R. Frank, *Kommentar zum Strafgesetzbuch*, note 3, Section 51.
[3] H. Oppenheimer, *The Criminal Responsibility of Lunatics* (1909), p. 156.

simply refused to answer this question.[1] The majority of German psychiatrists and jurists, however, discovered a more practical method of overcoming this difficulty. The wording of the legal provision—it was said—was so unreasonable that the intention of the legislator must have been different. It could not be supposed that the legislator had wished to interfere with the philosophical struggle between determinism and indeterminism. Criminal responsibility must rather be dependent upon the 'normal ability of the individual to be determined by normal motives',[2] an ability which must be assumed in every normal human being. The practical difficulties which are presented even by this formula, particularly those of distinguishing between the insane law-breaker and the habitual criminal, have never been overlooked. Sometimes, the psychological requirement of sect. 51 has been watered down even so far as to indicate merely that the mental disease, in order to exclude criminal responsibility, should have weakened the intellectual power or emotional restraint to a considerable degree.[3] All these attempts to transform an impracticable metaphysical into a practicable psychological element—a mainly qualitative into a mainly quantitative requirement—have, step by step, been accepted by the German courts, especially by the Supreme Court of the Reich, at least during the last thirty years. The following words used by Dr. Sullivan[4] with regard to the McNaghten rules can, therefore, be applied even more to the former German Code: 'In practice,' he writes, 'the legal doctrine of responsibility has been innocuous; it has not produced its logical consequences, because it has never been fully applied.'

'The free determination of the will', said the German Supreme Court in 1929, 'is excluded when, as a consequence of mental disturbances, certain ideas and feelings or influences dominate the will to such a degree as to exclude the possibility of determining the will through reasonable considerations. Where there are present incentives towards a certain action as well as counteractive considerations, the will of the actor is free only if he is capable of weighing the two elements against one another. . . . If there is present a morbid impulse so strong that the counter-

[1] See Bumke, *Lehrbuch der Geisteskrankheiten* (2nd ed., 1924), pp. 364–5.
[2] See Frank, note 3, Section 51.
[3] See Lobe in *Kommentar der Reichsgerichtsräte zum Strafgesetzbuch*, note 2, Section 51.
[4] W. C. Sullivan, *Crime and Insanity*, 1924, p. 230.

THE TREATMENT OF MENTAL DISORDERS

active considerations, although existent, are unable to prevail, free determination of the will within the meaning of sect. 51 is excluded.'[1] This example may suffice to show how strongly the emotional element has been emphasized in the practice of the German courts. In order to justify punishment it is not sufficient that counter-active considerations existed; the offender must also have had the possibility to carry them into effect. This is the defence of irresistible impulse in its purest form, and in this form it has now become written law in Germany. It was the law concerning juvenile offenders that, in this case as in so many others, served as the forerunner of general legal reforms. Whilst the Code of 1871 provided that juveniles were not punishable when they were incapable of realizing that their actions were contrary to the law, the Act of 1923 dealing with the establishment of juvenile courts enacted that juveniles between fourteen and eighteen years of age were not punishable when, 'in consequence of their intellectual or moral development, they are incapable of understanding the unlawfulness of their action or of acting in accordance with this understanding'. The same test is now, by an Act of November, 1933, applied to the insanity problem.[2] The first part of sect. 51 of the Penal Code, in its new formulation, runs as follows: 'An act is not punishable when the actor, at the moment of his action, in consequence of mental disturbance, of mental disorder or imbecility is incapable of understanding the unlawfulness of his action or of acting in accordance with his understanding.' It is commonly accepted that this provision is nothing but a restatement of a law that has already been applied for several decades.[3] The psychiatrists, supported by the courts, have succeeded in improving a rather unfortunately worded legal provision, with the result that their view became first unwritten and finally written law.

The defence of irresistible impulse has also been explicitly accepted by many other modern continental Codes, the Italian Code of 1930 (art. 85–8), the Russian Code of 1926 (sect. 11), the Yugoslav Code of 1929 (art. 22), the Polish Code of 1932 (art. 18),

[1] *Reichsgerichtsentscheidungen in Strafsachen* (Official Collection of the Judgements of the Supreme Court in Criminal Cases), LXIII, p. 48 (author's translation).
[2] On this Act, see the author's paper in *Journal of Criminal Law and Criminology*. Vol. XXVI, November, 1935, pp. 517 et seq.
[3] See, e.g., the decision of the Supreme Court of 29th January, 1935, LXIX, p. 112.

the Turkish Code of 1926 (art. 46), the Belgian Act of 9th April, 1930 (art. 1, 7, 10), as well as by several continental draft Codes. The Italian Code (art. 90) makes the reservation that 'conditions of emotion or passion do not exclude, nor do they lessen, responsibility'.[1] This reservation is nothing but the self-evident principle existing in most legal systems that emotion and passion, being at the bottom of many criminal actions, are as such, i.e. if they are not an outcome of mental disease, unable to exempt the offender from responsibility.[2] It must, however, be understood that emotion and passion have sometimes to be taken into consideration as mitigating circumstances, and the Italian Code itself contains a few provisions of this kind.[3] The prohibition contained in art. 90 is, therefore, probably intended chiefly as a safeguard against the excessive leniency of lay judges—although it must be borne in mind that Italy abolished the jury system in 1931 in favour of the German *Schöffen-System* which greatly restricts the powers of the lay judges.

The French Code Pénal of 1810 differs from the majority of continental Codes. Its art. 64 runs as follows: '*Il n'y a ni crime ni délit lorsque le prévenu était en état de démence au temps de l'action ou lorsqu'il a été contraint par une force à laquelle il n'a pu résister.*' The latter part of this provision would seem, at the first glance, to contain the irresistible impulse test. Among French lawyers, however, the view prevails that this part is not concerned with mental disease at all, but refers to compulsion by external forces.[4] The problem of mental disorders is to be solved exclusively by means of the term 'démence'. What, then, is the meaning of 'démence' in French criminal law? Jurists and psychiatrists agree that this term is extremely vague; in fact, French writers seem to be just as pleased with the vagueness of the term 'démence' as many English with the vagueness of the McNaghten rules.[5] Moreover, it is commonly acknowledged that the legal meaning of 'démence' is much wider than its medical meaning, and that it covers not only intel-

[1] Official English Translation.
[2] See, e.g., Garraud, *Précis de droit criminel*, pp. 666 et seq.; Vidal and Magnol, *Cours de droit criminel* (7th ed., 1928), p. 309.
[3] Art. 62, Nos. 1-3.
[4] Garraud, op. cit., pp. 690 et seq.; the opposite view seems to be supported by Vidal and Magnol, p. 289.
[5] See, e.g., Henry Verger, *L'Evolution des idées médicales sur la résponsibilité des délinquants* (1923), pp. 15, 89; Garraud, op cit., pp. 622, 625-6; and, on the other hand, Humphreys, *Cambridge Law Journal*, I, p. 312.

THE TREATMENT OF MENTAL DISORDERS

lectual, but also emotional defects.[1] That, in spite of its vagueness, French jurists are, on the whole, quite satisfied with the present legal position, is also proved by the fact that in the French *Avant-projet* of the General Part of a new Penal Code, published in 1932, the term 'démence' was retained without any reservation.[2]

An important contrast between English and French law, on the one hand, and German law, on the other, concerns the *question of proof*. According to the McNaghten rules, every man is presumed to be sane until the contrary is proved,[3] and the same principle is valid in French law,[4] although the attitude of the latter may be somewhat doubtful.[5] Some other continental countries, however, do not adopt such a general presumption of sanity. In German law, e.g. the question of insanity does not constitute an exception to the principle that every man is presumed to be innocent until his guilt is proved; the presumption of innocence refers also to insanity. That may seem strange to those who believe that the presumption of innocence is not accepted at all in continental criminal law. As far back as 1890, however, the German Supreme Court[6] upheld the rule that a conviction is possible only when the prisoner's sanity has been proved beyond any doubt. 'The contrary', said the Court, 'would be inconsistent with the idea that only a guilty person should be punished.' That, of course, does not mean that in every criminal case the prisoner must be examined by a psychiatrist that his sanity may be proved. It means merely the so-called 'risk of non-persuasion', i.e. if the court having heard the evidence is still doubtful as to the prisoner's state of mind at the time of the crime, the case, according to German law, as in about twenty of the North American States,[7] must be decided in

[1] See Verger, op. cit., pp. 23, 89, etc.; Garraud, pp. 621–2.
[2] Art. 122 of the Avant-projet reads: 'Est exempt de peine le prévenu qui était en état de démence au temps de l'action'. Professeur Donnedieu de Vabres, however, recommends a provision similar to the present German Law (see his remarks in *La Giustizia Penale*, 1923, Part II, pp. 3 et seq.).
[3] See now the interesting case Sodeman v. King (*The Times Law Reports*, May 28, 1936, and [1936] 2 All E.R. 1138).
[4] See Garraud, op. cit., p. 608; Roux, *Droit criminel* (2nd ed., 1927), I, p. 170.
[5] See Oppenheimer, op. cit., p. 250.
[6] Vol. XXI, p. 131. As to the Swedish practice see Olof Kinberg, *Basic Principles of Criminology* (Copenhagen, 1935), pp. 346, 368.
[7] See Henry Weihofen, *Insanity as a Defence in Criminal Law* (1923), pp. 148 et seq.; Sheldon Glueck, *Mental Disorders and the Criminal Law* (1925), pp. 41 et seq.

favour of the prisoner, whilst in this country and in France the prisoner must be convicted. And when we consider how frequently the question of insanity cannot be answered with absolute certainty, the importance of this difference becomes evident.

In English law, a successful plea of insanity invariably leads to detention in a lunatic asylum during Her Majesty's pleasure, i.e. usually for a very long period or even for life. According to English Criminal Statistics for 1933, for instance, there were detained in institutions on 31st December, 1933, 21 lunatics charged with manslaughter. Out of these 21 there were 7 at that time detained for more than five years, and 11 for twenty years and over.[1] The *punishment* for manslaughter, however, is, according to the same source, usually imprisonment for a comparatively short term, and only very seldom penal servitude, particularly penal servitude of more than three or four years. The same relation is to be found in the case of many other offences. In many continental countries, however, the setting up of the defence of insanity means, or meant, only the small risk of being detained by the administrative authorities for a comparatively short period. The prisoner, even if charged with a minor offence only, is under such a system obviously much more than in this country tempted to take refuge in the defence of insanity. This was the position in Germany until 1933, and is still the position in France.

What may be the practical consequences of such a state of affairs? There are in German law two principles of great importance—acceptance of the irresistible impulse test and absence of a 'presumption of sanity'—both working in favour of the prisoner and sometimes even being combined with a particularly lenient treatment of insane offenders. Is not such a combination inevitably bound to create an extremely dangerous weakening of criminal law? When answering this question two aspects of the matter ought to be distinguished: any failure to deal efficiently with prisoners acquitted on the ground of insanity may involve consequences of the most serious kind, and the majority of continental countries have, therefore, during the last years, improved

[1] Twenty years later, the corresponding figures for 'Broadmoor Patients', as they are now called (Crim. Just. Act., 1948, sect. 62), are as follows: 13 patients detained for manslaughter on 31.12.53, of whom 6 were at that time detained for 5 years or more and 2 for 20 years and over. On the other hand, of 45 persons sent to prison for manslaughter only 5 had sentences of over 4 years (*Criminal Statistics for England and Wales for 1953*, pp. 40 and 87.)

THE TREATMENT OF MENTAL DISORDERS

their criminal legislation in this respect by empowering the courts to send to institutions for mental diseases—if necessary for life— every person who commits a crime in a state of insanity, if the protection of society requires such a measure.[1] But we are here at present only concerned with the question of how to define and how to prove insanity, and so far as these questions are involved I do not think that the admission of the defence of irresistible impulse and the shifting of the burden of proof to the prosecution have led to results dangerous to society. We cannot, it is true, prove this statement by means of statistical data. In most countries there are, unfortunately, no figures available to show accurately for each type of offence the number of prisoners acquitted or otherwise discharged on account of insanity. Moreover, even if such figures were available, they could be used for international comparisons only with the utmost caution, since so much depends upon the particulars of criminal procedure in the various countries. With this reservation, I should like to draw attention to the following figures concerning two offences which most frequently give rise to the setting up of the defence of insanity, murder and indecent exposure. Out of 122 persons tried for murder in Germany in 1932, 100 were convicted, 21 were acquitted—insanity being only one among the possible reasons for acquittal—and one case was otherwise disposed of. In England, however, out of 53 persons tried for murder in 1932, only 19 were convicted, 5 were found insane on arraignment, 10 were acquitted and 18 found guilty, but insane (one case: no bill), and still higher is the percentage of persons found insane on arraignment or guilty but insane according to the statistics given by Lord Atkin's Committee in 1924.[2] Now consider the example of indecent exposure: out of 3,521 persons tried in Germany in 1931 for this offence, 3,100 were convicted, 400 acquitted, whereas in England in 1933 out of 1,575 persons proceeded against only 1,093 were convicted (228 were discharged, whilst in 242 cases the

[1] See, e.g., sects. 42b and 42f of the German Act of 24th November 1933; art. 222 of the Italian, sects. 11 and 24 of the Russian, art 60 of the Polish, sect. 53 of the Yugoslav Penal Code, the Swedish Abnormal Delinquents Act of 1928, the Belgian Act of April 9, 1930, art. 72 of the French Avant-projet of 1932. See also the Swiss Fed. Penal Code of 1937, sects. 14–17; Denmark (1930), sects 16, 17, 70; Czechoslovakia (1950), sects. 11 and 70; Yugoslavia (1951), sects. 6 and 61.

[2] See Report, p. 25. The complete figures for 1900–49 are now reproduced in the *Report on Capital Punishment*, 1953, pp. 298–300.

CRIMINAL LAW

charge was proved and order made without conviction). These figures seem to prove that the chances of escaping punishment on account of insanity were in Germany at least not greater than in England.[1]

I would like to mention—without attaching too much weight to the results—an interesting private enquiry held in Berlin in 1931 among a few thousand juvenile workers of fourteen to seventeen years of age, on problems of guilt and punishment.[2] Although many of these boys and girls criticized rather severely what they regarded as the sometimes excessive leniency of the penal methods of that period and especially the fact that the death penalty was in their opinion too rarely carried out, no one complained about the leniency of sect. 51 of the Penal Code. Another still more convincing fact to disprove the view that the wide formulation of the conception of insanity and the absence of a presumption of sanity must undermine the protection of society against crime is that even the present régime in Germany has not only not changed, but in November, 1933, expressly confirmed the previous legal position. Moreover, during the present discussions about the new German Penal Code the idea of abolishing the defence of irresistible impulse has, as far as I am aware, never occurred to the legislators. And the same may be said of the position in Italy and Russia.

The most serious objection against the irresistible impulse test is certainly that it may sometimes be impossible, even for an experienced psychiatrist, to say whether or not an impulse was really irresistible. In his *Psychology of the Criminal*[3] Dr. M. Hamblin Smith even said: 'It is impossible to say, in any particular case, that an impulse was irresistible; all that can be said is that the impulse did not appear to have been successfully resisted.' Difficulties of this kind have certainly very often been experienced by German psychiatrists, but they as well as the lawyers have always realized that legal formulations of psychiatric terms must not be taken too literally. Dr. W. C. Sullivan was certainly right in saying: 'Criminal responsibility is a purely legal question. . . . The

---

[1] In *The Criminal Law and Sexual Offenders*, published by the British Medical Association (1949), p. 9, attention is drawn to the large number of persons charged, but found not guilty.
[2] Mathilde Kelchner, *Schuld und Sühne im Urteil jugendlicher Arbeiter und Arbeiterinnen* (1932, Beiheft 63 zur Zeitschrift für angewandte Psychologie).
[3] 2nd ed., p. 179.

THE TREATMENT OF MENTAL DISORDERS

law may fix whatever limits it thinks fit.'[1] But, on the other hand, we must bear in mind the warning which a famous German jurist, nearly a century ago, expressed in the following words: 'It is a pity that no legislator will ever succeed in finding a formulation which may truly express the right principle. The law-maker can use his powers to prohibit certain actions and to impose punishments. But his authority ends when he interferes with the realm of science by regulating matters which the most accomplished psychologist may hardly be able to describe so that his formulation is neither too narrow nor too wide.'[2] It seems that every legal system produces the type of psychiatrist that it requires. If the law adheres to a narrow formulation of insanity, the psychiatrist will do his utmost to strip off the legal fetters; if the law is elastic and wide, the psychiatrist will be reluctant to use the opportunities offered to him lest he endanger the vital interests of the State. I should like to emphasize that during the course of my work in German criminal courts I experienced only very few cases in which the psychiatrist experts took a view that did not duly consider the protection of society.

In spite of this, I am afraid it would not be advisable to follow a recommendation which has sometimes been made[3] to renounce every legal definition and to leave the question of insanity as a question of fact entirely to the jury.[4] The French Code, which goes in this direction and has been followed, among others, by the law of New Hampshire[5] and recently by the Chinese Penal Code,[6] is apparently too vague. And it may perhaps be added that a country which still preserves trial by jury in its pure form may be even more in need of some legal buttresses than those continental countries which allow the lay assessors to discuss the whole matter, in some form or other, with the learned judge behind closed doors.

---

[1] *Crime and Insanity* (1924), p. 233.
[2] C. I. A. Mittermaier, in his foreword to the 3rd edition of Feuerbach's *Aktenmässige Darstellung merkwürdiger Verbrechen* (1849).
[3] E.g., by the Medico-Psychological Association of Great Britain in their proposals to Lord Atkin's Committee, or by Dr. Prideaux in his, otherwise admirable, Cambridge Address (*Cambridge Law Journal*, I, p. 321).
[4] See *Report on Insanity and Crime* (1923), p. 4; Dr. W. Norwood East, *Forensic Psychiatry* (1927), pp. 63 et seq.
[5] See Sheldon Glueck, *Crime and Justice* (1936), p. 100; Oppenheimer, op. cit., p. 85. See now also the Report of the Royal Comm. on Cap. Punishment, 1953.
[6] See art. 19 of the Code of 1935.

CRIMINAL LAW

There is still another feature of continental criminal law that also acts somewhat as an antidote against possible dangerous effects of the defence of irresistible impulse. It is the idea that the offender, although insane at the time of committing the crime, may nevertheless be legally responsible because he had got himself intentionally into a state of temporary insanity knowing that he might, in this state, later commit a crime. This idea of the so-called *actio libera in causa* has been accepted by some continental Codes, the Italian, Swiss and Norwegian for instance. In France and Germany, however, the idea has been mainly developed by doctrine,[1] and the courts have accepted it with great reluctance and in exceptional cases only. In some of the numerous cases of mass murder which occurred in Germany after the war of 1914–18, the sanity of the murderer at the time of his crimes might have been doubtful. Nevertheless, he was held fully responsible, since—according to the view of the experts—he must have known after the first murder that, if he put himself in a state of sadistic emotion, he would lose his self-control and probably commit more murders. This argument might, however, ignore the possibility that in such cases the murderer, if really insane, may never have been in a position to restrain himself from further acts leading to the desired end.[2] [In the words of the Royal Commission on Capital Punishment of 1953 (p. 111), cases should be exempt from responsibility not only where the accused was incapable of preventing himself if he had tried to do so, but also where he was 'incapable of wishing or trying to prevent himself....']

The same idea of *actio libera in causa* lies, to a wide extent, at the bottom of the continental law on *drunkenness*. It cannot be denied that a high degree of intoxication may produce a state of temporary insanity which, from the standpoint of pure logic, would make the offender legally irresponsible. It is only the fact that he has usually put himself voluntarily in this position that justifies a different method of treatment. The French Code Pénal does not explicitly take cognizance of crimes committed in a state of drunkenness. It is, however, recognized in French law that voluntary drunkenness does not constitute a defence, if it was caused

---

[1] See Garraud, op. cit., pp. 671 and 665; von Liszt-Schmidt, *Lehrbuch des Strafrechts* (26th ed., 1932), sect. 37 V.
[2] See, e.g., the description of the Kürten case by Margaret Seaton Wagner, *The Monster of Düsseldorf*, pp. 191 et seq.

THE TREATMENT OF MENTAL DISORDERS

with the intention of committing a crime. If this latter condition has not been fulfilled French jurists are inclined to treat the offender as a person who is merely guilty of criminal negligence.[1] The Italian Code takes a more severe attitude: 'Drunkenness not arising from an accidental event or from *force majeure*—according to art. 92—shall not exclude or diminish responsibility. If the drunkenness was pre-ordained for the purpose of committing an offence, or for providing an excuse, the punishment shall be increased.'[2] The Russian Code (art. 11) limits itself to the laconic footnote that its provisions dealing with insanity are not applicable to crimes committed in a state of drunkenness, and similar provisions are to be found in the Turkish Code and the French *Avant-projet*.[3]

Of special interest is the development in German law. The German Code did not deal with the problem of drunkenness before 1933. Therefore, a person who had committed a crime in a state of complete drunkenness was punishable only if he had intentionally produced this condition, although he knew (or ought to have known) that he might, in his drunkenness, commit an offence of such a kind as he later actually did commit.[4] This, of course, was very difficult to prove; consequently, acquittals frequently occurred that aroused public indignation. Drunkenness as such was not punishable. Detention in reformatories for inebriates after acquittal was the business not of the courts, but of administrative authorities who were often afraid to burden their communities with heavy expenses. In this respect, the position was probably not much different from that in this country under the Inebriates Act of 1898. I should like to illustrate some of the existing difficulties by referring to an extreme case with which I had to deal as an examining magistrate (*Untersuchungsrichter*) many years ago. A man had killed a boy of fourteen who had been entirely unknown to him, without any reason and without a quarrel, in a fit of raving frenzy after drinking some comparatively

---

[1] See Vidal and Magnol, op. cit., p. 301; Garraud, p. 660; Roux, *Cours de droit criminel* (2nd ed., 1927), I, p. 170.

[2] Official English translation.

[3] See also the Danish Penal Code of 1930, sects. 18, 72 and 73; and the Czechoslovak Penal Code of 1950, sects. 21 and 70; the Yugoslav Penal Code of 1951, sect. 6(3).

[4] See the author's remarks in *Journal of Criminal Law and Criminology*, Vol. XXVI, pp. 528–9.

CRIMINAL LAW

small quantities of beer and cognac. Immediately after his arrest he fell into a profound sleep, and later, when informed of his crime, he attempted suicide. When I interrogated him some days after his arrest, he maintained that he knew nothing of the crime, and, after several examinations, the psychiatrists agreed that this statement seemed to be true. It was obviously a case of pathological drunkenness—to use this not commonly approved term[1]—as the serious effect could be explained not by the quantity of alcohol consumed, but by a special susceptibility to its action. The problem was whether, under such circumstances, it was possible to punish the man according to German law as it was before 1933, since he had acted in a state of temporary insanity. He was punishable only if he had wilfully produced his drunkenness, although he knew or ought to have known that he might in this state commit a crime of such a character as he did later actually commit. It was, therefore, necessary to make a careful study of the earlier life of the prisoner, which showed that he had never committed a crime in a state of drunkenness, or otherwise. Several years before the homicide in question he had, however, in a state of drunkenness been involved in a brawl in the course of which he had been thrown from a bridge and badly injured. After this misfortune, so he stated, he had never had any alcohol until the day of the homicide when a friend had enticed him to drink. These facts were, in the view of the prosecution, not sufficient to prove that the prisoner knew or ought to have known that he might kill or injure another person in a state of drunkenness. Therefore, as a conviction could not be expected, he had to be released, without being committed for trial at all; and, since he was neither insane nor a habitual drunkard, the administrative authorities refused to send him to an institution.[2] A few weeks later he called at my office and asked me for protection, because, as he told me, the relatives of the dead boy, who lived in his neighbourhood, were threatening to beat or even to kill him. This example shows in a striking manner how dangerous it may be when the law is too logical or considers only one aspect of the matter; it may provoke self-help even in the form of lynch justice.

[1] See Norwood East, *Forsenic Psychiatry*, 1927, p. 251.
[2] A similar case is reported by W. C. Sullivan, *Crime and Insanity* (1924), p. 67, and referred to by Glanville Williams, *Criminal Law: The General Part* (1953), p. 371, who rightly draws attention to the difficult problems presented by such cases to the administration of criminal justice.

THE TREATMENT OF MENTAL DISORDERS

Nevertheless, the solution of punishing a crime committed in a state of complete drunkenness exactly as in the case of a sober person has been favoured in Germany neither by the former nor by the present régime. It has always been maintained that such a method does not sufficiently take into consideration the fact that the guilt of the offender does not consist in the commission of the particular crime, but only in his drunkenness. Take the case of three friends who have put themselves wilfully in exactly the same condition of drunkenness. On their way home, one of them smashes a window, the second assaults a policeman, and the third has the misfortune of killing a person who crosses his path. The guilt of these three men, it has been said, may be exactly the same; how can a system be justified which deals with them in completely different ways according to the different gravity of the consequences which, by chance, they have brought about? It has, therefore, been suggested that there should be a special offence of aggravated drunkenness, according to which a person who, wilfully or negligently, puts himself in a state of drunkenness is to be punished with imprisonment or with a fine when he commits a crime in this condition. The penalty, however, must not exceed the limits set by the statute which is actually violated. Although even under such a law there will certainly be a difference in punishment between the man who smashes a window and the man who kills a person, this difference will be comparatively small, and the offender will not be punished for murder, manslaughter, etc., but for aggravated drunkenness only. This method has been adopted by the German Statute on 24th November, 1933. It may not be without interest to quote some remarks from the Report of the Official Committee, as they reveal a certain difference between National Socialist and Fascist penal theories: 'It may be possible'—says the Report—'to provide uncompromisingly, as does the Italian Code, that such an action is to be treated as if it were committed in a state of full responsibility. That, however, would be a *fictio juris et de jure* which would be in harmony neither with a law that is based upon the idea of guilt nor with the natural popular opinion that regards a person who kills another in a state of voluntary drunkenness as punishable, but not as guilty of murder or manslaughter'.[1] It may be added that the solution adopted by the Act of 1933 is not entirely without

[1] See *Das kommende deutsche Strafrecht* (Allgemeiner Teil, 1934), pp. 42–3.

CRIMINAL LAW

supporters even outside Germany.[1] The difference between it and full responsibility for a crime committed in a state of drunkenness (*actio libera in causa*) is that in the latter case the offender gets drunk in order to commit a crime under the protection of the defence of drunkenness.[2]

POSTSCRIPT

Although there have been no explicit changes in the English law of insanity since this paper was written, certain interesting developments have nevertheless taken place to which the attention of the reader should be drawn. Not only has the subject been fully treated in the 'Report of the Royal Commission on Capital Punishment of 1953'[3] and in its Minutes of Evidence, further important contributions to this perennial discussion have recently been published by legal writers, notably by Professor Glanville Williams in his outstanding book, *Criminal Law: The General Part*,[4] and in a subsequent paper on 'The Royal Commission and the Defence of Insanity',[5] also by Mr. Justice Devlin in his lecture on 'Criminal Responsibility and Punishment: Functions of Judge and Jury'.[6] On the psychiatric side, Dr. Edward Glover's *Notes on the M'Naghten Rules*[7] and his comments on the Report of the Royal Commission[8] should be mentioned. While nothing even approaching a comprehensive review can here be attempted of the present position as it appears in the light of such recent developments, the following points might be made in view of their special relevance to the subject of our earlier paper:

(1) The *Burden of Proof* in relation to insanity. It was one of our principal criticisms of the English law of insanity that, against all

---

[1] e.g., Dr. J. F. Sutherland, then Deputy Commissioner in Lunacy for Scotland, in his book on Recidivism, 1908, p. 17, writes: 'There is something, indeed much, to be said for this view, in any rational system of jurisprudence.' Vidal-Magnol, op. cit., p. 302, note 1, also approves of this method.

[2] See Adolf Schönke, *Strafgesetzbuch*, Kommentar, art. 33a, note 1.

[3] 'Report of Royal Commission on Capital Punishment, 1953' (Cmd. 8932), Chapter 4.

[4] Glanville Williams, *Criminal Law: The General Part* (1054), Chapter 9.

[5] In *Current Legal Problems*. Ed. by G. W. Keeton and G. Schwarzenberger on behalf of the Faculty of Laws, University College, London (London, Stevens & Sons, Ltd., 1954), pp. 16 et seq.

[6] *The Criminal Law Review*, September, 1954, pp. 661 et seq.

[7] *The British Journal of Delinquency*, Vol. I, No. 4, April, 1951.

[8] Ibid., Vol. IV, No. 3, January, 1954.

THE TREATMENT OF MENTAL DISORDERS

the established principles of criminal procedure, it places this burden on the accused instead of fixing it unmistakably on the prosecution. This criticism is still valid. Even if, as the Royal Commission and Mr. Justice Devlin have pointed out,[1] the jury are told in the judge's summing-up that 'the burden of proof on the defence is lower than that on the prosecution, it being sufficient if they prove insanity on the balance of probabilities and not beyond a reasonable doubt', even this still seems to place an undue burden on the shoulders of the defence and may in some cases of conflicting expert evidence well lead to unjustifiable verdicts of guilty.

An interesting attempt has been made by Professor Glanville Williams to show that actually in English law, too, the burden of proof rests on the prosecution and that the prevailing view to the contrary is due to a confusion between evidential and ultimate or persuasive burden of proof.[2] According to him, the only burden that rests on the accused is that he has to raise the issue of insanity, i.e. the 'evidential' burden of introducing the evidence; once this has been done the 'ultimate' evidence, or the 'risk of non-persuasion of the jury', is on the prosecution. Glanville Williams admits, however, that these distinctions which seem obvious to him are 'consistently ignored in the literature and in judicial statements'. It is to be hoped that in any future revision of the McNaghten rules the present anomaly may be brought to an end. Unfortunately, no recommendation in this direction has been made by the Royal Commission on Capital Punishment. With regard to another, closely related, procedural issue the Commission has, however, taken the right view by recommending that the trial judge should be given power 'to raise the issue of insanity, to call relevant evidence and to put the issue to the jury'.[3] If this recommendation should be accepted, together with Glanville Williams' interpretation, the 'evidential' burden of proof, too, would be taken away from the accused, and there would be no difference any more in this respect between English and Continental procedure.

(2) The defence of 'irresistible impulse'. This conception is no longer regarded as a satisfactory solution of the difficulties created

[1] Report, p. 81; Devlin, p. 675.
[2] *Criminal Law: The General Part*, sects. 102 and 224/5.
[3] Report, p. 277, No. 36.

by the narrowness of the McNaghten rules. In the Report of the Royal Commission it is rightly pointed out that the conception is inadequate not so much because it is impossible to distinguish between an irresistible and a merely unresisted impulse—such a distinction, the commission holds as did the present writer in his paper, might often be very difficult, but is not impossible. The conception is, however, regarded as too narrow because it seems to limit the defence to acts committed 'suddenly and impulsively after a sharp internal conflict', excluding cases where the crime was coolly and carefully prepared over a period of time.[1] To these objections Professor Glanville Williams adds the criticism that 'any rule based on the idea of irresistible impulse' . . . lands in the metaphysical quagmire of determinism'.[2] While this is perfectly true, it also applies to most other formulations if they are taken literally.

As will have been obvious to the careful reader of the original paper the formula 'irresistible impulse' was used there not in any specific sense but rather as a collective to cover all those attempts made in Continental law to include the emotional element in their definition of insanity producing criminal irresponsibility. It was used as it seemed to be the only phrase available at the time in English legal literature to describe that emotional factor. In fact, as clearly shown in our discussion of the changes in sect. 51 of the German Criminal Code and in the references to other Continental Codes, the phrase 'irresistible impulse' was meant to cover the broader formula now recommended by the Royal Commission as an alternative, i.e. disease of the mind making the accused 'incapable of preventing himself from committing the act'.

Whatever formula will be adopted to replace the obsolete McNaghten rules the main problem for the future will be in whose hands the power to apply it should rest. The Royal Commission proposes to leave it to the jury to decide whether the accused was, at the time of the act, 'suffering from disease of the mind to such a degree that he ought not to be held responsible' (p. 276). In the view of the present writer, this would result in haphazard and amateurish verdicts. 'To make problems of modern psychiatry clear to the average juror is impossible if presentation and discussion have to take place in the straitjacket form of jury

[1] Report, p. 110.
[2] *Current Legal Problems*, p. 22.

THE TREATMENT OF MENTAL DISORDERS

proceedings.'[1] Since this was written the strongest possible confirmation has come from Dr. Denis Hill in his evidence before the Royal Commission,[2] and it is encouraging to see that Professor Glanville Williams also takes the view that the question of insanity should be removed from the jury and left to a body of three psychiatric experts, possibly sitting as assessors with the judge.[3] When asked by the Royal Commission whether he thought that, as an expert witness in murder trials, he 'could successfully explain the Electro-encephalogram and the lessons to be drawn from it to an ordinary jury' Dr. Hill had to reply in the negative. This might well be regarded as symptomatic of the general position, and using the E.G.G. as a symbol of modern science one might be tempted to summarize the position in the formula: either the jury or the E.E.G.—one cannot have it both ways in a criminal trial. Exaggerated as this is, it contains some truth.

(3) *The defence of Drunkenness.* In his admirable chapter on the subject[4] Professor Glanville Williams points out that drunkenness is not generally an aggravation of crime and may well lead to reduced punishment. Apart from capital crimes, however, where the present law is over-severe, he regards the legal position as satisfactory as sufficient latitude is given to the Courts. Any criticism should therefore be directed against the sentencing policy of the judges and the lack of adequate facilities for treatment. The question arises, however, whether these two considerations, i.e. the rigidity of the present law of murder and the lack of guidance to judicial policy in non-capital cases, might not speak in favour of a special provision on the lines of the German law (now sect. 330*a* of the Criminal Code).[5]

[1] *Criminal Justice and Social Reconstruction*, p. 247.
[2] Minutes of Evidence, 1950, p. 313.
[3] *Current Legal Problems*, pp. 26, 29.
[4] *Criminal Law: The General Part*, Chapter 10.
[5] On the whole problem see now the careful comparative survey by Rolf Heuermann in *Materialien zur Strafrechtsreform*, Vol. II (Bonn 1954, Dr. Hans Heger, Godesberg), pp. 209 et seq.

APPENDIX TO CHAPTER 13

THE CRIMINAL LAW AND MENTALLY ABNORMAL OFFENDERS

WHEN the Council of the International Society of Criminology did me the honour of inviting me to prepare for this Congress a General Report on the subject of " The Criminal Law and mentally abnormal Offenders " I realised that I would have to tackle a topic on which everything that could reasonably be said had already been said, a topic where the words from Goethe's *Faust* seem to apply with particular force:

" Wer kann was Dummes, wer was Kluges denken,
Das nicht die Vorwelt schon gedacht? "
(Who can think of anything, be it stupid or clever, that has not yet been thought of before?)

Or, to turn from poetry to music, I felt like a conductor who has been invited by a record company to produce yet another recording of, say, Beethoven's Fifth Symphony (which, I believe, has already been recorded twenty-five times) and who nevertheless feels the urge to produce something original, instead of simply trying to imitate, say, the Toscanini or Ansermet or Furtwängler, or Klemperer or Karajan touch.

I should like to invite you to regard the present Congress as some sort of a Summit Conference No. 2, with objects not too dissimilar from those of Summit Conference No. 1, but we hope with better results. Let us try to conceive of the law and its associates as standing in the place of the Western Allies and of psychiatrists and their confederates as representing the Soviet Union with its satellites, with

---

* A lecture delivered on September 6, 1960, at a Plenary Session of the Fourth International Congress of Criminology at The Hague. Published in the Congress *Proceedings* (pp. 465–81) and reprinted in *The British Journal of Criminology* (formerly *British Journal of Delinquency*), Vol. 1, No. 3, January, 1961. Reproduced with the kind permission of *The British Journal of Criminology*.

the possibility of sociology as a third force lurking somewhere in the background—all this, of course, implying no political value judgments whatsoever as for our present purposes East and West are equally near and dear to our hearts. Let us then see whether some practicable disarmament agreement could be worked out and whether all three parties could be persuaded to join a Common Market.

Sometimes, when looking at the literature of our subject, one gets the feeling that the differences between East and West are still very wide in spite of all the various state visits and other, more informal, travellings, or, shall we say, International Congresses. To one like myself, a lawyer by theoretical and practical training, a sociologist by naturalisation and a " psychiatrist " by association, but actually belonging to none of these three great professions and representing nobody but himself, anxious to see those dangerous gaps and misunderstandings reduced to the utmost minimum, the present Congress seems to offer a valuable opportunity.

Obviously, my subject centres largely, though not exclusively, around the relationship between the forces of the law, on the one hand, and the psychiatric profession, on the other, and it is here that most of the controversies and misunderstandings have arisen. It is a disturbing fact, however, that sociologists, too, have occasionally contributed to them, and their views cannot, therefore, be entirely ignored.

A distinguished and otherwise progressive English lawyer has recently said,[1] in an attempt to define the role of the psychiatrist in criminal proceedings: The judge's patient is not the offender; his patient is society—" the diseased body politic," as he calls it; and as the psychiatrist is concerned only with the offender there is, he concludes, not much room in court for the psychiatrist before the verdict, though he might be useful afterwards in advising on the kind of sentence to be imposed. While there is some grain of truth in these statements they seem to me to draw a one-sided, over-simplified, and distorted picture of the real situation. It is of course true that psychiatry is in the first place interested in the individual, just

[1] On the following text, see now Walter Raeburn, *The British Journal of Criminology*, Vol. I, No. 2, October 1960, p. 102 *et seq.*, and Editorial Note, pp. 97–98.

as sociology is in the first place interested in society and other social entities. The law, however, is concerned with both, society and the individual, although it is indisputable that wherever their interests clash the law has to give precedence to society. The relationships involved are in fact much more complex than would appear from the statements quoted before. Society, for example, is not merely the patient of the judge; it is also his boss, as it is the boss of the psychiatrist, too. Society is, on the other hand, the victim of the offender, but it is at the same time responsible for him and may even be partly responsible for his crime. We might perhaps say the offender is the patient of society through the medium of both the judge and, in certain cases, the psychiatrist. This being so, the judge cannot simply leave the offender to his fate and concentrate exclusively on his other patient, society.

Similarly, the relationship between law, psychiatry and sociology cannot be reduced to a simple formula. Under certain aspects, psychiatry and sociology belong together as primarily fact-finding disciplines, opposed to the normative character of the law; and they are both often regarded as deterministic in contrast to the indeterministic tendency of the criminal law. As far as their methods of fact-finding are concerned, however, psychiatry and sociology stand in different camps, the former relying mainly upon intuitive and uncontrolled clinical observation, the latter mainly upon objective, controlled, statistical techniques. What about sociology and the law? It is in their criticism of the psychiatrist's alleged neglect of the interests of society and of his preference for vague terms and imprecise techniques; in their use of generalisations instead of the individualistic bias of the psychiatrist; in their rejection of the exaggerated claims of some psychiatrists that all crime is due to mental abnormality that the lawyer and the sociologist are in agreement. It is interesting to observe, however, that especially in recent years, while lawyers have on the whole become somewhat more tolerant of psychiatry, certain sociologists—in particular in the United States—have been inclined to outdo the lawyers in their ferocious outbursts against psychiatrists. The explanation may be found in the simple fact that lawyers have at last become aware that, for good or ill, in their practical work they have to come to terms with psychiatry as an often indispensable auxiliary force, whereas the sociologist, whose share in the diagnosis and treatment of crime has so far often remained largely theoretical, can afford to maintain a purely negative attitude. Looking at the vast amount of time and energy spent in recent years by some of our sociologists in their efforts to show how vague and unscientific most psychiatric terms are and how great the disagreement is among psychiatrists even about their most fundamental concepts [2] one cannot help feeling that, while these criticisms are useful reminders to psychiatrists not to allow their imagination, their scientific research and techniques to become too wildly undisciplined and subjective,[3] they leave the essence of psychiatric work basically untouched. It is fairly obvious that among psychiatrists, working clinically and intuitively, there should be even more disagreement and that they should produce even less evidence for their claims than is the case with lawyers and sociologists. On the other hand, should not members of these last-mentioned professions and, we have to add, members of the medical profession outside psychiatry, too, be honest enough to admit that there is far too much vagueness, jargon, too much unnecessary hairsplitting and frequent lack of unanimity even about fundamentals in legal and sociological literature, too? One of the sociologists referred to before even goes so far as to hint vaguely at the " methodological and philosophical reasons why it is perfectly legitimate for judges and lawyers to disagree, but not permissible for psychiatrists to do so." [4] There is in my view no human profession where it is " not permissible " to disagree; nor can there be any " methodological and philosophical reasons " to prevent a scientific worker from disagreeing with his fellows. In so far, I am happy to concur with Professor Jerome Hall, who writes: " Indeed, a lack of disagreement (among psychiatrists) would in many cases raise doubts regarding the

---

[2] See in particular Michael Hakeem, " A Critique of the Psychiatric Approach to Crime and Correction," in *Crime and Correction, Law and Contemporary Problems*, School of Law, Duke University, Vol. XXIII, No. 4, Autumn 1958, p. 650 *et seq.*; Barbara Wootton, *Social Science and Social Pathology*, London, 1959, Chaps. VII and VIII.
[3] For an illuminating discussion of the basic differences in research techniques used by experimental psychologists, on the one hand, and by psychoanalysts, on the other, see Gardner Lindzey in his introductory chapter to *Human Motives*, New York, 1958, p. 8 *et seq.*
[4] Hakeem, *loc. cit.*, p. 668.

integrity or competence of the witnesses,"[5] and we are all happy to see how eager psychiatrists usually are to demonstrate their integrity and competence. In short, the many undeniable weaknesses of present-day psychiatry should not be used as reasons or excuses for the exclusion of psychiatrists from any stage of criminal proceedings, but should rather force the lawyer to devise a system which would combine freedom of movement and expression for the psychiatrist with proper safeguards for the administration of justice. These safeguards can only be found in suitably formulated laws and, even far more important, in an adequately trained judiciary. Regarding the latter point, without anticipating my subsequent remarks it is obvious that the position will differ fundamentally according to whether the crucial decisions are entrusted to a professional judge or to a jury. One can at least try to train the former, but one cannot train the latter, and however detailed the instructions given by the judge in his summing-up they can be no substitute for proper training.

II

After these brief introductory remarks I have now to pass to a discussion of some of the most important specific problems of my subject. The time at my disposal does not permit any reflections of an historical nature, nor is there any need for them after Dr. Guttmacher's lecture. There is, however, one personal remark which I find difficult to suppress. Looking back over developments in the past fifty years one can safely say that considerable progress has been made not only in psychiatry but also in the criminal law which, in many countries, has become more discriminating, more sophisticated, and more efficient in its dealings with our problems. Even some thirty years ago, when I was still a criminal court judge, our work was in some respects comparatively simple and correspondingly unsatisfactory. All we had to do, all we could do, was to decide whether the accused was legally responsible for his actions and, if he was found irresponsible on account of insanity, to acquit him. What happened afterwards to those found irresponsible was not our

[5] Jerome Hall, *Studies in Jurisprudence and Criminal Theory*, New York, 1958, p. 278 (reprinted from the *Yale Law Journal*, 1956, Vol. 65).

concern. In most jurisdictions things are now very different, and the task of the judge has become correspondingly more complicated, but perhaps also less unsatisfactory.

1. The first of those specific questions which I have to discuss is that of *definition* in order to determine the scope of the subject. I have no time to read out full literal quotations of the various legal definitions to which I shall have to refer, but an admirable comparative survey of the position in many countries up to the year 1953 is fortunately available in the Report of the English Royal Commission on Capital Punishment [6]; a shorter one may be found in the American Law Institute's Tentative Draft No. 4 of their Model Penal Code,[7] and a third survey up to 1954 has been given in German in the " Materialien zur Strafrechtsreform." [8]

How, then, do we propose to define the term " mentally abnormal," how has it been defined in the various criminal legislations? Perhaps the most important lesson to be derived from a study of the enormous literature is that we should never limit our investigations to one particular legal system but rather treat the matter on the widest possible international and comparative basis. Before an international audience such as this the comparative approach has to be taken for granted, but elsewhere, too, it is essential to avoid those pitfalls of narrow parochialism into which even some of our most eminent legal writers have fallen. If one knows of no other solution than, say, the M'Naghten Rules one may easily succumb to the temptation to regard them as indispensable and almost as a law of nature. Only if we realise that there is no particular magic about these Rules and that there are in fact many other formulae which have actually been used elsewhere without any disastrous consequences to society, only then shall we be willing to listen to reason.

Leaving aside all those refinements for which there is here no

---

[6] Report of the Royal Commission on Capital Punishment 1949–53. London, H.M.S.O. 1953, Cmd. 8932. See in particular p. 75 *et seq.* on English and Scottish law, and p. 105 *et seq.* and Appendix 9, p. 407 *et seq.* on the position abroad, p. 102 *et seq.* on " the inadequacy of the M'Naghten Rules " and p. 275 *et seq.*, on the recommendations for their reform.

[7] The American Law Institute, Model Penal Code, Tentative Draft No. 4, Philadelphia, April 25, 1955, Appendix A, p. 161 *et seq.*

[8] Hans Heinz Heldmann, Zurechnungsfähigkeit, Zurechnungsunfähigkeit und verminderte Zurechnungsfähigkeit, in Materialien zur Strafrechtsreform, 2. Band, Rechtsvergleichende Arbeiten I. Allgemeiner Teil, Bonn, 1954, pp. 345–365.

time we can, I believe, at least for the first stage of this discussion, safely content ourselves with a broad distinction between the world inside and outside the M'Naghten Rules. I know of course that according to many writers these Rules do not intend to give a definition of insanity, but in their actual application it can hardly be disputed that they have this effect. As Dr. Guttmacher has already shown, the Rules are still substantially adhered to, either as common law or as statutory law, in Great Britain and nearly all parts of the British Commonwealth—modified in some states of Australia and in South Africa through the addition of the irresistible impulse test— and they are also in force in most states of the United States, except New Hampshire and the District of Columbia, but in fourteen states they are also modified through the irresistible impulse test. This does not mean, of course, complete uniformity throughout in the interpretation and application of the Rules. The High Court of Australia, for example, in 1952 interpreted the word "wrong" in the Rules in a much wider and more reasonable sense than has been done by the English Court of Criminal Appeal.[9] And with regard to the United States, Professor Glueck wrote many years ago that "perhaps in no other field of American law is there so much disagreement as to fundamentals and so many contradictory decisions in the same jurisdictions."[10] The essence of the Rules and the principal criticisms to which they have been subjected for over a century can be taken as generally known. In a nutshell, these criticisms may be summarised under eight headings as follows:

(a) The notorious "right and wrong" test of the Rules concentrates exclusively on the element of knowledge, ignoring the elements of will and emotion and—not surprisingly in 1843—also ignoring the unconscious.

(b) The test expects psychiatrists to deal with a question to which they can have no meaningful answer, since "knowledge of right and wrong" is not a psychiatric concept, nor is it in their view a test of

---

[9] See J. E. Hall Williams, *The British Journal of Delinquency*, Vol. V, No. 1, July 1954, p. 72 et seq.; Norval Morris, "The Beattie Smith Lectures," *The Medical Journal of Australia*, March 8, 1958, p. 2; Glanville Williams, *Criminal Law: The General Part*, London, 1953, p. 323 et seq., where a very detailed critical analysis of the M'Naghten Rules can be found.

[10] Sheldon Glueck, "Mental Disorder and the Criminal Law," quoted from Henry Weihofen, *The Urge to Punish*, London, 1957, p. 37.

MENTALLY ABNORMAL OFFENDERS

insanity.[11] Even to the lawyer the test is too narrow, since *mens rea* is wider than mere knowledge.[12]

(c) The Rules are limited to cases of gross insanity, ignoring the much more frequent " non sane non insane " category, to use Sir Norwood East's phrase,[13] in other words the various types of neurotic and psychopathic offenders, and also ignoring the mentally defective group.

(d) Even within these narrow limits the Rules, in conjunction with the peculiarly Anglo-American system of cross-examination, greatly restrict the freedom of the psychiatric expert to say and to explain to the best of his ability what he regards as the crux of the matter, thereby forcing him to make statements in court which he himself may well regard as distortions of the truth.

(e) The vagueness of the Rules makes the outcome of an individual case unpredictable. This is a criticism which I am reproducing not because I believe other tests to be capable of giving more predictable results—they don't!—but because the mistaken view has so often been expressed that *only* the M'Naghten Rules are clear and simple enough to be administered with any degree of certainty by a jury.[14] Only recently Lady Wootton has written, and I was sorry to hear yesterday that Dr. Guttmacher apparently agrees with her: " Once we allow any movement away from a rigid intellectual test of responsibility on M'Naghten lines, our feet are set upon a slippery slope which offers no real resting place short of the total abandonment of the whole concept of responsibility." [15] My reply to this is simply that the path is always slippery, with or without the Rules, but that it is hardly more slippery and definitely more in agreement with modern scientific views without than with them.

(f) By establishing an unrealistic and much too narrow test the Rules inevitably hand the final decision over to the administration, *i.e.*, in England to the Home Secretary and his advisers who are not

---

[11] Report of the Royal Commission on Capital Punishment, p. 80; Philip Q. Roche, *The Criminal Mind*. Fifth Isaac Ray Lecture, New York, 1958, pp. 104 *et seq.*, 109 *et seq.*
[12] John Reid, " Understanding the New Hampshire Doctrine of Criminal Insanity," *Yale Law Journal*, Vol. 69, No. 3, January 1960, p. 386.
[13] Sir Norwood East, *Society and the Criminal*, London, 1949, Chap. XIV.
[14] East, *op. cit.*, pp. 35 and 299.
[15] Barbara Wootton, *Social Science and Social Pathology*, p. 249.

CRIMINAL LAW

bound by them, thereby often reducing the solemn judgment of the court to a mere farce.

(g) By requiring the defence to establish insanity the Rules depart without adequate reason from the fundamental principle of criminal procedure that the burden of proof is on the prosecution.[16]

(h) By restricting their application to the jury courts the Rules introduce a dual system of criminal justice, one for the more serious crimes and another for the less serious offences dealt with by the magistrates' courts.

This last point, of course, implies more praise than criticism since, as the Rules are so bad, it is all to the good that they are at least not applicable to the great masses of criminal cases. Moreover, recent British legislation has done much to improve the legal position. I can here only refer to certain provisions of the Criminal Justice Act of 1948, the Magistrates' Courts Act of 1952, the Homicide Act of 1957, and the Mental Health Act of 1959.[17] In particular the last-mentioned statute, which for the first time explicitly recognises the legal existence of the psychopath, which even gives a definition of " psychopathic disorders " and provides that mentally disordered and psychopathic offenders may be sent by the court to a mental hospital instead of being punished, seems to offer an opportunity greatly to reduce the iniquities of the M'Naghten Rules. The Homicide Act of 1957 is also of considerable importance in so far as it admits in the English law of murder the defence of diminished responsibility which has already been available in Scotland for over a century, with the effect that the penalty has to be reduced from that for murder to that for manslaughter and may, therefore, in suitable cases be a short prison sentence or even no " punishment " but only probation. On the other hand, here too the burden of proof for the existence of an abnormality of mind which " substantially impaired " the offender's mental responsibility is placed on the defence.[18] It is doubtful, moreover, whether this provision will be treated by the courts as

---

[16] On the burden of proof under the M'Naghten Rules, see above, pp. 287, 296–297, and Glanville Williams, *op. cit.* (above, note 9), p. 352 *et seq.*

[17] Criminal Justice Act, ss. 4 and 26; Magistrates' Courts Act, ss. 26 and 30; Homicide Act, s. 2; Mental Health Act, ss. 4 and 60.

[18] See J. E. Hall Williams, " The Homicide Act, 1957," *The Modern Law Review*, July 1957, pp. 382–383.

covering psychopathic disorders, and it is also regrettable that no provision whatsoever is made in the Act for the treatment of such abnormal offenders convicted of manslaughter.

Passing now to the world outside the M'Naghten Rules one can perhaps say that there is more uniformity between the various national legislations and recent drafts than there is diversity. It is true that some of the provisions, notably article 64 of the French Penal Code of 1810, the Cuban Code of Social Defence of 1936, article 35, and the Swedish Act of 1945 [19] simply refer to insanity, " démence " or " mental disorder " without trying to define their meaning and also without explicitly requiring any particular psychological effect, although the Swedish Act seems at least to require that the crime was committed " under the influence " of the mental disease, *i.e.*, a causal link between crime and disease. This method has sometimes been described as " purely biological." [20] It is also true that a few of the present legislations, again notably the French Code, do not mention the " non-sane non-insane " group and, consequently, make no provision for diminished responsibility. However, the strong link which unites most of the other legislations outside the realm of the undiluted M'Naghten Rules is, first, that they recognise the force of the irrational, emotional element, traditionally referred to as " irresistible impulse "; secondly, that they include mental deficiency and the " non-sane non-insane " group including psychopathy; and, thirdly, that they place the burden of proof on the prosecution. When I use the term " irresistible impulse " I am of course fully aware of its growing unpopularity and of the criticism made of it by the Royal Commission on Capital Punishment and by many psychiatrists, too.[21] Weihofen has called it " another example of the nineteenth-century penchant for using absolute terms as ' rhetorical flourishes.' " I am using the term not as a cut-and-dried legal formula but rather as a symbol of the " irresistible impulse " of

---

[19] On the Swedish Act of 1945, see Gösta Rylander, " Treatment of Mentally Abnormal Offenders in Sweden," *The British Journal of Delinquency*, Vol. V, No. 4, April 1955, p. 262 *et seq.*; Thorsten Sellin, *The Protective Code, A Swedish Proposal*, Department of Justice, Stockholm, 1957, p. 19.
[20] See Heldmann, *op. cit.* (note 8, above), p. 348.
[21] Report of Royal Commission on Capital Punishment, p. 109 *et seq.* and *passim*; Guttmacher in the American Law Institute's Model Penal Code Tentative Draft No. 4, Appendix B, p. 174 *et seq.*; Henry Weihofen, *op. cit.* (note 10, above), p. 66 *et seq.*; Philip Q. Roche, *op. cit.* (note 11, above), p. 179 *et seq.*

CRIMINAL LAW

the human mind to shake off the fetters of a purely rationalistic dogma. In perhaps the majority of countries outside the English speaking world we have the corresponding phrase "inability to recognise the wrongness of his action or to act in accordance with his insight," or something similar,[22] and it is particularly significant that this phrase is also used in two of the most important recent European Drafts, the French " Avant-projet de Loi concernant les délinquants anormaux " of 1959 and in § 23 of the Western German " Entwurf des Allgemeinen Teils eines Strafgesetzbuchs " of 1958.[23] Again, I am not saying that there is complete unanimity here and absence of doubtful points. There are differences, for example, on the question of what kind of knowledge and understanding of the significance of his action the offender is required to possess: is it an understanding of its legal or of its moral meaning? The German Code says at present: " das Unerlaubte der Tat," whereas the new Draft proposes to say, in conformity with the Swiss Code: " das Unrecht der Tat." The French Avant-projet uses the formula: " le caractère délictueux," the Czechoslovak Code: " the dangerousness of his action to society," the Yugoslav Code says simply: " the significance of his action." The Belgian " Loi de défense sociale " of 1930 makes no mention at all of the intellectual element, but requires only the offender's lack of ability, as a consequence of his mental abnormality, to control his actions.[24] While such differences may well have some practical consequences in a limited number of cases, they can, however, hardly destroy the picture of uniformity to which I have referred.

Now, although I believe that this formula, so commonly used, " inability or impaired ability to recognise the wrongness of his action or to act in accordance with his insight " is on the whole an adequate expression of what we have in mind for the insane and for

---

[22] See, *e.g.*, the Argentine Penal Code of 1921, art. 34; the Bulgarian Code of 1951, art. 13; the Czechoslav Code of 1950, art. 11; the German Code of 1871, art. 51, as amended in 1933; the Italian Code of 1930, art. 85; the Soviet Russian Code of 1926, s. 11; the Swiss Federal Code of 1937, art. 10; the Turkish Code of 1926, art. 46; the Yugoslav Code of 1951, art. 6.

[23] On the French Avant-projet see the interesting and detailed analysis in *Les Délinquants anormaux mentaux*. Ouvrage publié sous la direction de Georges Levasseur. Introduction comparative de Marc Ancel. Paris, 1959; on the German Draft Entwurf des Allgemeinen Teils eines Strafgesetzbuchs mit Begründung. Bonn, 1958.

[24] Belgian " Loi de défense sociale à l'égard des anormaux et des délinquants d'habitude," art. 1.

MENTALLY ABNORMAL OFFENDERS

the " non-sane non-insane " groups respectively, it has one weakness to which attention was drawn twenty years ago in the Report of a Belgian Commission set up to study the reform of the Act of 1930 [25]— a weakness which has often been felt but which legislators have so far found almost impossible to remedy. What I am aiming at is the fact that, according to the principles of criminal procedure, our formula has to be used explicitly in the judgments of the courts, in other words, the offender has to be told in the clearest possible language that he is regarded as a person incapable or only inadequately capable of controlling his actions. He arrives at the institution where he is supposed to receive his treatment and of course he feels in duty bound to live up to his official reputation, which may actually make him untreatable and a dangerous nuisance to the whole institution. The dilemma which we have to face is that, when framing our legislation for dealing with mentally abnormal offenders, we have not merely to solve an abstract scientific problem, but in addition we are addressing a public—in fact the widest possible audience, *i.e.*, the whole community—and a public, including the offender, which is just as incapable of understanding our formula in the way it is meant as the offender is incapable of controlling his actions. Is it perhaps preferable to tackle the problem from another end, from that of punishment, and define this category of offenders as " persons unable to be influenced by *ordinary* punishment " and, therefore, to be subjected to other measures? If I understand it rightly, this is the technique of the Danish Penal Code of 1930, articles 17 and 70; it is even more imprecise than the other formula, but it may give better practical results.[26]

A few remarks have still to be added on the rather involved and

---

[25] Commission chargée d'étudier la révision de la loi du 9 avril 1930 (Extrait de la *Revue de Droit Pénal et de Criminologie* 1940), pp. 10-11. In a somewhat different context, *i.e.*, for the application of arts. 14 and 15 of the Swiss Federal Penal Code, the psychological effect on the offender of the legal formula used by the courts has been stressed in the interesting article by the Swiss psychiatrist Professor Hans Binder, Psychiatrische Probleme gemäss, art. 14 and 15, Str. G. B., *Schweizeriche Zeitschrift für Strafrecht*, Vol. 74, No. 1, 1959, p. 70.

[26] From the Danish literature on the subject only the following may be quoted: Knud Waaben in his *Introduction to The Danish Criminal Code*, Copenhagen, 1958, p. 11 *et seq.*; Georg K. Stürup, " L'établissement pour psycopathes de Herstedvester," *Revue de science criminelle et de droit pénal comparé*, Nouvelle Série 1958, No. 3, Juillet-Septembre, p. 593 *et seq.*; and with special reference to the treatment of recidivists Stürup, Summary of Proceedings, Third International Congress on Criminology 1955, London, 1957, p. 201 *et seq.*

CRIMINAL LAW

much discussed position in the United States. As previously stated and also mentioned by Dr. Guttmacher, the State of New Hampshire and the District of Columbia, which of course includes Washington, have rejected the M'Naghten Rules, the former already since 1870,[27] the latter only since 1954, when the District of Columbia Court of Appeal passed its famous decision in the *Durham* case. The essence of the New Hampshire rule, which owed its origin to the collaboration of an eminent psychiatrist, Dr. Isaac Ray, and a distinguished lawyer, Judge Charles Doe, and which has been repeatedly reformulated, is that, since no satisfactory legal tests of insanity can be found, only medical criteria should be used and that the decision should be left to the jury whether the accused suffered from a mental disease which had taken away his capacity to form a criminal intent. One can see that this doctrine has had a certain influence on the Royal Commission on Capital Punishment, whose principal majority recommendation [28] was also to leave the crucial question to the jury, a proposal which would make any consistent policy impossible because, as already stressed before, the jury cannot be trained.[29] The *Durham* rule, which in its turn was partly inspired by the proposal of the Royal Commission, states that " an accused is not criminally responsible if his unlawful act was the product of mental disease or mental defect," reminding us somewhat of the Swedish Act of 1945. This *Durham* decision has been under fire from various quarters, including Jerome Hall and the American Law Institute, who criticise in particular the vagueness of the term " product." [30] The American Law Institute's own Draft is essentially, I feel, a return to the European formula discussed before. It establishes irresponsibility if the offender " lacks substantial capacity either to appreciate the criminality of his conduct or to conform his conduct to the requirements of law," but it excludes the psychopath altogether from its scope and, unfortunately, it leaves the all-important question open who should bear the burden of proof.[31]

[27] On the history and meaning of the New Hampshire doctrine see the detailed account by John Reid (above, note 12). Also Weihofen, *op. cit.*, p. 4 *et seq.*, and briefly Report of Royal Commission on Capital Punishment, pp. 105 and 411.
[28] Report of Royal Commission, p. 276, under 19.
[29] See above, p. 298, also p. 239.
[30] Jerome Hall, *Studies* (above, note 5), pp. 288-289; American Law Institute's Tentative Draft No. 4, Comments, p. 159.
[31] Tentative Draft, pp. 193-194.

MENTALLY ABNORMAL OFFENDERS

Of a different character is the Maryland Defective Delinquent Statute of 1951, which defines a defective delinquent as " an individual who, by the demonstration of persistent aggravated anti-social or criminal behaviour, evidences a propensity toward criminal activity, and who is found to have either such intellectual deficiency or emotional unbalance or both, as to clearly demonstrate an actual danger to society so as to require . . . confinement and treatment. . . ." [32]

To sum up this part of my discourse, many of you will have got the feeling that I have been spending too much of my limited time trying to unravel the mysteries of definition. I have done so because, after fifty years of watching this fascinating game—fascinating at least for those actively engaged in it—I have come to the conclusion that it is more or less futile. Certainly, some sort of a legal formula there has to be, and I am far from implying that when we try to establish that Common Market which I described as the ultimate object the type of goods to be offered in such a Market does not matter—it does. But far more important than an ideal definition of insanity and diminished responsibility, which we shall never achieve anyhow, is the harmonious co-operation between well-trained lawyers and psychiatrists, each of them willing to listen to reason and to play his own part instead of trespassing on the field of the other.

2. Assuming now that we have found a fairly satisfactory definition not only of insanity but also of the " non-sane non-insane " group and that we have placed the burden of proving the absence of any of these mental abnormalities squarely on the shoulders of the prosecution—which of course does not mean a legal presumption that every offender is abnormal but merely that a final doubt has to be resolved in favour of the accused—what else do we expect the criminal law to do in this field? In my discussion of these other problems I have to be careful not to trespass too much on the subjects allotted to my distinguished co-rapporteurs.

Naturally, there is, first of all, the question of the *legal consequences* of mental abnormality. Here we are no longer satisfied

[32] See H. M. Boslow, D. Rosenthal and L. H. Gliedman, "The Maryland Defective Delinquent Law," *The British Journal of Delinquency*, Vol. X, No. 1, July 1959, p. 5 et seq.

with a purely negative solution, *i.e.*, with an acquittal or something equivalent to it for insanes and with the "dosage" system[33] of "attenuating circumstances" for the "non-sane non-insane" ones, which has been so popular in most legislations and often means only that the more dangerous an offender is the less is done for and to him. Whether or not we have to retain these more lenient penalties for cases of "diminished responsibility" depends largely on the question of whether we prefer a single-track or a double-track system. If we prefer the former, the penalties will be altogether replaced by measures of security and treatment; whereas in the case of a double-track system using both penalties and measures we have to consider how to produce something reasonably coherent, balanced and efficient out of the two basically conflicting parts. What is the present position, and what are the trends for the future? Generally speaking, it seems that present-day legal systems are more willing to accept the single-track idea for mentally abnormal offenders than they are in the case of habitual offenders. This is only natural, since the insistence of public opinion on at least some sort of punishment is less strong where mentally abnormal offenders are concerned. We find, for example, in the Belgian Act of 1930 the single-track system adopted for abnormals against the double-track system for habituals. English law is on single-track lines for both habituals and abnormals, in the sense that the court cannot impose at the same time a penalty and a measure of security and treatment, but it is left to the discretion of the court which one to choose.[34] The Swedish Act of 1945, too, is on single-track lines. Some of the countries which still adhere to the double-track system try to avoid the undesirable cumulation of penalties and measures by employing the so-called "vikariierende" system, *i.e.*, the courts have to, or may, abstain from carrying out the penalty before the offender is sent to the appropriate hospital or other institution. This is the system used in Switzerland and Maryland, where it is mandatory, and also proposed in the German Draft Code where it is, however, left to the discretion of the court whether or not a prison sentence should be

---

[33] See Marc Ancel in his Introduction to *Les Délinquants anormaux mentaux* (note 23, above), p. XIII.
[34] For habitual offenders, Criminal Justice Act, 1948, s. 21; for abnormal offenders, Mental Health Act, 1959, s. 60.

carried out before the measure.[35] If this is not done, the question remains whether it has to be carried out after the offender's discharge from the hospital, etc. This can actually be done in Switzerland and Maryland and under the German Draft Code, although the time spent in that institution has to be, or can be, deducted from the prison sentence. Of special interest is the discussion of this question in the very important recent French symposium, edited by Professor Georges Levasseur and introduced by M. Marc Ancel, *Les Délinquants anormaux mentaux*. Here the single-track system has been adopted, though apparently with slightly varying degrees of enthusiasm by the different contributors.[36] The editor himself, while accepting this system, takes the view that even with regard to " non-sane non-insane " offenders, *i.e.*, the " délinquants anormaux " of the Avant-projet, the idea of moral retribution is not entirely out of place and that most measures of security and treatment could well be combined with a penalty, a combination which, however, should not mean a mechanical succession in time of penalty and measure but rather an organic fusion of both. This leads to the conception of a " medico-repressive " régime for this category, which actually appears in article 29 of the Avant-projet and is fully discussed by several contributors to the symposium.[37] As a formula, this seems to be admirable, provided it does not mean subordinating the psychiatric aspects altogether to the repressive ones and also provided we recognise with Levasseur that it poses more problems than it solves—for example, how far should the law applicable to this mixed régime be moulded according to penal and how far according to medical considerations? I am confident that the practical experiences collected over the past twenty-five years in institutions such as Herstedvester, Utrecht, Rheinau in Switzerland, Belmont and Wormwood Scrubs in England and similar ones, supplemented by the discussions of the present Congress, will offer some guidance on these problems. Moreover, the law should also make provision for the

---

[35] Swiss Federal Penal Code, arts. 14 and 15; Maryland Defective Delinquent Law, § 9 (b); German Draft Code, §§ 24, 86, 93, 94, and the " Begründung," pp. 84, 93–94. On the Swiss reform project, see Erwin Frey, *Internationales Colloquium über Kriminologie und Strafrechtsreform*, Freiburg, 1958, pp. 27–28.

[36] Georges Levasseur, *Les Délinquants anormaux mentaux*, p. XII (Marc Ancel), Levasseur, p. 6 *et seq.*; Germain, p. 114 *et seq.*

[37] See, *e.g.*, Levasseur, p. 25 *et seq.*; Vullien-Dublineau, p. 66; Germain, p. 120.

CRIMINAL LAW

treatment at large on probation for suitable cases, and it is encouraging that article 32 of the Avant-projet, following the example of recent English and German legislation, and in conformity with a Swiss Draft,[38] permits probation with medical and social treatment, limited, however, to cases of " délit."

I am now finally passing to one of the most intricate problems of our subject, the extent of *judicial control* of the measures applicable to mentally abnormal offenders. It is here that we can observe certain differences between Great Britain and other countries in that the principle of judicial control is more strictly adhered to in the latter.[39] Although the language of the English Mental Health Act, 1959, is so extremely involved that one hesitates to make any categorical statements at all, it seems to me that the powers here given to administrative authorities, notably the Secretary of State and the newly created Mental Health Review Tribunals, are more extensive than the powers allotted to such authorities in other legislations or recent Drafts.[40] In part, this contrast finds its outward expression in some Continental countries in the existence of a special court or judge, such as the " juge de l'exécution " of the French Avant-projet, which contains particularly detailed provisions on the subject, or the German " Vollstreckungsgericht."[41] The Belgian Act of 1930 provides for mixed Commissions composed of lawyers and one psychiatrist, and the position seems to be similar in Sweden.[42] The French Draft, art. 59, leaves even the choice of the institution to the court and any subsequent change to the juge de l'exécution, and M. Germain, while calling this a " revolutionary innovation," thinks that it will be welcomed by the administration.[43] Personally, while I am in favour of strengthening judicial control in this field—always provided the judges are well selected and trained for the job—I do

---

[38] Criminal Justice Act, 1948, s. 4; German Penal Code, § 24 (1 No. 3) and Draft Code, § 78 (2). See the brief account by Dr. Michael Craft, *The British Journal of Delinquency*, Vol. X, No. 3, January 1960, p. 222 *et seq.*, on a " Psychopathic Unit " for delinquents on probation sent there by the courts as a condition of their Probation Order. Craft stresses that " neither labels of psychopath or of defective are welcomed by patients who are more prepared to enter a hospital with a Special Training Unit."
[39] Germain in Levasseur, p. 127 *et seq.* On the Swiss Draft, see Frey, *loc. cit.*, above, note 35, p. 27.
[40] See Mental Health Act, 1959, ss. 65, 66.
[41] French Avant-projet, Chap. V; German Draft, §§ 86, 93, 94, 96, 97.
[42] Belgian Act of 1930, Chap. III; on Sweden see Sellin, *op. cit.*, pp. 19-20.
[43] Germain in Levasseur, p. 119.

not think that the choice of the institution should be left to the court. In Britain in particular the whole trend of developments has been in the opposite direction, and the last traces of judicial selection of institutions have been abolished or will soon be abolished either by law or by practice.

One word only about provisions for the compulsory detention of mentally abnormal persons not yet convicted of crime, but regarded as dangerous. While the English Mental Health Act gives certain powers of detention for such persons, the French Avant-projet rejects them.[44] To do justice to the considerations involved one would have to enter into a full discussion of the concept of "social defence," for which there is no time.

In fact, I have already exceeded the span of time allotted to me, but even so all I have been able to do is briefly to touch upon a few problems of a vast subject. I should like to conclude, as I began, with a few observations of a general nature. First, in the light of past experiences we should make sure that in our enthusiasm for reform we should never produce new legislation which permits the application of far-reaching measures, in particular long-term detention, without first making sure that the desired facilities for treatment are actually available. Secondly, in my introductory remarks I referred to the need for a " Common Market " between lawyers and psychiatrists and also for international discussions of common problems. In the course of this lecture I have repeatedly mentioned recent legislation and Drafts in some of the principal European countries, such as the French Avant-projet and the English Mental Health Act of 1959, which latter was preceded by the very elaborate Report of a Royal Commission.[45] Surely, a recurrent exchange of ideas between those actively engaged in these great and simultaneous enterprises might have been most fruitful, but here, too, the barriers of tariffs and customs have been still too high, it seems, to establish a real " Common Market."

---

[44] Mental Health Act, 1959, s. 44; Marc Ancel and Levasseur, *op. cit.*, pp. XXVI *et seq.* and 11.
[45] Report of the Royal Commission on the Law relating to Mental Illness and Mental Deficiency 1954–57, London, H.M.S.O., 1957.

INDEX OF SUBJECTS

Abortion, 270, 273
Actio libera in causa, 292
Adultery, 278
Aftercare, 240
Aider and abetter, 42, 43, 266
Alternatives
 to capital punishment, 240
 to short prison sentences, 245 et seq.
American Institute of Criminal Law and Criminology, 209
American Juvenile Courts, 211 et seq.
American law of insanity and mental deficiency, Appendix
American Prison Association, 183, 185, 187
American prisons. *See* Prisons
Anti-semitism, 54
Anti-social behaviour, 261
Anti-social character formation, 141
Approved Schools, 246
Artificial insemination, 278-9
Association of Scandinavian Criminologists, 274
Asthenic type, 76 et seq.
Athletic type, 76 et seq.
Attendance Centres, 249-50

Balfour Committee on Royal Commissions, 237
Blackout during the War, 93
Blasphemy, 270-1
'Born criminal', 72 et seq.
Borstal Institutions, open and closed, 126, 218
Borstal System, 84, 124, 169, 245-246
British Colonies, collective punishment in, 48 et seq.
British Columbia, 188-9
 John Howard Society of, 188
Broken homes, 34, 36, 87, 134-5
Brussels 'European Seminar', 3

Burden of proof, 287, 296-7

California
 adult authority, 175 et seq.
 Correctional Industries Commission, 181
 forestry camps, 29, 31, 177
 Intensive Parole Supervision Project, 219-20
 migration into, 170
 prisons, 167, 175 et seq., 183, 186
 Sexual Deviation Research, 205 et seq.
 Training Schemes for Prison Staffs, 187
Cambridge Evacuation Survey, 86
Cambridge-Somerville Study, 120, 123, 128, 138, 142, Chapter 6, Sect. IIIb
Capital punishment, Chapter 10
Causes of crime, research into, 118, 133
Chicago, Commission on Race Relations, 196
 Race Riot, 201
Christie case and Evans case, 241
Church membership, 123
Class distinctions in prison, 37
Classical School of Criminology, 70
Classifications, legal and sociological, 76-7
 penological, 169, 174, 177, 204
'Cocoanut Grove' Fire, 55
Codes of behaviour, official and unofficial, 8, 36, 38
Collaborators, 274-5
Collective responsibility and punishment, 25, 26, Chapter 3
 under Nazi rule, 50 et seq.
Compulsory labour outside prison, 253
Concentration Camps. *See* Nazi system of Collective Punishment
Conduct norms, 262
Conference on the Scientific Study of

INDEX OF SUBJECTS

Juvenile Delinquency, 22, Chapter 6, Sect. II
Continental Criminal Law, Chapter 13, and Appendix
Control Group Techniques, 117, 120 et seq., 131, 142, 147 et seq., 254
Corporal Punishment, Report on, 125
Corporations, responsibility of, 43, 46
Correlations, statistical, 134
spurious, 123
Corruption, 276
Counsellors, 147 et seq.
Criminal anthropology, 69 et seq.
'Criminal by tendency', 75
Criminal Groups, 51
Criminal Justice Act 1948, 5, 244–5, 250–1, 263, 288
Criminal Justice Administration Act 1914, 246
Criminal Law, 206, Part Five
Sociology of, Chapter 12
Criminal statistics, 87, 99, 101, 109, 227, 288
Criminal super-ego, 21
Crimino-biological School, 75, 78, 79, 80, 81
Criminology, 155
American, Chapter 8
and Criminal Law, Chapter 12
International, 208
Currency offences, 112

Degrading penalties, 26
Deserters, 111 et seq.
Detention Centres, 249–50
Diminished responsibility, Appendix
Dismissal and binding over, 249
Domestic Relations Court, New York City, 215
Drug addiction, 188
Drunkenness, 88, 188, 292 et seq.

Ecological study of delinquency, 131, 136
Education of prisoners, 84
Elmira Reformatory, 84
Endocrinology, 83
Epilepsy, frequency among criminals, 72
État dangereux, 208
Ethiopian Penal Code, 50
Evacuation during the second World War, 86 et seq.
Experimental research in criminology, 127, 137, 146 et seq., 218–20

Family problems, 8, 278. *See also* Broken homes
Female delinquency, 266–7
Fines, non-payment of, 246–8, 254
First offenders, 96, 102, 246
Follow-up studies, 13, 125–6, 133, 152, 253–4
Free will, 283–4, 298, and Appendix
French Code Pénal of 1810, 286, 292

Generalizations, 54
Genocide, 276
George Junior Republic, 29 et seq.
German Criminal Law, Chapter 13, and Appendix
Germany, changes in crime rate after first World War, 82
Glossatores, 46, 47
Group values and attitudes, 8 et seq., 16 et seq., 21 et seq., 44, 267 et seq., 273, 277. *See also* Collective Responsibility and Punishment
Groups, national, racial, religious, 276
Guilt, feeling of, 22
collective. *See* under Collective Responsibility and Collective Punishment
individual, 25

Habitual criminals, 102, 143, 185, 193. *See also* Professional Criminals and Recidivism
Hague Congress 1950, 242, 254–6
Hawthorne experiment, 20
Heredity, Chapter 4, 139 et seq.
Highfields project, 217
Holmes *v.* Director of Public Prosecutions, 278
Homes for neglectful mothers, 111
Honesty, 21
Howard League for Penal Reform, 27, 96, 129, 165, 223

Idiographic discipline, 261, 263, 273
Ill-treatment and neglect of children, 110–11
Imitation, 110, 184
Immigrants, 9, 86, 192, 194 et seq.
Incorrigible criminals, 79
Indeterminate sentences, 37, 176, 179, 186
Individual case study technique, 123, 137, 238
Industrial psychology, 23

INDEX OF SUBJECTS

Insanity. *See* Mental Disorders
Intake system. *See* Referee system
Intelligence quotient of inmates, 34
International Penal and Penitentiary Commission (I.P.P.C.), 86
 The Hague Congress of the, 242
International Society of Criminology, 210
International Society of Social Defence, 208 et seq.
Interview technique, 12
Irresistible impulse, 285 et seq., 297-8, and Appendix
I.S.T.D., 27, 34, 94, 129, 238, 282
Italian Penal Code of 1930, 74, 285 et seq., 293

Jails, American, 169, 178-80
Japanese community, 17, 60
Jurisprudence, 264, 267
 'Gestalt', 279
 Sociological, Chapter 12
Jury, Chapter 10, 286, 291
Justice, 127-8, 207
Juvenile Courts, 87, 211 et seq.
Juvenile offenders, 5, 87 et seq., 106-7, 129 et seq., Chapter 6, Sect. II and III

Kefauver Committee, 195-6
Kenya, collective punishment in, 49
Kriminalbiologische Gesellschaft, 75
Kriminalpolitik, 270 et seq.

Langley Porter Clinic 192, 206-7
'Laws', criminological, 101, 263
Leadership in prison, 38
Leisure, 39, 89
Leptosome type, 76 et seq.
Life history technique, 13, 36, 137
Life imprisonment, 240
Liverpool Police Juvenile Liaison Scheme, 214
London School of Economics and Political Science, 86, 130
Looting during the War, 95 et seq., 102 et seq.
Lynching, 201
Lynskey Tribunal, 277-8

McNaghten Rules, Chapter 13, and Appendix
Malaya, collective punishment in, 49
Manic-depressive (or circular) insanity, 75

Mass atmosphere, 280
Mass-Observation on Juvenile Delinquency, 21, 23
 'Puzzled People', 270-1
Maturation, 158
Maximum security prisons, 36
Mental deficiency, 36
Mental disorders, Chapter 13. *See also* Manic-depressive Insanity and Schizophrenia
Mental Health Act 1959 (England), Appendix
Methodology of criminological studies, 10 et seq., Chapter 6, 142, Chapter 10, and Criminal Law, Chapter 12
Migration, 169-70
Money payments (Justices Procedure) Act 1935, 247
Multiplicity of causes, 119
Murder, 109-10, 121, 197, 225 et seq., 278
 grading of, 229 et seq.
 subjective element in, 230 et seq.

Nazi system of collective punishment, 50 et seq., 58
National Association for Mental Health, 129
Negroes, 7, 170, 179, 192, 196 et seq.
New Jersey, 175, 177, 183, 186, 194, 199-200, 213, 217
New York City
 Juvenile Aid Bureau, 216
 Juvenile Court, 194, 213, 215
Nomothetic discipline, 262-3, 273
Non-sane non-insane offenders, Appendix
Norms, legal and other, 262, 265
Norwegian statistics of recidivism, 126
 System of suspended prosecution, 252
Nuremberg Charter and Judgement, 47

Operational research, 129
Oregon, 168 et seq., 178-9

Parole, 185, 219-20
Pennsylvania, 172 et seq., 179, 200, 231
Penology, 40, Part Four, 243, 260-1, 263, 272
Philadelphia Municipal Court, 200, 213
 Crime Prevention Association, 217
 Juvenile Court, 212, 215

INDEX OF SUBJECTS

Police Forces, Understaffing of, 112
Negroes in, 197
Preventive Work by, 216
Political Influences in American Prison Administration. *See* Prisons, American
Population Movements in England during the second World War, 86
Positive School of Criminology, 69
Poverty and Crime, 105
Pre-delinquents, 147 et seq.
Prediction, 6, 40, 118–19, 124, 140 et seq., 150 et seq., 160 et seq., 207
Preliminary investigations in Juvenile Courts, 215
Pre-sentence enquiries, 5
Prevention of Crime, 20, 146 et seq., 202, 207, 216–17
of Corruption Acts, 276–7
Primitive societies, 44, 45, 54, 57
Prison Commission for England and Wales, 240, 242, 246, 251
Prison Statistics, England and Wales, 243 et seq.
Prison Statistics, Scotland, 244
Prisons
American, Chapter 7
education in, 168, 182–3
Federal System, 187, 198
Labour in, 39, 174, 180–2, 240
mobility, its effects on, 168
politics in, 37, 170, 184
racial segregation in, 200, 203–4
riots in, 38, 167, 183–5
See also Jails, American
English, 181. *See also* Psychological Treatment, Short-term Imprisonment, Prison Statistics, Prison Commission
Probation and Probation Officers, 17, 20, 24, 26, 27, 88, 90, 91, 124–5, 248–9, 263
in U.S.A., 214
Professional Criminals, 21, 96. *See also* Habitual Criminals
Profiteering in Wartime, 98, 105
Property, attitudes to, 23, 104
Psychiatric examinations in Juvenile Courts, 215
Psychological methods of study, 7, 9
Psychological treatment in Institutions, 33, 240, 242, 252–3

Psychopathic Sex Offenders Laws, 205 et seq.
Psychopathy, 139 et seq.
Pyknic Type, 76 et seq.

Q Camps and Hawkspur Camp, Chapter 2, Sect. II
Questionnaire Method, 13, 236–7

Race, Chapter 8, 276
Race relations and riots, 196, 201
Racial segregation, 203. *See also* Prisons
Recidivists, 20, 34 71, 91, 94, 102, 108, 126, 139 et seq., 240
Referee system, 213–14
Reihen Untersuchung, 140
Research, criminological, 7, 128 et seq., Chapter 8, especially 217 et seq., 253, 254, 256
See also Control Group Technique, Ecological Study, Experimental Research, Individual Case Study Technique, Interview Technique, Operational Research, Statistical Technique, Typological Method
Research Techniques of Royal Commissions, Chapter 10
RowntreeCed Cocoa Works, 25
'Ruler Punishment', 45

Scandinavian Child Welfare Councils, 211 et seq.
Scapegoats, 54, 55
Schizophrenia, 75
Schools, closing of, during the War, 88
Schools for maladjusted children, 28
Second World War, crime in the, Chapter 5
Official History of, 85
Sentencing policy of the Courts, 97, 108, 126, 176–7, 185–6, 197, 239, Chapter 11
Sexual offenders, 205 et seq., 251, 289. *See also* Psychopathic Sex Offenders Laws
Sexual problem in prisons, 37
Shared responsibility and self-government, 28, 31 et seq., 60
Shelter life during the War, 92
Small Groups, study of, 41
Smuggling, 111

322

INDEX OF SUBJECTS

Social case work, 149 et seq.
Social control, forms of, 280
Social groups. *See* Group values and attitudes
Social groups in Prison, 38
Social psychology, 17, 267
Social Survey, 238
Social workers, 4
Sociological study of the Adult Offender, Chapter 1, Chapter 2, Sect. III
Sociologists employed in prisons, 16, 35, 177
Sociology Departments, 190
Sociology of Criminal Law, Chapter 12
Sociometric technique, 12
Soviet Union, 253, 255
Specificity of social and anti-social conduct, 21
Standon Farm Report, 59, 110
Statistical techniques in criminological research, 11, 120 et seq., 134
Stealing from employers, 19 et seq.
from docks, 24
from gasmeters, 20
Subjective judgements, 10
Suicide, 226
Supreme Court of the United States, 53, 202, 203
Suspension, conditional of prosecution, 252
Swedish Prison Act 1945, 272

Tuskegee Institute, Alabama, 201
Twin research, 80, 121, 128
Typological method in criminological research, 12, 81 et seq., 122-3
Kretschmer's types, 75-6

Unemployment in prisons. *See* Prison Labour
in Wartime, 93 et seq.
United Nations, Department of Social Affairs, 3
Report on Probation, 126
War Crimes Commission, 276
United States of America
employment of sociologists in prisons, 16
law of adultery, 278
See also American, Prisons, and individual States of U.S.A.
Utah, 168

Value judgements, 273, 278. *See also* Group values and attitudes
Verwahrlosung, 139 et seq.
Violence, crimes of, 111

Wages, wartime increases in, 95, 105
Washington, State of, 185
White collar crime, 21, 105, 193
Workers' Committees and Factory Courts, 25 et seq.

'Young Offenders', 129-30

INDEX OF AUTHORS

Adler, Mortimer J., 118, 133, 271
Allport, Gordon W., 13, 146 et seq., 262, 279
Ancel, Marc, 208, 310, 314, 315, 317
Andenaes, Johs., 115, 255
Aschaffenburg, Gustav, 69, 73, 75–76, 80
Atelsek, Frank J., 202
Axelrad, Sidney, 198

Baer, Adolf, 70, 72
Bagot, J. H., 132
Barnes, Harry Elmer, 178–79
Bates, Sanford, 175, 183, 185, 195
Becker, Howard R., 12
Bemmelen, J. M. van, 25, 274
Benedict, Ruth, 60
Bennett, James V., 184
Benney, Mark, 137
Berenda, Ruth W., 18
Beth, Marianne, 262
Bettelheim, Bruno, 51, 58–59
Binder, Hans, 311
Birnbaum, Karl, 72, 76
Bisno, Herbert, 4
Bixby, F. Lovell, 217
Bjerre, Andreas, 226
Bleuler, Eugen, 69, 76
Boslow, H. M., 313
Bossard, James, 3–4
Bowlby, John, 23, 90, 131, 136
Bowman, Karl M., 205
Braithwaite, R. M., 249
Brearley, H. C., 227
Brennan, James J., 216
Brockway, Z. R., 84

Brogan, D. W., 201
Bronner, Augusta F., 121
Brown, Wilfred B. D., 25
Buchan, Alistair, 203
Bumke, E., 283–84
Burbank, Edmund G., 173
Burgess, Ernest W., 10, 13, 191
Burt, Sir Cyril, 119, 129–30, 137

Cabot, Richard Clarke, 146 et seq.
Campbell-Johnson, Alan, 277
Cannat, P., 255
Cantor, Nathaniel, 74
Cardoza, Benjamin, 231
Carr-Saunders, Sir Alexander, 117, 130
Christiansen, Karl O., 12, 274
Clark, Robert E., 200
Clemmer, Donald, 12, 35 et. seq., 178
Clinard, Marshall B., 103, 191, 195, 263
Cole, Margaret, 86
Commager, H.S., 46, 53, 203
Cornil, Paul, 3, 165, 184, 186
Craft, Michael, 316
Cross, Rupert, 268

Dallemagne, Jules, 70
Dallin, David, J., 253
Daniel, G., 71
Daube, David, 45–46, 57
Devlin, Mr. Justice, 296
Dickson, W. J., 23
Doe, Charles, 312
Dollard, John, 13–14
Donnedieu de Vabres, 287

INDEX OF AUTHORS

Dostoevsky, F. I., 63
Duffy, Clinton T., 170
Dunham, H. Warren, 9

East, Sir Norwood, 120, 132, 242, 294, 307
Ehrlich, Eugen, 155, 265, 275
Eisenstadt, S. N., 8
Elkin, Winifred A., 132
Elliott, Mabel A., 170, 186, 194–95, 197, 202–03, 216
Ellis, Havelock, 69, 72
Eriksson, Torsten, 218
Exner, Franz, 84, 144, 165
Eysenck, H. J., 237

Fauconnet, Paul, 45, 46, 48
Fenton, Norman, 177
Ferguson, Sheila, 85
Ferri, Enrico, 69, 71–72, 74
Feuerbach, Anselm von, 71, 291
Fink, Arthur E., 119
Fitzgerald, Hilde, 85
Flynn, Frank T., 180, 184
Fox, Evelyn, 91
Fox, Sir Lionel W., 272
Fox, Vernon, 184
Frank, Reinhard, 283–84
Frankel, Emil, 186, 195
Franklin, Marjorie E., 27–28
Frazier, E. Franklin, 204
Frey, Erwin, 139 et seq., 208, 315, 316
Friedlander, Kate, 141
Friedmann, Wolfgang, 51
Fry, Margery, 214

Garraud, R., 286–87, 292
Gates, E. C., 104
Germain, Charles, 315, 316
Gibbens, T. C. N., 206
Giles, F. T., 251
Gillin, John Lewis, 121–22
Ginsberg, M., 45, 54, 265
Givskov, Carl Christian, 274
Gleidman, L. H., 313
Glover, Edward, 296
Glueck, Eleanor T., 7, 34, 83, 120,

Glueck, Eleanor T. (contd), 122–23, 144, 146, 155 et. seq., 191–93, 216
Glueck, Sheldon, 6, 34, 83, 120, 122–23, 144, 146, 155 et. seq., 191–93, 216, 287, 291, 306
Göransson, Gösta, 253, 255
Gordon, Walter A., 219
Goring, Charles, 69, 72–73, 84, 117
Gorphe, François C., 239
Grammatica, Filippo, 208
Graven, Jean, 50
Greeff, Etienne de, 208
Greenwood, Ernest, 118
Gross, Hans, 69, 70
Gruhle, Hans, 74, 76, 80
Grünhut, Max, 120, 249
Grygier, T., 7, 250
Gunther, John, 166, 170, 199, 202
Gurvitch, George, 265, 267
Guttmacher, Manfred, 304, 306, 307, 309, 312

Hakeem, Michael, 303
Hall, Jerome, 261–62, 303, 304, 312
Hall, Patricia, 25
Hanbury, H. G., 47
Hartshorne, Hugh, 21, 23
Healy, William, 15, 121, 129
Heldmann, Hans Heinz, 305
Hentig, Hans von, 197
Heuermann, Rolf, 299
Hill, Denis, 121, 299
Hippel, Robert von, 271
Hobhouse, L. T., 45
Holland, Vyvyan, 64
Hooton, E. A., 73, 117, 190
Hubert, W. H. de B., 242
Humphreys, Travers, 286
Hurwitz, Stephan, 256, 275
Huxley, Thomas, 167

Isaacs, Susan, 86

James, John, 41
Jaspers, Karl, 61 et seq.
Jescheck, Hans Heinrich, 276

325

INDEX OF AUTHORS

Johnson, Guy B., 197
Jolly, J. C., 110
Jones, Howard, 60
Jones, Maxwell, 17
Jones, P. Asterley, 268
Jung, C. G., 64

Kahn, Alfred J., 194, 213
Kallmann, Franz J., 121
Kamenetzki, 82
Kautsky, Benedict, 51
Kelchner, Mathilde, 290
Kelsen, Hans, 57
Kenny, C. S., 48, 232, 278
Kephart, William M., 197
Killian, Frederick W., 213
Kinberg, Olof, 74, 80, 82, 287
Koenig, Samuel, 200
Korn, Richard, 41
Kretschmer, Ernst, 75
Kurella, Hans, 69

Lander, Bernard, 195, 198
Lange, Johannes, 70, 80, 121
Lattes, Leone, 73, 74
Lee, Frank F., 203
Lee, George E., 55
Leitch, Alexander, 132
Lejins, Peter, 118
Lemkin, Raphael, 276
Lenz, Adolf, 75, 81
Levasseur, Georges, 310, 315, 316, 317
Levit, S. G., 80
Lewin, Kurt, 17
Lewis, H. D., 63
Lindesmith, A. R., 9
Lindner, Robert, 226
Lindzey, Gardner, 301
Liszt, Franz von, 69, 71, 76, 292
Lobe, Adolf, 284
Locke, H. W., 25
Lombroso, Cesare, Chapter 4
Lombroso-Ferrero, Gina, 77, 84
Lowie, Robert H., 45
Lundberg, George A., 13
Lunden, W. A., 12
Lynd, Helen M., 11

Lynd, Robert S., 11

McCorkle, Lloyd W., 41
MacCormick, Austin H., 170, 184
McDonald, Lawrence R., 202
McGee, Richard A., 169, 172, 175, 181
MacIver, R. M., 134
Magnol, 286, 296
Mandelbaum, David G., 204
Mangus, A. R., 206
Manouvrier, L., 70
Marshall, T. H., 119
Martin, John Bartlaw, 184
Maudsley, Henry, 282
May, Mark A., 21, 23
Mayo, Elton, 23
Mead, Margaret, 17, 18, 60
Meek, C. K., 48
Merrill, Francis E., 194, 202–03
Merton, Robert K., 9, 11
Mezger, Eduard, 74, 75, 76, 78, 79, 80, 81, 271
Michael, Jerome, 118, 133, 271
Mittermaier, C. I. A., 291
Moberly, Sir Walter, 64
Monachesi, Elio D., 14
Monckton, Sir Walter, 111
Montagu, The Hon. Ewen E. S., 251
Moreno, Ludwig, 12, 203
Moroney, M.J., 123
Morris, Norval, 306
Motz, Anton, 206
Muller, N., 17, Chapter 2, Section I
Mullins, Claud, 19
Murphy, G., 267
Murphy, L. B., 267
Myrdal, Gunnar, 197–98

Nagel, W. H., 11, 15
Nelson, Elmer K., 189
Newcomb, Theodore M., 267
Nicolaevsky, Boris I., 253
Niebuhr, Reinhold, 187
Nimkoff, Meyer F., 281

Ogburn, William F., 281
Ohlin, Lloyd E., 6, 178

INDEX OF AUTHORS

Oppenheimer, H., 283, 291

Padley, Richard, 86
Page, Sir Leo, 12, 244
Paneth, Marie, 132
Parkes, James, 54, 55
Paterson, Sir Alexander, 138, 165, 168
Pear, T. H., 104, 132, 262
Phelan, Jim, 40
Piaget, Jean, 56
Ploscowe, Morris, 206, 278–79
Porterfield, Austin L., 198, 228
Pound, Roscoe, 267
Powers, Edwin, 120, Chapter 6, Section IIIb
Prideaux, G. F. E., 291
Printzlien, Conrad P., 252
Purcell, Victor, 49

Raeburn, Walter, 301
Raphael, Winifred, 25
Ravden, May, 131
Ray, Isaac, 312
Reckless, Walter C., 10, 118, 133, 191, 199
Reid, John, 307, 312
Reinemann, John Otto, 27, 197, 213, 215, et seq.
Reiss, Albert I., 7, 120
Reiter, Hans, 75, 213
Reiwald, Paul, 22
Rhodes, E. C., 117, 130
Riedl, Martin, 76, 78, 79
Roche, Philip Q., 307, 309
Rodger, Alec, 132, 137
Roesner, Ernst, 82, 84
Roethlisberger, F. J., 23, 24
Rohden, Friedrich von, 75, 76, 78, 79
Rooy, H. van, 16
Roper, W. F., 13, 244
Rosanoff, Aaron J., 80
Rose, A. G., 237
Rose, Arnold M., 202
Rosenthal, D., 313
Roth, Cecil, 55
Rubin, Sol, 120

Ruggles-Brise, Sir Evelyn, 71, 84
Russell, Bertrand, 54, 55
Rylander, Gösta, 283, 309

Saldaña, Quintiliano, 74, 81
Saleilles, Raymond, 36
Sauer, Wilhelm, 75
Schlapp, Max G., 83
Schönke, Adolf, 296
Schwartz, Edward E., 198
Scudder, Kenyon J., 170, 180
Seelig, Ernst, 77, 272
Sellin, Thorsten, 74, 117, 118, 136, 187, 191, 236, 262, 309, 316
Selling, Lowell, S., 10
Sharp, E. Preston, 194
Shaw, Clifford R., 11, 13, 191
Shaw, Otto L., 31
Sheldon, Henry D., 179
Shils, Edward A., 116
Sieverts, Rudolf, 80
Simey, T. H., 23
Smith, Edward H., 83
Smith, N. Hamblin, 290
Sorensen, Robert C., 12
Sorokin, Pitirim, 155
Spencer, John C., 12, 17, 244, 250
Sprott, W. J. H., 23
Stable, Mr. Justice, 269
Stafford-Clark, D., 121
Stocks, P., 120, 132
Stone, Julius, 264, 267
Stouffer, Samuel A., 56, 204
Strahl, Ivar, 237
Stürup, Georg K., 311
Sullivan, W. C., 284, 290, 294
Sutherland, Edwin H., 11, 22, 26, 73, 77, 80, 84, 191 et seq., 206, 209, 260
Sutherland, J. F., 296

Talbert, Robert H., 198, 228
Tappan, Paul W., 118, 169, 190–92, 199, 206, 213–15
Taylor, F. H., 121
Teeters, Negley K., 27, 178, 179, 184, 192, 197, 200, 213, 215, 216–17, 255

INDEX OF AUTHORS

Thrasher, Frederick, 120
Timasheff, N. S., 260 et seq., 268
Titmuss, Richard M., 85
Thomas, W. I., 11
Tocqueville, Alexis de, 187
Topping, C. W., 188–89
Troyat, Henry, 63
Tullio, Benigno di, 74
Turner, J. W. Cecil, 48, 232, 278

Vardy, John, 133
Vechten, Courtlandt C. van, 195
Vedder, Clyde B., 200
Velfort, Helen Rank, 55
Verger, Henry, 286–87
Vervaeck, Louis, 81
Vidal, 286, 296
Viernstein, Theodor, 79
Vullien-Dublineau, 315

Waaben, Knud, 311
Waddington, C. H., 156
Wagner, Gertrude, 104
Wagner, Margaret Seaton, 292

Wallack, Walter M., 184
Weber, Max, 116
Weeks, H. Ashley, 217
Wegner, Arthur, 276
Weihofen, Henry, 287, 304, 309, 312
Werk, van de, 27
Wertham, Frederic, 226
Wheeler, G. C., 45
Wilkins, Leslie T., 7, 124, 218
Willemse, W. A., 75, 77, 79, 81
Williams, Glanville, 53, 232, 237, 294 et seq., 306, 308
Williams, J. E. Hall, 239, 306, 308
Wills, W. David, 27, 28, 132
Wilson, Margaret S., 209
Wines, F. H., 119
Witmer, Helen, 120, Chapter 6, Section IIIb
Wootton, Barbara, 301, 307

Young, H. T. P., 120, 132

Znaniecki, F., 11

PATTERSON SMITH REPRINT SERIES IN
CRIMINOLOGY, LAW ENFORCEMENT, AND SOCIAL PROBLEMS

1. Lewis: *The Development of American Prisons and Prison Customs, 1776-1845*
2. Carpenter: *Reformatory Prison Discipline*
3. Brace: *The Dangerous Classes of New York*
4. Dix: *Remarks on Prisons and Prison Discipline in the United States*
5. Bruce et al: *The Workings of the Indeterminate-Sentence Law and the Parole System in Illinois*
6. Wickersham Commission: *Complete Reports, Including the Mooney-Billings Report.* 14 Vols.
7. Livingston: *Complete Works on Criminal Jurisprudence.* 2 Vols.
8. Cleveland Foundation: *Criminal Justice in Cleveland*
9. Illinois Association for Criminal Justice: *The Illinois Crime Survey*
10. Missouri Association for Criminal Justice: *The Missouri Crime Survey*
11. Aschaffenburg: *Crime and Its Repression*
12. Garofalo: *Criminology*
13. Gross: *Criminal Psychology*
14. Lombroso: *Crime, Its Causes and Remedies*
15. Saleilles: *The Individualization of Punishment*
16. Tarde: *Penal Philosophy*
17. McKelvey: *American Prisons*
18. Sanders: *Negro Child Welfare in North Carolina*
19. Pike: *A History of Crime in England.* 2 Vols.
20. Herring: *Welfare Work in Mill Villages*
21. Barnes: *The Evolution of Penology in Pennsylvania*
22. Puckett: *Folk Beliefs of the Southern Negro*
23. Fernald et al: *A Study of Women Delinquents in New York State*
24. Wines: *The State of the Prisons and of Child-Saving Institutions*
25. Raper: *The Tragedy of Lynching*
26. Thomas: *The Unadjusted Girl*
27. Jorns: *The Quakers as Pioneers in Social Work*
28. Owings: *Women Police*
29. Woolston: *Prostitution in the United States*
30. Flexner: *Prostitution in Europe*
31. Kelso: *The History of Public Poor Relief in Massachusetts: 1820-1920*
32. Spivak: *Georgia Nigger*
33. Earle: *Curious Punishments of Bygone Days*
34. Bonger: *Race and Crime*
35. Fishman: *Crucibles of Crime*
36. Brearley: *Homicide in the United States*
37. Graper: *American Police Administration*
38. Hichborn: *"The System"*
39. Steiner & Brown: *The North Carolina Chain Gang*
40. Cherrington: *The Evolution of Prohibition in the United States of America*
41. Colquhoun: *A Treatise on the Commerce and Police of the River Thames*
42. Colquhoun: *A Treatise on the Police of the Metropolis*
43. Abrahamsen: *Crime and the Human Mind*
44. Schneider: *The History of Public Welfare in New York State: 1609-1866*
45. Schneider & Deutsch: *The History of Public Welfare in New York State: 1867-1940*
46. Crapsey: *The Nether Side of New York*
47. Young: *Social Treatment in Probation and Delinquency*
48. Quinn: *Gambling and Gambling Devices*
49. McCord & McCord: *Origins of Crime*
50. Worthington & Topping: *Specialized Courts Dealing with Sex Delinquency*

PATTERSON SMITH REPRINT SERIES IN
CRIMINOLOGY, LAW ENFORCEMENT, AND SOCIAL PROBLEMS

51. Asbury: *Sucker's Progress*
52. Kneeland: *Commercialized Prostitution in New York City*
53. Fosdick: *American Police Systems*
54. Fosdick: *European Police Systems*
55. Shay: *Judge Lynch: His First Hundred Years*
56. Barnes: *The Repression of Crime*
57. Cable: *The Silent South*
58. Kammerer: *The Unmarried Mother*
59. Doshay: *The Boy Sex Offender and His Later Career*
60. Spaulding: *An Experimental Study of Psychopathic Delinquent Women*
61. Brockway: *Fifty Years of Prison Service*
62. Lawes: *Man's Judgment of Death*
63. Healy & Healy: *Pathological Lying, Accusation, and Swindling*
64. Smith: *The State Police*
65. Adams: *Interracial Marriage in Hawaii*
66. Halpern: *A Decade of Probation*
67. Tappan: *Delinquent Girls in Court*
68. Alexander & Healy: *Roots of Crime*
69. Healy & Bronner: *Delinquents and Criminals*
70. Cutler: *Lynch-Law*
71. Gillin: *Taming the Criminal*
72. Osborne: *Within Prison Walls*
73. Ashton: *The History of Gambling in England*
74. Whitlock: *On the Enforcement of Law in Cities*
75. Goldberg: *Child Offenders*
76. Cressey: *The Taxi-Dance Hall*
77. Riis: *The Battle with the Slum*
78. Larson et al: *Lying and Its Detection*
79. Comstock: *Frauds Exposed*
80. Carpenter: *Our Convicts*. 2 Vols. in 1
81. Horn: *Invisible Empire: The Story of the Ku Klux Klan, 1866-1871*
82. Faris et al: *Intelligent Philanthropy*
83. Robinson: *History and Organization of Criminal Statistics in the United States*
84. Reckless: *Vice in Chicago*
85. Healy: *The Individual Delinquent*
86. Bogen: *Jewish Philanthropy*
87. Clinard: *The Black Market: A Study of White Collar Crime*
88. Healy: *Mental Conflicts and Misconduct*
89. Citizens' Police Committee: *Chicago Police Problems*
90. Clay: *The Prison Chaplain*
91. Peirce: *A Half Century with Juvenile Delinquents*
92. Richmond: *Friendly Visiting Among the Poor*
93. Brasol: *Elements of Crime*
94. Strong: *Public Welfare Administration in Canada*
95. Beard: *Juvenile Probation*
96. Steinmetz: *The Gaming Table*. 2 Vols.
97. Crawford: *Report on the Penitentiaries of the United States*
98. Kuhlman: *A Guide to Material on Crime and Criminal Justice*
99. Culver: *Bibliography of Crime and Criminal Justice: 1927-1931*
100. Culver: *Bibliography of Crime and Criminal Justice: 1932-1937*

PATTERSON SMITH REPRINT SERIES IN
CRIMINOLOGY, LAW ENFORCEMENT, AND SOCIAL PROBLEMS

101. Tompkins: *Administration of Criminal Justice, 1938-1948*
102. Tompkins: *Administration of Criminal Justice, 1949-1956*
103. Cumming: *Bibliography Dealing with Crime and Cognate Subjects*
104. Addams et al: *Philanthropy and Social Progress*
105. Powell: *The American Siberia*
106. Carpenter: *Reformatory Schools*
107. Carpenter: *Juvenile Delinquents*
108. Montague: *Sixty Years in Waifdom*
109. Mannheim: *Juvenile Delinquency in an English Middletown*
110. Semmes: *Crime and Punishment in Early Maryland*
111. National Conference of Charities and Correction: *History of Child Saving in the United States*
112. Barnes: *The Story of Punishment*. 2d ed.
113. Phillipson: *Three Criminal Law Reformers*
114. Drähms: *The Criminal*
115. Terry & Pellens: *The Opium Problem*
116. Ewing: *The Morality of Punishment*
117. Mannheim: *Group Problems in Crime and Punishment*
118. Michael & Adler: *Crime, Law and Social Science*
119. Lee: *A History of Police in England*
120. Schafer: *Compensation and Restitution to Victims of Crime*. 2d ed.
121. Mannheim: *Pioneers in Criminology*. 2d ed.
122. Goebel & Naughton: *Law Enforcement in Colonial New York*
123. Savage: *Police Records and Recollections*
124. Ives: *A History of Penal Methods*
125. Bernard (Ed.): *The Americanization Studies*
    Thompson: *The Schooling of the Immigrant*
    Daniels: *America via the Neighborhood*
    Thomas et al: *Old World Traits Transplanted*
    Speek: *A Stake in the Land*
    Davis: *Immigrant Health and the Community*
    Breckinridge: *New Homes for Old*
    Park: *The Immigrant Press and Its Control*
    Gavit: *Americans by Choice*
    Claghorn: *The Immigrant's Day in Court*
    Leiserson: *Adjusting Immigrant and Industry*
126. Dai: *Opium Addiction in Chicago*
127. Costello: *Our Police Protectors*
128. Wade: *A Treatise on the Police and Crimes of the Metropolis*
129. Robison: *Can Delinquency Be Measured?*
130. Augustus: *A Report of the Labors of John Augustus*
131. Vollmer: *The Police and Modern Society*
132. Jessel: *A Bibliography of Works in English on Playing Cards and Gaming*. Enlarged
133. Walling: *Recollections of a New York Chief of Police*
134. Lombroso: *Criminal Man*
135. Howard: *Prisons and Lazarettos*. 2 vols.
136. Fitzgerald: *Chronicles of Bow Street Police-Office*. 2 vols. in 1
137. Goring: *The English Convict*
138. Ribton-Turner: *A History of Vagrants and Vagrancy*
139. Smith: *Justice and the Poor*
140. Willard: *Tramping with Tramps*